Does Class Matter?

*Colonial Capital and Workers'
Resistance in Bengal (1890–1937)*

Does Class Matter?

Colonial Capital and Workers' Resistance in Bengal (1890–1937)

Subho Basu

OXFORD
UNIVERSITY PRESS

OXFORD

UNIVERSITY PRESS

YMCA Library Building, Jai Singh Road, New Delhi 110 001

Oxford University Press is a department of the University of Oxford. It furthers the
University's objective of excellence in research, scholarship, and education
by publishing worldwide in

Oxford New York

Auckland Bangkok Buenos Aires Cape Town Chennai
Dar es Salaam Delhi Hong Kong Istanbul Karachi Kolkata
Kuala Lumpur Madrid Melbourne Mexico City Mumbai Nairobi
São Paulo Shanghai Taipei Tokyo Toronto

Oxford is a registered trade mark of Oxford University Press
in the UK and in certain other countries

Published in India
By Oxford University Press, New Delhi
© Oxford University Press, 2004

ISBN 0 19 566599 6

Typeset in A Garamond 9.5/11.5
By Le Studio Graphique, Gurgaon 122 001
Printed by Sai Printopack Pvt. Ltd. New Delhi 110 020
Published by Manzar Khan, Oxford University Press
YMCA Library Building, Jai Singh Road, New Delhi 110 001

Contents

Acknowledgements

This book was originally conceived of as an MPhil thesis at the Jawaharlal Nehru University, New Delhi in 1986. It underwent radical transformations at several stages: it was submitted as fellowship dissertation at the Centre of South Asian Studies, University of Cambridge in 1993 and finally for doctoral degree at the History Department of the University in 1994. Since then I was constantly engaged in revising it to incorporate new researches and developing a clear focus.

It is not surprising that in this long process of work on Bengal's jute industry, I have incurred many debts. Prof. Tarashankar Banerjee of Visva-Bharati University had first inspired me to explore these ideas and had always provided me with research connections in his native region in Bhatpara. I also benefited from discussions with Prof. Ashin Dasgupta, my boyhood hero and model historian. Their untimely demise had robbed me of the opportunity to present this book to them. In Calcutta Prof. Suranjan Das has taken care and interest in the progress of this work and has provided unqualified support for the completion of this work.

At JNU Prof. Majid Siddiqi and Sabyasachi Bhattacharya have taken care to teach me how to frame arguments and develop a coherent research strategy. At Cambridge my supervisor Dr R.S. Chandavarakar encouraged me to explore new ideas concerning labour history, sorted out my inchoate arguments, corrected patiently my language, and benignly tolerated my intolerant outbursts. Dr Gordon Johnson constantly prodded me to finish this draft and provided unconditional support in every aspect of my life at Cambridge. Dr Lionel Carter was also an enthusiastic supporter of my research. Prof. David Washbrook had offered new insights as PhD examiner and during seminar discussions at Oxford. Prof. Ranajit Dasgupta, a pioneering researcher in the jute labour movement, helped me in many ways. His untimely departure had sadly robbed me of his insights into the subject. At Amsterdam, during a conference, I came to know briefly Prof. Dipesh Chakrabarty. His charming manner and kind tolerance of my virulent criticism of his work had impressed me highly.

Among colleagues, Dr Samita Sen literally spent hours improving the quality of this manuscript when it was being prepared for submission as a doctoral dissertation. Arjan De Haan, a formidable jute wallah, shared the accommodation in Calcutta and spent sleepless nights in debating the future of socialism. Though we had never agreed, I benefited from his researches and ideas immensely. I met two other passionate jute wallahs at Cambridge: Prof. Parimal Ghosh of Calcutta and Dr A. Cox of Dundee, both of them have a profound influence on my research and life in general. Dr Joya Chatterji took particular care at a time of near homelessness in England by arranging accommodation and even food. Dr Sanjay Bhattacharya paid meticulous attention to the draft of the thesis and suggested valuable changes.

Life in Cambridge would have been dull and monotonous without the presence and assistance of Bidyut Chakravarty, and Anil Sethi. They contributed much to the making of this book in their own ways. Sugata, Sarmistha, Dwaipayan, Anjan, Gargi, Somak, Debasish, Abdul, Damayanti, Sikha, Sangeeta, Jayanta, Aparajita, Vinayak Srivastava, Gargi, Vinay, Vinayak Chaturvedi, Nandini Gooptu, Nandini Gondhalekar, Prakash, Riaz, Sudeshna, Gopal, Arnab, Mousumi, Nilmani, Ranjit, Lubya, Toto, William, Ornit, Manas, Mohua, and Sarah Glynn made life easy with their friendship and companionship. Shafiur Rehaman and Laura Itzaki over the years became more than friends and took responsibility for my well-being at Cambridge.

During my stay at Plymouth, I gained immensely from the friendship and familial care of Alan and Sue Cousins. Bob Keys, Nigel Mace, and Dave Guardian turned out to be sympathetic and understanding colleagues. In London, members of the South Asia group at SOAS—Peter Robb, David Arnold, and Averill Powell provided support, help, and comments. Daud Ali and Sugra Bibi were more than friends. They transformed their home into our home too. At Edinburgh, Crispin Bates acted as more of a concerned brother than friend. Markus is a new comrade and friend from SOAS. I would also like thank Dr Marina Carter for her careful and diligent editing of this manuscript. Surajit and Mousumi deserve special mention for their care and attention to me in Calcutta and Leicester. Comrade Harshev, Preet Bains, and Indrajit Chakrabarty had offered me shelter and assistance during my stay in London. Nilanjan, Suchetana, Urvi, and Bodhisatta also boosted my morale in many ways. Yet none of these people are responsible for the errors that remain in this monograph. In Illinois, my colleagues have gone out of their way to make my stay comfortable. Richard Soderlund and Katherine McCarthy transformed their home into mine. Muhammad Tavakoli, Ali Riaz, Anthony Adedze, and Victor Devinatz provided company and made my stay in this distant land into a home away from home.

This long acknowledgement would remain incomplete without mentioning my research assistants Souvik, Zaim, and Jyoti. They worked tirelessly to collect and organize information for this research. Shri Satyajit Chaudhuri and his colleagues at the Haraprasad Shastri Research Institute in Naihati, Shri Amitabha Bhattacharya, the late Minister of Commerce of West Bengal, Shri Bidyut Ganguli, Shri Debaprasad Bhattacharya, and Shri Paresh Pal of Bhatpara Municipality helped in many ways to conduct research in the mill belt. I would like to thank the staff of the West Bengal State Archives, National Library, Central Secretariat Library, Bangiya Sahitya Parishad, Chaitanya Library in Calcutta, Joykrishna Library in Uttarpara, Bhatpara Saraswat Samaj, National Archives of India, Nehru Memorial Museum Library at Delhi, Dundee University Library and Archives, Dundee District Record Office, India Office Library in London, Cambridge University Library and the Centre of South Asian Studies Library at Cambridge.

Finally, my friends and family members are untiring sources of support. Baro Mashi and Baro Mesho, and Dulumashi and Indronil Mesho have taken care of my comfort even over a distance of 5000 miles. Mungli, Budhi, Tipu, and Dan have also helped and consoled me in times of crisis. My father- (Bapi) and mother- (Ma) in-law have always expressed their support. Bikraman Nair had actually enabled me to travel abroad by arranging my passports from Calcutta. He took the utmost care of my welfare in his own way during my visits to Calcutta. It is sad that my father Santosh Kumar Basu, who inspired me to study History, is no more to appreciate the book. However, my Ma—my source of inspiration, my elder brother, Saura and Sutapa Boudi—an ever-caring couple, are all around. Mallika Banerjee knows that this book would not have seen the light of day without her companionship through thick and thin of life. I dedicate this book to Ma, Baba, Dada, Boudi, and Mallika.

1

Introduction

Understanding Labour Politics in Bengal: Problems of the Idea of 'Peasant-Worker'

In 1937, during the second general strike in the jute industry, Debendranath Sen, a leader of the Congress Socialist Party, candidly described in his party bulletin the contrast between the superficial commonplace assumption about workers' inability to initiate collective action and the hard reality of labour politics:

It is well nigh impossible for a man not intimately known to them, to entertain any great regard for them, least of all credit them with any great capacity for heroic action of the kind they have done. Even in a meeting, where they become (sic) together by a sense of collective unity, they evince no great enthusiasm. Not unoften (sic) a speaker finds it difficult to hold on, his audience seems so dull and devoid of life. But when the meeting has been dissolved and the bulk of the audience has dispersed, some of the workers would be found assembled in small groups, carrying on conversations in an amazingly animated way. They would then be seen arriving at momentous decisions in a strikingly short time and setting to work those out in a still more striking fashion. And strangest of all, these decisions have very often little connection with the speaches (sic) they had heard just a few minutes before.[1]

A skeptic may question the objectivity of Sen's report. Undoubtedly, he had an interest in exaggerating worker's revolutionary inclinations and Sen's socialist ideology might have dictated his choice of words. However, the crucial element in Sen's report was not his portrayal of heroic revolutionary workers but the underlying surprise at the evidence of such robust autonomy and the ability of workers to organize the strike themselves. Sen was not alone in discovering such unexpected events. Almost a decade before Sen wrote his report, a colonial official during the 1929 strike wave in Bengal expressed his disbelief at the rapid spread of the strike. He even suspected that the literacy rate among workers was higher than it was thought to be.[2]

Interestingly, there exists a commonalty in these narratives—a sense of bewilderment at the ability of workers to mount powerful industrial actions.

This bewilderment may, in some respects, be attributed to the way labour politics unfolded in Bengal in the period between 1890 and 1939. Workers' agitations in this period were characterized by a certain paradox. There were occasions when intense industrial action, marked by workers' solidarity, was followed by communal rioting between Hindus and Muslims, upcountry workers and Bengalis. Numerous strikes were organized in the jute mills yet formal labour organization remained weak. Few trade unions existed and those which did had only a handful of members and very little influence. During strikes, workers faced the concerted repressive apparatus of the European managers and the colonial police. Yet, the workers did not form a ready-made political constituency of the Congress which was also confronting the colonial state in Bengal in this period. Contemporary observers were left confused and many readily concluded that workers in Calcutta were motivated more by their primordial loyalties and rural mentalities than by a sense of belonging to a class. They lacked the ability to organize and sustain industrial action.

This book examines the conundrums that came to characterize labour politics in late colonial Bengal and contests the notion that Calcutta workers were a politically innocent migrant peasant workforce. It argues that workers in Calcutta deployed sophisticated political strategies in dealing with their employers, the managers of the colonial state, and even nationalist politicians. It considers workers' politics in its widest sense, including the social organization of the neighbourhood, daily conflicts at the workplace, and the institutional politics of trade unions and political parties, municipal boards, and provincial councils. Focusing primarily on the politics of the jute workers, who constituted the core of the industrial workforce in the mill towns located around Calcutta—the centre both of colonial power and of nationalist politics in Bengal—the book explores the interaction between workers' politics, nationalist movements, and the colonial state at various levels in the period between 1890 and 1937.

During this period, fundamental changes occurred in the relationships between the labour movement and various political parties in Bengal. The 1890s witnessed the beginning of a labour movement for better working conditions, higher wages, attempts at unionization, and the preservation of what workers regarded as their customary rights regarding hours of work, leisure, and holiday. In this period industrial workers received little support from the Congress or other political organizations but exerted pressure on the government through confrontation with law-enforcing agencies on the streets of the capital. Although in the Swadeshi period nationalist politicians joined hands with a segment of labour to put pressure on European-owned mills and imperial economic interests, it was especially from the end of the First World War that labour came to play a crucial role in major movements in Bengal.

Between 1918 and 1920 Bengal witnessed widespread industrial strikes that provided a powerful momentum for organizing the Khilafat non-cooperation movement. Political parties now began to see the advantages of developing links with, and establishing a foothold among, the jute mill labourers. Congress leader C.R. Das evinced an active interest in recruiting the support of workers. The 1920s saw the rise of socialist and communist movements in Calcutta and the surrounding mill towns. By 1929, the jute industry was experiencing its first general strike, which received widespread public support. Soon a sweeping retrenchment radically reduced the number of jute workers and struck a debilitating blow at the ability of labour to enter into a collective action to prevent employers' labour rationalization strategy. Yet, by 1937 a second general strike among jute industrial workers influenced the process of the formation of the first elected Bengal government (although with a highly restricted franchise limited to only approximately 10 per cent of the population) and also significantly informed its policies. All these factors indicate the salience of labour as a major player in Bengal politics.

Why was it that the industrial labour force was regarded as politically insignificant and still struggling to emerge from the quagmire of social relations into which it was born? The answer may well be located in the way both colonial official and Indian historians constructed the image of the migrant labour force. For almost half a century, colonial officials and mill owners contrasted the attitudes of their Indian employees with the apparently disciplined and efficient labourers in Britain.[3] The conclusion was drawn, in colonial discourse, that '[t]he habits of the Indian factory operatives are determined by the fact that he is an agriculturist or a labourer on the land'.[4] This notion of 'peasant-worker' had been given universal form in colonial discourse exhibiting a common attitude towards wage labour in predominantly agrarian societies. For example, the life of African workers when looked at through the lens of the colonial official appear strikingly similar to the representation of Indian labourers in colonial discourse. Even on the eve of decolonization in Africa, a leaflet on the labour situation in dependencies of the United Kingdom mentions in 1957.

The majority of the African do not accept continuous work as a necessary part of their lives. Most African worker-labourers, that is as opposed to office workers and domestic servants take jobs only for as long as it takes them to earn the money to pay their taxes, or to buy something that they need, after which their wives have been cultivating in their absence.[5]

The oxymoron 'peasant-worker' highlights several dichotomies. It contrasts the industrialized West with the predominantly agrarian non-Western countries, the supposedly atomized world of peasant production with the collective world of factory work, and finally, the resilience of peasant attitudes towards work and the inconsistencies of such attitudes in industrial production organization. From this perspective, India or sub-Saharan Africa was conceived to be a transitory place where workers had one foot in the rural world and the other in the urban industrial complex.

Whilst historians in Western Europe today question linear theories of process of proletarianization, of the English working classes[6], such understandings of the Indian workers as ignorant, simple minded and lacking commitment to factory work continue to resonate in the writings of many historians of India.[7] Drawing upon the belief that workers were actually migrant peasants, most historical accounts of Bengal nationalist politics dismiss workers as an insignificant political force wholly dependent on *bhadralok* leadership.[8] Indeed, workers are seen as malleable for communal action and prone to sectarian violence.[9] Thus, in writing about the working class, scholars have argued that rural ties had paralysed workers' sense of collective interests and transformed their political action into spasmodic disorganized peasant jacquerie.[10] This notion of migrants is paradoxically strengthened by the almost conventional assumption by historians that the colonial state colluded with expatriate capital to orchestrate labour migration from the rural hinterland to the cities.[11] Such views strengthen the image of migrants as hapless victims of colonial capitalism and throw little light on workers' strategies of resistance and survival.

In more recent historical writings this particular emphasis on the dichotomy between agriculture, usually characterized by the atomized world of pre-capitalist subsistence production, and industry, generally marked by labour herded by capital, is contested. It is recognized that there existed a symbiotic relationship between the two in shaping workers' work, social life, and political consciousness. In European history the notion of peasants' inability to organize themselves because of the isolationist nature of their household-based production has given way to the idea of an ensemble of relations which determine the conditions of production and reproduction of peasant enterprise and which could include cooperation among peasants for harvesting, grazing, use of common lands, and forest resources.[12] In the Indian context the return of the peasantry as a crucial historical force is celebrated in recent historiography.[13] Given this new understanding of peasant resistance, it is indeed problematic to argue that the workers were unable to organize themselves because of their peasant roots. More importantly, migrants did not seem to be silent victims of colonial capitalism but important agents, making their own strategies of resistance, survival, and furthering of their particular interests. In the context of declining rural resources, urban labour constituted a crucial element in their survival strategies and migrant workers worked hard to preserve it. This indicates that the melting down of the barrier between town and country operated contrary to the way many scholars believed it to. This erosion of the boundary between town and country is well observed in many context in sub-Saharan Africa.[14]

In Bombay, Chandavarkar demonstrates that rural connections did strengthen workers' collective bargaining power. Rural bases enabled workers to prolong their strike action in urban areas.[15] Workers, so the argument goes, were neither atomistic in terms of their social organization, shepherded by jobbers, caste elders or trade union leaders, nor were they naturally solidaristic.[16] It has thus far been taken for granted that the jute industry in Bengal, controlled by a British-dominated cartel, and the cotton textile industry in Bombay, owned primarily by Indian industrialists, followed sharply contrasting courses.[17] However, this argument about the process of labour force formation and politics in Bombay is also applicable in Bengal. This monograph demonstrates that rural social ties constituted a powerful base for urban workers to maintain their existence in an overcrowded and uncertain labour market marked by low wages. Rural ties did not act as a hindrance to the development of industrial action of urban labour. On the contrary, as in Bombay, rural social ties enabled workers in Calcutta to intensify their resistance against colonial rulers.

It is true that in urban areas, migrants depended upon their fellow villagers, members of the same caste, religion, and linguistic group for support and help. However, it would be highly simplistic to believe that these communities were the simple transposition of rural community networks in an urban context. The life pattern of jute workers prevented the direct transposition of a rural social structure in urban regions. Most workers were adult male migrants who spent their childhoods in the villages and their adult working lives in the cities, except for brief annual periodic visits to rural areas. Moreover, the radically different process of proletarianization of single female workers who in many instances entered into complex conjugal partnerships with their male colleagues from different linguistic and religious groups also suggest the limited scope for the transfer of community values across generations. All these point to the absence of watertight community structures based on caste, language or religion. These ties were overlapping and they were negotiated in a complex manner in everyday life where intense competition for jobs, higher wages, and shelter constituted rather fragile threads for weaving stable communities. Rather these ties acquired new meanings in the urban industrial milieu and became activated in a variety of ways in different political contexts. The political implications of these nexuses can be better understood by investigating such episodes in detail. This work investigates the significance of such ties both in their quotidian forms and their different and diverse meaning during a period of confrontation.

Affiliations of caste, religion, and region did sometimes lead to violence, but such violence cannot be divorced from wider political currents. For instance, communal antagonisms were influenced by the policies of the colonial state. Colonial officials pleaded the rule of local conventions in adjudicating conflicts over social and religious rituals. This forced various religious groups to outbid each other in inventing traditional customs. Politically, the introduction of the separate electorates in 1909 and their extension in 1919 increased the competition between Hindu and Muslim elites for office. At the same time communalism rose sharply in Bengal. In addition, the domination of Bengali Hindu landlords over the Congress alienated the predominantly Muslim peasantry in east Bengal. The growing gulf between the 'bhadralok' Congress and Muslim peasant leaders in Bengal also had repercussions on the labour movement. Increasingly, European mill owners formed cross-party alliances in the assembly with Muslim politicians against the Congress. The socialists who were prominent in labour politics were closer to the Congress and had little contact with Muslim leaders who enjoyed wider support among the peasants. This prevented the formation of cross-party alliances between the representatives of the peasants and the workers.

The politics of labour thus could not be abstracted from wider social, political, and economic contexts. The complexity of these situations indicates the manifold transformations of caste, religious, regional and linguistic ties in the process of interaction with the strategies of the employer, policies of the state, the unfolding of diverse types of nationalist movements, and the rise of socialist politics. Communal conflict and the process of the emergence of 'class' is integrally related to these multiple forms of contest for the loyalty of labour both as the producer of commodities important to imperial economic relations and (because of that) as a potentially important constituency of wider political movements in Bengal.

In this context, political movements concerning labour may be categorized into two separate clusters of political ideologies and activities. It is possible to interpret Bengal politics as a process of contestation between a cluster of ideas and movements articulating the interests of the working classes and a melange of nationalist ideologies that could not be isolated from the politics of caste, language, and religion. It is indeed true, as many historians have argued, that religious and caste consciousness were often pressed into the making of industrial action even where socialists and communists played a crucial role in mobilization.[18] However, they tend to overlook the fact that primary goal as well as the organizational mechanism and language of political mobilization of the movements purporting to articulate the 'class interests' of labour, transcended loyalties to caste, region, and religion and aimed at achieving a horizontal unity among classes. This horizontal unity among different segments of workers materialized in concrete forms during moments of resistance and strikes despite being challenged by other forms of loyalties. A second crucial factor is that the expression of class solidarity is not above contestation as class is not a homogenous totalizing notion. By imagining class to be a totalizing notion historians— both supportive and critical of the discourse of class-based politics—tend to engage in heuristic debates that too often lead us into a *cul-de-sac*.

Class as Theoretical Construct: Interpretations of Workers' Politics in the Existing Historiography

The word 'class' is used loosely in this book as indicative of the making and unmaking of a particular form of social entity in terms of the lived experience of the social relationships centred around industrialization and modern political mobilization through trade unionization, nationalist movements, and the coming of a rudimentary form of representative democracy. In classical Marxian terms class signifies a social group with a common relationship to a means of production, common means of surplus product and a common relationship to those who sell their labour to earn their livelihood. This classic Marxian definition is predicated upon the commodification of money, land, and labour. For historians this description remains a heuristic construct aloof from the experience of workers. Marx himself used the term 'class in itself' to denote such a situation. He argues that when a class becomes aware of its interests *vis-à-vis* other classes, it becomes a 'class for itself'—i.e. possessing the willingness and the capacity to pursue its interests.[19] In this context, the classical Marxian analysis provided us with a conceptual framework rather than a clear indication of experience-related process of class formation.

E.P. Thompson's seminal work on the subject indicates ways to overcome this problem of using class in historical writings. He views the formation of class as a social, cultural, and discursive process rooted in the experience of workers in terms of relationship with other social groups defined through action, reaction, change and conflict.[20] Thompson thus emphasizes the shared experience of the process of the making of class. Thompsonian descriptions, as Ira Katznelson points out, have four distinctive levels.[21] At the first level, class is an economic concept merely describing and mapping out the position of workers in a particular social context; at a second level, class indicates a particular form of social relationship in industrial capitalist society based on both their position in production relations and in terms of their consumption of commodities and services; at a third level, class moves beyond these distinctive categories to indicate dispositions. Dispositions point towards how workers interpret, relate, and develop their own responses to situations. At a fourth level, Thompson indicates the process of collective action, the realm of politics. The framework promotes an open-ended analysis based on class without a deterministic causal relationship. It enables us to trace workers' politics and the politics of other social groups through a class perspective in a more precise manner. It argues class as a social construct is open to a process of making and unmaking which, in the end, depends on a wider political and economic process of making and unmaking which, in the end, depends on a wider political and economic process stretching from the local to the global through various stages. It thus emphasizes the role of workers as makers of their own history from an open-ended class perspective with a focus on a political process different from traditional Marxist idioms of history. Importantly, this theoretical method is empirical and not teleology driven.

A further point of distinction from existing Marxist historical writings on the subject is essential. Marxist historians, often operating within a structuralist mode, analysed the emergence of industrial working-class in terms of recruitment, wage structures, and patterns of unionization, and assumed that the workers were naturally solidaristic. The exclusive focus on the workplace and trade union activity has sometimes led to the conflation of class, movement, and leadership.[22] The serious flaw in this analysis is the neglect of the every day social organization of workers both in workplaces and neighbourhoods. The analysis of quotidian[23] world of workers may enable us to understand how workers tried to organize their work and leisure by defining their notion of time and space. Indeed, managerial strategies tried to give concessions to workers' customary practices within industrial discipline. Most industrial conflicts occurred when management made attempts to tighten work discipline by changing everyday work practices in order to meet fluctuations in the market or to increase profit margins. Thus, industrial conflicts took place when management changed working hours, moved from multiple to single shifts or tried to curb certain privileges enjoyed by skilled workers, and threatened to terminate jobs.

The analysis of the everyday world of work and leisure draws our attention to the hierarchy among workers based on skill, wages, the length and nature of their job contracts, and differences in living standards. The existence of this hierarchy implied that different working groups had different interests *vis-a-vis* the management of the factories. Weavers, for example, stood out from other social groups in the factories as they were indispensable to management in the short run while women employed in the sewing section had little bargaining power as their skills could be learnt easily. The insecurity of employment also implied that every worker was competing with each other for jobs. Solidarities that led to strikes emerged through prolonged and intense negotiations amongst the workers themselves. Industrial actions were preceded by complex negotiations among weavers, spinners, rovers, and beamers—workers of the main departments of the jute mills. Meetings were held for hours on open grounds beside the slums. When important elements, representing different segments of workers were convinced that strikes or unions were required to resolve their intransigence with the management, support for collective action gained ground. Grocers, slum owners, and moneylenders were persuaded to support the strike. Collective decision-making was essential to resist pressure from these elements as strikes would mean a halt on repayment of loans, rent, or advances made for purchasing of essential food items.

Indeed, complex arrangements with grocers, slum owners, sardars, and moneylenders were essential for the everyday survival of workers. Powerful social entrepreneurs such as *sardars, burrababus* (head clerks) grocers, wine sellers, and moneylenders provided workers with jobs, shelter, low priced food, and loans. Sardars were generally portrayed as a powerful authority, combining the roles of the village headman and community elder in the neighbourhood as well as foreman and jobber in the factory. Factories employed several sardars and only a few among them enjoyed powerful positions in the neighbourhood, building such stature by entering into alliances with other powerful social entrepreneurs such as burrababus. Once such a sardar established a powerful presence within the mill and slum, he was recognized by the managers as workers' representative. However, sardars had to tread on rather precarious ground, divided between workers' grievances, managers' demand, and the needs of allies such as burrababus.[24] In other words, different segments of workers depended upon wider networks of social nexuses centring around different types of social entrepreneurs within mill towns. Such strategies obviously produced a varied geometry of alliances between ordinary working men and women on the one hand and sardars, neighbourhood toughs, and police on the other. Many aspects of these ties were drawn upon during industrial conflicts by both the mill management and strikers. As a consequence, the process of class formation and class action remained a contested process whereby different segments of workers pursued different strategies of alliance among themselves against the state and capital. By focusing upon the quotidian social world at the workplace and neighbourhood, it is possible to understand the context for workers' participation in wider politics, industrial action, and mass movements, particularly in the periods when managerial strategies tried to reshape work practices. Sadly enough, instead of analysing such everyday politics of workplace and neighbourhoods, structural Marxist accounts explained the political consciousness of Bengal workers in terms of the universal paradigm of class.[25]

Recent postmodernist attempts at moving beyond a structural Marxist paradigm by analysing the quotidian politics of jute mills have proved to be fruitful. In the work of Leela Fernandes[26], quotidian politics within the factory has come to acquire a new significance. Fernandes argues that the everyday struggles for power between managers and workers are the product of political processes. Following Stuart Hall[27], she aims to problematize categories by analysing the political processes of the construction of categories. She points out how by excluding women, trade union leaders narrow the premise of class as a category. Many of these issues have also been raised by authors such as S. Sen and R.S. Chandavarkar.[28] However, Fernandes's emphasis on the hegemony of trade unions and the manufacturing of workers' identity imply a rather mechanical process with no reference to the historical context within which workers not only resisted such processes of domination, but subverted any attempt to represent outsiders on their behalf. Indeed, such claims ignore the agency of workers in claiming their own identity as producers of commodities even if such identities are putatively refracted through caste or regional loyalties.

In recent historical writings Marxist analysis, in general, has come under intense criticism from 'subaltern historians'. The origin of subaltern studies can be traced back to the end of the 1970s when Indian politics witnessed a powerful change. The decade of 'radicalism' culminating in a Maoist insurrection in Eastern India came to an end. In such circumstances, the Congress claim to represent the nation and its interpretation of the freedom struggle obviously dissatisfied young historians. More pronouncedly, they also came to believe that rigid and formulaic orthodox Marxism did not provide an adequate alternative to existing historiography. On the other hand, they revolted against the Namierism of the 'neo-colonialist' Cambridge school. Internationally, this was the period when class as a master identity in western industrialist society suffered a steady erosion; sociologists and historians became engaged in explaining and exploring these changes and their impacts upon 'identity formations'. Raymond Williams[29] and Stuart Hall[30] focused on reinterpreting Marxian analyses from a humanist tradition. Gramsci became a new source of strength for Marxist historians engaged in reinterpreting history. These trends no doubt excited the would-be subaltern writers.[31] But these were not the only trends that influenced their ideological set up. At the same time, in France, the post-structuralist anti-humanist writings emerged as a powerful strand of thought through the writings of Foucault. In the United States, in Indian studies Cohn laid emphasis upon recovering and using indigenous sources as well as rereading the colonial archives to write a new history through a combination of anthropological and historical methodologies.[32] In these circumstances, Said's work on cultural underpinnings of imperialism registered an important presence in the historical research on the cultural aspects of imperialism.[33]

Subaltern studies in India and later on the New Social Movement in Latín American studies claimed heritage to many of these new trends. Contributors to the early volumes of *Subaltern Studies* combined a Thompsonian concern for history from below with vigorous empiricist researches. Increasingly, this empirical idiom was replaced by Saidian concern and contributed crucially to the new genre of literature namely postcolonial studies.[34] It was particularly true from volume IV onwards when subaltern writings veered towards a more clearly post-modernist direction tearing away from its early Thompsonian and Gramscian moorings. However, even in the early stage the quest for an autonomous peasant rebel consciousness led subaltern scholars to re-emphasize the communitarian concerns of the peasantry. The focus clearly is on the peasantry as a community in place of the rigorous analysis of social stratification within peasantry.[35] Indeed, such trends were not surprising since many subaltern scholars traced their antecedents to the Maoist Naxalite movement in Bengal. Naxalites at the heyday of their struggle characterized India as a semi-feudal and semi-colonial social formation and thus externalized capitalist exploitation in agriculture. In practice they celebrated *adivasi* cultural particularism relating the present agrarian struggles with the past forms of struggle through an ethnic idiom. The Naxalite base among adivasi communities in Bengal obviously created an ideological space for linking their struggles with ethnic identities along with romanticization of supposedly subsistence producing poor homogenous peasant communities.[36] The focus in this historiography, as was evident in the seminal writings of Ranajit Guha[37], was clearly on the spontaneously violent but ethnicised peasant as the subject of her/his own history. In many ways these sophisticated and brilliant analyses tended to bring forth an image of a static peasant rebel with her/his political consciousness submerged in a routinized symbolic violence which could not be understood in terms of bourgeois rationality and discursive processes. Ironically, these analyses, in their implications, confirm many colonial assumptions about the Indian peasantry as being prone to violence, irrational, and trapped in primordial ethnic identities.

Not surprisingly, this trend in subaltern writings has found expressions in the analysis of working class politics. In his well-known research on Calcutta workers, Dipesh Chakrabarty argues that the pre-capitalist hierarchies of Indian society play a fundamental role in shaping labour politics.[38] For Chakrabarty, jute workers were trapped within the pre-capitalist loyalties of caste, religion, and region. In this way, Chakrabarty replicates the basic assumptions of the colonial and 'orientalist' discourse. For him, bhadralok trade union leaders in Bengal created zamindaries of their own and workers served merely as retainers. More importantly, in an account which professes to emphasize how workers made their own history, babus have been assigned too dominant a role. Judged against the universalist yardstick of class and class formation, this historiography tends to highlight the 'peculiarities of Indian working class', and it becomes a list of failures, the absence of strong trade unions, the weakness of political parties aspiring to represent the working classes and the inability of workers to make a significant impact on Bengal politics in general.

In Calcutta's context, labour did insert their agency in making their own politics. This book demonstrates that during industrial action various segments of the jute work-force compelled the state and its employers to rethink their strategies as much as it shook many bhadralok labour activists to come out of their self-constructed image of downtrodden masses ready to hum the tune sung by them. More than this, the Workers and Peasant Party in Bengal asserted its presence in politics on the back of labour radicalism. At the discursive and ideological level, socialist political formations in Bengal owed their existence not so much to the prompting of the Comintern but to the interaction between the politics of industrial labour in the inter-War period and the city's radical intelligentsia.[39] This did not imply that workers readily accepted socialist politicians as the champions of labour. Workers' support to such politicians depended upon the immediate political and economic relationship between workers and employers and among different groups of workers themselves. In other words, workers deployed conscious political strategies to defend their interests and displayed robust independence in formulating such political strategies.

Are Trade Unions Representatives of Workers' 'Class Consciousness'? Workers' Politics, Unionization and Workers' Consciousness in late colonial Bengal

The issue of trade union formation in this context deserves particular attention. The process of consolidation and organization of trade unions in contingent upon the relationship between different levels of state and managers of capital and different segment of workers themselves. Trade unions could be used to produce particular forms of stable industrial relations and to restrain wider expressions of grass roots level labour democracy. The establishment of trade unions, in that sense, did not imply a reflection of the maturity of workers' consciousness in all contexts. The crucial importance attributed to the emergence of trade unions as manifestations of workers' consciousness in labour history writing could be traced to two different sources, depending on the ideological orientation of historians.

The salience of trade unions in politics was institutionalized in the work of Henry Pelling. He traced the emergence of trade unions and their relationship with the Labour Party, demonstrating how the trade union movement gradually gave birth to a party that came to acquire a mass base and eventually formed the government in the country.[40] No doubt, Pelling also demonstrated that the labour Party had to distance itself from trade union organizations once it formed the government, but his treatment of the transformation of the trade union movement into a political party of governance in an industrial society became a powerful narrative of the political relationship between the workers' movement, trade union organization, and the formation of a party capable of governance. While Pelling's contribution was based on the experience of the British trade union movement, from a completely different perspective a wider conceptual framework was formulated by Lenin. Lenin associated trade union consciousness with the spontaneous consciousness of the working class; he categorized this as a lower level of political consciousness. Lenin argued that the socialist consciousness of the working class constituted the higher level of political awareness.[41] In the context of labour history, Eric Hobsbawm applied Leninist theory in a historically nuanced manner. Echoing Lenin, Hobsbawm has argued that:

Without either, [trade union consciousness and socialist consciousness] the workers may, for political purposes, be completely negligible, indeed invisible, like the very substantial mass of Tory working men who have always existed in Britain, without affecting, in more than the most fleeting and marginal way, the structure, the policy and programme of the Conservative Party, which could not win a single election without them.[42]

It would be wrong to deny the validity of this realistic observation but in a mechanical reading this analysis could make the absence of stable trade unions synonymous with workers' inability to bargain with employers, or lack of effective resistance to the strategies that appeared to have contradicted their interests. This equation between the process of unionization with workers' growing political maturity does not delineate distinctions between the desire to form unions and the impediments towards the translation of that desire into practice. We thus know little about management's strategies towards unionization and how such strategies influenced and informed workers' politics. Were unions that were on offer in Calcutta capable of furthering labour's everyday negotiations and struggles for more democratic work conditions and a higher standard of living? Or did they aim to restrain the grass roots level labour radicalism? How did such unions operate and why and when did workers join such unions? In what circumstances did they retreat?

The answer to these questions demands a survey of the nature of the governance of mill towns and the institutional shape of the colonial state at the local level. A crucial constraint on labour activism was managerial hostility to trade unions and their domination over local political institutions. The managers of jute mills served as chairmen of municipal boards of mill towns and honorary magistrates. They used such power to suppress strikes. The mill managers could deploy the police force, declare political assemblies unlawful and try workers in local courts. In this context, the lack of organization among workers might have reflected a 'calculated' strategy on their part. As indeed, in the face of other odds, lightning strikes might have been preferred alternative since they had the potential to catch the management unawares and consequently perhaps avoid victimization.

The manager Raj in the mill towns integrated conflicts and tensions within the workplace with tensions related to the issue of urban governance. Sanitation, epidemic control measures, general concerns over/about the development of salutary living conditions came to be informed by tensions among workers, mill managers and local landlords (particularly because of arbitrary destruction of slums). The general body of workers was often excluded from the political management of the town. This impinged on the collective political consciousness of workers and alienated them from the local state machinery. In periods of long strikes, managerial domination over local self-governing institutions transformed industrial conflicts at the work-place into a confrontation between the town administration, police, and workers. In workers' perceptions the colonial state often became the protector of the interests of capital rather than a neutral umpire of industrial conflicts. It is for this reason that the process of making the politics of workers was integrally related to their everyday experience of the operation of mill town administration. These institutionalized forms of conflicts characterized the relationship between workers and the colonial state at different levels and constituted a primary ground for labour radicalism. Strikes thus became politically explosive particularly when they coincided with anti-colonial upsurges. Indeed, in the immediate post World War I period, it was the labour offensive that transformed the non-cooperation movement into formidable urban civil disobedience in Calcutta. Yet various efforts at the establishment of trade unions in this period proved to be ephemeral. Here again workers rejected not the principle of unions in themselves but an attempt to restrain their radicalism. The Gandhian nationalists preached the ideology of cooperation between capital and labour and also sought to isolate labour from nationalist movements. They remained opposed to militant industrial action which limited their influence on the labour movement in Bengal. In the end, these Gandhian-sponsored unions collapsed. Workers rejected their attempts to restrain them from joining nationalist politics or organizing their collective political action. In these years, in the midst of confrontation, repression, and failed attempts at unionization, socialist ideologies gradually fructified in the form of nebulous communist and socialist groups.

Political movements articulating the language of empowerment of workers often appealed to workers' sense of dignity and provided impetus to workers for participation in anti-colonial mass upsurges. Against such a background, alliances were formed between workers and socialists.[43] Yet socialists were crucial mediators and not arbitrators of workers' political action. The relationship between socialist activists and workers was contingent upon internal consensus among workers' representatives and their appreciation of the efficacy of socialist strategies. Often for the majority of workers, organized unions did not provide any evidence of immediate tangible gain. However, when managerial strategies impinged on their customary work practices and threatened the security of their jobs, if the political and economic conditions appeared to be congenial for collective bargaining, workers mounted enormous pressures on management through industrial action in alliance with socialist groups.

Even in such circumstances, attempts at 'political education' by socialists proved to be difficult. Historians have pointed out impediments towards such 'political education' in terms of job insecurity, early marriages, linguistic differences between bhadralok organizers and ordinary workers and unintelligible ideological bickering among different socialist activist groups in late 1920s and early 1930s. The importance of such factors is obvious but possibly a more important factor in this context was the workers' distrust of bhadralok 'do gooders'. The crucial significance of the latter could be best understood by analysing the social structure and spatial organization of the mill towns which reminded workers of their supposed social inferiority to Bengali bhadralok inhabitants. The bhadralok enjoyed substantial positions in the municipal administration of the mill towns and as a 'class' utilized such positions to marginalize workers in the economy of these towns. In such circumstances, it is not surprising that even sympathetic bhadralok union leaders were not readily trusted by workers. In many instances, bhadralok nationalists had to establish their credentials by highlighting their long-term association with the labour movement and their sacrifice for the sake of it. It would be wrong to interpret such political language as a reflection of a hierarchical relationship implicit within a pre-bourgeois culture. Such attempts were simply a reflection of the bhadralok attempt to gain credibility in the eyes of their labour constituency. Grass roots-level labour leaders often shrewdly manipulated bhadralok union organizers from diverse political backgrounds.[44]

The intention here is not to present a cynical picture of labour politics in which pragmatic rationalism guided the activities of a grass roots-level working-class leadership. The impact of the Russian and failed German revolutions after the Great War had a distinct echo in Calcutta's labour politics. Urban industrial areas witnessed in the inter-War period prolonged political campaigns by political and social activists of various hues. On the one hand, there were moderate Gandhians such as C.F. Andrews or K.C. Roychowdhury, and on the other there were communist emissaries from the UK as well as indigenous socialist and communist activists, many of whom were trained in the Soviet Union, advised Chinese revolutionaries, or came from Mesopotamian war fronts bringing tales of nationalist revolutionary ferments there. Against the background of such intense political campaigning in the course of industrial action for a prolonged period, workers' politics were radicalized beyond the usual collective bargaining tactics. In 1937, for example, workers made attempts to develop rudimentary grass roots level factory committees that tried to establish control over the production organization in factories. Such organizations made attempts to establish workers' democracy whereby workers' representatives from all departments of the factory formed a chain of committees and tried to exercise control over work practices in every department. But the success of such organizations was contingent upon the wider political power equation in the province. Provincial politics was at the time experiencing a growing communal polarization where the established political organization exhibited little interest in the wider democratic struggle that could forge political nexuses between peasant associations demanding land reforms and workers' movements aiming at reforms in industrial relations.

Politics of Capital, Policies of the Colonial State at Different Levels And the Making of Workers' Politics

The investigation of such a historical conjecture requires an analysis of the interaction between labour politics, the politics of capital, and policy measures of the political institutions of the colonial state in India at different levels. Contemporary nationalist accounts and later Marxist historiography depict how well-organized British capital, enjoying the close patronage of the colonial state, exerted through their cartel—the Indian Jute Manufacturers' Association (hereafter IJMA)—monopsonisitc pressure on the raw jute market and exercised a monopolistic control over the market for finished products.[45] This historiography depicts a starkly contrasting power equation between a well-organized cartel of the jute mill owners enjoying close proximity to the colonial state and disorganized migrant peasants earning a meager livelihood for survival. This situation became far more complicated in the inter-War years with the rise of Marwari traders and mass nationalist movements. Gradually, Marwaris not only made their entry into the IJMA but also a few Indian firms that outside the cartel refused to abide by IJMA's attempt to limit output in accordance with the demand in the market. The government, now partially restrained by the nationalist movement, could not intervene in favour of British traders directly and thus remained seemingly neutral on the issue. This signalled the beginning of a slow decline of the British expatriate hold on industry.[46] A very recent Cambridge thesis brilliantly reasserts the old dogma that it was the rise of Marwari traders that united Anglo-Scottish IJMA bosses and fundamentally restructured the industry.[47]

In recent researches, these assumptions have come under increasing critical scrutiny. The IJMA, it has been argued, was not as powerful as it seemed to be. The cartel was always weak and their seeming agreement on working hours to control production in order to regulate the price of gunny bags—the staple product of the jute industry—was punctured by intense internal rivalries and competition.[48] The rise of the Marwaris in the inter-War years, against the background of the shrinkage of the market, further accelerated these internal rivalries. Expatriate traders had few resources to fall back upon. The colonial state never trusted expatriate business leaders. The tension in the relationship between the colonial state and expatriate traders, according to this set of arguments, can be traced back to the days of the East India Company. These expatriate traders represented the buccaneer free traders who challenged the East India Company's monopoly in the early nineteenth century. The colonial state was thus more a threat than a stable ally. The extent of their hostility was manifest in their social lives as English bureaucrats evaded the company of those traders whom they derisively called 'boxwallahs'. Conflicts with Marwaris appeared to be the nemesis of these expatriate traders because of the particular forms of their business organizations. The managing agency houses and the organizational invention of these traders were suitable in the context of the nineteenth century when they could overcome the paucity of capital by raising funds from the public while managing it through a small cabal of shareholders. A small percentage of the shares would be under the control of the managing agency itself. But they would distribute the remaining shares in such a way that no single group of shareholders would be able to dominate the companies. The managing agents and their trusted allies would constitute the board of directors. The affiliated companies would pay large fees to managing agencies for such management. Legally these companies were autonomous but managing agents would exercise control over them on everyday issues.[49]

In the twentieth century, such agency houses faced the obvious crisis: Indian shareholders demanded more voice in running the firms. The management agency structure appeared to be unnecessarily bureaucratized and centralized but not always effective in maintaining the affiliated company's interests; more ominously old colonial enclaves such as tea, jute, and coal were now outmanoeuvred in terms of the prospect of expansion in newly emerging sectors of the economy such as chemical, steel, and cement.[50] It appears from this historiography that the seemingly omnipotent old British colonial capital was really a vulnerable paper tiger. Haunted by assertive Indian capital, deserted by the colonial state, busy protecting their old confines, these managing agents were presiding over a business empire that was fast disappearing. Given the internecine conflicts among the captains of the jute industry, is it possible to conceive of a homogenous capitalist class? If business politics could be reduced to a morass of juggling interest groups, was it then possible to write a history of labour politics in terms of the contestation between two social classes? How can we interpret these two diametrically opposite views of the history of capital?

The task is indeed very difficult here. Only at their own peril, can historians reject both of these arguments in their totality. A nuanced approach would shy away from such sweeping generalizations. First, theoretically speaking, class may never be taken as a totalizing concept. Class as a historical process was always contested and conflicted by diverse forms of loyalties and interest groups and yet emerged as a political and social entity. It is possible to chart the making and unmaking of social classes and class conflict amid such a seemingly chaotic picture of confrontation and conflicts. It is also plausible to argue from this perspective of class formation as a contested process that class politics in Bengal seemed to have emerged from class struggle even in the absence of a clearly defined stable class structure. This class conflict, centred around the jute industry, in turn deeply influenced the politics of predominantly agrarian regions in Bengal.[51] If we explore this argument in detail in the context of the history of industrial relations in Calcutta and Bengal, it would be possible to explain how the conflicts within industrial relations impinged on the wider politics of Bengal.

The intervening point in this context could be the nature of the relationship between capital and the colonial state in relation to labour politics. First, it would be a gross error to imagine that the relationship between labour, capital, and the colonial state was structured through a uniform polity framework at all levels of industry and the state. Rather, there existed differences in such relationships at different levels of the colonial state. At the grass roots level, the colonial state relied upon the Scottish managers of the mills to govern the mill towns. These managers constituted the thin 'blue line'[52] that supposedly maintained discipline among the unruly mob of migrant workers outside the 'traditional' structure of their rural society. Thus, managers acted as chairmen of the municipalities, judicial magistrates, and the head of local auxiliary forces. Thus the relationship between labour, capital, and the colonial state was forged at the grass root level through the mediation of manager ràj.

A second crucial point, not always recognized, is that the relationship between capital and the state varied at different time periods in accordance with the growing political salience of labour due to changes in international and national situations. In the nineteenth century, both colonial capital and the state often agreed that issues concerning labour unrest could be left in the hands of mill managers and local police forces. It was clear that labour did not enjoy enough political clout at that time to attract the special attention of the state. The situation altered when various segments of labour tried to search for assistance from outside political groups such as the nationalist leadership. At the same time, many among nationalist politicians recognized that labour constituted powerful political constituency which could be used to put pressure on imperial economic nexuses. More importantly, in the 1920s, labour gained further political attention when it became clear that a combination of labour unrest and nationalist mobilization could undermine the hold of the colonial state over the city and its environs. The emergence of socialist and communist organizations played a crucial role in the process. Again, the situation was treated carefully as labour was no longer a matter of regional importance but of international significance. The Russian and German Revolutions created a fear of communist infiltration. In the United Kingdom, radical members of the TUC voiced their disquiet over the labour situation in India. Leaders of the Labour Party tried to evolve a subtle policy of encouraging moderate leaders to establish their hold over emerging trade unions in order to marginalize radical socialists and communists. At the same time a new legal structure was established to deal with labour unrest under the auspices of ILO conventions. However, the colonial state's ultra-sensitive attitude towards communists deepened and took shape with the Meerut conspiracy case. In such circumstances, despite the colonial repressive machinery being used to suppress the general strike of labour in 1929, industrial action led to frequent intervention by the state. These issues were no longer treated as a bipartite matter. At the local level, the state obviously committed the police to arrest strike-leaders and contain the spread of industrial action. But more importantly, the state intervened as a seemingly neutral umpire, albeit refusing to give ground to the demands of socialist and communist politicians. By 1937 with the emergence of the electoral political system the state became an integral part of such negotiation despite serious misgivings within the IJMA about the intention of the state. In other words, the relationships among state, capital, and labour evolved in accordance with the overall process of the growing political clout of labour as significant actor in both international and Indian politics. Such relationships were not static, nor were they based on clearly formulated alliances between the colonial state and expatriate capital. It was contingent upon the power equation among labour movements, the strength of nationalist politics, and a perceived ominous threat from the growing influence of communists and socialists. It is not suggested here that the captains of jute industry did not enjoy a close relationship with the mangers of the colonial state. Benthall himself was a member of the Viceroy's council, while labour leaders such as Dutta Mazumdar and Zaman were frequent visitors to His Majesty's Prison. But the government had to take into account the rapidly changing political power equations at the ground level. The salience of this political process may how be better understood if we focus on the third factor, the evolution of business politics in the jute industry.

Though the IJMA was established in 1884 to voluntarily create a working hours agreement in order to dominate the market, it had never been able to enforce effectively a working hours regime among members. The lure of profit tempted individual companies to expand their loom capacity and violate the agreement through time-cribbing within individual mills. In the 1920s, the IJMA faced an even deeper crisis as the international market reached saturation point even as IJMA mills added new looms and constructed new factories to take advantage of the boom years during the Great War. The real crisis of the IJMA occurred as managing agencies dipped into the reserves to construct new mills and expand the old factories. They also had to raise funds by selling shares, and to pacify the shareholders they had to provide a steady dividend. Thus the real profit margin plummeted and smaller managing agency houses were tempted to emulate mills run by Indians on longer hours. As a consequence, between 1928 and 1939 the IJMA mills entered and exited from diverse forms of working hours agreements but failed to resolve the problem. The entire experiment aimed at driving the 'pirates' or non association mills out of operation did not produce any result. In the end trade feuds only further depleted the IJMA's resources.

Despite the trade feud, it would be wrong to imagine that both Europeans and Indians wished to destroy their business rivals totally. Historians working on the subject have revealed a far more complex picture. Managing agencies raised their capital in India. Most of this money came from Marwari traders who acted as *banias* or brokers to these managing agents. Marwari traders were obviously rewarded in the form of bulk share holding. As the twentieth century progressed they made their presence felt in the board room of the companies of these Managing Agents on the basis of their shareholding strength. The British captains of the IJMA were unable to prevent their entry as their business operation depended upon the steady flow of finances from the Marwari traders. At the same time, Marwari traders knew that undermining these companies would also affect their own interests. After all, they benefited immensely from their shares in these companies. They thus had mutual interests in running the industry.[53] These mutualities were recognized by traders themselves and the trade feud never became an all-out war.

How did these trade feuds and the mechanism of operation of the IJMA influence labour politics? As the IJMA mills repeatedly tried to adjust and readjust their working hours, such strategies impinged on the every on the everyday work practices, wages, and jobs in the mills. This was integrally related to the nature of organization of work according to the shift system, length of working hours, and the pattern of payment of wages. In 1886, soon after the formation of the IJMA, the short time working hours agreement led to complaints among workers over the lack of work and subsequent decline in wages. However, by 1896 when electricity was gradually being introduced in the factories and the composition of labour slowly changed due to the influx of migrant workers, the attempt at tightening the work discipline provided the grounds for the first spate of strikes in the jute mills. It is difficult to calculate wages for jute mills workers because of the reluctance of mill managers to reveal wages in their mills, but one could fairly guess that weavers, who were paid a piece rate or wages according to the amount of cloths being cut and woven, were interested in a particular type of working hours arrangement in comparison to beamers who were paid wages on an hourly basis. A second crucial factor in this regard could be the shift system that arranged work either through single shift which meant one long stretch of working hours and/or through multiple shifts when working hours were divided between different groups of workers in smaller shifts extending to four hours at a stretch. The multiple shift required rather larger number of workers to operate it and was adopted only when markets were expanding rapidly. In the 1920s, with competition stiffening in both international and local markets, the IJMA changed the shift system in individual factories. By 1926 nearly 59 per cent of the mills moved back into the single shift system from the double shift system.[54]

This switch from single to multiple shift contributed to the dislocation of labour, and labour unrest became a regular feature of the industry.

Numerous strikes occurred in individual mills. More importantly, those mills which were under the multiple shift system operated 13½ hour working days but for four days a week. This left the multiple shift system with two days of theoretical margin. Workers were paid an allowance for these two idle days. However, by 1928 the IJMA entered into a great debate over the usefulness of short-time working hours agreement and decided to adopt a 60 hour working week. The IJMA selected such a course of action due to pressure from its constituents for a fuller utilization of their productive capacity in order to drive out the non IJMA mills from the market as well as to compete with new mills in Europe and Latin America. It was decided that the IJMA would implement this new agreement from 1 July 1929.[55] Thus the political process of the formation or an alliance among different segments of capital was informed and influenced by changes in the global capitalist economy as much as by changes in local political and economic alignment among industrialists. For workers, however, such agreement only meant longer working days and a decline in wages. This sparked off the first general strike. In other workers, the dynamics of business politics were such that at the point of their agreement the IJMA's strategies sparked off wider labour resistance that challenged and contested such IJMA strategies. In a way, when business strategies radically threatened everyday work practices and wages, it led to an industry-wide strike by labour.

Similarly, on the labour side the general strike was a product of both local and international intervention by different political interests in shaping the labour movement. There were emissaries of the British Communist Party who were sent to Bengal to organize workers. The first Labour Party government was under pressure from the TUC to look into the affairs of Indian labour. The newly formed ILO was making demands on the Indian state to enact legislation for workers. There was a new expectation that India would experience radical industrialization after World War I. Thus, despite the change of the government in London new legislation was put into place to create the machinery of industrial relations in India.[56] At the same time, alarmed by the growing popularity of Communists among Bombay workers, the Indian state took repressive measures and launched the infamous Meerut conspiracy case. As Calcutta workers attracted the attention of both nationalists and diverse segments of the international trade union and socialist movements, the threat from the IJMA to the everyday work place issues provided a new political context for the explosive general strike in Bengal. Thus the long-term political and economic processes at global and national levels intervened at the everyday level of work organization on the shop floor. It was in these circumstances that Bengal's labour politics changed. The process of the formation of political strategies of the different segments of capital and the working classes could not be isolated from the global political and economic changes although the strategies of each groups came from within these social classes rather than from the outside.

Soon after the general strike the IJMA realized the fullest depth of the crisis that had struck the jute industry with the oncoming depression. Throughout the 1930s, it led an successful battle for a working hours agreement but transferred its losses to labour through radical retrenchment. In the meantime, individual agency houses tightened work discipline within factories. They evolved a sophisticated political strategy to revive their fortune. Indeed, while they faced hostility from local British bureaucrats, they were successful in securing political concessions from the British government in London during the Round Table Conference of 1932. In the communal award of 1932 they obtained a large statutory representation in the Bengal Legislative Assembly. Benthal and his associates in Bengal pursued a powerful strategy of forming a coalition among propertied elements as an investment in the future against the remote possibility of a radical government harmful to colonial economic interests. To European traders, 1937 did not represent inevitable doom. Rather they made a new confident beginning through cobbling together a ramshackle coalition Ministry of the Muslim League and non-Congress elements. They put forward a robust agenda to recover their declining economic fortunes through political negotiation. The coalition government became instrumental to IJMA control over the procurement of raw jute and experimentation with forms of labour administration. Their position was deeply shaken in this period by growing labour radicalism from 1937 onwards and the general strike that shook the entire industry.

In Bengal politics, the depression intensified the process of class polarization and the mushrooming of organization that purported to represent peasants and workers and demanded reforms in existing agrarian and industrial relations. At the same time, the depression was destroying the old symbiotic ties between the peasantry and landlords and communal polarization at all levels of Bengal politics. Both these processes were unsettling for British industrialists and Indian propertied elements alike. A section of Indian property owners and British industrialists came together in an alliance that committed itself to uphold existing property relations. The reforms introduced by this ministry in the sphere of land relations were watered down and did not go as far as promised during electioneering. On the labour front, the coalition among trade unionists won handsome victories on the charter of sweeping industrial reforms. Throughout the depression years labour faced retrenchment and radical reorganization in industrial discipline but the pressure of growing unemployment restrained bargaining strategies. Thus in 1937 jute workers mounted their second general strike against retrenchment in the jute industry. At the same time, the labour strike reinforced the bond between conservative political elites and the expatriate trading lobby. In order to suppress a class-based movement, this coalition made use of sectarian strategies, supporting pro-employer Muslim League unions directly. Initially, the general strike displaced sardars and burrababus from their key positions in maintaining industrial discipline and in many instances empowered workers' committees to maintain a radically democratic production organization in the factories. However, the government soon re-employed many of the sardars in the Muslim League trade union organizations while they ruthlessly suppressed factory committees. Strikes brought closures but did not remedy the situation. In the end, workers gradually withdrew their support from the factory committees which they had formed in earlier stages of the strike. These events left a bitter mutual distrust between Hindu and Muslim workers. No doubt communal riots occurred frequently in mill towns among workers themselves but those riots never led to the formation of communally separate trade unions. As communal feelings were already present at the grass roots level, the government's use of such strategies produced devastating results in the form of growing communal tensions in the mill towns. This new development in the late 1930s sadly transformed the nature of labour politics in the closing years of colonialism and paved the way for an ominous resurgence of mass communalism in Bengal. Thus the historic battle among social classes for the restructuring of industrial relations played a crucial role in transforming Bengal politics as a whole.

Historians are often wrongfooted in their emphasis on a totalizing notion of class. The assumption of ready-made solidarities among supposed social classes, centred around production relations in the factories, denied workers an agency in making their history. This book demonstrates how such solidarities were produced and dismantled in the process of political mobilization at a particular historic conjuncture. The book also points to the making of political strategies and alliances among social classes by investigating the long-term political and economic processes both at the regional and global levels. It also contests simplistic assumptions about the relationship between the colonial state, expatriate capital, and industrial labour. It demonstrates that any ready-made assumption about hostilities between imperial or nationalist interests is superficial without reference to wider political and economic processes that transformed the relationship between the different segments of capital and the different levels of colonial state, as well as the impact of such alliances upon the diverse segments of labour. It shows that these political processes informed the making and unmaking of the politics of social classes. It finally demonstrates that radical changes and realignments in the global capitalist economy and the political contests between forces defending different segments of capital at the global level and movements purporting to represent labour and diverse types of socialism informed and influenced the process of class formation at the local regional levels in the remotest corner of the British empire. It would be difficult to understand politics in late colonial Bengal without referring to them.

The study of Indian politics in this period from such a perspective would also imply that no social classes exercised hegemony in Bengal politics in this period. Rather, one could observe in the inter-War period a desperate attempt to establish political and economic hegemony by various types of coalition among propertied elements and how such attempts generated stubborn resistance from the working classes. The absence of such hegemony made the political and economic process more fluid and marked by bitter contestations among different segments of capital, between capital and different segments of labour, and between the retreating colonial state and the forces opposed to colonialism, and among different forms of nationalist movements and their putative constituencies. The unfolding of industrial conflict along class lines and the use of sectarian tactics to overcome the challenge of the working classes constituted a crucial element in such a moment. There were no predetermined paths cobbled out for major political actors in such a situation; actors themselves developed their strategies in response to wider political and economic processes. It also reveals that, though it may be fashionable to abandon the notion of class as a category of political analysis, there is enormous opportunity in using an open-ended notion of social class to understand the making and unmaking of classes and their strategies in politics. Indeed, it is particularly useful to make sense of labour politics and the aspirations of workers as agents of their own history provided we remove a teleological, economically deterministic perspective of class as a given category from the notion of working-class movements. The aim here is to produce a humane understanding of workers as makers of their own strategies and their struggle to shape Bengal's political and economic history for a more democratic and egalitarian society against the global background of the historic battle among different terms of socialism and imperialism. In a word, then, workers deployed self-conscious strategies, shaped by the conditions of the urban environment, in their negotiations with capitalists, as well as in their relations with the political institutions that operated within the apparatus of the colonial state in the global context of the transformation in capitalist economy.

Theoretical Concerns and Chapterization of the Monograph

The organization of this monograph follows a specific theoretically-informed narrative structure. The first chapter traces the pattern of the formation of the working classes by investing the significance of rural–urban relations in the life of migrants. It shows how workers used their village bases as source of security for survival in the urban labour market. From an analysis of the urban-rural relationship, it also examines the lived experience of the working-classes in terms of their community formations at the quotidian level in the mill towns. Indeed social class was not simply a heuristic social construct. Rather, workers entered into various sets of social relationships sharing particular behavioural dispositions which were manifest in their everyday life. Chapter 2 also explores the importance of religious, linguistic, and regional ties among workers to understand their influence in the social organization both in the workplace and the neighbourhood. Chapter 3 provides us with crucial background to another feature of life in industrial settings where entire regions came to be defined in terms of the social polarities between classes in the physical organization of the towns, and this found expression in the political governance of such towns and the development of the local political institutional structure. It analyses how the pattern of operation of institutional politics at the local level influenced the labour movement and examines why Indian professional elites, mainly bhadralok politicians who were also active in the local administration, remained hostile to the working-classes.

Chapter 4 describes the development of the labour movement in the late nineteenth and early twentieth centuries. It shows how workers evolved their forms of political action against the employers and the state. It also explains the reasons for nationalist reluctance to support workers in the late nineteenth century and the failure of swadeshi agitators to win the support of the workers. Chapter 5 examines changes in the labour movement in the post war years. On the eve of the non-cooperation movement, massive strikes by industrial workers widened the scope of popular anti-government agitations. Gandhian politicians, however, intervened to restrain labour militancy. Paradoxically, the growing participation of workers in the nationalist movement led to a decline in the support for Gandhian trade unions in the jute mills. Chapter 6 discusses how labour politics, after the collapse of non-cooperation witnessed both a growth in left-wing political struggles and sectarian clashes, which brought issues of class and community into active contradiction in the 1920s and 1930s. Chapter 7 discerns the process of changes in industrial workers' politics and the interaction between it and government formation in Bengal. It establishes how this process of interaction influenced and informed Bengal politics in general. This monograph examines workers' politics at four different levels. It starts from the level of formation of working classes through to the level of the emergence of class as lived experience of shared lives in urban areas marked by distinctive industrial social geography and style of governance. Finally, it surveys processes of collective action within the industry, and their impact on the wider politics of nationalist and socialist mobilizations.

Notes

1. *Congress Socialist*, 13 March 1937, No. 10, p. 13. Quoted in A. Cox 'The Calcutta General Strike of 1937' draft paper, p. 27.

2. A government official observes regarding the 1929 general strike 'The fact that the contents of these pamphlets seems to have been so quickly assimilated by such a large body of workers suggest that there must be in the jute mill area considerably more literacy than the census statistics show'. *Royal Commission of Labour in India* (here after *RCLI*) Vol. V Part I, The Note of Gilchrist, p. 144.

3. Communication from Secretary, Government of Bengal (hereafter GOB) to Government of India (hereafter GOI) dated 13 May 1879, National Archives of India (hereafter NAI) General No. 31 of January 1880. Quoted in R. Dasgupta 'Material Conditions and Behaviourial Aspects of Calcutta Working-Class', Occasional Paper Centre for Studies in Social Sciences, Calcutta, 1975, p. 13.

4. *Report of Indian Factory Labour Commission* (Vol. I Report and Appendices) London, 1908, p. 18.

5. *Labour in the United Kingdom Dependencies,* Central Offices of Information, Reference Pamphlet, London 1957, p. 13.

6. See for example, P. Joyce, 'Work' in F.M.L. Thompson (ed.), *The Cambridge Social History of Great Britain 1750–1950, II,* Cambridge, 1990; and also P. Joyce, *Visions of the People: Industrial England and the Question of Class.* Cambridge University Press, 1991, Ch 1. Though Joyce tends to reject the classical notion of class explained by Marxist scholars in totality and brings forth a post-Marxist critique, many of the questions raised in his work chart out the problems associated with the classical assumption of proletarianization of the working class. This does not mean that this work accepts such post-Marxist critique, rather it simply points out the problems of transposing historical theories mechanically from one context to another.

7. Arjan de Haan in his highly valuable study tends to reaffirm many of these assumptions though his own findings point in a different direction. He argues 'To understand the perspective on employment [of jute workers] one has to consider this from the perspective of the village. Somebody born and brought up in the village has a different perspective on work and living in the city and working in a large-scale enterprise. I assume that people in the village are used to irregularity in production. Life in the village is very insecure; crops are insecure, depending on rains and floods and prices show large variations …. In this sense, the workers dismissed in 1931 may not have been surprised: they left with the money they had earned, went back to their home, and waited for the next opportunity, perhaps the next season.' Arjan de Haan *Unsettled Settlers: Migrant Worker and Industrial Capitalism in Calcutta,* Rotterdam, 1994 p. 28. This portrayal presents the picture of a highly idealized peasant worker unwilling to resist retrenchment in the factories as he did not have a notion of life-long work. Yet de Haan fails to mention that the general strike of 1937 was actually a protest against the continued practice of large-scale dismissal of workers.

8. Rajat Ray, *Social Conflict and Political Unrest in Bengal 1875–1927.* Delhi, 1984; J.H. Broomfield, *Elite Conflict in Plural society: Twentieth Century Bengal,* Berkeley, 1968; L. Gordon, *Bengal: The Nationalist Movement 1876–1940,* Delhi, 1974.

9. Broomfield, *Elite Conflict in Plural society: Twentieth Century Bengal,* Berkeley, 1968, Dipesh Chakrabarty 'Communal Riots and Labour: Bengal's Jute Mill Hands in the 1890s', *Past and Present,* 91, May 1981, pp. 140–169. Only exception to such historiography is Sumit Sarkar's *Swadeshi movement in Bengal 1903–1908.* New Delhi, 1973; and also 'The conditions and nature of subaltern militancy: Bengal from Swadeshi to Non-cooperation', in Ranajit Guha (ed.) *Subaltern Studies III,* New Delhi, pp. 271–320.

10. This argument is forcefully voiced by Rajat Ray, a historian of Bengal politics. He dismissed Calcutta workers as an insignificant political force who 'showed themselves incapable of any combination.' Ray locates the cause of the absence of trade-unions in Bengal in the 'rural connections' of the workers. According to him '[w]orkers were still tied to their native village, where they went back every summer to look after their families and lands. There was, therefore, no question of their undergoing a thorough process of urbanization and losing their traditional rural identities.' R. Ray, *Social Conflict and Political Unrest in Bengal 1875–1927*, Delhi, 1984, p. 38.

11. The emphasis in this literature is on the extra coercion and pressure on the countryside exercised through the colonial state and the migrants being forced out of their habitats. This argument constitutes the fundamental premise of the writings of J. Bremaan in *Of Peasants, Migrants and Paupers: Rural Labour Circulation and Capital Production in West India*. Oxford, 1985; *Labour Migration and Rural Transformation in Colonial Asia*. Comparative Asian Studies 5, Free University Press, Amsterdam, 1990, Guy Standing, 'Circulation and Labour Process, in Guy Standing (ed.), *Labour Circulation and Labour Process*. London, 1985. Such arguments imagine a ready-made alliance between colonial state and expatriate capitalist class which in reality was far more complex and varied in different periods. Such relationship was conditioned by the permutation and combination of political power equations between nationalist movements, pressures from Indian capitalist class, and workers themselves.

12. R. Hilton, 'Peasant Society, Peasant Movements and Feudalism in Medieval Europe', in H.A. Landsberger (ed.), *Rural Protest Peasant Movement and Social Change*, London, 1974.

13. Peasant movements and rural politics came to constitute one of the core areas of post-colonial history writings. A.R. Desai, D. Dhangare, Eric Stokes, Peter Reeves, and later on Majid Siddiqi all pioneered the move in this direction. Eric Stokes' celebrated work on the Return of the Peasants captured the powerful role of peasantry in nationalist movement. The writing of peasant history and peasant consciousness acquired a new dimension with the rise of subaltern studies. R. Guha's primary motive was to discover a distinct form of peasant consciousness that was autonomous of elite domination. For an interesting discussion of these issues, see C.A. Bayly's review article 'Rallying Around the Subaltern'. In Vinayak Chaturvedi (ed.), *Mapping Subaltern Studies and the Postcolonial*, London, 2000.

14. A new powerful paradigm of inquiries in the South African context is put forward by S. Marks and R. Rathbone when they argue 'African migrants still have access to land and first generation proletarians still have a consciousness in part informed by their rural class position. While shaped by their precolonial experience, however the nature of the African working class clearly cannot be understood outside the imperatives of late nineteenth-century imperialism and South Africa's mining

economy'. S. Marks and R. Rathbone (ed.), *Industrialisation and Social Change in South Africa: African Class formation, Culture and Consciousness 1870–1930*, Harlow, 1982 p. 8. Apart from highly industrialized South Africa, such observations were made regarding the dock workers of Mombassa though in a different way. It is observed that the independence of dock workers of Mombassa could be attributed to their persistent rural connections. Frederick Cooper, *On the African Water Front*, New Haven, 1987.

15. R.S. Chandavarkar, *The Origins of Industrial Capitalism in India: Business Strategies and the Working Classes in Bombay, 1900–1940*, Cambridge, 1994.

16. Ibid.

17. A.K. Bagchi has drawn attention to the contrast between Calcutta and Bombay in terms of industrial growth and investment pattern in his *The Private Investment in India 1900–1939*, New Delhi, 1980, pp. 117–57.

18. See Dipesh Chakrabarty, *Rethinking Working Class History Bengal 1890–1940*, Princeton, 1989, p. 217.

19 To quote Marx, 'economic condition had first transformed the mass of the people of the country into workers: The combination of capital has created for this mass a common situation, common interests. This mass is thus already a class as against capital, but not yet for itself. In the struggle, of which we have noted only a few phases, this mass becomes united, and constitutes itself as a class for itself. The interests it defends become class interests. But the struggle of class against class is a political struggle, K. Marx 'The Eighteenth Brumaire of Louis Bonaparte', in Marx and Engles, *Selected Works Vol. 3.* Moscow, 1969, pp. 479.

20. E.P. Thompson 'The Peculiarities of the English' originally published in R. Milliband and J. Saville (eds), *Socialist Register*, London, 1965. Republished in E.P. Thompson, *Poverty of Theory and other Essays*, London, 1978.

21. I. Katznelson, *Working—Class Formation: Nineteenth Century Patterns in Western Europe and the United States,* London, 1986, pp. 14–23.

22. See Panchanan Saha, *History of the Working Class Movement in Bengal,* Delhi 1978; Ranajit Dasgupta, 'Structure of the Labour Market in Colonial India', *Economic and Political Weekly,* (hereafter *EPW*) Special No. November 1981; Ranajit Dasgupta, 'Factory Labour in Eastern India—Sources of Supply 1855–1946', *Indian Economic and social History review* (hereafter *IESHR*), Vol. 8, No. 3, 1976; Ira Mitra concentrates only on political leaders in her article on the trade union movement in Bengal. Ira Mitra, 'Growth of Trade union Consciousness among the Jute Mill workers', *EPW*, Special Number, November 1981. Parimal Ghosh, *Colonialism, Class and a History of the Calcutta Jute Millhands 1880–1930*, Hyderabad, 2000; Parimal Ghosh in his analysis of the working-class conflict integrates urban workers' experience with their rural social background and argues that jute workers' 'conflicts' with the colonial state was primarily conditioned by their experience of overall colonial exploitation, In his view, jute workers' perception of European supervisors' attitude

in the industry was coloured by their experience 'of the oppression of the indigo planters' in north Bihar villages. Sanat Bose, 'Industrial Unrest and Growth of Labour Unions in Bengal 1920–24' *EPW*, Special Number, November 1981, Sanat Bose in his article focuses on the perceptions of the political parties on labour politics but ignores the impact of such politics on the daily life of jute workers.

23. I am indebted to Deep Kanta Lahiri Choudhury for drawing my attention to different possible historical meanings of the word quotidian.

24. This explanation follows the nuanced and creative interpretation provided by R.S. Chandavarkar in his *This Origins of Industrial Capitalism in India: Business Strategies and the Working-Classes in Bombay, 1900–1940,* Cambridge, 1994.

25. Ranajit Dasgupta, a prominent Marxist labour historian of Bengal, observes that working-class agitations in the late nineteenth century were arrested to the primitive stage of individualistic protests marked by incipient class consciousness due to circumscribed industrial growth. Dasgupta views the 'working-class movement' as an unilinear progress towards class consciousness marked by various stages of transition. He thus explains labour politics in the late nineteenth century Bengal as an era of transition from 'individualistic protests to class protests'. Ranajit Dasgupta, 'Material conditions and, behavioural aspects of Calcutta working class 1875–99' Occasional Paper No. 22, Centre for studies in Social Sciences, Calcutta 1979; also his *Migrant Workers, Rural Connexions and Capitalism. The Calcutta Jute Industrial Labour 1890s to 1940s,* Indian Institute of Management, Calcutta, 1987, and his more recent work *Labour and Working Class in Eastern India: Studies in Colonial History,* Calcutta, 1994.

26. Leela Fernandes, *Producing Workers: The politics of Gender, Class and Culture in the Calcutta Jute Mills.* Philadelphia, 1997.

27. S. Hall, 'What is This "Black" in Black Popular Culture?', in Gina Dent (ed.) *Black Popular Culture,* Seattle, 1992.

28. Samita Sen has put forward a pioneering hypothesis regarding how the male-centred language of trade union politics tends to marginalize women workers in trade union politics. However, Sen sometimes overstates her case as there were also instances of how grassroots-level factory committees are used by women to voice their concerns particularly in moments of conflict. S. Sen, *Women and Labour in Late Colonial India: The Bengal Jute Industry,* Cambridge, 1999; R.S. Chandavarkar has put forward the hypothesis regarding the contested nature of identities as category in the context of Bombay working classes. See R.S. Chandavarkar, *The Origins of Industrial Capitalism in India: Business Strategies and the Working Classes in Bombay, 1900–1940,* Cambridge, 1994.

29. R. William, *Marxism and Literature,* Oxford, 1977.

30. Stuart Hall, *The Hard Road to Renewal: Thatcherism and the Crisis of the Left,* London, 1988.

31. For a perceptive analysis of the subject please see V. Chaturvedi, 'Introduction' in V. Chaturvedi (ed.), *Mapping Subaltern Studies and the Postcolonialism,* London, 2000.

32. B.S. Cohn, *An Anthropologist among the Historians and other essays,* Delhi, 1987. This is a collection of articles written over a longer period of time but reveals his methodological concerns. In the introduction to the book, Ranajit Guha repeatedly referred to Cohn's contribution to the development of this new methodology that combined anthropological queries with historical investigation. Recently Cohn wrote a new monograph on the subject entitled *Colonialism and its forms of knowledge: The British India.*

33. E. Said, *Orientalism,* London, 1978.

34. See V. Chaturvedi, *Mapping Subaltern Studies,* p. xii. Said himself stated in the foreword of the selected subaltern studies that 'in reading this selection from Subaltern Studies one becomes aware that this group of scholars is a self-conscious part of the vast post-colonial cultural and critical effort.' 'Foreword' *Selected Subaltern Studies* New Work, 1988, pp. v–x Quoted in V. Chaturvedi, *Mapping Subaltern Studies* p. xviii, end note 49.

35. Partha Chatterjee, *Bengal 1920–47: The Land Question,* Calcutta, 1984.

36. E. Duyker, *Tribal Guerrillas: The Santals of West Bengal and Naxalite Movement,* New Delhi, 1987, In a perceptive comparison with *Sendero Luminoso* (The Shining Path)—the Peruvian Maoist movement, Tom Brass points out the similarities among the Maoist formulations across continents and their proclivity to combine anti-urbanism, anti-imperialism, ethnic chauvinism, and peasant essentialism. Tom Brass, 'Moral Economics, Subalterns, New Social Movement and the Re-emergence of a (Post-) Modernized (Middle) Peasant', in V. Chaturvedi, *Mapping Subaltern Studies.*

37. R. Guha, *Elementary Aspect of Peasant Insurgency in Colonial India,* Delhi, 1983.

38. D. Chakrabarty, *Rethinking Working-Class History: Bengal 1890–1940,* Princeton, 1989.

39. Suchetana Chattapadhaya, 'Muzaffar Ahmed: The making of an Early Communist' (A thesis in progress, School of Oriental and African Studies, University of London) traces this process very effectively.

40. Henry Pelling, *A History of British Trade Unionism,* Harmondsworth, 1963; *The Origins of the Labour Party,* Oxford, 1954.

41. V.I. Lenin, *What is to be done?* (Originally published in 1902); Translated into English by Joe Fineberg and George Hanna. Introduction and Glossary by Robert Service, London, 1988. Lenin's view in this regard is contradicted by the Polish-born German revolutionary Rosa Luxemburg who emphasizes more on direct struggle by working class rather than being patronized by professional revolutionaries

or intellectuals. For details see Iring Fetsher 'Class Consciousness' in Tom Bottomore (ed.), *A Dictionary of Marxist Thought* (Second Revised Edition) Oxford, 1991, p. 91.

42. E.J. Hobsbawm (1971) Notes on Class Consciousness in *Worlds of Labour: Further Studies in the world of labour,* London, 1984, p. 27.

43. The term socialist is used here deliberately. In strict sense we find historians describing various politicians as Communists and Leninists while these politicians spent their lives in opposing the influence of Communist Party of India. On the other hand, in labour politics many politicians changed their sides very rapidly. Only a few had their connections with the official Communist Party. Many identified with Marxism and Leninism but refrained from joining the Communist Party while many worked with the Communist Party but remained non-Leninist in their political beliefs.

44. It is Tanika Sarkar who had put across this thesis and drawn attention to the possibility of exploring in depth such an argument. T. Sarkar, *Bengal 1928–1934 Politics of Protests,* Delhi, 1987.

45. For such an analysis see Amiya Bagchi's classic account *Private Investment in India, 1900–1939.* Cambridge, 1972; A.K. Dasgupta 'The Jute Industry in India 1857–1956' in V.B. Singh (ed.), *Economic History of India 1857–1956,* Bombay, 1956; Saugata Mukherji 'Some Aspects of Commercialization of Agriculture in Eastern India, 1891–1938' in Ashok Sen, P. Chatterjee and S. Mukherji (eds), *Perspectives in Social Science, II: Three Studies on the Agrarian Structure of Bengal Before Independence,* Delhi, 1982; R. Dasgupta, *Labour and Working Class in Eastern India: Studies in Colonial History,* Calcutta, 1994.

46. D. Chakrabarty, *Rethinking Working Class History Bengal 1890–1940,* Princeton, 1989.

47. A.R. Cox, 'Paternal Despotism and Workers' Resistance in the Bengal Jute Industry 1920–40', Cambridge PhD thesis, March 2000.

48. O. Goswami, *Industry, Trade and Peasant Society: The Jute Economy of Eastern India 1900–1947,* Delhi, 1991.

49. Ibid., pp. 12–13.

50. M. Misra, *Business, Race and Politics in British India,* Chapter 3, 'Industry and Innovation', pp. 86–103.

51. This interesting proposition about the relationship between class struggle and class formation was originally made by E.P. Thompson in the context of eighteenth century England where he observed interestingly the existence of class struggle even though class in its institutional form did not come into existence. The evidence for this, according to Thompson, could be located in the polarization of antagonistic interests and the corresponding dialectic of culture. He also warns us— which is particularly valuable in Calcutta's context: In the eighteenth century

resistance is less articulate, although often very specific, direct, and turbulent. One must therefore supply the articulation, in part by de-coding the evidence of behaviour, and in part by turning over the bland concepts of the ruling authorities and looking at their undersides. If we do not do this we are in danger of becoming prisoners of the assumptions and self-image of the rulers: free labourers are seen as the loose and disorderly sort, riot is seen as spontaneous and blind; and important kinds of social protest become lost in the category of 'crime'. E.P. Thompson, Eighteenth century English society: Class Struggle without Class, *Social History* Vol. 3, No. 2, p. 154.

52. For details of comparative study of colonial policing see David M. Anderson and David Killingray, *Policing the Empire: Government, Authority and Control, 1830–1946,* Manchester, 1991.

53. This has been correctly pointed out by Dipesh Chakrabarty. D. Chakrabarty, *Rethinking Working-Class History,* pp. 57–8.

54. *RCLI* Vol. V Pt. I, *Evidence Bengal,* pp. 127–8.

55. *RCLI* Vol. V Pt. II, *Evidence Bengal,* pp. 127–12.

56. In the 1920s various labour reforms came into existence which no doubt had an impact on industrial relations in Bengal. The amended Factories Act 1922, the Workmen's Compensation Act 1923, the Trade-Union's Act 1926, the Trade Dispute's Act 1928, the Maternity Benefit Bills 1929, and the Payment of Wages Act 1933. The concerns regarding labour in the highest echelon of British government is evident in the Private Office Papers of the Secretary of State for India. Notes on Trade Union Congress Deputation to the Secretary of State, July 23, 1924, Private Office Paper, Secretary of State, L/PO/1/14, IOL.

2

Rural–urban Migration, Caste, Religion, and Class

Situating Workers' Politics in the Bengal Jute Industry 1890–1937

This chapter investigates the nature of rural-urban migration of jute mill workers. It further examines the social world of workers in the mill towns. It argues that the periodic migration of industrial workers to their villages was not necessarily a reflection of their lack of commitment to urban jobs. Rather, trapped between diminishing returns from the agrarian economy and an overcrowded labour market, jute industry workers needed to maintain their village ties for survival in industrial areas.[1] Thus, contrary to the common assumptions of scholars, workers were unsettled settlers because of the lack of investment in urban infrastructure, the nature of urban ecology, and public health system.

This chapter further argues that though in urban areas migrants depended upon their fellow villagers, members of the same caste, religion, and linguistic group for support and help, these identities were by no means fixed or permanent. Caste, religious, and linguistic affiliations always intersected with each other.[2] The overlapping and changing nature of these identities militated against the possibilities of the development of community identities based on kinship ties.[3] In addition, migrant workers always had an oscillatory existence in both rural and urban areas. Some workers maintained two different households in urban and rural areas. In urban working-class households, the sexual relationship between women and men often cut across caste and language boundaries. Jute workers were thus not divided into various separate watertight communities governed by a specific set of caste or religious norms; instead these features of their social life might have limited the possibilities of 'self conscious construction of communities' among them.[4]

Sardars, who were sometimes perceived as representatives of a modified version of the village authority structure,[5] were also not a homogeneous group acting as leaders of different labouring communities. Power and authority in the workplace and outside depended on a combination of forces and was constantly negotiated between different social groups. Some sardars, who established a powerful presence in factories, combined their control over the workplace with influence in the slums where they further competed with grocers, liquor sellers, and local toughs.[6]

Despite their diverse social backgrounds, workers shared common grievances over low wages, long working hours, increasing intensity of their workload, and unsafe working conditions, which resulted in serious accidents. Through periodic strikes mill hands created pressure on the managers to improve living conditions in the mills. The survival strategies of industrial workers included both dependence on the social network based on kinship ties and collective bargaining. Crucial to these networks and work culture within the factories was the notion of custom (*dasturi*), fairness (*insaf*) and honour (*izzat*). These are complex social signifiers through which workers developed their ideology of everyday work-practice. Even in organizing strikes these notions played an important role in creating a unity among workers.

In other words, the significance of caste, language, and religion-based nexuses can be better understood if we situate them in the contexts of everyday social and economic insecurities of urban working-class life as well as in moments of conflicts and political mobilization. These networks, in different contexts, provide workers with complex markers to identify themselves as workers, as Muslims, or as Bengalis. In the process of political mobilization social ties were thus infused with different meanings in order to construct seemingly homogenous community identities for the purpose of political mobilization.

Migration Pattern and Survival Strategies of Industrial Workers in Calcutta-Howrah Industrial Belt

Calcutta in the late nineteenth century became a vast and thriving city. It functioned as the transit point for Indian raw materials to the outside world, labour for the overseas colonies, and manufactured products for distribution within India. The dramatic rise of Calcutta as the 'second city' of the empire was accompanied by industrial growth in the immediate neighbourhood of the metropolis. New investments in various industrial activities transformed the hitherto rural riverine regions of Howrah, Hooghly, and the 24 Parganas into a highly urbanized and densely populated area. The influx of single male migrant workers changed the demographic composition of the locality. Pivotal to this process of industrial expansion and urban growth was the jute industry. Jute mills stretched over an area of 20 miles along the banks of the Hooghly, both north and south of the city. The jute mill belt was confined to 6 miles on both sides of the Hooghly.[7] Expansion in the jute industry in the riparian belt gave birth to numerous towns essentially centred around the mills and thus created a vast suburban belt surrounding Calcutta. By 1912, there were 61 jute factories in this region employing nearly 200,000 workers.[8] Many of these workers continued to migrate to and fro from villages to the town across five hundred miles from the interior of eastern United Province (hereafter UP) and Bihar. The roots of such circular migration can be explained clearly by examining rural and urban contexts of the workers' world.

The changes in the rural economy of Bihar and east UP crucially influenced the pattern of formation of the migrant work force in Bengal. The districts of north and central Bihar and east UP were located in the middle of the vast and fertile plain of northern India. In the closing decades of the nineteenth century these districts witnessed far-reaching social and economic transformations. By the 1890s, due to rapid population growth, the demographic pressure on land increased significantly.[9] Virtually all cultivable land were brought under the plough.[10] This in turn had an adverse effect on pastures.[11] Pastoral communities in Bihar and east UP were forced to give up pastoral pursuits and became cultivators.[12] As pressure on land increased, family holdings were increasingly subdivided. Villages in east UP and Bihar became mosaics of little pieces of land, each piece belonging to a different holding.[13] Such subdivision and fragmentation of holdings increased the cost of cultivation and reduced the returns.[14]

The steady growth of population and the relentless extension of cultivation also adversely affected the natural resources for agriculture. Bihar and east UP were not areas of heavy rainfall.[15] Here cultivation to a great extent relied upon irrigation. But marshes and creeks, which were sources of water supply, dried up and tanks were filled up for new cultivable land.

The proportion of irrigated areas to total cultivable land was stagnant in this period.[16] This made agriculture far more dependent on the monsoon and the failure of which could have disastrous consequences.[17] Central Bihar, which was primarily a rice-producing area, often suffered from drought in the late nineteenth century.[18] Agriculture in north Bihar was similarly dependent on irrigation from private wells but these were insufficient for local needs. Perhaps the peasants' need for water was most aptly reflected in the Bhojpuri saying:

Charat barse Adra, urat barse Hast
Kitna Raja Dandi le, sukhi rahe grihast.[19]

(If rain falls at the end of Hast September, the cultivator will be happy no matter how much of grain the landlord takes from him.)

Population growth apart, the Permanent Settlement introduced by the British in Bihar since the 1790s, tightened the control of the landlords over diminishing rural resources and thus served to deepen the agrarian crisis. It has frequently been argued that the Permanent Settlement initiated, or at least accelerated the commercialization of the agrarian economy, especially of land, primarily through the sale of estates of defaulting *zamindars* (revenue collectors enjoying proprietary rights over land) and tenants.[20] In reality, the zamindars, who often combined money-lending with the income from landed estates,[21] acquired land from indebted peasants.[22] Tenants were frequently forced off the land and as landless labourers they lived on the edge of starvation. Increasingly, as zamindars acquired large landed estates, land distribution became extremely unequal and the average size of peasant holdings decreased.[23]

Moreover, the zamindars imposed various forms of exactions on the peasantry that never appeared in the government's calculations, like forced labour on zamindars' land, homage, or appropriation of the produce of orchards.[24] The zamindars were also entitled to tax the tenants for the maintenance of tanks and roads, even though they spent little on the development of rural estates.[25] Tenants were also subjected to arbitrary levies known as '*abwabs*'.

During the nineteenth century these zamindars, the so called 'natural leaders' of the people and guardians of agricultural progress, increasingly became absentee landlords.[26] The collection of revenue and village administration in most of the cases were left to the *thikadars*. Originally tax collecting officials, these thikadars, in the nineteenth century, leased an area and paid rent to the landlords. By this arrangement the thikadars were entitled to proprietors' rights on the land. Often these *thikas* were sold to the highest bidder. The thikadars, for their part, also raised rent and extracted levies from their tenants whenever they could.[27] 'There can be no doubt whatever', declared the Lieutenant Governor of Bengal in 1877, 'that the combined influence of zamindars (landlords) and ticcadars (land speculators) has ground the ryots (farmers) of Behar to a state of extreme depression and misery ...'.[28]

In the late nineteenth century, commercialization of agriculture led to a further decline of the conditions of the peasants. In this period, the improvement in the road and especially rail networks helped to open up distant markets for the local agricultural products of Bihar and east UP.[29] In Bihar this wider access to the market enabled the zamindars and affluent tenants to store produce until prices rose and make large profits. However, poor peasants enjoyed little from expanding market networks. Spiralling rent from the land forced poor peasants to sell their crops to the zamindars. Moreover, in order to maximize profits, zamindars in many areas tried to switch over from *nagdi* or cash rent to *bhaoli* or produce rent. This attempt at the reintroduction of produce rent also possibly depleted the stock of food crops which peasants stored for consumption. In a period of increasing prices of food crops this perhaps pushed them further towards the edge of starvation. This presumably led to constant conflicts between landlords and tenants over the forms of the revenue payment.[30] The mood of peasant bitterness was aptly captured in a local saying:

Du dana me sen ek dana jamidar lehala aur ek dana asami ke dehala.

(Of two grains the landlord takes one and gives one to the cultivators.)[31]

In the late nineteenth century, with the deepening of the agrarian crisis, numerous small peasants faced starvation. It was reported that in some districts of Bihar the size of peasant holdings was so small that peasant families could not even afford 'two meals a day'.[32] Wages of agricultural workers were low and remained stagnant for a long time.[33] Hunger was a condition of life for the rural poor. Following the suicide of a twenty year old woman at Etawah in 1872, a local official observed that

her husband was an agricultural labourer, and that, in addition to his wife he supported an aged mother. His daily earnings when in regular employment during the whole day were twenty five chittacks (fifty ounces) of behjur. His wife in weeding times obtained fifteen chittacks or thirty ounces of behjur. He only eats salt once in eight days ... oil, spices or vegetables he never tastes. The three grown up people were, he says, always in state of hunger.[34]

The implication of the story was that the woman had been driven to suicide by hunger. Prisoners in the local jails, who were also day labourers, told him that starvation had compelled them to steal. Throughout the late nineteenth century the purchasing power of the 'poorer classes' in this rural region constantly declined.[35] Famines and scarcities marked the region from 1860s onwards.[36] By the 1890s the rural population became vulnerable to diseases and succumbed to epidemics of malaria, *kalazar* and the plague.[37] Population which had been growing since the early nineteenth century now started to decline.[38] It became clear that an alternative source of income was essential for the survival of the rural population.[39] The famines, starvation, and epidemics caused large-scale exodus of people from these regions to Bengal and Assam.

With the introduction of the railways, migration became much easier. The railway journey from Bihar and east UP to Bengal took only two days, which made it possible for the migrants to return to their villages more frequently.[40] The volume of migration was so large that the railway companies made significant profits to reduce the cost of travel which in turn stimulated further migration.[41] By the first decade of the twentieth century, migrants from Bihar and east UP districts were found all over eastern India and overseas colonies. A sizeable section of Bihar peasants were employed in jute presses, railway sites, and road construction in east Bengal.[42] In addition, migrants from this region were sent as indentured labourers for the tea gardens.[43] The overseas colonies also received a large share of these migrants. Between 1889 and 1900, nearly 15,162 residents of Ghazipur alone were registered for travelling to British Guyana, Trinidad, Natal, and Mauritius.[44]

At the very point when the flow of migration from Bihar and east UP quickened in the 1890s, the jute industry in Bengal began to grow rapidly. This mass movement of migrants to Calcutta and the neighbouring emerging industrial areas not only ensured an abundance of labour, but provided an impetus to the proliferation of jute mill towns as well. In fact, from 1896 some of the mills in 24 Parganas had begun to replace local labour with 'up country' mill hands.[45] The most densely-packed migrant-dominated industrial enclave in the region was the Kankinara–Jagatdal–Bhatpara–Naihati belt, wherein twelve Jute mills and three other large factories and 85,000 people were packed in an area of 5.5 square miles.[46] The contrast between the population density in the region in the late nineteenth and the early twentieth centuries is more clear from the description of the peaceful, retired villages by Breverly in the Bengal census report of 1872:

Even in the neighbourhood of Calcutta the so called townships are mere collections of villages. Villages closely situated and densely populated it is true, but still with small pretensions to be designed [as] towns. The villages are grouped together for municipal purposes, and are thus shown in the census tables as towns: but cattle graze, and rice were sown and reaped in their very midst.[47]

The recent and the rapid growth of the mill towns was also reflected in the changed linguistic composition of their residents. The compiler of the 24 Parganas district gazetteer in 1914 commented 'that some mill towns are now practically foreign towns planted in the midst of Bengal.' In Bhatpara, according to same source, 'four persons speak Hindi to each person speaking Bengali.' In Titagarh 75.1 per cent of the inhabitants were Hindi speakers while only 11 per cent speak Bengali (apart from 8 per cent Telegu and 4 per cent Oriya speakers).[48]

The mill settlements on the western bank of the East India Railway, namely, Sreerampur, Rishra, Uttarpara, Baidyabati, and Bhadreswar, underwent similar changes as the flow of migrant workers also increased in these areas from the 1890s onwards.[49] For example, between 1891 and 1911, during the peak period of the influx of migrant workers from Bihar and east UP, Sreerampur and Baidyabati added nearly 94 per cent and 163 per cent to their population.[50] In Hooghly district the highest population density was also found in the Sreerampur subdivision. By 1911, the Sreerampur subdivision, which is a narrow riparian strip, contained five municipal towns and had as many as 5,098 persons per square mile. The census of 1911 recorded 50,740 jute industrial workers in Hooghly district.[51] Similarly, Calcutta's twin city Howrah witnessed rapid industrial development in these decades.[52]

However, this sudden transformation of hitherto unknown rural areas into a highly urbanized industrial belt was confined to a narrow enclave. In the early twentieth century, two-thirds of the industrial undertakings in Bengal were located in Calcutta and the metropolitan districts of Howrah, Hooghly, and 24 Parganas. The operatives at work in the mills in these metropolitan districts constituted over half of the total industrial work-force in the province. In 1911, the rest of the province, with an area of 70,000 square miles and a population of 38.25 million, had only two hundred mills which employed 35,000 workers.[53] Urban expansion in Bengal was also limited to this region. In the same year, Calcutta, Howrah, and the suburban municipalities contained two fifths of the urban population while the rest of Bengal, at the turn of the century, remained mostly rural.[54]

A steady flow of labourers from declining agrarian economic regions continued to serve these mill towns for the first half of the twentieth century. Gradually an effective information network developed in rural Bihar on the availability of jobs in the industrial areas of Bengal.[55] However, the volume of migration to these industrial districts quickly exceeded the rate of growth of employment and created a glut in the demand for labour. This was reflected in the stagnant wage rates of the industry in that period. According to Foley, wages had increased by a mere 10 per cent between 1890 and 1905.[56] Foley's statement was also supported by other enquiries conducted during the period. According to the report of K.L. Dutta, the average real wages of the workers witnessed little increase in the last decade of the nineteenth century.[57] This factor obviously necessitated the mainte-nance of a rural base for adult male migrants.

Single adult males were preponderant among the migrant workers. The uncertainties of life in an unknown, distant land perhaps initially discouraged the migration of women and children.[58] Most adult male migrants were marginal farmers or agricultural workers who had negligible plots of land in rural areas and which were looked after by their wives and children.[59] These men wanted to supplement their rural resources with urban employment. Moreover, few workers earned enough to support their wives and children in the mill towns. In 1929, according to one calculation, a working-class family of husband, wife, and three children required Rs 7 per week to subsist in the mill towns, but an average mill worker at that time earned only Rs 5 per week.[60] As late as 1946, a survey of family budgets showed that expenses exceeded income in 70 per cent of working-class households in the urban areas.[61] This further indicates that workers could not maintain their families in the mill towns on urban wages alone. This separation of migrant male workers from their wives and children in turn reinforced the need for periodic migration to the villages.

The wages of single workers, too, met only the subsistence expenses in urban areas.[62] This left workers with little savings. The IJMA records were often eloquent on the remittances sent by the workers to their villages, which to them reflected the affluence of the workers in the mill regions. These calculations of the amounts of money remitted were based on the postal money orders sent from the mill town post offices. But this crude sample included diverse social groups from traders down to casual labourers. A glance at the postal money orders in Bhatpara between 1918 and 1921 reveals the absurdity of the claim that money orders reflected the affluence of the workers. In each year, the total value of money orders sent from the post offices in the town exceeded the total wages of the workers of Bhatpara.

TABLE 2.1

The amount of money orders sent from post offices in
the town of Bhatpara and the total wages of the workers

Year	Amount of money orders sent from the post offices of Bhatpara town (in Rs)	Total wages of the workers in the town of Bhatpara (in Rs)
1918	778,861	579,096
1919	925,983	595,013
1920	1,268,612	835,455

Source: The first column of this Table is taken from the Annual Administrative Report on the Bhatpura Municipality (AARBM) 1922; the second column from *AARBM* 1918 (p. 14), 1919 (p. 14), 1921 (p. 17).

The need for a rural base became necessary for migrant workers for health reasons too. The wages of jute mill workers provided them with bare subsistence. They were often hungry, and some were malnourished. In 1929, Dr Batra, a Bengal Government health official, found that the jute workers' average calorific food intake was much lower than that of prisoners in Bengal.[63] Dr Batra further observed that those workers who did not return to their village each year suffered most from diseases related to malnutrition.[64] Most workers lived in privately owned slums which, according to Foley, suffered from 'overcrowding and a serious neglect of the [sic] sanitation.'[65] Thomas Johnston, the Scottish Labour MP, who visited

Kankinara bastee in Bhatpara in 1925 has left us with a vivid picture of conditions of living in the slums of the area:

Two thirds of the workers in this industry ... are housed in vile, filthy, disease-ridden hovels, called basti. These ... are one-storyed blocks of mud plaster on wicker and matting with thatched roofs; [there are] no windows or chimneys ... the smoke simply oozes through the thatch if it cannot get out through the doorway, which is so low that one has to go down almost on hands and knees to enter. The basti have neither light nor water supply; the floors are earthen; sanitary arrangements there are none; and usually access ... can only be had along a narrow tunnel of filth where myriads of mosquitoes and flies breed and the stench is such that one fears to strike a match lest the atmosphere, being combustible, should explode ... .[66]

These slums were put together on the lands of the local zamindars who reaped enormous profits from them.[67] As mills expanded, and the demand for tenement rooms increased, the zamindars raised the rents. Rising rents, in turn, forced the workers to share small rooms in larger groups in the already over-crowded slums. The mill managers often turned a Nelson's eye to the conditions in which their workers lived and absolved themselves of any responsibility for it. They even invested little on improving such housing as they themselves constructed. In the mill housing, four or five workers shared small rooms.[68]

It is not surprising that such congested insanitary dwelling places created an unhealthy environment in the mill towns. This was particularly evident in the repeated occurrences of epidemics in working-class slums.[69] The causes of epidemics in the mill municipalities were undoubtedly rooted in the insanitary conditions of the over-crowded bastees. The Bhatpara Municipality makes the point clear in its annual report in 1902:

Cholera may be said to have prevailed in a rather epidemic form first amongst the coolies in the Brick fields at Samnagar and at Athpore and then in the coolie bustees at Mirpur and Kankinara. These have all along been condemned as the most insanitary bustees.[70]

However, municipalities located the main cause of such insanitary environment in the 'unclean habits' of workers. The currency of these stereotypes among the members of the municipality was reflected in their annual report on town administration in 1918 which states that

The ill-ventilated rooms and the *coolies* [italics in original] crowding together on small patches of land, supplemented by the *natural unclean habits of the people living in them,* [emphasis mine] afford an excellent breeding place for germs of all sorts of diseases.[71]

It was found that although there was 'scarcity of good drinking water', it was a less important factor for these diseases (including the water-borne viruses) in comparison to the 'unclean habits of workers'.[72] But despite their lamentation about the lack of good drinking water, mill managers were unwilling to pay for it.[73]

In these circumstances workers naturally preferred to go back to their villages when they fell ill. Municipal boards which were dominated by the mill managers, might also have preferred this periodic migration. In Bhatpara, the Municipal report of 1922 unambiguously declares, that it 'is a place for working people and not for the sick, and idlers ....'[74] In fact, if contagious diseases were noticed among the coolies, the management immediately threw those workers out of their dwellings. In 1918 during the influenza epidemic the municipality reports that

It was indeed a very hard task to trace out stray cases of such diseases happening in the midst of thousands of rooms inhabited by low class coolies who would do their best to conceal such incidents from municipal authorities. But it must be said to the credit of the sanitary Inspectors that scarcely any such case escaped detection.[75]

The detection of disease was often followed by harsh measures. The sick could be evicted and then their 'clothes and other belongings would be burnt.'[76]

The high infant mortality rates in working-class slums also reflected the insanitary conditions of the mill towns. According to the municipality report of Bhatpara in 1931, 108 out of 822 deaths reported in the town were of children under one year and 93 were from one to five years of age.[77] Women workers, in many cases, went back home to give birth to their babies and returned when the latter became old enough to work in the factories.[78] Mr Johnston, a member of the British parliament from Dundee, was told by an old man in a Kankinara slum that half of the babies in the bustee died every year.[79]

The Bhatpara municipality in 1922 proudly claimed that the 'death rate here would be lower than other towns. Towns similarly circumstanced, such as Titagarh and Garulia have also low percentage of births and deaths.'[80] In part this was true because workers during illness went back to their villages. However, even then the crude figures provided by the municipality itself did not bear this out. Though such figures were extremely unreliable, they provide a rough indication that the birth rate in the Bhatpara mill municipality was not always higher than the death rate. It was possible that the high rate of infant mortality swelled the death rate in the mill towns because most of the adult workers, as the municipality report claims, went back home when they were ill.

TABLE 2.2
Annual birth and death rates in
the mill town of Bhatpara per thousand

Year	Birth rate	Death rate
1902	17,	30
1907	22.4	29.2
1913	10.6	9
1917	11.4	11
1921	10	12
1922	9	7
1925	16	22.3
1926	15	18.6

Sources: This Table is based on the AARBM Reports 1902 (p. 2), 1907 (p. 3), 1913 (p. 2), 1917 (p. 13), 1921 (p. 14), 1922 (p. 13), 1921 (p. 14), 1922 (p. 13), 1925 (p. 16), 1926 (p. 20).

Mill managers made only the most superficial attempts to improve the situation. In the 1920s they opened baby clinics and crèches in the mills. But a report of a mill doctor mentions that

The conditions of these (workers') children is often pitiful because those looking after them are either too old or too young to find employment in the mills, or are the sick, and the blind or an occasional out of work. The mother does not return to feed her infant between 5.15 a.m. and 10.45 a.m. or between 1.15 p.m. and 6.45 p.m. and the mixtures which the children are given when they cry is enough to ruin all but the strongest digestion and to swell the death rate enormously. Many are doped with opium and die eventually from inanition.[81]

These high rates of infant mortality might have also discouraged workers from bringing their wives and children to the mill towns. Thus their villages, for most workers, were the only source to supplement their earnings from factory employment. By fragmenting these experiences and juxtaposing rural and urban industrial lives as two separate domains, historians tend to miss the crucial significance of rural-urban nexuses in the survival strategies of workers in urban areas. Periodic migration to rural areas did not reflect a lack of commitment to urban industrial settings. On the contrary, hopes and aspirations of the rural poor, driven out from their village habitats by push factors, were linked with the opportunities available by employment in the mills. In other words, the migrant jute workers did not lack a commitment to urban jobs, but low wages and inhospitable living conditions in the mill towns compelled them to retain their rural ties for survival in urban areas. The periodic migration to the rural areas was a reflection of that survival strategy rather than a simple rural mentality.

Meaning of Community: Religion, Caste, and Gender in Delineating the Social Organization of Jute Workers

Migrant workers in Bengal mill towns developed social networks based on caste, religious, and regional affinities in order to get jobs, loans, and housing. In times of need they depended upon these networks for help. Yet a detailed investigation of the social organization of workers does not reveal clearly-formulated, neat categories of ethnic identities; rather we find a complex process of formation of social ties that was the product of urban industrial work settings. For example, family members played a crucial role in helping mill workers obtain employment in the factories. The search for employment in the jute mills was expensive and time consuming. Migrants often took loans in the villages to come to the jute mills.[82] The support of relatives was essential to the migrants as they often had to wait for months to find employment. New arrivals also needed the right contacts in the mills to get employment.[83] In most cases, migrants came to the mill towns with their relatives or fellow villagers who helped them to find employment in the jute mills.[84] Workers who had no relatives in the urban areas depended upon their fellow villagers or 'country men' for support.[85]

Yet such ties were not clearly delineated and often language, caste, and religious ties overlapped with each other. This was evident in the census of mill workers conducted by individual factory authorities, which indicated that notions of belonging to a community varied among different social groups. This point is further exemplified in the mill census table on the next page. The Manager of Victoria Jute Mill conducted this census on the basis of information supplied by the workers. This information shows that workers used various categories of affinity to describe their identity. Telegus and Bilaspuris were classified on the basis of their region, but Hindustani-speaking people were identified on the basis of language. Among them caste, religious, and linguistic affiliations always intersected with each other and there was no singular interpretation of them.

TABLE 2.3

Distribution of workers according to region and religion in the coolie line of Victoria Jute Mill in 1931

	Men	Women	Children	Total
Madrassi	672	576	66	1314
Bengali	2	1	–	3
Bilaspuri	116	85	19	220
Oriya	18	–	–	18
Hindustani	166	99	45	310
Mussalman	2	–	–	2
Total	976	761	130	1876

Source: The Manager's report to the Directors of Victoria Jute Mills in 1931. Thomas Duff Company Records, Dundee University Archives, Dundee Ms 86/v/8/1.

The censuses taken in the Shyamnagar Jute Mill by the Thomas Duff Company reveal that the 'Madrassi' line was often occupied by both Oriyas and Telegus. Similarly, 'Muslims' and 'Hindustanis' from Bihar and east UP resided side by side in the 'Bilaspuri lines.'[86]

Conjugal living in an overwhelmingly male environment also often tended to challenge the hold of caste and religion. Working-class women and men in the mill towns often selected their household partners from among people of different regions and religions. Predominantly adult male migrants who were separated from their wives for long periods, dominated the mill towns. Migration patterns undoubtedly varied between linguistic groups. Oriya workers, for example, were mainly adult single male migrants.[87] There were only 62 women migrants to Calcutta per one thousand Oriya males.[88] In contrast to Oriyas, a large proportion of women labourers were to be found among Telegu migrants. According to Mr Williams, the manager of the Kinnison Jute Mill, in the 1920s single male Oriya workers often co-habited with Telegu women.[89] There was no uniformity in the social norms which regulated such inter-caste and inter-communal relationships. For instance, Telegu women were refused housing in Madrassi lines if they had a Hindustani partner.[90] But no exclusion was applied to the alliances between Hindustani men and Bengali women. In the Lothian Jute Mill, Curjel found that 'upcountry workers' generally selected their partners from Bengali women.[91]

The majority of single adult Bengali women workers were mostly widows, or otherwise alienated from their families. In the mill towns these women selected their partners from diverse social backgrounds.[92] In many cases, these male partners had two different '*Samsars*' or 'household establishments', one based in the mill towns, and the other in the villages. Manikuntala Sen, a communist activist in the 1940s, recalled her experience of such relationships. Women who co-habited with men to whom they were not formally married, put a vermilion mark on their forehead, but did not use it on their hair partings, which was the mark of marriage among Bengali Hindu women. These relations cut across boundaries of religion, region, or caste. In fact, Manikuntala found that among these couples the men were upcountry workers while the women were Bengalis.[93]

Caste-, language- and religion-based identities were also intersected by hierarchies based on skill, wages, nature of employment, and gender. The main divisions among workers occurred in terms of skill required for operating different machines in various stages of production. The raw jute passed through six different departments of a factory called batching, softening, preparing, spinning, weaving, and sewing. The departments of spinning and weaving constituted the most important sections of jute factories because this is where jute was put into looms and transformed into cloth for burlaps. The nature of the employment and training of weavers and spinners differed from that of the other workers. This was evident in the time taken by labourers to learn the work in different departments of the factory. In the opinion of the Chairman of the IJMA in 1906, ordinary coolies, shifters, and women in the preparing and hand sewing department generally took one week to learn their work, whereas spinners and weavers needed a year to learn their skill. In addition, good spinners were to be graduated from the shifter's work.[94]

The social and economic distances between skilled and unskilled workers in terms of work-place hierarchy, wages, and the regularity of employment had an effect on life outside the factory. Relatively affluent adult male skilled workers like weavers often prevented their wives from working in the factories, while much poorer labouring families worked collectively for survival. 'It is noteworthy here, as elsewhere,' Curjel wrote in 1921 that, 'the weavers were the autocrats of the mill and their women folk did not work.' She observed that the rooms of weavers were screened with *purdah* and 'were much lacking in light and ventilation'. She wondered at the end of her description 'Was the pseudo-purdah a symbol of social superiority as published in the news papers?'[95] In contrast, the story of Ramkalyan and his wife Parvati in 1929 illustrates the living conditions of the poor families in the urban areas. Ramkalyan and Parvati were up at 5 a.m. every day, and worked in the first shift till 11 a.m. After a recess of half an hour, they laboured till 7 p.m. At the end of the day Parvati cooked food and Ramkalyan with his children collected coal from the mill or brought wood from the fields. Their entire family worked, including their five year old girl and two year old boy.[96] These differences between weavers and ordinary labourers were evident among Muslim workers also. Muslim weavers, who were better off than other workers, confined their wives to purdah. But poorer Muslim women worked in mills side by side with their partners like other women.[97]

Thus, although caste, regional, and religious ties were important for workers in the mill towns and provided them with some security in an uncertain urban environment, social identities and affiliations were fluid. Within communities defined by caste or religion, language or region, the occupational hierarchies, divisions of labour, wage differentials, and gender differences divided the workers whom historians and anthropologists lumped together in a single cultural category. Even sexual relationships between women and men in urban areas cut across caste and region. These overlapping social ties made community identities of workers extremely ambiguous, fragile, and incapable of recreation.

The Role of Sardars in the Work Place and in the Slums

Colonial officials portrayed *sardars* as the leaders of the labouring communities based on caste, religion, or region. Sardars were also seen as all-powerful labour leaders by contemporary Indian politicians. Sardars undoubtedly played crucial roles in labour management of the jute factories. The mill managers entrusted the sardars with considerable power to employ, resolve disputes, and even to dismiss workers in order to maintain labour discipline. As a result, the sardars commanded considerable influence over the work force. They maintained contacts with the workers in the slums and bazaars of the mill towns. *Badli* workers often approached sardars for employment in the factories and asked for their help in getting housing and loans. In periods of distress, common workers looked towards sardars for assistance.

The power of the sardars in the mill management also increased because of the presence of a handful of Europeans for managing the factory administration.[98] A typical jute mill employed 15 to 20 Europeans, one for every two or three hundred Indians, who often looked after two or three departments.[99] Moreover, European factory officials could not communicate clearly with Indian workers and clerks because they did not speak Hindustani.[100] They depended upon the sardars to communicate with the workers. In this division of labour, European supervisors limited their role only to taking the final decision in labour management.

However, the power of the sardar in the industry had its limitations. In every department there were two or three sardars. Each sardar had 15 to 20 workers under him. Most of these departmental sardars wielded relatively little power. Among 4,000[101] workers there were nearly two hundred sardars, the most powerful of whom was the head sardar or the main foreman of the department. In the jute mills, the most important sardars were the 'head-sardars' in the weaving section. They exercised widespread influence over the factory. Yet the large number of sardars and the competition among them for the support of the workers limited their influence.

Sardars also had to share power with other intermediaries at work. The most crucial aspect in power relations of jute mills was collaboration between sardars and *babus* or clerks. The non-technical departments in jute factory were dependent on the clerks, called *babus*. The head clerk was known as the *burrababu*. He supervised the distribution of the raw jute within the factory, maintained a list of workers, and even disbursed salaries. He was the de facto head of the day-to-day administration in the mills. Burrababus were aided by departmental clerks, numbering nearly 10 to 20, who performed various functions—from counting the bales of raw jute to time keeping in the factories. Burrababus also exercised tremendous influence over the factory management.[102]

Sardars and burrababus depended upon each other to control the workers. This was perhaps most visible in the way sardars extracted bribes from the workers for the services he rendered to them.[103] These fees were shared with the burrababus who maintained the records of employment in the factories.[104] Daily fluctuations in the numbers of the casual workforce enabled sardars to create 'ghost' lists of workers with the result that babus and sardars shared the extra money from the inflated wage bills.[105] Even in the unions in jute mills burrababus and sardars collaborated with each other.[106] For example, in 1908 the two office bearers of Kankinara Mohammedan Association were Kazi Zahir Uddin, a mill clerk, and Muhammad Zulfiqar, a sardar.[107] In other words, the nature of the work of burrababus and sardars was complementary and it was difficult for the sardars to ignore the burrababus. This also limited the authority of sardars who, on their own, might not have been able to influence the everyday working of the mills and would thus attract few clients for his services.

Sardars who exercised a wide influence over the workers developed their bases through networks in the slums and bazaars. Sardars gained influence among the workers as providers of essential services. Influential sardars often took the slums of workers on lease from zamindars and also functioned as *mahajans* in the slums.[108] They sometimes negotiated the terms of supply of essential items to new workers from local grocers. As a result, sardars had to compete with various other influential people in the bazaars and slums.

Few influential sardars could ignore the social networks of bazaars which were centres of life in the mill towns. In the narrow and dingy lanes of the bazaars thousands of shopkeepers eked out their livelihoods. Many mill-hands ran small shops to supplement their earnings from the factories. Temples and mosques were also situated in the middle of these bazaars. In the Bhatpara area, both the Hanumanji Temple of Kankinarah and the Jumma mosque of Jagatdal were located in the bazaars. On the *hat* [marketing] days, wrestlers, gamblers, dancers, and snake charmers entertained crowds in the small open spaces in and around these bazaars. Bazaar gossip also formed the main source of information for the town population.[109] It was in these bazaars that sardars had to deal with other powerful people to gain influence over the workers.

Liquor sellers, neighbourhood bosses, money lenders, and grocers all established an impressive degree of influence over workers in the bazaars. However, such diffused networks of power relationship also prevented the sardars from exercising unlimited influence over workers, who could turn to many other patrons for support. The sardars who aspired to exercise influence over workers had to compete with patrons in bazaars and slums for developing their own mechanism of resource mobilization for their clients. Yet, it was difficult for sardars to provide all such services to the workers.

The most important locations for social interaction among workers were the liquor shops in the bazaars.[110] The numbers of wine shops in mill areas increased rapidly and became important places of recreation for workers.[111] In 1896 C.C. Steven a police officer posted at Barrackpur noted that between 1877–8 and 1883–4 consumption of liquor in the 24 Parganas more than trebled.[112]. He ascribed the cause for the increase in the consumption of alcohol to the influx of workers into the area.[113] All these areas constituted the heartland of the jute mill belt. Samaresh Basu, a noted novelist and trade-unionist, describes *tari* drinking as a major form of social recreation among the workers. In Jaggaddal, young women and men gathered for drinks at particular households and spent the night together. Social interaction between various groups of workers took place around communal drinking of tari.[114] In other words, liquor sellers played an important role in the social life of the jute mill workers.

The very organization of the liquor trade made wine sellers powerful men. In the late nineteenth century Bengal, the liquor traders had to maintain widespread connections with the local officials to subvert various forms of bureaucratic control. The distillery system gave local officers tremendous power.[115] These distilleries had a large army of employees. The quantity of spirit manufactured was entered into a register kept by every distillery. Shopkeepers, who drew liquor from the distillery, were issued a pass by the *darogas* (officers in charge of police stations). Wine merchants also had to bribe the police in order to avoid unnecessary interference, which also enabled them to build up connections with the local police officers. These connections with local officials made them powerful figures in the mill towns. Workers spent large amounts of money on liquor and were often indebted to the liquor sellers. Bankim Chandra, as a deputy magistrate, observed that sometimes liquor was sold on credit in exchange for grain, and some of the workers 'give almost the whole of the week's earnings [to the liquor sellers] when they come out on Sunday.'[116] Sardars thus had to compete with local liquor sellers in the bazaars to gain influence over workers.

The other powerful actor in the slums and bazaars of mill towns were the local toughs, more popularly known as *goondas*. A description of the mill town goonda is sufficient to indicate the importance of such persons in the local power structure of working-class neighbourhoods. Sarju Tewari, a local tough of Baranagar, was born in 1891 in the village of Nautan of Chapra District, Bihar. He was a gambler and blackmailer and ran a protection racket at the jute mills. He became so powerful that he could evade police control. For example, when on one occasion he assaulted a police constable, the police could not produce any evidence against Tewari in court. In 1920, more than 100 people petitioned the sub-divisional magistrate, Barrackpur, for protection from his activities. In the last case instituted against him, fifty witnesses produced by police officers included local bhadraloks, mostly clerks in the jute mills.[117] Men like Sarju often wielded much clout in the mill towns.

These men were feared, hated and respected by the local poor. They were the typical bosses of the working-class slums in mill towns. They ran gambling dens, liquor shops and extortion rackets. At the same time goondas could not maintain their influence without satisfying their fellow residents- particularly those who sought help. In this situation sardars did not enjoy unlimited influence in bazaars and slums; they always had to contest and collaborate with liquor sellers and goondas for influence in slums and bazaars.

Sardars also had to compete with other important people in the bazaars and slums for a position of influence. Sardars had to arrange loans for workers in times of need. They were also asked to negotiate credit from grocers for the workers.[118] Yet sardars were not the only men who could provide loans. Mill *durwans* in factories, grocers, and boatmen in the slums also lent money to the workers. Grocers were the most important moneylenders in the slums.[119] When all other sources of debts within slums and factories were exhausted, workers went to the *kabuli* moneylenders. Generally speaking, loans up to four months corresponding to wages of four weeks' were given by the kabuli money lenders without any security, but they insisted on personal security on higher sums.

Few sardars were in a position to provide widespread services to the workers in slums and bazaars. In many cases poor sardars themselves were in debt and did not have money to support other workers. For example, Palaia of the Titagarh No. 2 Jute Mill spent Rs 300 in his daughter's marriage and incurred a debt of Rs 200, which forced him to pawn his wives' ornaments. In fact, he became dependent on the earnings of his two wives and was not in a position to enter into competition with other workers.[120]

Even powerful sardars could not freely impose their whims on ordinary workers. In order to maintain their influence sardars always had to be receptive to the needs of ordinary workers. Their influence among workers depended upon their ability to provide help. The relationship between sardars and their clientele was defined by the notion of custom. Sardars were supposed to be service providers as well as representatives of workers. As patron he was expected to lead the community during industrial action and represent the grievances of the workers. Yet sardars could not apply pressure beyond a certain point on the managers as they might lose their jobs. They remained trapped in their positions. The emergence of trade unions and in periods of industrial action, the authority of sardars over workers weakened. In such circumstances, sardars often could not resist any combined action by the workers and became powerless during strikes. During the general strike of 1937, the Director of the Thomas Duff and Company lamented in a letter that the burrababus and sardars 'had lost all control over workers' and the 'sirdars said the workers at the time would listen to nobody but the strike leaders who had great influence over them.'[121]

Ironically, in such circumstances, the more the management relied upon the sardar and appointed him to powerful positions within the mill town administration, the more he became estranged from ordinary workers. By the 1930s it became clear that the days of the sardar were numbered. In fact Edward Benthal, the powerful partner of Bird and Company, regularly corresponded with his brother about the introduction of work councils to communicate directly with workers and the institution of a labour officer to keep a watch on workers' activities.[122] In other words, sardars were increasingly deprived of power over the labour management.

Thus, the sardars' authority over the workplace and slums was based not only on the rural community loyalties of workers but mainly on their ability to provide support to them. More importantly, the institution of sardars came into existence due to the need for the everyday management of the workplace. Workers needed sardars to understand the demands the management placed on her/his work; sardars remained the workers' most important contact with the management. As service providers and patrons of local networks among workers, sardars appeared to be indispensable to the managers. The sardar's role was much larger than mere jobbers or recruiters. In fact, his position as recruiter decreased as a steady flow of workers to mill towns was established. As changes in the political structure within the industry and the province brought diverse forms of institutions into existence, the sardars were increasingly marginalized and became anachronistic. Thus, by positing the sardari system as a primordial social institution reflecting a pre-capitalist rural social structure historians gloss over the real significance of the social institution of sardars.

Interpreting Mutuality of Interests and the Mechanism of Workers' Protests

If rural communities were not reproduced in urban industrial settings, with sardars as village chiefs, could we talk about urban production relations providing a framework of shared experience for the industrial workers that tightened bonds within communities? Here, problems of community formation based on a shared working experience are a much more crucial problem. For example, social distances between weavers and general workers stood in the way of identification of common grievances. Weavers, particularly, earned much higher salaries than other workers.[123] Furthermore, weavers were not paid on the basis of time like most other occupations but according to the output.[124]

Divisions between skilled and unskilled workers were strengthened by the fact that most of the unskilled workers were employed on a daily basis. Mill managers generally divided the entire jute workforce into three categories—daily or *badli*, temporary, and permanent. The badli workers, who constituted a vast majority of the jute mill work force, were recruited on daily basis at factory gates.[125] Sibnath Bannerjee, the prominent socialist labour leader of the1930s, explained in an interview later that most of the workers in jute industry were badlis.[126] The temporary workers were those who had worked for six months and had some job guarantee. They did not have to wait for jobs at the mill gates everyday. The labour turnover statistics in the Victoria Jute Mill of Thomas Duff Company defined permanent workers as those 'employees who work in the mill year after year, periodically go on leave and as a rule return to the same job. [They] Must have at least one year's service.'[127] The jute industry mostly employed casual labourers, except for the spinning and the weaving departments.

These casual workers had little job security. In 1935 records show that in a single year nearly 27 per cent of the total workers left their jobs and new workers constituted 19.5 per cent of the total work force.[128] In Victoria Jute Mill in the same year, nearly 31 per cent of the workers left their jobs and were replaced by new recruits who constituted almost 13 per cent of the total work force.[129] Many of the badli workers were often dismissed from factories ostensibly for lack of efficiency.[130] Among jute workers, only the weavers were not employed on a daily basis, as their work required much more time to learn than that of the other workers. The managers sometimes permitted weavers to recruit new helping hands on their own.[131] These divisions due to the regularity of work further distinguished weavers from other workers.

There were also sharp divisions between women and men in terms of employment and skills. With the increasing flow of adult male migrants, women were recruited into departments with low wages. Even for the same jobs women were paid much less than the male workers. Sewing departments in the mills were named *magi-kol* by workers, indicating the dominance of women.[132] These women workers were mostly single migrants and nearly all of them were casual workers. According to a survey conducted in 1929 in 11 jute mills of Bengal, most of the workers had a very short industrial career. Of the 74,963 workers covered in this survey, only 4.33 per cent had worked for more than thirty years in the industry. These statistics show that approximately 81.2 per cent of the workers worked for less than ten years and about 65.9 per cent were employed for less than five years. In addition, only 15.33 per cent worked less than ten years. But this survey also indicates the sharp gender divisions in terms of continuity of work. Nearly 72 per cent of the women were employed for a period of less than five years, but it was only 61 per cent in the case of men. Only 5 per cent of the men worked more than thirty years, but among women it was only 2 per cent who worked more than thirty years.[133] This survey suggests that women workers were mostly daily employees and had much less continuity in employment than male workers. The fluidity of labour market formation and its segmentation thus raise the inevitable questions of why and how did workers mount such powerful strike waves in the jute industry from the 1890s to 1940 if there were no identifiable communities in urban settings?

The answer could be found in the workers' notions of mutuality of interests (despite the numerous divisions existing among them) centred around shared grievances over long working hours, wages, managerial practice of inflicting physical punishments, and arbitrary dismissals. It would be wrong to perceive that workers were always ready to engage into industrial action to redress these grievances. Such grievances indicate the existing level of frustration and anger over the condition of work in the factories.

Industrial conflicts occurred when workers perceived that managers violated what they regarded as customary rights (*dasturi*). For example, workers developed their own code of resistance to long working hours by refusing to be tied down to the machine throughout the working period. They moved around, took short breaks, and even smoked bidi or had food during such self-created recesses. The management made only selective interventions to regulate such behaviour and activities which the workers regarded as customary work practices. Related to such a custom was the notion of fairness (*insaf*). Workers regarded the violation of such customs as unfair treatment or denied justice (insaf). These developments unsettled the workers, who raised objections to what they perceived as gross violation of customary practices within the factories.[134]

Izzat, or sense of social honour, plays a crucial role in causing conflicts. Physical punishments often caused conflicts as they appeared to have undermined the notion of social honour of the workers. In September 1888, in Sealdah court, a case of assault was brought against John Miller of the Sealdah Jute Mill by a worker. According to a contemporary newspaper account Miller had sworn at him when he asked for leave. When the worker asked for his wages held in arrears, he was set upon and kicked by Miller.[135] Such incidents, not uncommon in the jute mills, provoked violence and was often regarded by workers as an infringement of their sense of social honour. Socially constructed honour remained another flexible parameter created by workers themselves to define their code of conduct. As time passed, most workers regarded physical punishment as a dishonourable practice.

However, such notions evolved and changed in accordance with the alteration in the political environment, economic situation, and managerial work culture. The most crucial example of such changes in these notions is the concept of the honour of women. Male workers viewed women colleagues as a repository of social honour only when such 'honour' was threatened by outside elements. During Hindu-Muslim riots, perceived insulting behaviour towards women became a symbol of communal dishonour. During strikes, managers' behaviour towards women also aroused suspicion. Yet, at the beginning of industrial action, male workers often attacked departments dominated by women to cause chaos and anarchy in order to stop work. Women then ceased to be the repository of social honour.

In the nineteenth and early twentieth centuries an important determinant of combined action among workers was the issue of long working hours. According to A Cobbe, the manager of Chapdani Jute Mill, most of the jute factories in 1879 that worked on an 'average for about twelve hours all the year around'. In 1890, the Indian Factory Commission reported that as a general rule factories worked 'from daylight to dusk, that is taking extreme limits in summer from 5 a.m. to 7 p.m. or 14 hours with half an hour's interval ....'[136] Sukhni, an eight year old girl, told the Indian Factory Commission in 1890 that she came to work 'when the whistle sounds before day light', left at 9 a.m. only to return at 12 noon for another shift until 6 p.m. in the evening.[137] Rajoni, another woman worker, also told the same commission that she used to wake up at 4 a.m., go to the mill at 5.30 a.m., and would get to rest only after 10 p.m..[138]

From 1896 onwards, after the introduction of electricity, the jute mills were able to extend their working hours even further. In 1908 it was common practice for the jute mills to work from 5 a.m. to 8 p.m. and when market conditions permitted, some extended their hours even further.[139] Most jute mills worked in a multiple shift system. The workers, except in the weaving and sewing departments, were divided into a number of shifts, allowing each worker an interval of two hours before the resumption of work or the start of a second shift.[140]

After the war, the IJMA adopted a 13.5 hour working day and limited the working week to 4 days. In practice, the remaining days were used to clean the machinery in the maintenance department workshop.[141] In 1922, factory managers told Curjel that workers generally worked more than 13 hours a day.[142] The nature of factory work was monotonous, as factory officials often admitted. In the 1890s, it involved standing for 13 hours where a 'quantity of fluff always floated in the air and whir of machines created continuous noise pollution.'[143]

In 1929, Babunya told a moving story of her experience in the factory: 'I leave my home at 5 a.m. in the morning to come to work in the mill, and go at 9.30 a.m., I come again to work at 11. I do not get sufficient time to do proper cooking. If I am late at work the babus reprimand me. I feed my children after 9.30 when I go home. ... As I cannot be at home to serve food to my husband he takes it himself, it becomes cold by the time he takes it.'[144] Babujan, a male worker, stated that he ate his food twice daily—'whatever has been cooked between work times in daylight hours.' He slept after work till dawn and had no physical recreation.[145]

The long working hours in the jute industry sometimes contributed to an increase in the number of serious accidents at work. In Bengal the number of accidents increased during the First World War when the jute industry expanded rapidly and ignored even rudimentary safety measures.[146] Most of these accidents occurred at the end of the day when workers were exhausted. Some serious accidents also occurred due to managerial negligence of safety standards in the factories. In fact, out of 85 serious accidents in 1916, 26 were attributed to managerial negligence. Sometimes extreme poverty compelled workers to steal oil from running gears for use as fuel at home. At the Shyamnagar Jute Mill a man was fatally injured while attempting to collect oil from softener gear wheels.[147] The absence of training for new workers also caused accidents. In 1916 at the Delta Jute Mill, a new worker unknowingly switched on the machines, killing another worker in the carding section. At the India Jute Mill a man was killed by getting drawn up between the rollers while cleaning the machines in motion.[148] Victims of accidents also included children. At the Naihati Jute Mill, a boy of seven years was injured when he got drawn round the delivery roller shaft of a drawing machine.

After the introduction of the 1923 Compensation Act, managers often blamed workers for inflicting injury on themselves in the hope of receiving payment.[149] But contrary to the claims made by the managers, those mills where unsafe working conditions had led to large number of accidents were avoided by the workers.[150] Behari Rai, a worker in the Angus Mill, told the Royal Commission that he had been recommended by returning migrants to go to Angus because it was known to be free from accidents.[151]

Managers usually held a week's wages of the workers and paid them in arrears. This was intended to curb the movement of mill hands from one factory to another.[152] But it also made workers far more vulnerable to the pressures of the management and perhaps contributed towards their increasing indebtedness. Workers' dissatisfaction with the situation was more pronounced in the tragic statement of a child labourer, Mongrul, that 'I have not been ill recently. Formerly, I was well fleshed but I am now weak as I do not get enough food.'[153]

Long working hours, lack of adequate safety measures, withholding of wages, and managerial violence were the common grievances around which workers came to feel a mutuality of interests. Thus, when—in the period of expansion in the industry or during the Depression—managers imposed new work discipline, workers regarded it as a violation of custom and as an absence of fair dealing. In everyday life, arbitrary dismissals were regarded as unfair only when they violated the notion of such customary practice. The notion of such customary practise was also contingent upon political awareness of what is customary. Thus earlier during the Depression there was little opposition to repeated dismissals by the management but in 1937 with the ascendancy of the 'red flag union' and the gradual elimination of the threat of economic uncertainties of the Depression period, any dismissal became politically the most contested issue.

Industrial action grew out of the interplay of religious and regional loyalties and of widely-shared grievances at the workplace through such social signifiers of dastur (customary practices), izzat (social honour) and insaf (fairness). For example, in the last decade of the nineteenth century when working hours increased without any corresponding rise in wages, workers demanded holidays. Yet, strikes in this period witnessed a curious combination of religious demands and workplace grievances. Workers demanded holidays on religious occasions and combined it with demands for higher and regular payment of wages. They constructed these demands in terms of violation of customary practices or dastur. In this way, religious protest and anxiety, along with social and economic grievances of workers could transform into an overall unity among workers.

Regional loyalties also found full play in labour politics in the *swadeshi* period when Bengali workers organized strikes in sympathy with the movement against Partition, even if they were informed by more immediate concerns about wages and working conditions. Regional differences in this period led to clashes between upcountry workers and Bengalis. In 1928, a left wing socialist trade-unionist praised Bauria workers for beating upcountry men when the latter had allegedly tried to break a strike.[154] In this context, regional loyalties played upon the sentiment of izzat or social honour of workers. Thus, while regional loyalties could divide workers; they could also, in particular circumstances, strengthen their unity—as the general strike of 1929 showed, particularly when they fitted into the workers' own social signifiers.

Identity, thus, should be regarded as flexible and fluid and it could acquire different shapes according to the changes in the social, economic, and political circumstances. By overplaying regional and religious identities, historians tend to play down other important sources of division among workers, such as those based on skill, employment, and departmental differences. Indeed, prior to any wider industrial action workers carried on protracted negotiations among representatives of different departments. Each department placed their grievances before a public gathering of workers before reaching a conclusion. Most strikes were organized on the basis of work-related grievances within the department. Thus any treatment of workers as a homogenous entity because of given religious, regional, or caste background, or loyalties on the basis of economic location within the workplace would lead to misconceptions about workers' politics. Identities— whether based on ethnic ties or class—were products of political action, negotiations, and the construction of social signifiers through which workers interpreted their own world. Identities were not given nor automatically homogenous and totalizing.

Conclusion

The notion of uniform and readymade 'class consciousness' or 'community consciousness' offers inadequate explanations for complex community networks among workers. Such frameworks reduce diverse forms of social ties among workers to primordial loyalties based on caste, religion, and region. In contradistinction to existing historiography, this work describes such ties as survival strategies of workers in a new industrial environment. While thousands of workers competed with each other for employment, they needed to rely on their own social networks for survival. Isolated from their families and villages, engaged in a hard struggle to preserve their position in an overcrowded labour market characterized by uncertain employment conditions, workers had few other alternatives. However, despite the apparent uniformity of such nexuses, a detailed investigation reveals that these ties were flexible, permeable, and overlapping. Similarly, labour conditions did not lead towards uniform experience of work; there existed salient divisions among workers in terms of employment patterns, skills, and gender. Thus there existed a multifaceted rubric of contradictions beneath all the forms of seeming uniformity in workers' lives. However, the working of these social ties in shaping broader identities were contingent upon the immediate political contexts in which labour politics developed.

This monograph, in the following chapters, explores how policies of the colonial state at various levels and the growing nationalist movement defined political contexts in which diverse forms of social ties acquired different meanings. The next chapter investigates the nature of governance in mill towns in order to understand the immediate political context in which labour politics unfolded. The pattern of municipal governance in mill towns institutionalized the contradiction of interests between management and workers on a wider plane. This impinged on the workers' perception of the colonial state and significantly influenced their political alliances.

Notes

1. This was clearly also the case in Bombay as R.S. Chandavarkar has explained it in detail in his work, *The Origins of Industrial Capitalism in India: Business Strategies and the Working Classes in Bombay, 1900–1940*, Cambridge, 1994.

2. In fact community is more a symbolic construction as Cohen noted that the most significant factor in the construction of Community, 'boundary' which 'encapsulates the identity of Community'. 'They exist in the mind of the beholders ... This being so the boundary may be perceived in different terms, not only by people on opposite sides of it, but also by the people on the same. This is the symbolic aspect of Community boundary ...' A.P. Cohen, *The Symbolic Construction of Community*, p. 12.

3. Since historians hardly provide a clear explanation of the term, we shall draw here upon anthropological understandings of the word community. In the discussion on Community in South Asia, Humphrey and Carrithers talk about five distinct features that make a Community: '(i) a common culture, belief, and practice, as well as some common interests'; '(ii) significantly different from the surrounding society in their culture, beliefs, practices, and interests'; '(iii) consciousness of an identity as member of a Community'; '(iv) effective as a collectivity in social, political, and/or economic life'; '(v) able to reproduce itself.' Michael Carrithers and Caroline Humphrey (eds), *The Assembly of Listeners*, Cambridge, 1991, pp. 4, 6–7.

4. In recent writings on Indian history, 'processes of Community formation' became social phenomena that replaced earlier focuses on 'class formations'. In an important work on Banaras, Sandra Freitag declares that '... The authors have shared an interest in looking at every-day activities to see what these could tell us about shared values and motivations, processes of identity formation, and the self-conscious constructions of Community that have marked the last century and a half in South Asia ...' Sandra Freitag (ed.), *Culture and Power in Banaras: Community, Performance, and Environment 1800–1980*, Berkeley, 1989, p. xi.

5. Tanika Sarkar, in her seminal work on Bengal politics, argues that '[t]he very oppression which the sardars embodied was not only far more personalized but was also deeply familiar to the worker. With his patronage functions, his caste and kinship

connections, with his ownership of land and bustees and his control over the caste panch, the sardar and the system based on his control in several significant ways replicated the village authority structure within Bengali industrial suburbs while, at the same time, subtly modifying the known aspects, through the additional new functions that were tied to the factory floor/urban slum control'. See *Bengal 1928–1934 The Politics of Protest*, Delhi, 1987, pp. 65–6.

6. In his recent work, R.S. Chandavarkar has questioned the concept of sardars as undisputed leaders of workers in India. See *The Origins of Industrial Capitalism in India*.

7. *Royal Commission on Labour in India, vol. V, part 2*, London, 1931, pp. 126–7, (hereafter *RCLI*).

8. S.R. Deshpande, *Report on an Enquiry into Conditions of labour in jute mills in India*, (hereafter Deshpande Report), Delhi, 1946, p. 6.

9. For example, in Arrah, at the centre of the plains of the Sahabad district, the density of the population was 782 persons per square mile. J.A. Hubback, *Report on the Survey and Settlement operations in the districts of Sahabad 1907–1916*, Patna, 1917, p. 18. Ghazipur, in east UP similarly had experienced a rise in the population till 1891 which reached 737.3 per square mile. B.N. Ganguly, *Trends in Agriculture and Population in the Ganges valley: A study in the Agricultural Economics*, London, 1938, p. 10 (hereafter *Trends in Agriculture*).

10. J.A. Hubback, see above, pp. 10, 18, 115–23.

11. According to the District Gazetteer of Saran, 'The cattle are generally of poor quality ... owing to appropriation of all available land for cultivation, pasturage is insufficient ...'. L.S.S. O'Malley, (Revised by A. Middleton) *Saran District Gazetteer*, Patna, 1930, p. 67.

12. For details see O'Malley (revised by J.F.W. James) *Sahabad District Gazetteer*, (Patna, 1924), p. 46. Also O'Malley, (revised by A. Middleton) *Saran District Gazetteer*, p. 44. H.R. Nevill, *Ghazipur District Gazetteer*, Allahabad, 1909, pp. 84–6.

13. Orders of Government, No 898/1–710 of 15 June 1889, Nainital, By order W.C. Benet, Secretary to Government, North Western Province and Oudh, attached to William Irvine, *Report on the Revisions of Records and Settlement in Ghazipur District 1880–1885*, Allahabad, 1886, p. 3.

14. See C.M. Fisher, 'Indigo plantations and Agrarian Society in North Bihar in the Nineteenth and Early Twentieth Centuries'. Unpublished Cambridge PhD thesis, 1976, p. 230.

15. See O'Malley (revised by J.F.W. James), *Sahabad District Gazetteer*, p. 16.

16. H.R. Nevill, *Ghazipur District Gazetteer*, p. 44.

17. See O'Malley (revised by J.F.W. James), *Sahabad District Gazetteer*, p. 87 and O'Malley, (revised by A. Middleton), *Saran District Gazetteer*, p. 74.

18. *Selection of Papers Relating to the Famine of 1896–97 in Bengal, Vol. 1. (October to November)*, Calcutta, 1897, pp. 3–4.

19. D.L. Drake, *Azamgarh District Gazetteer*, Allahabad, 1911, p. 23.

20. B.B. Chowdhury, 'Land market in Eastern India, 1793–1940 Part II: The Changing Composition of the Landed Society'. *IESHR*, Volume XII, April–June 1975, Number 2, pp. 133–67. Also see his 'The Process of Depeasantization in Bengal and Bihar, 1885–1947', *IHR*, Volume II, Number 1, pp. 105–65.

21. D.T. Roberts, *Report on the Revision of Records of part of Balia District 1882–1885 AD*, Allahabad, 1886, p. 53.

22. See C.J. O'Donnel, *The Ruin of An Indian province: An Indian Famine explained. A Letter to the Marquis of Harlington, Secretary of State in a Liberal and Reforming Government*, London, 1880, pp. 16–17. (hereafter *The Ruin of An Indian Province*).

23. William Irvine, *Report on the Revisions of Records and Settlement in Ghazipur district 1880–1885*, pp. 10–11, 61.

24. A.N. Das, *Agrarian Unrest and Socio-Economic change in Bihar*, New Delhi, 1983, p. 37.

25. J.A. Hubback, see 9 above, p. 28. See also W. Irvine, *Settlement Report Ghazipur*, p. 61.

26. In Ghazipur out of the seventy-two families, only forty-one were resident. Thirty families were entirely non-resident. See also William Irvine as above.

27. See O'Donnel, *The Ruin of An Indian Province*, p. 22.

28. Ibid., p. 19.

29. For details, see Ian David Derbyshire, 'Opening up the interior: The Impact of Railways on the North Indian Economy and Society', Unpublished PhD thesis, Cambridge, 1985, pp. 261–72.

30. See 15 above, O'Malley, pp. 97–9.

31. G.A. Grierson, *Bihar Peasant Life*, Patna, 1926, (second edition), p. 197.

32. G.A. Grierson, *Notes on District of Gaya*, Calcutta, 1893, p. 90.

33. See *Minute by the Honourable Sir Richard Temple, KCSI, Lieutenant Governor of Bengal Dated 31st October 1896*, Calcutta, 1898 pp. 4, 35 (hereafter *Temple Minute*). Also see *Selection of Papers Relating to the Famine of 1896–97 in Bengal*, pp. 3–4, and *Temple Minute*, p. 35.

34. W.C. Plowden, *Census of India Vol. III, General Report and Statements, Census of North Western Province 1872*, Allahabad, 1878, p. lxvi.

35. See *Selection of Papers Relating to the Famine of 1896–97*.

36. E. White, *Report on the Census of North Western Province and Oudh and the native states of Rampur and native Garwal*, Allahabad, 1882 (Census of India 1881), p. 27; and also see *Selection of Papers Relating to the Famine of 1896–97*, pp. 76–92.

37. Ira Klein, 'Population Growth and Mortality Part 1—The Climatric of Death', *IESHR*, Vol. 26, No. 4, (December, 1989), p. 393.

38. See 11 above, O'Malley, p. 35; B.N. Ganguly, *Trends in agriculture*, pp. 10, 123.

39. *The Saran District Gazetteer* summed up the situation clearly: 'It (Saran) never produces sufficient for its own consumption, and imports consequently exceed exports, the cost of the surplus being met largely from the earnings of natives of the districts employed elsewhere.' L.S.S. O'Malley, (Revised by A.Middleton), *Saran District Gazetteer*, p. 91.

40. The traditional route to Bengal lay along the age old Badshahi *sarak*. A large number of people took their annual sojourn from west to east and east to west along this road even before the introduction of the railways, but the journey was slow and time-consuming. Anonymous, *A letter to the share holders of the East Indian and the Great Western Bengal railways on their present position and future prospects*, London, 1847, p. 8. But with the deepening of the agrarian crisis in Gangetic Bihar the flow of migration to Bengal increased manifold. For details see also Ian David Derbyshire, 'Opening up the interior: The Impact of Railways on the North Indian Economy and Society', Unpublished PhD thesis, Cambridge, 1985, pp. 261–72.

41. See, for example, details on Trihoot railways *Progress and Administrative Report on Railways in Bengal 1885*, p. 11.

42. GOB, Com Dept, Com Branch, 1914, A progs File No 1-w 5(1), WBSA. And (GOB) Com Dept, Com Branch, 1914, File no.1-w 5(1), Letter No 3326J, WBSA.

43. H.R. Nevill, *Ghazipur District Gazetteer*, pp. 78–9. However one official, F.J. Mohanan, Chief Secy to the Chief Commissioner of Assam, in a letter to the Secretary to the GOB expressed his concern on the unpopularity of Assam among the emigrants. General Dept Emigration Branch, February 1904 and General Dept Emigration Branch, July 1904, A6–15, WBSA.

44. See R. McLeod, *Annual Report on emigration from the port of Calcutta to British and Foreign colonies, 1890*, Calcutta, 1891, pp. 7–8.

45. In the 1890s, the Kankinarah Jute Mill employed entirely upcountry workers. Of the 4,500 workers employed in the Shyamnagar Jute Mills, nearly 3000 were from Bihar and east UP. Report on Police Supervision in the Riverine Municipalities in Bengal, Nos 6–11, Judicial Police 1896, WBSA, p. 28.

46. *RCLI Vol. V, Part II*, oral evidence of S.C. Bhattacharya, p. 255.

47. Quoted in O'Malley, *24 Parganas District Gazetteer*, pp. 65–6.

48. Ibid., pp. 65–6.

49. O'Malley, *Census of India 1911, Vol. V, Part I*, p. 178.

50. This calculation is based on the statistics of the growth of population provided in O'Malley's, *Census of India 1911, Vol. V, Part II*, p. 12.

51. See above, Part 1, p. 9. Munindra Deb Roy in his book *Hooghly Kahini* provides us with an interesting picture of the growth of these mill towns. *Hooghly Kahini*, Calcutta, 1901, p. 88.

52. B.R. Chakraborty and O'Malley, *District Gazetteer of Howrah*, Calcutta, 1909, p. 14.

53. Ibid., p. 532.

54. O'Malley, *Census of India 1911, Vol. V, Part I*, pp. 8–9.

55. B. Foley, *Report on labour in Bengal*, Calcutta, 1906, para 83.

56. Ibid., p. 10.

57. K.L. Datta, *Report on an Enquiry into the rise of prices in India, Vol. III*, pp. 194–5.

58. For details see C.J. O'Donnel, *Census of 1891, Vol. I*, Calcutta, 1893, p. 112.

59. Of the twenty life histories of jute workers collected by the *RCLI*, thirteen almost had no income from land at all. *RCLI, Vol. XII*, p. 359. Another survey at Jagatdal shows that 605 of the workers from there had no land at all. K.A. Chattapadhaya, *Socio-Economic Survey of Jute Labour*, Department of Social Work, Calcutta University, 1952, p. 30.

60. *RCLI Vol. V, Part II*, p. 132.

61. *Deshpande Report*, p. 26.

62. Ibid.

63. *RCLI Vol. V, Part I*, pp. 31–2.

64. Ibid.

65. Foley, *Labour in Bengal*, p. 11.

66. *RCLI Vol. V, Part 1*, Note by Dr Batra, p. 31.

67. For example in Bhatpara four markets which housed such slums belonged to the zamindars. *AARBM*, 1921, p. 15.

68. *RCLI Vol. V, Part II*.

69. General Dept Miscellaneous Branch Nos. 1–33, August 1893, WBSA; *Annual Report on the Working of Factories Act 1898*, General Dept Miscellaneous Branch, No 25, August 1899, WBSA; General Dept Miscellaneous Branch, Nos 26–7, September 1898, WBSA. Also see B. Foley, *Report on Labour in Bengal*, p. 12.

70. *AARBM*, 1902, p. 14.

71. *AARBM*, 1918, p. 12.

72. *AARBM*, 1918, p. 12.

73. *AARBM*, 1918, pp. 7–8.

74. *AARBM*, 1922, p. 13.

75. *AARBM*, 1918, p. 12.

76. *AARBM*, 1918, p. 12.

77. *AARBM*, 1931, p. 34.

78. *RCLI Vol. V, Part 1*, p. 52.

79. Ibid., p. 254.

80. *AARBM*, 1922, p. 13.

81. Dr Jean Orkney, 'Report on the Titagarh health centre', 1931, Manager's Report to the Director 1932, No. 2 Titagarh Jute Mill p. 9. V/8/2/1932 TDA, DUA.

82. See for details *RCLI, Vol. XI*, pp. 360–2.

83. The story of Fagua in the novel *Asamapta Chatabda* is illustrative in this case. Fagua came to the mills with his cousin who was a lorry driver and tried to obtain a temporary employment but did not know whom to approach. Fagua had to wait three months to find a right patron. Mohanlal Gangapadhaya, *Asamapta Chatabda*, Calcutta, 1963, pp. 38–52.

84. See *RCLI, Vol. XI*, pp. 362–4.

85. Ibid., p. 360.

86. Manager's Report to Directors 1934, Shyamnagar Jute mill Ms 86/v/8/5 Thomas Duff and Company records 1934, Census of workers living in the coolie lines.

87. *Census of India, 1891 Vol. I*, p. 112

88. *RCLI, Vol. V*, p. 9–14.

89. Com Dept, Com Branch, April 1923, B77, Appendix B,WBSA.

90. Com Dept, Com Branch, April 1923, B77, Appendix B, Interview with John Williamson of Kinnison factory, WBSA.

91. Com Dept, Com Branch, April 1923, B77, Appendix B, Interview with Mr Malish of Beliaghata Jute Mill, WBSA.

92. *Report of Indian Factory Commission, 1890*, p. 88.

93. M. Sen, *Sediner Katha*, p. 124.

94. B. Foley, *Labour in Bengal*. Appendix quoted in D Chakraborty, *Rethinking working-class history*, 1989, p. 91.

95. Com Dept, Com Branch, April 1923, B77, Appendix B, serial no 9, WBSA.

96. *RCLI, Vol. XI, Part II*, p. 356.

97. Com Dept, Com Branch, April 1923, B77, Appendix B, Interview with Mr Dewar of Kharda Jute Mill, WBSA.

98. For example, in 1893 a jute mill employed nearly 2,542 operatives. General Miscellaneous, August 1893. Report on the working of 1891 Factory Act, Walsh special inspector to the secretary of GOI, WBSA. By 1925, an ordinary jute factory employed nearly 4,000 workers and in some mills the number even reached 8,000. A later estimate made in the 1930s put the figure at around 4,000. D H Buchanan, *Development of Capitalistic Enterprise in India*, Newark, 1934.

99. D.H. Buchanan, *Capitalistic Enterprise*, 1934, p. 246 These men were employed mainly in the technical section of the jute mills. The limited number of Europeans increased their work load in the factories which tied them to machines and left them with little time to devote their attention to workers.See for details of work load Manager's report to Director, Angus Jute Mill, 1936, p.42, TDA, DUA.

100. The mill managers encouraged European assistants to learn Indian languages to bridge the gap between workers and the factory officials. In the 1920s, Thomas Duff and Company gave European personnel a bonus if they learnt an Indian language. In 1930 those who passed the 'government examination in colloquial Hindustani were paid the usual Rs 400 as language bonus'. Manager's report to Director Ms 86/v/12 Victoria Jute Mill, 1930, p.38. In the Titagarh Jute Mill 1929, out of 14 European employees only one passed the Hindustani exam, while in the Titagarh No. 2 Mill only one out of eleven Europeans was successful. TDA Dundee University Archives Manager's report to director Ms 86/v/11 Titagarh Jute Mill 1 1929, p. 46.TDA, DUA.

101. The average number of workers employed in a mill in a typical mill town such as Bhatpara increased from 2,800 in 1902 to 3,483 in 1907 to 4,131 in 1913 and finally to 4,244 in 1921. *AARBM* 1902, p. 17, the second column, 1907 p. 17, 1913 p. 16, 1921 p. 17.

102. Mohanlal Gangapadhaya's *Asamapta Chatabda*, provides a detailed picture of burrababus' control over the workplace.

103. RCLI, Report, p. 24.

104. RCLI, Report mentions that, 'The jobber subsidises the head jobber and it is said even members of supervising staff share the bribe.' p. 24.

105. The manager of Caledonian Jute Mills informed the Royal Commission of Labour that sardars and babus shared the wages of ghost workers with the workers who often did two men's jobs. *RCLI*, Vol. V, Part II, pp. 144–5. Quoted in D. Chakrabarty, *Rethinking Working-class History*, p. 98.

106. Chapter 4 and 5 provide a detail discussion of sardars in leading strikes and forming trade unions.

107. *IFLC, 1909*, Vol. 2 witness No. 176, p. 263–5.

108. Foley, *Labour in Bengal*, p. 11.

109. D.R. Wallace, *Romance of Jute*, Calcutta, 1908, p. 9.

110. Report on Police Supervision In Riverine Municipalities, Judicial Police Nos. 1–33, p. 30, WBSA.

111. The presence of numerous shops could be located in the mill town of Bhatpara. For details see Municipal Meetings Proceedings Of Bhatpara, Friday 20 April, 1905–6.

112. *Report of the Excise Commission 1883–84*, Calcutta, 1884, p. 199.

113. Ibid., also see *Report on the consumption of Tari in Bengal*, Calcutta, 1886, p. 7.

114. Samaresh Basu, *Jagatdal*, Calcutta, 1946, pp, 120–6.

115. *Report of Excise Commission 1883–84*, Calcutta, 1884, p. 286.

116. Ibid., p. 220.

117. Home Police Confidential File No 219/25, 1925, WBSA.

118. According to J.M. Mitra, Registrar of the Co-operative Societies of Bengal, 70–90 per cent of the labourers were in debt. *RCLI, Vol. V, Part 1*, pp. 294–6.

119. *RCLI, Vol. V, Part 1*, pp. 294–6.

120. *RCLI, Vol. XI*, p. 358.

121. Private Official letter from the Director to the Managing agents, Thomas Duff and Company, 10 June 1937 Mss 81/6/81, p. 9, TDA, DUA.

122. Paul Benthall to Edward Benthall, 21 July 1937. He objected to the formation of workmen committees proposed by his brother on the ground that they would be soon captured by the agitators and argued for the employment of labour officers to communicate with workers. Benthall in a letter on 7 August 1937 retorted 'probably it is better to be in regular touch with the actual workers rather than completely out of touch with the labour and the agitators'. CSAS Benthall Papers, Box 12.

123. For detailed discussion of salary of workers, see Ranajit Dasgupta 'Material Conditions and Behavioural Aspects of Calcutta Working-Class 1875–1899', Occasional Paper No 22, Centre for Studies in Social Sciences, Calcutta, 1979, p. 48.

124. Weavers were mainly piece workers. *RCLI, Vol. V, Part I*, pp. 96–100.

125. Interview with George Harrison, a supervisor in Naihati Jute Mill during the period 1950–55. Dundee 7 August 1992.

126. Sibnath Bannerjee private papers, interview, NMML. This was confirmed by Mr George Harrison who estimates the number of badlis at around 80 per cent and the temporary workers at around 10 per cent. Rest were permanent. Badlis were recruited on daily basis and temporary workers had jobs for three months. George Harrison, worker in Budge Budge jute mills from 1950–55. Interview 7 August 1992, Dundee.

127. MS 86/V/8/6, Manager's Report to the Directors, 1935, Victoria Jute Mill, p. 64, TDA, DUA.

128. MS 86/v/8/6, Manager's Report to the Directors, Titagarh Mill, No. 1, 1935, p. 71, TDA, DUA.

129. MS/86/v/6, Manager's Report to the Directors, Victoria Jute Mill, 1935, p.64, TDA, DUA.

130. Ibid.

131. See *IFLC*, 1908, p. 5.

132. M. Sen, *Sediner Katha*, Calcutta, 1978. 'Magi' is Bengali slang for woman, though initially the word meant elderly women.

133. *RCLI, Vol. XI, Part I*, pp. 348–9.

134. For example, a petition to the District Magistrate of 24 Parganas by jute workers in March 1931 noted that workers were not allowed to even attend 'nature's call' freely. WBSA, GOB Political Department, Political Branch d/o No. 126.

135. R. Dasgupta, 'Material Conditions and Behavioural Aspects of Calcutta working-class 1875–1899', p. 29.

136. *IFC Report, 1890*, para 13

137. Ibid., pp. 77–88.

138. Ibid., pp. 77–88.

139. *IFLC Report, 1908, Vol. I*, pp. 8–10.

140. Ibid.

141. *RCLI, Vol. V, Part 1, Evidence*, pp. 127–8.

142. Com Dept, Com Branch, April 1923, B 77, Appendix B, WBSA.

143. *Report On the Working of Factory Act*, General Miscellaneous-25, 6 April 1894, WBSA.

144. *RCLI, Vol. V, Part 2*, pp. 75–81.

145. *RCLI, Vol. XI*, p. 355.

146. For details of such accidents see Com Dept, Com Branch, 1917, September, A 26, File no R-48(2), *Report on the working of the Indian Factories Act 1911 in Bengal, Bihar, Orissa and Assam for year 1916*, p. 18, WBSA.

147. Ibid., p. 19.

148. Ibid., p. 18.

149. See for example, Manager's report to Director, Victoria Jute Mill 1930, p. 53, TDA, DUA.

150. Ibid., p. 20.

151. *RCLI, Vol. XI*, p. 355.

152. See for details of this practice workers' testimony to the Indian Factory Commission. *IFC 1890*, pp. 77–88.

153. *RCLI, Vol. V, Part II*, pp. 75–81.

154 According to a CID report, Kalidas Bhattacharya, a left wing labour leader, in a public meeting on 2 December 1928, eulogized the strikers for their being able to beat the Hindusthani workers instead of being beaten by them. Meerut conspiracy Case Progs, Exhibits SL 2737, NAI.

3

The Manager Raj and Local Elites

Collaboration and Confrontation in the Administration of Mill Towns, 1880–1930

Introduction

In 1918, David Mudie, manager of a local jute mill and chairman of the Bhatpara mill municipality, wrote to his superiors advising against the introduction of elections to the local municipal board arguing that '[t]he labour class form the majority of its population who are unfit to exercise an election franchise and who are quite fitly [sic] represented by the managers of the mills they work in.'[1] Mudie was merely echoing the common opinion of mill managers in the industrial towns of Bengal that workers were best represented by their managers. In their self-perception managers regarded themselves as *ma-baap* (parental authority) of their employees, believing that they should exercise corrective influence over the 'irrational' but 'simple', 'child-like' mill hands.[2]

The paternalistic views of Scottish mill managers were in tune with the dominant ideology of the British colonial bureaucracy in India.[3] The managers of jute mills established a stranglehold over mill town administrations in Bengal in the early twentieth century. They dominated municipal boards, controlled the local police force, and acted as judicial magistrates. They maintained their control over the municipal administration by forging alliances with propertied high caste Indians, generally from white collar professions.[4] Thus the local administration of mill towns, dominated by Scottish mill managers and propertied Indians, tried to 'control' the social life of the urban residents, mainly industrial workers, through sanitary measures, municipal taxation, and police supervision.

The mill managers' control over municipal boards, local police, and judiciary informed the working-class perception of town administration and colonial government. The involvement of propertied Indians in town administration generated opposition among workers against them. The marriage between town administration and managerial authority at workplaces widened the scope of political confrontation between workers and the mill management and transformed industrial disputes into an overall experience of class.[5] This created a political environment in which militant left-wing nationalists enjoyed greater support from the workers, because of their seemingly uncompromising political struggle against the colonial government and their exclusion from the cloistered circles of institutional politics.

The Manager Raj and the Industrial Working-class

The British liked to claim that the purpose of local self-government was to educate Indians to rule themselves; in fact, local government institutions were introduced by the Government of India seeking primarily to cheapen the cost of government. Hence municipalities were lumbered with police and conservancy charges, while it was hoped that the principle of representation and a small stake in local power would offset the unpleasantness of higher local taxation.[6] Yet, in devolving power to these municipal boards the British adopted their traditional methods of maintaining a balance between different 'interest groups'.

In Bengal, British mill managers, representing the jute industry, were appointed as commissioners in municipal boards of industrial towns. The history of the Bhatpara municipality, a large mill town on the east bank of the Hoogly, clearly bears this out. The 1884 Bengal Municipal Act introduced municipal administration to the large town of Naihati, also on the east bank of the Hoogly.[7] Located on the junction of the East Bengal and the East India railway, Naihati became the centre of the jute industry in the late nineteenth century.[8] The population of the municipality was heterogeneous but Naihati housed a powerful local Indian landed gentry. European managers of jute mills felt uneasy in a town where the local gentry exercised such powerful influence over local affairs of the municipality. Hence they demanded the vivisection of the municipality, ostensibly to allow for the adequate representation of the factories located in the town.

In 1899, the Bengal government created a new municipality called Bhatpara comprising factory areas of Naihati. The mill managers were confident that only they would be elected as the chairmen of the new municipality. Thus, T.W. Clark, a local mill manager argued in the municipal meeting that '*when one of the managers of the mills must always be the chairman of the municipality*—the area should be divided to enable the chairman to function more efficiently' [emphasis mine].[9] Mill managers also planned a new division of the municipality in 1925 to resist movements by *bhadralok* ratepayers for the introduction of an elected municipal board. The political rhetoric of mill managers evolved around the theme of improvement of the living conditions of workers, which they claimed would be neglected if bhadralok demands for elections were met. They proposed the creation of a separate municipality for the bhadralok-dominated areas.[10] Thus, the industrial interests of British capital were favoured in demarcating municipal areas in Bengal. This was particularly evident in the constitution of town boards in industrial municipalities like Bhatpara.

Bhatpara was placed under the first schedule of the 1884 Municipal Act which empowered the government to nominate the commissioners 'by name or official designation.'[11] Henceforth, Scottish mill managers constituted a majority of commissioners in Bhatpara till the enactment of the 1932 act.[12] Even this act contained a provision that in industrial towns the government would have the power to 'increase the number of appointed commissioners ... in order to secure proper representation of such industry or industries and labourers employed therein ...' This clause ensured the domination of European managers over the industrial municipalities after 1932. They enjoyed the support of the colonial government, which was evident in the way they could influence the creation of new municipalities and control the municipal boards through government nominations. However, the nomination of Scottish mill managers to the municipal board did not embitter their relationship with workers as much their policies concerning the maintenance of public health did.

Newly-created municipalities also became the most important vehicles for the introduction of improved sanitary measures which were increasingly viewed as an essential requirement for the stability of the empire.[13] The rapid growth of mill towns without any urban planning posed enormous problems for the development of 'clean and loyal' towns for British mill managers. The population of the mill town of Bhatpara quadrupled between 1901 and 1931.[14] The majority of the town's residents were mill workers and their dependants.[15] The constant expansion of the population made a mockery of the minimal sanitary programmes adopted by the mills.[16] The population explosion also increased the pressure on land, and in industrial towns like Bhatpara, within two decades, land prices increased thirty to fifty times.[17] This made accommodation extremely expensive in the mill towns and caused overcrowding in the bastees, especially near the mills.[18] This physical proximity of working-class habitations to the factories made the maintenance of a healthy environment a prerequisite for their efficient operation.

Mill managers regarded repeated outbreaks of cholera and smallpox epidemics as the main threat to the health of the operatives. They tended to overlook other diseases caused by malnutrition, like tuberculosis, which killed as many people as cholera did.[19] Cholera and smallpox concerned mill managers because they afflicted the mill towns annually, killing a large number of people in a slum or *coolie* line in a very short space of time and causing panic among workers. Because of the severity of their impact on the work of jute mills, managers took the harshest possible measures to combat these diseases. However, mill managers ignored them when they occurred on a small scale. For example, in 1918 the municipal report observed:

The general health of the town was throughout the year good, there having been no outbreak of cholera, smallpox, or plague. During the whole year no death from plague or small pox was reported, *though there were 39 deaths from cholera which was certainly the minimum that could be expected in a town with a population of 60,000.* [emphasis mine.][20]

Mill managers thus felt able to tolerate 39 deaths from cholera because it had a minimal impact on the production system. The chairman of the Bhatpara Mill municipality stated in a municipal report of 1918 that considering the scale of over-crowding in local slums, mill towns depended only on the mercy of God to save themselves from epidemics.[21] But in the mill towns God was often harsh: in the following decade, cholera and smallpox often affected Bhatpara.

The repeated occurrence of epidemics often unleashed panic among workers. In the twenties, epidemics assumed alarming proportions which threatened the smooth functioning of the mills. For example, in 1919, a sudden outbreak of influenza epidemic afflicted about 20 per cent of the town's population. When the influenza epidemic subsided, smallpox appeared in a sporadic form at Bhatpara and Jagatdal. Vaccination and re-vaccination were pursued actively and its spread was arrested. Again 'in March, cholera committed a havoc in some private bustees' at Jagatdal and led to several deaths. The worst feature of the disease 'was that there were more deaths than cures, and that the sufferers collapsed in less than 24 hours.'[22] Bewildered managers took the harshest measures to suppress the epidemics:

The cause of the outbreak was attributed to the pollution of tanks in the neighbourhood and the water of the polluted tanks was (sic) disinfected with Permanganate of Potassium and Chloride of Lime, especially the latter, which was abundantly supplied by the paper mills and alliance mills free of cost ... Guards were placed against the use of their polluted tanks. The affected houses were also similarly disinfected, and the sufferers' clothing were burnt to ashes.[23]

TABLE 3.1

The impact of Cholera and Smallpox in
the mill town of Bhatpara

Year	Smallpox Attacks	Smallpox Deaths	Cholera Attacks	Cholera Deaths
1923–24	47	17	112	70
1924–25	716	282	50	43
1925–26	225	96	274	182
1926–27	45	18	158	115
1927–28	60	12	228	142
1928–29	26	11	337	208
1929–30	41	8	221	142
1930–31	143	51	60	37

Source: For 1923–24,1924–25,1925–26,1926–27 AARBM 1927 p. 21; for 1927–28 p. 23, for 1928–29, 1929–30, 1930–31 AARBM 1931, p. 32.

The ponds, which were the only source of drinking water, were also closed to workers. However, managers did not stop at such measures. At times they knocked down slums located in the vicinity of factories. In 1917 the Annual Administrative Report of Bhatpara municipality noted that 'The clearing out of private *bustis* from the plot of land opposite the Alliance Mill has made the place cleaner and tidier and will have a beneficial effect on the sanitation of the place.'[24] Workers thus lost their dwelling places and even their jobs due to the sanitary measures adopted by mill managers. Such measures readily provoked the anger of the working-classes.

Workers normally tried to evade the attention of the municipality during epidemics.[25] They mounted stiff resistance to mass vaccination measures during a smallpox epidemic in 1925. Bhadralok residents of mill towns also aided them.[26] This resistance was attributed to the superstitions of ignorant natives. Public health measures continued to be informed by crude notions of the 'unclean habits' of workers. Health officers in the mill towns roundly blamed workers for their diseases. Facing a smallpox epidemic in Bhatpara, the health officer concluded: 'the cause of the spread of the disease was due more to the pernicious habits of the people of fouling open spaces and infecting tanks by washing soiled clothes and bedding in them, than to anything else'.[27]

However, superstitions or suspicion of western medicine was least among the causes of the working-class opposition to public health measures. This was evident from the success of an inoculation drive among workers in 1928 during a cholera epidemic in Bhatpara. The municipal commissioners expressed surprise when they found that in 'The worst affected places, ... people eagerly sought for the inoculation ...'.[28] In fact, an increasing number of working-class patients attended mill dispensaries in the town.

TABLE 3.2

The number of cases treated in the hospitals in
Bhatpara in the period 1902–20

Year	No of cases yearly	No of dispensaries	Town population
1902	12,228	5	21,450
1907	20,566	8	40,000
1913	61286	8	50,426
1917	56,438	9	60,000
1918	54,258	9	60,000
1921	69257	9	65,666

Sources: AARBM 1902, p. 11, 1907, p. 11, 1913, p. 13, 1917, p. 11, 1918, p. 10, 1921, p. 9.

Managers themselves admitted the need for the establishment of hospitals in mill towns.[29] The Chairman then commented that 'What is wanted for the maturity of the scheme is not money, but a spirit of enterprise and some power to take initiative, and I am sure that there must be amongst the European gentlemen living in the town, to push the work to the best advantage of the community, and thus earn the gratitude of the thousands of the labourers left under their care.'[30] Yet the municipal hospital did not come into existence for the next ten years. The 1927 Annual Report of the Municipality of Bhatpara briefly mentioned that the hospital could not be set up due to lack of adequate funds.[31] Opposition to European medicine by superstitious workers should be seen as a managerial excuse to avoid expensive public health measures.[32]

In fact, the absence of proper arrangements for water supply in mill towns also led to epidemics. Residents had to use local ponds not only for drinking water, but also for bathing and washing of their clothes and utensils as well. Municipalities often pleaded with the Bengal government for the introduction of a regular water supply scheme. Finally, in 1928, after having suspended the water supply scheme for a decade, mill managers in Bhatpara took up a new scheme of comprehensive town development which focused on improved water supply. The new water supply scheme made arrangements for the daily supply of water at the rate of 10 gallons per head for an estimated population of 120,000. This quantity was allocated through mills, in proportion to the labourers engaged in each factory. However, the bhadralok residential areas received the bulk of the water in comparison to the working class areas.[33] Water supply schemes were often utilized for combating strikes, and thus became a useful tool in the hands of managers during industrial unrest.[34] Hence, such schemes were regarded with suspicion by workers, which they felt were introduced to curb their independence.

As population increased in the mill towns, it became apparent to mill managers that comprehensive town planning was necessary to improve the sanitary condition of the towns.[35] For smooth functioning of the town administration, managers depended on their alliance with the local propertied elite who feared that such planning would impinge upon their properties and reduce the incomes they yielded.

The expanding areas of mill towns undoubtedly brought monetary gains to the *zamindars*. New *bazaars* were constructed on their land, slums came up on their estates, and zamindars encouraged more tenants to settle in the slums in order to increase their earnings from rent. This became a source of long-standing disputes between the local landlords and jute mills.[36]

Mills often made attempts to control bastees by enacting new municipal bye laws compelling zamindars to spend more on the improvement of housing. In Bhatpara, municipal politics witnessed intense conflict between zamindars and mills. The Bhatpara municipality repeatedly asked the local zamindar to improve the bastee lands. The zamindar retorted by complaining that municipalities imposed excessive taxes on his lands. On 7 September 1900, the municipality decided to take action against the landholders for the insanitary condition of the bastees on their lands.[37] Moreover, they threatened to take over the land if the owners did not take steps to improve the conditions of housing.

The construction of new roads in the mill towns became an important part of municipal schemes—seeking to avoid congestion and disperse the settlement of workers and reduce the extent of overcrowding. In 1925, the municipality acquired two new villages to distribute the population more evenly, in accordance with a revised town planning scheme. Zamindars quickly realized that such schemes threatened their income from overcrowded bazaars and bastees, and opposed them.[38] Such disputes had a long history and they ensured that the public health programmes had an uncertain future.[39] However, by denying representation on the municipal board to the working classes, mill managers allowed the municipal schemes to become prisoners of local propertied interests and lost the opportunity to transform such issues, which served their own needs, into matters of public concern that were sure to get the support of the workers.

Frustrated by their failure to secure the cooperation of propertied elites in town development schemes, managers sought to clean up the mill town in other ways. Artisan social groups, who had no connection with factories, were compelled by mill managers to leave the industrial towns. Local potters, for example, were perceived to pollute the sanitary condition of Bhatpara. In 1901, soon after the municipality was established, high rates of taxation were imposed upon them. Potters complained—but they had no effect, and eventually simply left the town.[40] Potters were soon joined by fishermen whose occupation, it was said, generated an odour 'too obnoxious' for 'civilized' mill managers residing on the riverbank. In the vicinity of Shyamnagar in Bhatpara, there was a large lake known as Bhattibil. Fishermen increasingly settled down around these '*bils*'.[41] But the new municipal sanitary scheme of flushing the town sewage into the lake threatened their profession and generated much protest from them.[42]

In the mill towns thousands of casual workers eked out their livelihood from local bazaars by hawking small articles, plying hackney carriages, and working in small cattle sheds in addition to their employment in the factories. But municipal restrictions, seeking to reduce overcrowding, began to impinge upon them. *Chamar* workers in jute mills, who also earned money from the hide trade, were displaced by the new municipal cattle pound laws which transferred this trade to local contractors. Similarly, some workers who kept cattle and sold milk were now subject to high taxes. In 1918, small traders and casual workers met a new license fee for cattle sheds with widespread resistance.[43] The tussle between municipality and cattleshed owners continued for a long time. This was extended to hackney carriage drivers who also soon faced new taxes and licensing policies.

These new taxes, it was claimed by the municipality, would restrict the unusual growth of petty trade and would prevent overcrowding of the bazaars.[44] In 1932 the annual municipal report observed that

Some of the Mill workers and Sardars have combined to establish another bazar at the northern borders of Kankinara and—as a preliminary—started some stalls for sale of vegetables only. ... but the municipal commissioners must not encourage competition by sanctioning new market in the close vicinity of an existing one, so long the latter is managed efficiently. The organizers of this proposed new market asked for a license which could not be granted for want of a certificate from the chairman.[45]

In fact, the municipalities encouraged wholesale traders to take over town businesses to reduce the risk of sanitary pollution and overcrowding of bazaars. Items in the list of dangerous trades, which were taken over by wholesale traders increased annually (See Appendix). These policies created a mistrust of the municipality among workers who lost their additional sources of earnings outside factories and even dwelling places because of the policies of mill administrations. Yet their wages in factories barely met their subsistence needs. Hence workers viewed most of these acts as part of the managerial attempt to exercise control over their work forces outside the mill compound and reduce their economic independence.

The implementation of such measures was accompanied by the force of coercive laws which imposed judicial punishments upon the workers and worsened the relationship between workers and the town administration.

Local municipal courts tried cases for the violation of the Birth and Death Registration Acts, the Vaccination Act, the Prevention of Cruelty to Animals Act, the Hackney Carriages Act, and the Food Adulteration Act. These acts were often arbitrarily implemented by police constables and poorly paid sanitary inspectors who utilized such opportunities to extract money from the workers rather than to improve the sanitary condition of the town.[46] Municipalities also encouraged police to bring an increasing number of cases to the court which enhanced their earnings from fines collected from these cases. The 1919 municipal report, for example, criticised police constables for the decline in the number of court cases and rebuked them for their failures.[47] The police thus often went into full-fledged action to impress municipal authorities.

These measures not only created hostilities between workers and police and the municipalities but also cast doubt upon the neutrality of the local judiciary. Workers quickly discovered that the magistrates who tried them for violation of these laws were mainly mill managers.[48] So they avoided providing information to the police which, they suspected, would in all probability be used by mill managers against them. Thus, the information collected under these regulations, for instance, compulsory birth and death registration, proved to be extremely unreliable. Finally, managers were compelled to declare rewards for reporting of births and deaths to encourage workers to come forward with information.[49] Yet workers continued to see these laws as part of the evil designs of mill managers to harass and oppress them.

The attempt of the British mill managers to improve living conditions provoked the hostility of the workers as these policies destroyed their livelihood and threatened their homes. At the same time these policies strengthened the hands of the local propertied elites. Despite their material gain from such policies, the Indian propertied elites always resisted any attempt by the mill managers or municipalities to improve the living condition of workers which they feared would affect their income. The mills, on their part, were not too keen to spend their money to provide better housing for their workers. As a result, the municipal attempts at sanitary reform proved a failure and served merely to generate hostility between workers and managers. Managerial attempts to exclude workers from the municipal boards not only led to bitter hostilities between them, but also created a complete mistrust among workers of their policies. This was further strengthened by managerial influence over the local police force in the mill towns, where the police often intervened in industrial disputes against workers.

Police Control and Manager Raj in Mill Towns

The police in colonial India, according to a recent work on Uttar Pradesh, 'had minimalist agenda of maintaining public order and was very little concerned with protecting the life and property of the common people.'[50] Police commanders were little concerned with any notion of 'policing by consent' as they were not accountable to 'representative bodies or the community'.[51] They openly defended the interests of propertied classes in general and European business interests in particular. In the jute mill towns of Bengal, the police were mainly controlled by British mill managers who, in addition, formed their own private forces to combat labour movements.

The relationship between the police forces and mill managers underwent various changes over different stages. In the last decade of the nineteenth century when labour unrest rocked mill towns in Bengal, the IJMA repeatedly appealed to the Bengal government to strengthen the police forces in the mill towns[52]. The IJMA's prayer resulted in a high-level enquiry into police arrangements in the mill towns led by the deputy inspector general of police in Bengal. The committee sanctioned new police outposts for Bhatpara, Shyamnagar, and Titagarh in 1895.[53] Even the remotest southern mill town of Budgebudge witnessed an increased police presence, including arrangements for its swift movement by steam boats.[54] Within two years of this new plan, however, the government appointed a special committee comprising the police and representatives of the Bengal Chamber of Commerce, a body of the British mill-owners and traders. The committee submitted a new plan to set up a military police station between Chinsura and Calcutta. It was suggested that mills could use their steamers to deploy military police in any emergency situation.[55] This system received a further boost after a series of strikes and riots in the mill towns in the first decade of the twentieth century. The district magistrate of the 24 Parganas stressed the need in the mill areas for the mobilization of the largest number of police to prevent rioting.[56] This found some support from nationalist newspapers like the *Amrita Bazaar Patrika*, which noted an increase in crimes in mill towns and attributed it to the presence of 'upcountry coolies'. The *Patrika* claimed that in the North-West Provinces anyone wanted for a crime would simply flee to the mill areas in Bengal.[57] With the coming of the First World War, the mill owners further demanded the armed policing of the jute mills.[58]

In 1915, a full-fledged plan was prepared for the introduction of a police defence scheme in the 'Hoogly mill area'. Interestingly, this scheme focused more on dealing with labour unrest than addressing ordinary crimes. The mill area was divided into fourteen distinct blocks. Each police station in the blocks was provided with a detailed list of the number of employees in the mills and was prescribed the amount of the ammunitions which they required in the local thana to control an agitation. Plans were made to support police actions by arms carefully stored in the thana. Knowledge of the local communication network was given primary importance in the scheme, with particular emphasis placed on the arrangement of the telegraph. Each thana was provided with a list of mills and their distance from the nearest police outpost. Principal roads leading to the mills were shown in specially prepared maps. Railway timetables were kept in the police stations to enable quick movement of armed forces from Calcutta. Police officers were also authorized to press ferries into service for rapid deployment of forces. In emergencies, the military was to be called to the area of conflict while the fixed reserves were also increased.[59].

In this scheme, executive power to tackle the situation remained in the hands of the honorary first class magistrates who could command 'any unlawful assembly of more than five persons to be dispersed'. If the assembly refused to disperse, the former were empowered to send for auxiliary forces to suppress any unrest in the mill towns.[60] Under the Auxiliary Force Act of 1920, the mills were provided with Lewis guns to tackle unrest. Under Section 18 of the Auxiliary Force Act, any company of the force could be mobilized into action in an emergency situation and Section 132 protected them from legal actions for their activities. Mills were connected by telephones with the general commanding officer of the areas.

In 1920–2, all the honorary magistrates in the 24 Parganas were jute mill managers. In practical terms mill managers were given legal cover to break the resistance of the workers and to repress any political activities.[61] European assistants in jute mills were recruited as members of the auxiliary forces who were empowered to meet emergency situation in mill towns. In Gouripur Jute Mill alone, 25 European assistants were members of the auxiliary force; in Bhatpara their number was 85.[62] The government was very conscious of the legal implications of the Auxiliary Force Act.[63] These powers were not simply confined to paper. In 1920, when nearly 30,000 workers were on strike, the government sought advice on the legal implications of the use of Lewis guns to suppress 'disturbances'.[64]

The Police Defence Scheme for the Hoogly mill areas brought all mill towns under the control of mill managers who held two offices, the chairmanship of the municipal board and the post of honorary magistrate of the mill town. They could unilaterally declare any gathering of workers comprising more than four persons as an unlawful assembly. The mill managers' control over the municipal administration, local judiciary, and the police system in the mill towns transformed local administrative institutions into a political machine for the repression and the control of workers' resistance. Because of the close links between the police and the mill managers, workers came to regard the police simply as the latter's coercive arm, which in turn, coloured their perception of the colonial state. The social distance between European managers and Indian workers further reinforced the fear of working class unrest among managers.

Isolation and Public Authority: A Survey of the World of European Mill Managers

A crucial aspect of the authority of British mill managers was the social distance maintained by them from Indian workers and town residents. This was manifest in the physical segregation of European residential areas, marked by long factory walls, from the rest of the Indian population. An examination of British social life within its walled-off residential complexes reveals an expatriate mind which shut its eyes to the surrounding working class population and looked towards Scotland for psychological and social comfort. Workers impinged upon their consciousness only when they posed a threat to British mill managers during strikes or communal riots.

The spatial organization of Bhatpara was typical of a Bengal mill town. Perhaps one may take here a glance at the colonial concept of the social order and its relationship with the physical organization of mill towns. The word *sahib*, an Arabic word meaning companion, was transformed into 'master' in Hindi, and generally the British were addressed as sahib[65]. But if sahibs continued to be master, the worker became coolie—and defined as 'a hired labourer ... a labourer induced to emigrate from India, or from China, to labour in the plantations of Mauritius, ... West Indies'; the Hobson–Jobson dictionary traced the roots of the word to a caste in western

India 'whose savagery, filth, and general degradation attracted much attention in former times or to Turkish *kol*, a word meaning '*Kuleh*' or a 'male slave and bondsman.' Between sahibs and coolies were the babus who comprised 'respectable' Bengali collaborators. Babus were often derided by the sahibs. 'The pliable, plastic, receptive baboo of Bengal', wrote Fraser's magazine satirically, 'eagerly avails himself of this system partly from a desire to obtain a government appointment'.[66]

The colonial conception of the social order was reflected in the physical organization of mill towns. An exclusive European quarter often occupied the river front. Buchanan described the mill towns thus:

Mills commonly face the water front and beside them stand the quarters for the European managers and European assistants. These are of similar construction and very attractive. Generally there are tennis courts, spacious lawns, which for a few rupees per month, the gardener keeps in luxuriant grass and beds of blossoming flowers. With tropical shutters and tropical touches in the architecture, these places are most inviting. Seen across the river or from a boat in mid stream on a crisp morning in winter .... a line of not too heavy smoke floating away from the great chimneys and the tropical setting mirrored in the glassy waters—the mill and its quarters present a picture not soon forgotten.[67] (See the map of Shyamnagar Jute Mill)

In the backyard of the mills were located the quarters of Bengali 'babu' or mill clerks and the staff of the jute mills. Workers in some mills were provided with quarters in the coolie lines. But often the mill lines were the exclusive preserve of the 'loyal workers'.[68] Most of the workers could not enjoy the luxury of paved mill lines; the city poor and common workers lived in 'bastees' outside the factory gate outside the factory wall.[69]

The social life of the Scottish supervisory staff in the mill towns revolved around factory, club, and golf course. They carved out a separate social enclave for themselves, ordered in the image of Scotland. When ships reached the Bengal shore, after a long journey from British ports, the sight of the mills was always said to bring joy to a newly recruited young Scottish employee. They searched for a new home and not strangers. Claude Henry, a Scottish mill assistant, wrote to his friend his impression of his arrival to a mill town in moving language:

The joy of swift motion after weeks of lazy humdrum sailing set upon us all and the land warmly populous, fertile, much cultivated, was in direct contrast to the barren lands seen on the voyage from England ... Plantation, palm groves, village native farmsteads with homely hay stacks, hens and cattle—gives picture of a populous and warm life. Later, great white buildings, each with its chimney ... and jetty, bulk out every mile or so from the rural scenery on either shore—the jute mills. At one of these we anchored at dark, about dozen miles (sic) below Calcutta.[70]

Life was, however, far from easy for these Scottish supervisors. After a few weeks spent learning the job, these men were introduced to what mill managers liked to describe as 'research'. This was the period when supervisors learnt how to control machines or select better quality raw jute.[71] The work schedule was so heavy at this stage that they became tied to the machines. Claude, the Scottish employee, was soon assigned his tasks and became *Karam Sahib* or 'head of the clerical department', but his duties were much wider than the name suggests. He was overseer of the store, supervised all imports of jute and machinery, and checked orders for raw jute. He spent his entire working day in the town bazaar or at the jetty. He worked from 5–30 a.m. to 7 p.m. 'The Europeans are liable to work the whole thirteen and half hours' but Claude records happily that 'we fit in times for meals and generally manage, two hours rest at mid day; at night one is glad to turn in at 9 o'clock.'[72] However, despite his day amongst workers, Claude did not in his letters to his friend back home describe Indian life at any length. This silence becomes pronounced when we look at sports and other forms of entertainment of British employees.

On holidays golf, tennis, and cricket kept the Scottish jute men busy. The manager of the Victoria Jute Mill wrote in his report in 1937: 'The health of the European staff has been good and the amenities enjoyed by them in the form of golf courses, swimming tanks, etc., contribute to this.'[73] Golf occupied an important part of the social life of Scottish employees. The Merchants' Cup Golf Competition was a big social event celebrated by all European companies in Bengal. All companies in Calcutta participated in the competition. In the early years, wines flowed freely on these occasions. An article in *The Statesman* in 1935 was nostalgic about the good old days of the pre-war period:

the battle for the Merchants' cup was concluded yesterday with an 82 by Ainslie to make ... Bird and Company winner for the first time. Except in the samiana, this has been one of the driest Merchant's cup in the history of the of competition ... in [the] bad old Barrackpore days when competitors foregathered on the 1st tee full of good spirits in contrast to the nervous sobriety of the present day.[74]

For some, tennis was the main entertainment. One mill assistant wrote back to his friend '[d]uring the weekend it's tennis all day long'.[75] On other important social occasions cricket matches were organized between the local XI and the Calcutta XI. Social activities of Scottish employees, including charities, evolved around old loyalties to Dundee while the local municipality languished from lack of a hospital. Mr McDonald, agent of Thomas Duff and Company, wrote back home to his colleague:

Mr Robertson will be pleased to hear ... that we continue as a result of various functions we have organised on behalf of the Dundee Royal infirmary to make good propaganda with collections. At the moment our figure stands at approximately Rs 6000. We still have a gymkhana at Shyamnagar North mill and a dance at Angus in the beginning of the November and I am quite hopeful of that when the time comes we shall be able to remit to the Infirmary something in excess what was sent by Begg Dunlop last year.[76]

On Friday evenings, dinner gatherings were organized where professional speakers were invited to speak on improving topics. These topics ranged from the Tibetan landscape to Everest expeditions. Magic lantern shows were another staple of these occasions. However, for all the scrupulous attention they paid to Indian natural life, these mill managers remained silent on the Indian people themselves.[77] The most important social occasion for Scottish employees in Bengal was the St Andrews day dinner. This was the occasion when Scotsmen gathered in main towns and made merry. Wallace recalled that in the late nineteenth century

partners of the Geo Henderson and Co used to make their residence at Baranagar in a bungalow in the mill compound, and the annual new dinner given by them to the assistants was quite an important function. Besides the host, there would be as many as 30 invited guests. The mill was honoured in 1870 by a visit from Lord Mayo and a party from government house, including Duke of Edinburgh who went up from Calcutta in company's launch.[78]

Thus, Scottish mill managers led a life typical of expatriate traders in Bengal. They denied Indian workers entry into that secluded mental world. They could enjoy in Bengal a social status of which they could not have dreamt in Scotland. Nonetheless, European social life in Calcutta was highly stratified, caste ridden, and hierarchical. The jute mill managers had little access to upper class European social life as represented by senior ICS officers and the governor's court. In colonial Bengal they were the untouchables among the expatriates.[79]

   In mill towns, however, these managers found themselves at the top of the heap. They controlled the local police force, chaired municipal boards, and even dispensed justice. Their interactions with workers were governed by carefully constructed social rituals marked by a strict sense of hierarchy. On festivals like Coronation Day, European and 'native gentlemen' were entertained in a specially erected pavilion at a distance from the workers.[80] In sports competitions, they presided and distributed the prizes. In schools, they were elected as honorary presidents.[81] In this way Scottish mill managers sought to project their power and status and assumed a lofty paternalism in relation to the workers; yet for all their pretensions they were like all other actors in the colonial power structure also dependent upon local collaborators among the Indian propertied elite. Despite their domination over the local administration, the sahibs also had to share power with the Bengali babus to run the local municipalities. The master script of this partnership was written by the government of Bengal who designed constitutional terms for the power-sharing at local municipal boards to ensure both British superiority and greater Indian involvement in local affairs.

Making of Local Elites: Bhadralok in Municipal Politics in Bengal

British colonial administrators imagined Indian society as a sum total of mutually hostile communities. They believed that it was their task to preserve peace and harmony by representing and balancing the interests of each, especially in local administration. They alone, they persuaded themselves, could protect and even liberate the Indian poor from the oppressive, indigenous elite. Yet to maintain political suitability, colonial bureaucrats sought to discover the 'natural leaders' of local communities whose collaboration they cherished. They ensured that locally powerful groups were well represented within the local administration. Indian propertied elites gradually appropriated the political language invented by British administrators and employed it to justify their supremacy over other social groups. The British search for political collaborators in the mill towns fell upon local professional elite groups who regarded themselves as bhadralok or gentlefolk. The bhadralok elite soon appropriated the political language of British administrators to establish their domination over local political institutions.

The period of the emergence of mill towns coincided with the strengthening of social networks among rising Indian professional social groups, more widely known as bhadralok. The term bhadralok included members of 'respectable classes' who did not earn their bread through manual labour. By the end of the nineteenth century, people belonging to the middle stratum of society who combined intermediary tenure holdings with employment in government services or the professions started to dominate the bhadralok community. The bhadralok perceived themselves as a mirror image of western 'middle class', the standard bearers of western enlightenment in Bengali society. Yet bhadralok ideology was not solely based on western education. It was also informed by their superior caste status.

Bhatpara, the largest mill town in the region, had always been a centre of upper caste Hindus.[82] Bhatpara became prominent during the late seventeenth century when it flourished as a centre of the philosophical school of *Nabya Naya*. Often the social decisions of the Hindu in Bengal depended on the brahmins of these settlements.[83] One important instance of such social judgment was the support offered by the Nadia Pundits to Krishnakanta Nandi when *Pandas* of the Jagannath temple in Orissa refused to accept his gifts as he was an unclean *Sudra*.[84] . The brahmins not only offered judgments but were also Sanskrit scholars. They were part of a wide intellectual network which included the most important settlements of Bengal, Bihar, and other parts of North India. Kashi occupied the central position in this brahminical culture. Marked by an eclectic cultural framework, the social discourses of Bhatpara brahmins often swung from liberal to orthodox positions. By the late eighteenth century, the brahmins of the region had an active interaction with Calcutta society. The British in the early nineteenth century, while drafting Hindu laws, relied upon the *sastric* interpretations of brahmins. The heyday of orientalist ideology in the late eighteenth century witnessed lively debates between Orientalists like Sir William Jones and the brahmins of traditional centres of Bengal.[85]

By the early twentieth century Bhatpara brahmins acted as arbiters of Hindu social customs and rituals and preserved them. Madhusudan Nayacharya, who spent two years in Bhatpara, left his impressions in an unpublished memoir. Madhusudan came to Bhatpara in 1919 as a student of *naya* and stayed with the family of Manmathanath Tarkathirtha, his teacher. There were two other students who came from Medinipur and East Bengal to study with the same *guru*. They constructed a mud hut near the Ganga. Tarkathirtha's source of income was the age-old ceremony of *Brahmin Viday* and the annual subscription offered by his students. Tarkatirtha's elder brother Shibchandra Bhattacharya, who was employed in the Sanskrit College at Calcutta, maintained the general expenditure of the household. Bhatpara's brahmin population followed a vegetarian diet and milk products constituted their most important food. Even at marriage ceremonies, guests were offered only vegetarian food.[86] Women members of brahmin families observed *pardah* and never appeared before outsiders. Even Manmathanath's wife did not serve food to the students. Bhatpara at that time was a stronghold of brahmins of the *Basistha Gotra*. One day, when Madhusudan came to know that his diet included *sradha anna* of people belonging to other gotras, he started cooking his own food in protest against this flouting of caste rules.

However, Basistha gotra brahmins never accepted non-brahmin disciples at that time. Chatuspatis, or traditional Sanskrit centres of Bhatpara, offered courses on naya and smriti. In 1921–2, Bhatpara hosted a meeting of the *Vangya Brahmin Sabha* which deliberated on the reforms of almanacs. Bhatpara brahmins sometimes could not maintain social norms regarding marriage. The limited number of brahmins led to marriages within *sapindas* (sub-castes delineated on the basis of the members' right to offer ablutions to their forefathers together). Girls at the time of marriage were 10 to 12 years of age and on the day of the marital ceremony at the husband's house known as *Boubhat*, only people belonging to the sapinda group were invited. Friends of the bridegroom were not allowed to meet the bride and they used to exchange greetings with only senior members of the family of the bridegroom.[87]

The brahmin community of Bhatpara, with a brilliant intellectual heritage, suffered an identity crisis at the turn of the century. Their material condition declined sharply. Bhatpara's brahmin population depended on the patronage of brahmin zamindars and grants of rent-free land formed the economic basis of the educational as well as the social life of the Bhatpara Pundits. But the British land revenue policies from the late eighteenth century spelt doom for the community.[88] Moreover, local patrons began to disappear as the resources of the brahmin zamindar families declined. Since Bhatpara brahmins performed religious services only for their brahmin disciples, the decline of the latter in social status and wealth heightened their own problems at the end of the century.

This was the period when jute mills expanded and marshy lands in the vicinity of Bhatpara were colonized. The new Bhatpara municipality, which came into existence in 1899, included the jute mill areas of Jagatdal and Kankinarah. By 1931, Bhatpara was the most densely populated industrial locality.[89] The jute mills changed the environment of Bhatpara's brahmin community. The local brahmins sneered at the prospect of an industrial culture invading Bhatpara society. But social practices in the late 1920s witnessed changes on a much more mundane plane, as slippers replaced the age old *kharams* and the *lungi* entered the brahmin household. The occupational structure of Brahmin scholars also underwent change. Economic and social changes compelled them to search for jobs outside the locality. While few refused jobs in government institutions, many sought employment in the service sector of Calcutta.

This new search for office jobs was also influenced by the improvement in communication networks with Calcutta which opened up new avenues of employment and changed the composition of the local bhadralok population. Suburban traffic developed rapidly in the early twentieth century. In 1910, 31, 776 return season tickets to Sealdah were issued.[90] The port commissioners' steamer service became popular with riverine municipalities in the Barrackpore subdivision. The result was that a growing army of clerks employed in Calcutta offices and living outside the city, commuted daily on the trains, trams or ferry services.[91] Even in the 1930s the Eastern Bengal Railway advertised in the newspapers: 'live in the suburbs and save house rent; buy a Rail cum Tram ticket'.[92] In 1932, a Calcutta newspaper reported that 'The Eastern Bengal Railway Puja Bazaar Special in which various mercantile firms of Calcutta are participating for exhibition and sale of their commodities of Calcutta left at 11 p.m., railway time on Saturday August 27 for a month's tour over the broad gauge and metre gauge sections of this railway.'[93] Employment and even the special seasonal purchasing by the suburban babus now came to depend on the railways.

The railways also changed the perception of time among the local population. Ramanuj Vidyarnab, a Sanskrit college professor from Bhatpara, narrated his experiences as a daily commuter in a poem, however unremarkable its literary qualities may be:

We go to toilets at a fixed time
We take our bath at a fixed hour
We yawn at a fixed moment
The clock controls our life;
Prayer becomes a hurried affair
We could just eat rice at lunch

Without clock our life plunges into darkness
Thus is our daily life.[94]

The poem goes on to narrate the daily journey to Calcutta—the card games, railway gossip, and other daily events in the office-goers' lives. Lamenting the lack of time in the newly emerging urban society, the poet sadly notes the erosion of traditional social customs including the *shistachar* or time-honoured manner of interacting with people with proper dignity.

The expansion of the railways, along with the drying up of income from land gave rise to a new social group within the mill towns. Professional people, lawyers, doctors, local pleaders, school teachers, and journalists became the social leaders of the towns. They were educated in similar local schools and increasingly constituted a cohesive social group. By 1901, Sreerampur (on the west bank of the Hoogly, had three schools which taught English and had 733 students on their rolls; Bhadreswar had one high school with 221 students, and Baidyabati had one English school and 4 primary schools.[95] These schools produced the future pleaders, teachers, and clerks of the mill towns.

These upper-caste Hindu urban professionals initiated new intellectual movements in late nineteenth-century Calcutta. By the early twentieth century, the bhadralok organized various associations for the educated. The main activities of these bhadralok elites centred around local libraries and literary associations which they established. In 1901 in Bhatpara, they started the *saraswat samaj*, literally a community of the learned.[96] Baidyabati, another mill settlement on the banks of Hoogly, had its own Young Men's Association.[97] These associations were formed primarily to discuss contemporary social and economic problems and discourse upon religious issues. The number of local journals from mill towns increased constantly. Kumardev Mukhopadhyay's *Education Gazette* acquired a prominent position among these journals. But the local backstreet literary magazines dominated the day. Most of these were conservative Hindu journals run by brahmin editors but were registered in the name of their female relatives, perhaps to avoid prosecution in case of financial failure.[98]

Along with these cultural associations, sport clubs were also set up. By bringing the local upper-caste youth together, these served to increase the social cohesion of the community. Young members of bhadralok households, responding to the colonial stereotype of the feminine nature of Hindus, opened gymnasiums and practised physical culture from the late nineteenth century. P. Mitra, the famous barrister and later organizer of the Anusilan Samiti, (a revolutionary organization) started a centre of traditional martial arts in Naihati.[99] In 1885, the first Sporting Association of Bengal came into existence in the mill locality of Garifa. It came to be known as Naihati Sporting. This club further expanded in 1905 and adopted a more Hindu name, the Hara Gouri Club. In 1919 this club became the United Sporting Club of Garifa.[100] In Bhatpara, a Lathi Khela Akhara (assocation for martial arts with bamboo poles) became prominent in 1905, and it was run by two local Brahmins—Harihar Bhattacharjee and Panchanan Bhattacharjee.[101] These sports associations also emerged as political centres for the bhadralok youth in the mill towns.

The mutuality of the bhadralok was marked by their sense of social superiority over the working-classes. A nostalgic passion for the pre-industrial past along with the self-glorification of their present achievements characterized the bhadralok mentality. It was in this context that the Sanskrit College professor, Ramanuj Vidyarnab of Bhatpara, poured his scorn on jute workers who flocked to the region after the establishment of the mills:

Well done, Bhatpara municipality:

Gone are the old jungles and bamboo groves

Of Kankinarah and Jagatdal

Their places taken by palaces and bazaar

Slums of meruas, factories and their sprouting chimneys,

The bazaars now bustle with the ghostly meruas

Buying and selling in their strange Hindi

On holidays,

They loaf about the town in groups,

Drunk singing songs that sound like howl of dogs.[102]

A strange nostalgic passion for an idyllic past, along with an animosity towards migrant workers, dominates the poet's feelings which also expressed the widely shared attitude of the bhadralok.

In their telling of the past stories of these settlements, these scholars and poets maintained a resounding silence about the presence of the labouring population. The bhadralok ideology of social superiority had its origins in the caste hierarchy of Bengal. This ideology was again informed and sustained by researches of the British officials into caste history. One notices an interesting ideological construction of the mythical past in the vernacular histories produced in rural Bengal in the early twentieth century. Nirod Baran Mishra Chakraborty's *Bangalar Jatiya Itihas* (National History of Bengal) is a fine juxtaposition of myth and history. [103] He makes an attempt to establish the origins of Badu Byas, a Brahmin sub-caste whose members trace their origins to Byas, composer of the Mahabharata. The myths and stories of the Puranas which find mention in his writings are persistently presented as 'history'. He claims Ayodhya is Goudha Desh, the original centre of brahminical culture and from where his caste fellows migrated to Bengal. But he also feels the need to turn to the works of Risley, Malcolm, and R.C. Dutt to sustain his claims.

The real significance of the text lies in its reflection of a resurgence of interest among Bengalis in the definition of their caste status which was in part stimulated by official investigations of the castes and tribes of Bengal, the census operations, and communal categories of the representative system of colonial rule. Social mobility and new-found prosperity also encouraged the bhadralok to reconstruct their caste histories. This trend was most pronounced in Calcutta but it soon gripped rural areas where numerous caste histories were produced. In this case, Nirod Baran Mishra Chakraborty himself was a member of the Bangiya Sahitya Parishad and Secretary of the Goudiya Brahmin Association. [104] The upper-caste Hindus in the mill towns now began to find their heritage in a mythical past of their own invention.

Bally, another mill town located across the river from Bhatpara, had a large *Kayastha* population who believed they had settled there since Adisura's time. The origin of Bally was traced by Prabhat Bandapadhyay to Adisura's time. The *Dakshin Radhi Kayastha* community had lived there, he claimed, since from Bijoysen's time. Purusottam of the Dutta family of Bally was said to have come to the town on an elephant with Bijoysen's army. Nishapati Ghosh, said to be the original founder of the Ghosh community in Bengal, was an inhabitant of Bally. [105] But Bandapadhyay does not even mention the labouring population, even though the local paper and jute mills could find a place in his description. In fact, for the most part, the labouring men remained invisible for bhadralok society. The working poor forced themselves into the attention of the bhadralok only as a threat. The bhadralok attempt to establish their superiority over the working-class was definitely rooted in their perceptions and practises of caste but they also justified their superiority with reference to the colonial discourse. The hostility of the bhadralok towards workers was further reflected in municipal politics.

Municipal Politics and Bhadralok Organizations

Colonial bureaucrats were ill at ease in dealing with the powerful Indian professional social groups in Calcutta and suburban mill towns. In the late nineteenth century, Indian professional elites were inspired by Queen Victoria's declaration proclaiming the equality of Indians in the British empire. But the paltry reforms in the late nineteenth century dashed their hopes. By the turn of the century the bhadralok became the most bitter critic of the colonial bureaucracy. This put the British rulers in a dilemma. They wanted to recruit the bhadralok into the colonial administration but were reluctant to devolve power to educated Indians. Municipal acts were designed to provide these bhadralok elites limited power within the parish. Unfortunately for the dissident bhadralok in the mill towns, municipalities became the pocket-boroughs of mill managers. Nevertheless, mill managers could not totally ignore the influence of bhadralok elites in mill towns.

The 1885 Act provided an informal guideline to mill managers about which Indians to recruit to the municipal boards. This municipal Act defined voters not only in terms of property-holding but also in terms of educational qualifications. [106] Though this clause was not operative in the mill towns, mill managers nominated local bhadralok for their 'leading role in local community'. For example, in 1927, faced with a cholera epidemic in the municipality, the chairman of Bhatpara municipality wrote in his report: 'I also trust that in this matter—the gentlemen class of the ratepayers—persons of lead and light—will first set an example and inoculate themselves, so that the cholera-inoculation may be popularized and the labour class of men may follow their example.'[107]

Moreover, both the government and the mill managers tried to win the support of the influential brahmins of Bhatpara who were not only locally powerful but had a pre-eminent position in society. Following an old custom, the British bestowed titles upon scholars in recognition of academic honours, and created a new honorific known as *Mahamopadhyay*. In Bengal, this title was bestowed upon distinguished Sanskrit scholars. Acceptance of the title by pundits gave the government a certain legitimacy not only in traditional academic circles but also among Hindus at large.[108] Between 1890 and 1910 there were six Mahamopadhyays living in the Bhatpara–Naihati region and were highly respected by the local bhadralok population.[109] Mill managers in Bhatpara also donated large amounts of money to local *chatuspatis* or Sanskrit schools to win the trust of the *pandits*.[110] On important occasions mill managers consulted the Bhatpara brahmins for their opinion on municipal affairs. For example, during the Orissa famine of 1905, the Bhatpara municipality formed a committee for fund raising comprising 'local notables'. A glance at the members of this committee would help us to identify what kind of personage was considered a notable in the managers' perception. In a meeting on 18 May 1900, the local notables who gathered in the house of the Chairman Mr T.W. Clark were mostly the Sanskrit scholars of Bhatpara while the others were local businessmen or employees of a local zamindar.[111] Brahmins constituted a substantial section of Indian members of the municipality till the end of the 1930s.

These municipalities provided employment for the local bhadralok. The number of municipal employees in mill towns increased significantly.[112] These employees played an important role in the town administration. For example, sanitary inspectors could deem workers' living quarters to be an unhealthy slum and order them to be demolished. Accountants were obviously much sought after by the local people as they managed and calculated taxes. The bhadralok utilized such posts to enhance their local influence and some made their career in municipal services. Shyamacharan Bhattacharya, a local brahmin who came from the neighbouring village of Kathalpara, made his career in the Bhatpara municipality. On 4 May 1900, Bhattacharya became vice chairman of the Bhatpara municipality. He continued in this office for the next three decades and drew a salary from the municipality. In 1901 he became a second class judicial magistrate of the town. In a single year Bhattacharya alone decided 163 cases in the municipal court. The Bengal government awarded him the title of Rai Bahadur in 1913.[113] Thus the local bhadralok established a considerable hold over mill town administration in Bengal.

Municipal administrations ushered in important social changes in these new urban settlements. Calcutta's industrial suburbs witnessed legal reforms hitherto unknown to them. Municipal laws tried to standardize several aspects of urban life. For example, the Hackney Carriage Act specified the size of the hackney carriages and the fares which they could charge, a development almost unimaginable in rural life.[114] Knowledge of these laws was made obligatory on the part of the drivers and even pedestrians. Similarly, land transactions, construction of houses, and taxes on property and water supply came under the jurisdiction of the municipal authority. This was accompanied by large-scale resource mobilization through local taxation.[115] Moreover, the expansion of paved roads and the provision of street lighting, and the construction of rail stations became symbols of progress in the industrial municipalities which had once been tiny hamlets located in marshy lands.[116] As administrative control over the town increased, a power structure was created to enhance the rule of law.

The bhadralok, who constituted a substantial section of the ratepaying population, aimed at complete domination of municipal administration and chafed under the control which mill managers exercised over mill towns. They formed new pressure groups and ratepayers' associations. By 1909, numerous such associations and bodies crowded the local political scene. The political activities of the ratepayers' associations were limited within the municipal boundaries.[117] In urban areas these municipality-based organizations created political platforms for local elite groups. All ratepayers' associations were dominated by professionals. In the Presidency division, the Baranagar Ratepayers' Association claimed that 'it is open to all the literate men of Baranagar municipality'. The association had 56 members, a majority of whom were assistants in government and mercantile offices in Calcutta, while some district court pleaders and *muktars* were also active in this association.[118] In Konnagar, a ratepayers' association was founded in 1884 and membership was open to 'anyone who paid annual subscription of 8 annas'. Clerks and landholders were preponderant among its 50 members. The Uttarpara Peoples' Association, which was established as early as 1862, limited its membership to `[a]ny adult men of good moral character and of respectable family'.[119] This political forum discussed social, political, moral and religious matters.[120] In some municipalities, small effective associations came into existence—more firmly based in particular wards— but once again, they confined membership to registered voters only.[121] There were some exceptions to such bhadralok pressure groups. For instance, the Bally Sadharani Sabha drew its members from persons residing within the limits of Bally municipality and was open even to non-residents who sympathized with the activities of the Sabha. But in this case, government servants, mercantile office staff, local merchants, lawyers and doctors dominated this association.[122]

The constitutions of these ratepayers' associations in mill towns show how the bhadralok appropriated colonial political vocabulary in organizing their associations. They organized associations of educated voters along the definition provided by the Bengal Municipal Government Act of 1885. For example, the Howrah municipality ratepayers' association defines its members as: 'Every person who is a graduate, undergraduate, or licentiate of any university, or holds a licence granted by the government authorizing him to practice as a doctor, a pleader, a muktar, a revenue agent or any literate person occupying a holding and paying municipal tax for it and pays an annual subscription of Rs 2.00 to the association'. These criteria were adopted broadly from the definition of voters in the Municipal Act of 1885.[123] Thus the bhadralok put into practice the colonial definitions of who should constitute the political nation.

Municipal politics thus gave a direction to the political activities of the bhadralok elite groups who formed cohesive political pressure groups through various types of local organizations. These associations operated within a particular political context in the mill towns, where the migrant workers and local poor constituted a majority of the urban population. This created an environment of political confrontation between the local poor and the urban educated bhadralok. In June 1893, the Secretary to the Barrackpore Peoples' Association complained to the Secretary, Bengal Government about the composition of the Municipal Board. 'The majority of the members [ratepayers]', he wrote 'are men who cannot realize the importance of electing really worthy men, and the result is that the elected commissioners are generally those who came in frequent contact with the lower classes and have influence over these people, but do not constitute as they should, the prick [sic] of the community in education, social position and a proper sense of duty. Those who are really worthy have no chance of success [and] keep aloof.' The representative of the peoples' associations then demanded changes in the municipal laws: '(1) to raise the money qualification of voters to Rs 3.00 per annum, and (2) to exclude [carters] and hackney carriage drivers from the voters' list' which according to him 'would lead to considerable improvement in the ensuing election.'[124] One notices here that bhadralok arguments, which claimed superiority over working classes, were rooted in the language of colonial administrators. The bhadralok believed that it was their superior role to educate the working masses, morally as well as in the arts of administration and politics. However, this assumption of superiority, posture of paternalism, and the political exclusion of the workers alienated and antagonized the latter.

The bhadralok claim to moral superiority was much ridiculed in popular Bengali theatre of the time which mainly catered to lower-class audiences in suburban towns. In 1888, a local cultural group of the 24 Parganas produced a farce on municipal politics in Bengal, called 'Vote Mongal Ba Debasurer Municipal Bibhrat.'[125] In this play, Bakasur, the legendary demon of the Puranas, contested the elections in the municipality of *Swarga* against the *Debatas*. The election generated much heat with both sides competing to buy votes and recruit *lathials*. Particularly revealing in the play was the dialogue between an 'English educated' young housewife and an old lady. The old lady innocently asks the young one, 'what is *michripal* and *vonte*?' The young lady promptly replies that michripal is actually municipality which goes to election every three years and this election process is known as voting. Another housewife tells the story of the tussle between two bhadralok, Indir Babu and Hutum Babu, for the vote of her husband. Finally, as night fell, Hutum Babu secured her husband's vote by offering him a dhoti and Rs 25.00, while even the young child in the family received a pair of new shoes from Simle of Calcutta.[126] This play exhibits a social distrust common among the urban poor towards the self-advertised moral superiority of the 'respectable classes'.

At the risk of alienating those whose support they might have needed in the future, the bhadralok-dominated ratepayers' associations started an intensive campaign in the early twentieth century for the introduction of a strict property qualification for the franchise in municipal elections. In 1910, of the eleven members of Bhatpara municipality, eight were connected with local mills. Under pressure from ratepayers' movements the Bhatpara town council in 1912 decided to increase the number of commissioners to enable 'proper representation' of the ratepayers in the municipality. However, the new commissioners again represented 'the mill interests'.[127]

The ratepayers of Bhatpara organized a movement against the domination of the mill interests. In 1923–4, the movement reached its peak when more than 710 petitions were filed for the proper representation of the ratepayers.[128] A.T. Bhattacharjee, Secretary, Peoples Association of Bhatpara, wrote to the Minister-in-Charge of local self-government, pointing out that 710 petitions were submitted to the District Magistrate for changes in the municipal constitution.[129] The petitioners demanded that members of the municipality should be nominated by the ratepayers' association only. This demand was a clear indication of bhadralok attempts to exclude any possible working-class representation in municipal councils.[130] The so-called Peoples' Associations wanted to capture political power for themselves and refused to share it with 'people below them' who constituted the vast majority of the urban population.

Even in those mill towns where commissioners were permitted to elect the chairman of municipal councils, official intervention in favour of mill managers effectively paralysed bhadralok aspirations. Often on local issues, the bhadralok in such towns became divided into two camps. This came to be known as 'party politics'. Local officials often played one group against another and the mill managers benefited from it. In Baidyabati, for instance, the chairman of the municipality, Mr Low, a local jute mill manager, left for England in 1913 and the municipal board met on 25 June 1913 to elect a new chairman. In the meeting, Becharam Sarkar a local teacher, proposed the name of Mahendra Chandra Lahiri, a pleader from Sreerampur for chairmanship of the municipality to avoid local factional fightings among the bhadralok.[131] This proposal was accepted unanimously, and placed before the district magistrate for his recommendation, but the latter promoted the cause of P.K. Mukherjee, a clerk in the local jute mill. The district magistrate expected that Mukherji would relinquish his chair when Low, a mill manager and erstwhile chairman, returned and help him to be reinstated. The vice chairman of the municipality immediately re-arranged the meeting of the municipal board but no side could secure a majority and P.K. Mukherjee became chairman by the casting vote of the vice chairman. The district magistrate's letter 'opened the eyes' of the local landlord, Bijay Mukherjee, who rushed forward to correct his past mistake and sided with P.K. Mukherjee. But others raised the issue with the local self-government minister. Finally P.K. Mukherjee won the day. But the municipality remained divided, with 'educated members', including a sub-judge, joining the anti-Mukherjee faction. The social background of P.K. Mukherjee was no doubt impressive in the local context. He had earlier served as headmaster of Borah English School. He had been a private tutor and private secretary to the Khaira Raj estate in Bihar. Finally, he settled down in Baidyabati where he resided in the Baidyabati–Chapdani mill complex for 17 years. But all these qualifications failed to convince his opponents and this event added another item to the nationalist list of British Indian bureaucratic injustice.[132]

The *Bengalee*, the leading moderate newspaper of the day raised the battle cry:

we have strongly condemned the action of the magistrate who had no business to send back the unanimous resolution of the commissioners for recommendation. The growing forces of public opinion have set the official mind in opposition to them. The line of cleavage is more distinct now than ever. The educated community are conscious of their growing strength. No class of men, least of all the members of bureaucracy, have been known willingly to part with power, and those who are in the forefront of the struggle, bear the brunt of official displeasure.[133]

Local issues thus crossed boundaries of locality and the overall political trends in Bengal transformed these local tensions into political confrontation with the Raj on a much broader plane. But it would be wrong to project the bhadralok participation in the nationalist movement as a unilinear progress from local politics to nationalist agitation.[134] The bhadralok elite expressed their claims to social superiority in a language borrowed from the official discourse, which they then tried to transform into a tool for establishing their own hegemony in local politics. This brought them inevitably into conflict with local colonial administrators. Yet bhadralok hostility to workers and their determined efforts to exclude the latter from the local political system, in turn, alienated the workers and generated doubts among them about the nature and purpose of bhadralok-led Congress movements.

Conclusion

The functioning of municipal administration in the Bengal mill towns influenced working-class perceptions of colonial political institutions. To safeguard the interests of expatriate traders, the colonial government encouraged the domination of mill town administrations by mill managers. The latter established a hold over municipal boards, local police forces, and the judiciary. Mill managers led a life segregated from the 'native coolies'. Their social isolation and lack of understanding of working-class problems impeded the development of the mill towns. Indeed, what is important in this context is not so much the managerial domination over the mill towns but their perception of the workers. Managers became imprisoned within their paternalist political culture of governance. Their rhetoric of governance, based on the notion of the inability of workers to represent themselves, prevented them from exploring alternative avenues of town governance strategy. They thus remained confined to a situation of confrontational relationship with workers who constituted the vast majority of town residents. This also resulted in a failure to improve living conditions of the towns.

In the absence of a democratic mechanism for transforming issues such as town planning and sanitation into a matter of public concern, mill managers resorted to extremely harsh measures of removing working-class slums from the vicinity of mills. During epidemics, they forced sick workers to leave their dwellings and their jobs and sometimes burnt their belongings. Restrictions were imposed on hawking and petty trading. As a result, many workers were dislodged from small-scale trade which supplemented their wages. In other words, confrontations between management and workers were not inevitable products of capitalist industrial relationships, but more a result of the inability of managements to appreciate the petty-bourgeois aspirations of diverse segments of workers to improve their living conditions. Thus the ideological construction of workers as childlike actually restricted the material prosperity of the working classes. This situation informed and influenced workers' perception of manager raj as the colonial system of governance in microcosm.

Workers naturally viewed the policies of local political institutions as part of the evil design of mill managements to harass them, and they did not distinguish too neatly between the local municipality, the police, and the judiciary from the *sarkar* or government. The institutionalized social hierarchy reflected in the spatial organization of mill towns, the political culture of governance, and secluded nature of authority further confirmed their views. Thus the policies of the mill town administration created hostile feelings among workers towards the government. More importantly, such hostility compelled managers to rely more on the collaboration of the bhadralok who were reluctant to offer it. This was essentially the irony of colonial capitalism.

Indian professionals who eagerly sought positions in local administrations, remained insensitive to the needs of the working classes. They asserted their self-perceived superior social position in municipal politics and strove to keep workers outside the local political system. But the bhadralok were also victims of the colonial situation. The jute mill towns were products of British investment in the industrial sector. The Indian Jute Mill Association of expatriate traders constituted a powerful lobby in colonial government circles and was able to resist, through official manipulation, bhadralok attempts to gain control over local self-governing institutions. Frustrated in their political aspirations at the local level, these new elite groups (i.e. bhadralok) looked elsewhere for political support. The politics of the bhadralok elites reveals the ambiguity and contradictions created by their intermediary social position. They wanted political power without social and economic changes. Thus mainstream bhadralok Congress-based nationalist politics did not always appeal to the workers as it often left them outside the political system of mill towns. It was in this political environment that many workers would seek alliances with left-wing political groups.

Leaders of left-wing political groups, despite their own bhadralok background, challenged the political establishment of the mill towns and earned the sympathy of the workers. However, these changes in working-class politics could not be described as a unilinear march towards revolutionary consciousness. The roots of the alliance between socialists and different sections of workers were anchored in the political culture of the governance and social organization of the mill towns themselves. From the twenties of this century, left-wing nationalists played important roles in establishing unions among jute mill workers. But the mill towns also witnessed the development of large-scale communal riots in these periods. Class, in this context, remained a much contested political identity that was in competition with other forms of loyalties such as caste, religion, and language. The last three chapters of this dissertation will explore the nature of the interaction between labour politics and the nationalist movement and try to explain how different forms of political mobilization led to this contest between class-based identity and diverse forms of fragmented identities based on language, religion, and region.

Notes

1. *AARBM*, 1918, p.1. James Bookless, another local mill manager and the chairman of Bhatpara Mill municipality, upheld the policies of nominated municipal boards in Bhatpara because, he argued the 'labouring class form a majority of the rate payers and contribute largely to its revenues ... any electoral franchise on its present conditions, instead of improving the tone of administration, might it is apprehended, tend to lower it.' *AARBM*, 1915, p. 1.

2. See Dipesh Chakrabarty, *Rethinking Working-Class History*, particularly the chapter on 'Protest and Authority', pp. 155–85.

3. In the late nineteenth century official committees categorized workers as the people who were to be represented and not to have their own representatives in municipal bodies. See for example *Report of the committee appointed by the govt of Bengal to prepare a scheme for the Amalgamation of the town of Calcutta with the urban portions of the suburb.* (This note was prepared by H.L. Harrison on 20 November 1885), Calcutta, 1887.

4. *AARBM*, 1915, p. 1.

5. R.S. Chandavarkar, 'Mill districts in Bombay between two wars', *Modern Asian Studies* Vol. 15, 1981, pp. 603–48.

6. Anil Seal, 'Imperialism and Nationalism in India' in Seal et al. ed., *Locality Province and Nation Essays on Indian politics, 1870–1940*, Cambridge, 1973, pp. 1–28.

7. *The Acts Passed by the Lieutenant Governor of Bengal in Council in the year 1884*, Calcutta, 1885, p. 10.

8. See Chapter 1 for details.

9. Bhatpara Municipal Minute Book, 21 November 1905.

10. *AARBM*, 1925, pp. 22–3. In this statement the chairman distinguished between bhadralok dominated Ward no. 1 and two other working-class inhabited mill areas to resist the introduction of elections in mill municipalities.

11. *The Acts Passed by the Lieutenant Governor of Bengal in Council in the year 1884*, Calcutta, 1885, p. 10.

12. *AARBM* provides detailed lists of commissioners in this period and Scottish managers constituted majority of them.

13. The appalling casualties inflicted on the British troops by cholera and dysentery led to a new appreciation of the importance of sanitation in government circles in this period. *Royal Commission on the Sanitary state of the army, Report from commissioners, parliamentary papers, xix, 1*, pp. 15–18 quoted in Anthony King, *Colonial Urban Development, Cultures, Social Power and Environment*, London, 1976, p. 103.

14. In 1901 the population of Bhatpara was 21,464. The census of 1911 recorded 50,426 inhabitants in the town which according to 1921 census increased to 65,609. In 1931, it finally came up to 85,000. *AARBM*, 1901, p. 1; *AARBM*, 1913, p. 2; and *AARBM*, 1921, p. 2.

15. Bhatpara municipality report always recorded a majority of its population as mill workers. See *AARBM*, 1901, p. 2; *AARBM*, 1913, p. 21 and *AARBM*, 1925, p. 22.

16. *AARBM*, 1913, p. 11.

17. *AARBM*, 1928, p. 24.

18. *AARBM*, 1925, p. 6.

19. Ira Klein 'Death In India', *Journal of Asian Studies* 32, 4 (1973), pp. 642–3.

20. *AARBM*, 1918, p. 12.

21. Ibid.

22. *AARBM*, 1919, p. 11.

23. *AARBM*, 1919, p. 11.

24. *AARBM*, 1917, p. 15.

25. The managers admitted that 'It was indeed a very hard task to trace out stray cases of such diseases, happening in the midst of thickly populated coolie

bustis, the owners of which would do their best to conceal such incidents from Municipal authorities.' *AARBM*, 1925, p. 12.

26. *AARBM*, 1925, p. 18. There was a difference between small pox vaccination and cholera inoculation. Small pox vaccination came from arm to arm vaccination which was extremely painful and often left behind severe deep ulcers and sometimes there were fatal complications. Moreover, smallpox vaccination also challenged deeply entrenched local cultural tradition of variolation which was quite common in Bengal. See for details David Arnold, 'Small pox and colonial medicine in nineteenth century India' (Chap 3) in D. Arnold (ed.), *Imperial medicine and Indigenous societies*, pp. 54–6. These factors, perhaps, contributed to resistance to mass vaccination attempt in mill towns.

27. *AARBM*, 1926, p. 18.

28. *AARBM*, 1928, p. 16.

29. *AARBM*, 1917, p. 18.

30. Ibid.

31. *AARBM*, 1927, p. 12.

32. It is not surprising that some workers refused medicine given by dispensaries for religious reasons too. Chakrabarty quotes from *The Royal Commission of Labour* report of evidence given by Kamala, a woman worker, who was looking after her husband. Kamala's husband refused to take medicine from the mill's dispensary because 'it will break his caste'. Chakrabarty concludes from this evidence that 'Such a communal sense of honour speaks of the non-individualistic, pre-bourgeois nature of identity that the jute mill worker had.' *Rethinking working-class history*, pp. 214–5. However, constantly increasing attendance in mill dispensaries did not suggest any widespread caste prejudice over western medicine on a large scale.

33. *AARBM*, 1931, p. 15.

34. In 1937 during the general strike in jute mills, managers cut the water supply to slums to force the striking workers to leave their habitations.

35. *AARBM*, 1927, p. 14.

36. Appendix AIJMA *Report of the Committee for 1896*, Calcutta, 1897.

37. Municipal proceedings of Bhatpara, 20 April 1900.

38. In 1931, the vice chairman of Bhatpara municipality complained against the zamindars' opposition to construction of new roads in this mill municipality. *RCLI Vol. V, paragraph II*, Oral evidence of S.C. Bhattacharya, 2 February 1930, p. 37.

39. Municipal minute book of Bhatpara, 8 February 1901.

40. Ibid., 19 July 1901, 6.30 p.m.

41. The last remaining remnant of the once powerful fishing community was a temple in Naihati constructed by the powerful *jalia* Kaibarta zamindar Rani Rasmani at the northern fringe of the town. Map 1899, Naihati Municipality, 2/1899, WBSA.

42. *AARBM*, 1931, pp. 36–7.

43. *AARBM*, 1917, p. 3.

44. *AARBM*, 1918, p. 12.

45. *AARBM*, 1932, p. 18.

46. Widespread distrust of police measures was evident in rumours among the town's poor during panic over plague in Calcutta. For example, at the time of the Calcutta disturbances of 19 May, police were rumoured to carry bottles of poison which they held to the noses unless bribed to desist. J.N. Cook's 'Report on plague in Calcutta 31 August 1898' in *Report of the epidemics of plague in Calcutta during the years 1898–99, 1899–1900 and to 30 June 1900*, Calcutta, 1900, p. 8 quoted in D. Arnold 'Touching the body: Perspectives on the Indian plague, 1896–1900' in R. Guha (ed.), *Subaltern Studies* Vol. V, New Delhi, 1987, p. 72.

47. *AARBM*, 1919, p. 14.

48. For example, in 1928 of six honorary magistrates presiding local courts three were mill managers and municipal commissioners. *AARBM,* 1928, p. 27.

49. *AARBM*, 1922, p. 13.

50. Gyanesh Kudesia, 'State Power and the erosion of Colonial Authority in Uttar Pradesh, India, 1930–42', Unpublished PhD thesis, Cambridge, 1992, p. 7.

51. See David M. Anderson and David Killingray, 'Consent, coercion and colonial control: policing the empire, 1830–1940', in David M. Anderson et al., *Policing the Empire: Government, Authority and Control, 1830–1940*, Manchester, 1991, p. 9.

52. *Report on Police Supervision in the Riverine Municipalities*, pp. 7–12. 'A petition from the Indian Jute Manufacturers' Association, advocating the employment of a police force at Barrackpur and of a civil magistrate either at that station or some other station'. WBSA Judicial Police Branch January 1896.

53. Bengal Judicial proceedings, Police department January to March; January A Nos 8–9.

54. Circular no. 138 Calcutta, dated 9 September 1895. Bengal Judicial proceedings, Police department January to March; January A Nos 8–9.

55. Parimal Ghosh, 'Communalism and Colonial Labour: Experience of Calcutta Jute Mill Workers, 1880–1930, *EPW*, Vol. XXV, No. 30, 28 July 1990, p. PE 68.

56. Home Dept Political Branch No. 64 B, File R/1 364, January 1909, WBSA.

57. *Amrita Bazar Patrika*, 12 June 1908.

58. Home Dept Political Branch No. A 10, File No 1-v/9 14, February 1915, WBSA.

59. Home Political (Confidential) No. 70B, 13 70 (i)/2, 1916, WBSA.

60. Home Political (Confidential) No. 307, Serial No. 1, November 1920, Appendix B, WBSA.

61. Home Political (Confidential) No. 307 Serial No. 1, November 1920.

62. Home Political (Confidential) No. 307 Serial No. 1, November 1920, WBSA.

63. Ibid.

64. Ibid.

65. Colonel Henry Yule and A.C. Burnell (eds), *Hobson Jobson Dictionary* (New Edition edited by William Crooke), Calcutta, 1986, pp. 781–2. A.K. Bagchi used the same conceptual framework in his review article 'Working-class consciousness', *EPW*, Vol. XXV, No 30, 28 July 1990.

66. Ibid, pp. 249–51.

67. D.H. Buchanan, *The Development of Capitalistic Enterprise in India*, Newark, 1934, pp. 244–5. Also see *AARBM*, 1902, pp. 17–18.

68. *RCLI, Vol. V, Part 1*, Note by Dr Batra, p. 31.

69. Thomas Metcalf has discussed at great length the security considerations behind construction of public places like railways stations. See Thomas Metcalf, *An Imperial vision: Indian Indian Architecture and Britain's Raj*, London, 1989. Also see G.H.R. Tillitson, *The tradition of Indian Architecture Continuity and Controversy and Change since 1850*, Yale, 1989.

70. Claude Henry to George Dott 15 January 1922. Personal and family papers of George Dott, 1909–1925 including letters from Claude Henry while working in a jute mill in India, (hereafter George Dott Private Papers GDPP), National Library of Scotland, Edinburgh.

71. Claude Henry to George Dott, 28 August 1922, GDPP, NLS.

72. Claude Henry to George Dott 15 January 1922, GDPP, NLS.

73. Manager to the Director Victoria Jute Mill, p. 38, TDA, DUA.

74. *The Statesman*, 27 July 1935.

75. Claude Henry to George Dott 15 January 1922, GDPP, NLS.

76. Private official letter McDonald to Band, 14 October, 1931, TDA, DUA.

77. Mary Pratt, in her analysis of the eighteenth and nineteenth century travel writing of European travellers has suggested that the latter while describing landscapes of these countries often cleared people from natural landscapes and projected an imaginary country available for improvement, without any indigenous cultural or political resources to resist western ambitions. Mary Louise Pratt, *Imperial Eyes Travel Writing and Transculturation*, London, 1992.

78. W.R. Wallace, *The Romance of Jute* 1908, p. 8.

79. Interview of Ian Melville Stephen India Office Library Oral Archives MSS EURT.7.65 part 2/4, p. 63, p. 2/4 See also Interview of Perceival Griffith, MSS EURT 31–32, Part 4-/5.

80. Municipal minute book of Bhatpara mill municipality, 24 October 1902.

81. The Public instruction section of *AARBMs* throws much light on the role of mill managers in presiding over local schools. For example, See *AARBM*, 1925, p. 21.

82. Debaprasad Bhattacharya, 'Bhatpara Swabhabe Swatantra', *Siladitya*, 1989, p. 61.

83. Ibid.

84. John McGuire, *The making of a colonial mind: A quantitative study of the Bhadralok in Calcutta 1857–1885*, Canberra, 1983, p. 26.

85. Alok Kumar Chakrabarty, *Maharaja Krishna chandra o Tatkalin Bangali Samaj*, Calcutta, 1990.

86. Madhusudan Nayacharya, 'Bhatparar Smriti', unpublished hand written manuscript, 1979, pp. 3–5.

87. Ibid., pp. 14–15.

88. Alok K. Chakrabarty, *Maharaja Krisna Chandra*, p. 120.

89. *RCLI, Vol. V, Part II*, Oral evidence of SC Bhattacharya.

90. L.S.S. O'Malley, *24 parganas District gazetteer*, pp. 60–1.

91. Ibid.

92. *Star of India* (daily newspaper of Calcutta) 17 August 1932 (Advertisement).

93. *Star of India*, 29 August 1932.

94. Ramanuj Vidyarnab, 'Daily passenger', a poem published in *Kanthamala*, Bhatpara, c. 1913.

95. Munindra Deb Roy, *Hugli Kahini*, Bansberia, 1310 Bengali era, (1901), p. 88.

96. Preface to *Catalogue of the Bhatpara library*, Bhatpara, 1991, p. 2.

97. Preface to *Baidyabati Young Men Association Library catalogue*, Baidyabati, 1990.

98. Home political Confidential File no 44, Serial no 1–4 Annual report on printed or published in Bengal during the year 1914, WBSA.

99. Prthviraj Mitra, 'Pramathanath Mitrer Samkhipta Jiban Charit', written in 1945 and reprinted in Satyajit Chowdhuri (ed.), *Pramathanath Mitra Bardhapak 1980*, Calcutta, 1980.

100. A.K. Ghosh, 'Amar jana Garifa United Sporting Club', in S.K. Mazumdar and A.K. Ghosh, (eds) *Garifa United Sporting Club Centenary Souvenir*, Naihati, 1985.

101. Tegart papers, Box III, Notes on 'Outrages in Bengal' (compiled in 1917), CSAS.

102. Translated by Dipesh Chakrabarty and quoted in his 'Trade union in a Hierarchical culture' in Ranajit Guha (ed.), *Subaltern Studies*, Vol. II, Delhi, 1984, p. 146.

103. Nirod Mishra Chakrabarty, *Bangalar Jatya Itihas*, Jhikhira Howrah, 1334 (Bengali era), circa 1927.

104. Ibid., Preface.

105. Prabhat Mohan Bandopadhyay, *Balir Itihaser Bhumika*, Bally, 1936, pp. 3–8.

106. *Municipal Manual for Bengal*, Calcutta, 1926, p. 2.

107. *AARBM*, 1927, p. 22.

108. However the political motive behind the title became so evident that scholars doubted the legitimacy of the title. Home Political Confidential Govt of Bengal, 1918, file No. 277 of 1912, serial No. 1–3. Instructions observed in making recommendations for the titles of Mahamopadhyay and Shams ul Ulema, WBSA.

109. Srijib Nayatirtha, 'Bangalar Samskrita pandit samajer ak bisrita adhaya', *Desh*, 20 June 1987, pp. 39–47.

110. *AARBM*, 1931, p. 22.

111. Municipal Proceedings Bhatpara Municipality 18 May 1900. In 1901 of the five Indian members in Bhatpara municipality three were brahmins. *AARBM*, 1901, p. 3.

112. See *AARBM*, 1901, p. 8 and *AARBM*, 1913, p. 10.

113. This short life history of Shyamacharan is based on the Municipal board proceedings of Bhatpara and the *AARBM*, 1915, p. 12.

114. Local Self Government Dept, Local Self Government Municipal Branch, December 1924, A 46, WBSA.

115. The resources of industrial municipalities increased dramatically. In 1899 Bhatpara municipality had an annual earning of Rs 7,494 (*AARBM*, 1901, pp. 4–5). By 1931 the receipts of the municipalities reached Rs 5,01,150. (AARBM, 1931, pp. 6–7). In 1899 the expenditure of the municipality was Rs 7,400 which in 1931 increased to Rs 5,07,456. (*AARBM*, 1931, pp. 6–7).

116. Munindra Deb Roy, *Hugli Kahini*, pp. 88–90.

117. Municipal Dept Municipal branch April 7 1909 File no M18-A No. 49, WBSA.

118. Ibid.

119. Ibid.

120. Ibid.

121. Ibid.

122. Ibid.

123. For details of such criteria see *The Acts passed by the Lieutenant Governor of Bengal in council in the year 1884*, p. 10.

124. Municipal dept Municipal Branch June 1893 No 36 File M2-R-1/22 April, 1909, WBSA.

125. Lila Natya Samaj, *Vote Mongal Ba Debasurer Municipal Bibhrat*, Calcutta, *c.* 1888, National Library of India, Calcutta.

126. Ibid. Third scene (Manas Sarobar) pp. 13–14.

127. Local self Government Dept Municipality Branch June 1924 A78 p.46, WBSA.

128. Ibid.

129. Ibid.

130. Ibid. M-12/7.

131. Municipal dept Municipal Branch proceedings for September 1916 B 115–116, WBSA.

132. Ibid.

133. *The Bengalee*, 18 July 1913.

4

Strikes, Riots, and
Swadeshi Unions, 1890–1908

Introduction

The previous chapters have examined how migrant workers depended upon their village bases to sustain urban jobs, developed social networks based on intersecting loyalties of caste, religion, and region, and were excluded from local political institutions of the Raj as a result of the alliance between managerial and *bhadralok* elites. This and the following chapters will seek to explore the relationship between the managements, workers' politics, and the bhadralok-led nationalist movement in the context of their interaction with the colonial state at various levels. I take the story chronologically to capture the complexities of events at various high points of nationalist politics and labour movements, which sometimes coincided and at other times moved apart. This chapter begins with the 1890s when the first major strike wave swept across industry and ends in 1908 when the *swadeshi* attempt to mobilize workers failed along with the collapse of the movement itself. Subsequent chapters deal with the non-cooperation movement and the rise of socialist politics in the 1920s, bringing the narrative to a close with the general strike of 1937.

The 1890s witnessed not only strikes over workplace grievances but also widespread riots on religious issues, agitation against plague regulations, and the emergence of a powerful nationalist movement. This escalated labour militancy, and various sections of workers confronted the European managers and law-enforcing agencies of the state, particularly the police. Through repeated confrontations with managers and the police over labour issues, in riots over supposedly communal matters, and in protests against plague regulations which were seen to discriminate against the urban poor, the working-class emerged as a potential constituency of the bhadralok-led nationalist movement. However, in this decade bhadralok nationalists were more concerned with protecting the interests of the rising Indian-owned industries to ensure India's economic well-being through industrialization. They therefore chose to ignore the grievances of workers. During the swadeshi movement (1905–8) they tried to mobilize workers chiefly through Bengali clerks who came from a similar bhadralok social background. Irrespective of nationalist help, workers deployed strategies of negotiation with the powerful combination of the employers and the colonial state.

Policing Strikes: 1895–6

In the closing decade of the nineteenth century, various groups of workers demanded restitution of their grievances through strikes. In most cases, strikes began as an attempt to induce managers to grant holidays on religious festivals, to increase wages, reduce working hours, and dismiss corrupt supervisors. The managers, unwilling to concede these demands, were faced with demonstrations outside mill gates. They responded by opening fire on groups of workers, and frequently called upon the police to contain workers' protests. The police dispersed the demonstrators by force and arrested workers at random. Such violent police intervention intensified the agitation, with the result that work-place conflicts now extended into the slums and streets of mill towns. The close collaboration among the mill managers, municipal administration, and the police served repeatedly to control and restrain workers. Confronted by the violence of the police and municipal administration, workers began to distrust these representatives of the state, especially of course, the police.

From the beginning of the 1890s several developments in the industry affected the workers adversely. The introduction of the electric light in 1895 made work throughout the night possible for the first time.[1] The significant increase in the workload which this entailed was not matched by a corresponding increase in wages.[2] This led to some discontent among workers. More importantly, managers began to fear a shortage of labour. Not only did night-work increase working hours, but the shift from short term to full-time working caused a greater demand for labour. Moreover, in this period, mills proliferated rapidly and existing mills expanded their loomage. This suddenly enhanced demand for labour caused labour shortages. Mill managers responded to this temporary bottleneck by trying to impose a more rigid work discipline. In this attempt they utilized the already established practice of 'keeping a week's wage in hand' to restrict the mobility of workers.[3] All these contributed to a general sense of dissatisfaction among the workers. For instance, the management's move to regulate absenteeism had on some occasions serious repercussions. While in the early years workers could easily take a day off,[4] in the changed circumstances, managers inadvertently interfered in the observance of religious festivals since they wished to prevent such ad hoc absenteeism. All absences, whatever the reason, were punished by fines and the withholding of wages.

For workers, holidays on religious occasions were especially significant because they provided a rare opportunity for festive enjoyment. These migrant workers, isolated from their families, confined to a factory for thirteen hours, inhabiting overcrowded slums, found in the collective celebration of religious festivals a respite from the monotony of mill life.[5] Various religious and regional festivals like Chhat, Annapurna puja, Id and Muharram were celebrated in the bazaars and streets of the mill towns. On these occasions local *akharas* invited wrestlers from Bihar and eastern UP and competitions were held for large audiences.[6] The Bhatpara municipality report of 1907 describes a carnival-like situation in the town on the day of Muharram:

The processions at the time of Muharram are gradually taking gigantic form and they now extend over a mile in length. Some ten to fifteen thousand people assemble on this occasion with over two dozens of Tazias and hundreds of wrestlers.[7]

It is not surprising that workers were angered when denied the opportunity to participate in the festivities. Their anger was not only directed at a perceived infringement of their customary religious practices, but was also regarded as both a deprivation of the few opportunities for collective entertainment they enjoyed and an encroachment on work-place rights they had come to consider as established.[8] Workers did not readily accept the curtailment of holidays on religious occasions. In the first instance, groups of workers sought to persuade the managers to grant them time off for at least part of the day. When these 'reasonable' requests were rejected arbitrarily, and fines imposed for leave taken without permission, discontent spiralled into strikes.

In the course of these strikes, workers often introduced other grievances such as demands for wage increases, and dismissal of unpopular factory supervisors, sardars, and durwans. Therefore, strikes which began over the issue of holidays could become a more general means of protest against a range of workplace-related grievances. Faced with this unexpected militancy of the workers, managers made use of their own magisterial powers to fire upon groups of workers and frequently called upon the police to assist them. The brutal suppression of these strikes led to an unprecedented intensification of the conflict between managers and police on the one hand and the workers on the other.

The way in which workers' determination to observe the Bakr-Id and Muharram of 1895 escalated into a full-scale confrontation with the management and the town administration is best illustrated by strikes in the Titagarh Jute Mill that year. In the Titagarh Jute Mill, the manager fined the Muslim workers who stayed away from work on Bakr-Id, and withheld their week's wages.[9] This measure provoked 'wild demonstrations' in front of European residences. The European employees responded by opening fire on the workers and called the police. The police arrested the 'ring leaders'.[10] The mill remained closed for two days.[11]

Neither case was marked by any tension among the workers themselves. Although both were Muslim festivals, the demand for holidays and the ensuing crises did not provoke any hostility from the Hindu workers who constituted over 65 per cent of the work-force in the case of Titagarh Jute Mill.[12] Rather, mill workers attacked the managers and the police.[13]

The management's attempt to tighten work-place discipline led to equally serious confrontations with the workers on a range of other issues like demands for increased wages and dismissal of unpopular supervisors. On these, as on the issue of religious festivals, managers changed their earlier accommodative policy. Whereas in the 1870s and 1880s, when spinning boys went on strike over demands like shorter working hours or more wages, their demands were disregarded, although no punitive action was taken against them[14], from the 1890s such strikes were treated with a new harshness. The frequent police interventions caused disputes previously confined to the mill compound to now spill over on to the streets, bazaars, and slums of the mill towns. For example, in June 1895 when the manager of the Kankinarah Jute Mill reduced the wages of spinners, the latter immediately went on strike.[15] The manager of the mill not only rejected the demand of the spinners but also tried to lock out the 'ring leaders'. A large body of workers gathered before the manager who immediately sent for the police. The police promptly arrested five workers which led to strikes in other departments. Nor did the trouble remain confined to the factory. The infuriated workers marched through the streets of the town and attacked the local police station.[16] Similarly, in August 1895 when the Budgebudge Jute Mill workers opposed the re-appointment of an unpopular overseer, the manager promptly ordered a 'lock out of all the operatives'. The workers attacked the European residences and the European assistants opened fire. The police on this occasion arrested twenty-one workers. This kept the tension alive in the factory for many days.[17]

As mentioned earlier, in most cases, workers' insecurities were reinforced by the management's practice of keeping 'a week's wages in hand'. In all the cases of strikes mentioned above, this issue contributed considerably towards the escalation of workers' militant action against the manager and his assistants. In one particular case, this practice was taken to an extreme. In 1895, the manager of Dunbar Cotton Mill at Shyamnagar sought the help not only of the police, but even of the 'armed forces' to enable a blatant enforcement of such a regulative policy. He kept 'three months wages in hand' to prevent his 'coolies' from leaving the mill for better jobs. When some workers went on strike, he not only refused to pay the wages, but also fined the strikers. The assistant manager made no secret to the police officer 'of their wish to coerce coolies returning to work by keeping back their pay'.[18]

The police showed themselves willing to assist and support the managers in their attempts to enforce stricter discipline on their work-force. The collusion between the various agencies of the colonial state, like the police and the employers and their associations like the Bengal Chamber of Commerce and the IJMA led to the deployment of a powerful coercive apparatus against the workers. Many senior police officers suspected that a 'conspiracy' lay behind every strike. The deputy inspector general of police in Calcutta, enquiring into strikes in jute mills in 1895 identified the following causes in the context of specific strikes: the practice of keeping wages in hand, physical assault, long working hours, lack of housing, denial of holidays, and malpractices of clerks.[19] Unhappy with these explanations, he is forced to conclude: 'It is hard to say what caused this disaffection which, admitted by all sides did not exist to such an extent last year.' In the end, however, he does discover a possible reason for the many strikes: 'Possibly agitators are abroad, and they [workers] may be incited to mischief by the native papers ...' In fact, he even predicted a peaceful end to the long year of unrest, 'when the large mills' extensions are completed ... when the labour market becomes over-stocked ... mill hands will grow less independent and matters will quiet down to their normal state.'[20]

In the late nineteenth century the Bengal government assured the IJMA that '[t]he Government ... will do all it can to afford moral support to the mill owners, both by increasing the police force and improving the magisterial jurisdiction.'[21] In other words, the government committed its support to mill managers in situations of industrial conflict and moreover empowered the managers with more control over local law and order machinery.[22] As a consequence, the police always acted in a partisan manner in favour of the mill management.[23]

On the ground, therefore, workers were confronted by a powerful alliance of the managers and the police. The unprecedented harshness with which their every attempt at redressing their daily grievances was met stiffened their resistance even as it engendered in them a greater fear of the various administrative agencies. In periods of protest workers appeared to have regarded the mere presence of police in the factories as threatening. For instance, in the Budgebudge Jute Mill so strong was the fear and distrust of the police that when the deputy inspector general of police in Bengal came to inspect the mill nearly 30 per cent of the workers deserted their jobs.[24] The fear and distrust of the police not only contributed to escalation of strikes, but was later to be the leitmotif of resistance to government policies and even direct confrontation with the state.

Policing Riots: 1896–7

In the 1890s, police intervention in situations of tension between Hindu and Muslim mill hands, often led to riots between various groups of Muslim workers and the police. The police, as indeed many other mill officials believed that the Muslim workers were turbulent and lawless people and therefore sought to closely scrutinize their activities.[25] This perception might have also been influenced by the notion of the 'bigoted and turbulent julaha' which gained currency in this period among the government officials serving in eastern UP.[26] Since a large number of Muslim weavers in Calcutta jute mills came from the same region and claimed to be from the 'julaha caste', mill managers often anticipated violence on occasions of minor disturbances concerning Muslim employees. The story of a 'riot' at the Lower Hoogly Mill in Gardenreach in 1896 provides an instance where the mill managers, apprehending an attack on the mill by Muslim workers, called for police and even army help.[27]

On this day of Bakr Id, 25 June 1896, some Muslim workers of the mill found that a few *chamar* workers had killed a pig in the mill compound. During the recess the next day, Muslim weavers went on strike demanding that the chamars be punished. Meanwhile, the Hindu head durwan had passed offensive remarks which provoked Muslims to demand the dismissal of the durwan. The manager refused to accept the demand and closed down the mill instead. Armed European assistants, anticipating violence, manned the mill gates and the district magistrate posted twelve additional armed policemen to help them.[28] At night, a Hindu durwan reported that Muslims were coming to attack the mill along with some outsiders. The manager removed all the Hindus to the European quarter and sent an emergency message to the district magistrate. The district magistrate asked for the help of the army and sent 100 troopers and infantry-men along with twenty-seven constables. However, after arriving at the spot the district magistrate found that Muslims had dispersed from the place without making much trouble.[29] The district magistrate then conducted a thorough enquiry to justify his appeal for military assistance.[30] Interestingly, this enquiry found that 'there was no ground to apprehend any disturbance in the mill on the occasion of the Bakr-Id'.[31] It appeared that the workers had long-standing grievances against the head durwan who was earlier also dismissed for ill treating a *mistri*. The Muslim workers, however, had no intention to use violence.[32] Even the alarm which was raised at night proved to be false.[33]

Why did the manager and district magistrate accept the story of the Muslim attack without proper investigation? The letter of the district magistrate to the commissioner of the Burdwan division provides the answer to this question. The magistrate wrote that he did not have any opportunity to 'ascertain what was going on in the mill' and rather 'thought it quite possible that a serious attack on the mills and Hindus employed there was contemplated,' because 'Mohammedans of Metiaburz and the locality are reported to be turbulent and disorderly'. He also asserted that 'there was no doubt that the manager and the others in the mill believed that such attack was imminent'. In other words, the magistrate and the manager of the mill, convinced that the Muslims were 'turbulent and disorderly', were willing to call for military assistance without any evidence of their culpability.[34] Thus, even when completely innocent, Muslim workers had to face police action merely because the magistrate thought that they were an endemically 'turbulent people'.

The grievances of Muslim workers against the police also increased when the government tried to control collective religious festivities according to local customs and imposed restrictions on the Muslim custom of cow sacrifice during Bakr Id celebrations in some mill towns. In fact, the government's search for customs led to a competitive scramble to establish the rights and precedences of different social groups. The claims of the migrant Muslim workers, who constituted a small minority in many mill towns, were often regarded by the police as innovations and they restrained the activities of Muslim workers on the day of Bakr Id. This generated hostilities among Muslim mill hands against the police. The Rishra riot on the day of Bakr Id in 1895 is a case in point.

Rishra was a densely-populated mill town with only a small number of Muslims working in the jute mills. The Muslims in Rishra were poor and few in number and had little power to assert their presence in town politics.[35] Trouble occurred in Rishra when the Government began recording local customs in order to facilitate decisions regarding controversial religious practises like cow sacrifice on the Bakr Id day. Muslims in Rishra generally sacrificed cows secretly without annoying their powerful Hindu neighbours. But in 1895, government interference made the migrant Muslim workers assertive about their 'long standing' customs of sacrificing cows in fear that they would be denied the opportunity to observe their religious rituals in future. In retaliation, 'upcountry-Hindu' traders became equally vocal about not allowing the Muslims to violate 'local customs' by sacrificing cows on the day of Bakr Id.[36] This competition for putative local traditions generated tremendous tension in the area. The sub-divisional officer, not recognizing that cow sacrifice often took place in the mill towns in a clandestine manner, maintained that Muslims were initiating a new practice to sacrifice cows on Bakr Id. This made the Muslim workers even more determined to 'pursue their rights' to sacrifice cows on the day of the festival.[37]

The local administration apprehended that cow sacrifice at a public place might cause a riot in this mill town, hence it imposed various restrictions on the Muslims. The manager of the Standard Jute Mill warned his Muslim employees against sacrificing cows.[38] The police surrounded the local mosque with an armed force to prevent cow slaughter. Instructions were given to the railway clerks not to sell tickets to the large number of Muslims coming down to Rishra. The administration also decided to detain any large group of low-class Muslims at the railway station and the local Imam of the mosque was arrested. The district magistrate reported that 'sulky' Muslim mill hands held the government responsible for these restrictions on their religious practises and believed that Hindu traders had influenced the government on the issue.[39]

The distrust of the police among Muslim mill hands is also evident in the Titagarh riot. On Bakr Id day in 1896 some Hindu durwans browbeat a Muslim mason working at the nearby mill construction site into giving them his *korbani* cow. The police were informed but there was a considerable lapse of time before the investigating officer arrived at the mill. Not surprisingly, the Muslim workers found in this delay an attempt to placate the Hindus. When the officer finally reached the mill, a group of hostile Muslim mill hands, forced him to look for the cow. After a futile search, the officer along with two Muslim constables tried to escape from the site of the dispute. Immediately, Muslim workers attacked him saying that the '*daroga* had joined the Hindu party and he is coming back with the police. Don't allow him to leave.' Evading them, the officer escaped from the place and informed the divisional commissioner and cantonment magistrate who arrived at the spot with a large police contingent. By the end of the day, the police arrested nearly thirty Muslims but only six Hindus, which might have further infuriated Muslim workers.[40]

It was thus not surprising that in 1897, just one year after the Bakr Id disturbances, Calcutta witnessed widespread anti-police rioting by Muslim workers. On the last two days of June 1897, the Talla riot paralysed life in Calcutta while Muslim workers attacked the police and Europeans for demolishing a mosque. On some occasions Hindu workers too joined Muslim rioters.

On 28 June, the police demolished an 'illegal hut' on the land of Sir Jotindra Mohan Tagore, a rich trader, financier, and landowner. The occupant of the place, an upcountry mason Himmat Khan, who claimed that it was a mosque, consulted Haji Nur Muhammad Zakariah—a trader and the *motwali* of the Nakhoda mosque in Calcutta, for advice in the matter. The Haji allegedly told Himmat Khan to reconstruct the hut[41] but he could not apprehend the depth of mass discontent that the destruction of the mosque generated.

From the night of 29 June 1897, groups of Muslim workers fought the police at various places in central Calcutta for two days—the protest actions developed into an upsurge against the government at large. Many Muslim workers had come to believe that British rule would end soon and the Turkish Sultan would take over the city. The workers also displayed a deep suspicion of all government institutions, so much so, that even the wounded refused to go to government hospitals fearing that they would be poisoned. It is significant that Muslim workers did not target the Hindus. In fact, according to the police commissioner, Hindu 'bad characters' joined 'low class' Muslims rioters in the agitation. The police and military who were called in to suppress the uprising fired at the crowd killing eleven people.[42]

This riot was not confined to the city only. On 6 July 1897 it spread to the mill towns. The most serious disturbances occurred in the mills located in the Bhatpara region. On the morning of 6 July a letter written in Bengali reached the mill operatives of Kankinarah which asked all true Muslims to join the Talla rioters in rescuing the mosque. Nearly 1,500 Muslim employees came out of the mill and decided to hold a meeting with other mill employees. With that purpose they marched southwards beating a tom-tom with sticks and gathered other Muslim workers from various mills on the way, informing the managers that they declared war against the government.[43] The procession then came down to Jagatdal Jute Mill where Muslim workers had already applied for leave but had been refused by the factory authorities. This led to violent clashes between the European assistants and workers. This battle continued for the next two hours with the Europeans freely using firearms to prevent workers from taking over the mill. News of this confrontation soon travelled to nearby Shyamnagar Jute Mill where the workers went on strike immediately.[44] The government acted promptly by alerting the army.[45]

This incident remained free from Hindu–Muslim tensions in the mill towns, although many Hindus were present at the site of the riot. In fact, Hindu workers proved to be sympathetic to the Muslim cause. In the post-riot days an appeal was pasted in the form of a notice at Howrah court in Persian and Bengali 'calling upon Hindus and Muslims to rise and loot the house of the district magistrate and the deputy district magistrate.'[46] The fellow-feeling between Hindu and Muslim mill hands in this period was even supported by the *Samay*, an ultra-conservative Hindu newspaper. Commenting on the notice, the *Samay* wrote that

There can be no doubt that its authors are low-class men. Just at present a very large number of up country Hindus and Mussalmans of low class can be seen in Howrah, who are very stout and strong in physique but most of whom are without employment .... The men are generally addicted to *ganja* and bear turbulent character. *The religious differences between upcountry Hindus and Mussalmans are not very great and they will live in the same room with only a mat partition between them.* [Emphasis mine][47]

Even the *Samay*, which elsewhere held that Muslims were inimically hostile to non-Muslims (*kafers*), was forced after the Talla riot to recognise the mutuality of interests that bound the urban poor together.[48] Thus, these riots in mill towns did not produce polarization among Hindu and Muslim workers. The Muslim workers in most cases directed their attacks against managers and the police. They felt a deep injustice at being subjected to unjust police supervision. The accumulated anger of the poor Muslims against the government caused the Talla riot.

The Talla riot reinforced stereotypes of the Muslims as a violent and lawless people, and the government passed a series of repressive measures directed particularly against the Muslim poor of Calcutta and surrounding mill towns. In 1897 the inspector general of police in Bengal declared that 'the excitability of a mob of Mussalman mill hands, renders disturbances with which they are concerned more serious than occurrences of a similar character in which other inflammable material [sic] take part.'[49] The government revised an earlier act to station punitive forces in 'lower class' Muslim areas and forced the inhabitants of the localities to pay for the expenses incurred in these actions.[50] In 1898, the IJMA executive committee also decided to put a stop to the recruitment of the upcountry 'Muslim mill hands'. According to *The Englishman*, IJMA felt concerned at:

... the gradual ousting from the jute factories of the *mild Hindus* by the *aggressive Mussalmans*. This was brought keenly before all in view of the riots of the past year. The latter class were kept in a state of ferment by their leaders, and would be a constant source of anxiety unless the former order of things could be established where by Hindu element would *preponderate*. [emphasis mine][51]

The language of the IJMA members in the meeting indicates the deep influence of communal stereotypes among mill-owners. This open discrimination against the Muslim workers obviously strengthened their grievances against the management for being unfair to them.

These developments, however, did not produce an all-encompassing political unity among Calcutta Muslims. During the Talla riot affluent Muslim groups did not have much sympathy for workers of their faith When the riots occurred in Calcutta the Muslim leaders were as much perplexed by them as the Hindu elites and the British professed to be. The

Dainik Chandrika clearly expressed the ambivalence of the Muslim elites in pointing out that:

the law abiding and respectful Mussalmans had no sympathy with the rioters. Many of them were forced to fly from Calcutta during the disturbance.[52]

As soon as the police brought the situation under control, rich Muslim leaders like Haji Zakariah, who was also motwali of the largest mosque in Calcutta issued a series of *fatwas*, appealing to the Muslims to exercise restraint. Initially he had argued that J.M. Tagore had promised to donate the land for the purpose of erecting a mosque but later shifted his position to propagate that the Koran did not prescribe construction of mosque on the land 'which is not *waqf*'.[53] It seems that a few elite Muslims like Haji Zakariah who were in touch with the workers issued these fatwas to prove their loyalty to the government. The government, however, immediately decided to use such fatwas in removing unauthorized Muslim huts from the city which were claimed by poorer Muslims as mosques. The chief secretary to the Bengal government informed the home secretary of India 'of the great value of these fatwas not only in reference to the present case, but as likely to facilitate the disposal of other disputes (also) which may now exist or hereafter arise in regard to huts used for worship without the authority of the owners of the sites. It appears to have become a common practice for Mohammedans of the lower classes in the suburbs of Calcutta to erect such huts ...'[54] Thus, Muslim leaders like Zakariah, in order to strengthen their claim to official favour, were ready to sacrifice the rights of their less privileged co-religionists.

The elite Muslim politicians were unable to understand why Muslim workers consistently fought police repression and their politics failed to address the issue. Even when some Muslim workers asked for help from the Calcutta-based Muslim leaders during the Bakr Id disturbances in 1896, the meeting of the Mohammedan Reformed Association—an organization of professional Muslims—passed a resolution congratulating their members 'for doing their best to prevent outburst of religious fanaticism by explaining to the concerned uneducated Mohammedans that their religious complaints would be constitutionally redressed by proper steps being taken both in the High Court and in the government.'[55] In essence, the Muslim elites tried to present themselves to the government as effective, loyalist power-brokers between the administration and the Muslim workers. The mood of the Muslim elites after the 1897 riot was captured in an Urdu poem which was published after the Talla riots in a journal called the *General and Gauhari Ashrafi*. The poem counselled 'ignorant Muslims' in the following words:

O Mussalman, danger befall you as you are making noise without reason ...
You should not devote your attention to the Talla affair.
Look at the kindness and favour of the government,
Look at the love of the queen for her subjects.
You must know you are ignorant.
Think and do not put the whole Mussalman community to the shame ...[56]

This poem is clear evidence of the fact that a section of the Muslim elites in the city opposed the riots. Thus, religious riots did not create a common political goal before the Muslims of Calcutta. It also did not lead towards permanent divisions among workers along Hindu-Muslim lines.

The above analysis demonstrates that although there were elements of Hindu- Muslim tensions in the mill towns, it was also true that on many occasions, various sections of workers confronted the police irrespective of their religious affiliations. Here, the context of political dominance of mill town administration by managers must always be kept in mind. The prejudices of the administration against Muslim workers and the stereotypes with which the managers and police operated helped create conditions in which Muslim workers had confrontations with the local law-enforcing agencies. The colonial officers' general perception about lower-class Muslims as being turbulent people contributed in no small measure to the highlighting of the religious dimensions of their identity even as this simultaneously coalesced with their identity as workers. In the context of religious issues, these affiliations played on each other in influencing workers' decisions and actions. When Muslim workers confronted the police, their Hindu colleagues sometimes sympathized with them and indeed occasionally put up a joint resistance against the police, as we have seen in the case of the Talla riots. Thus, it would be wrong to accord primordiality to any aspect of workers' identity which were created and recreated according to wider circumstances and contexts. It is also significant to note that during the so-called communal riots, various sections of workers decided their course of action independent of elite influence. This independent political action of workers against the government further manifested itself during the agitation against anti-plague regulations issued in 1898.

Policing the Plague, 1898

The 1898 plague in Calcutta killed only a few residents of the city but government's plague regulations scared many. The fear of plague regulations was widely prevalent in Calcutta even before its presence was announced by the municipal officials.[57] The news of the demolition of houses, burning of infected articles, and report of public dishonouring of Indian women by the police in Bombay, made the plague regulations extremely unpopular in Calcutta.[58] These stories gained further credence among slum dwellers in the summer of 1898 when the municipal health officer, Dr Cook, began destroying the houses of supposed plague victims after the discovery of a dead body in a central Calcutta slum.[59] Slum dwellers perceived a sinister design in these measures as they believed that 'the government has made up its mind to carry on plague inspection in right earnest to destroy the filthy bastis which are hotbeds of epidemics.'[60] The fear of the dreaded plague regulations increased further when on 27 April the Calcutta Corporation decided to form ward-level vigilance committees, empowered to enter any house to conduct a search for patients. Immediately, the Indian press in Calcutta started clamouring for more information regarding measures to control the plague. These measures led to 'wild rumours' about imminent quarantine of the city after the official declaration of the 'plague epidemic'.[61] People believed that those removed to the 'isolation hospitals' were being poisoned to death by the doctors to prevent the latter from spreading the contagion.[62] Such rumours created panic in the city and there occurred a large-scale exodus from Calcutta in fear of the 'draconian measures' adopted by the government.[63] The government sensed that by leaving the city in large numbers the people were indirectly protesting against the imposition of those measures in Calcutta which they adopted in Bombay to combat the plague. Even the ultra-loyalist *The Englishman* advised the government of the expediency of taking measures 'which might have had the effect of settling the minds of ignorant masses on fire against the ruling race.'[64]

The lieutenant governor decided to follow a cautious policy of winning over the professional elites who, he expected, would pacify the 'ignorant masses'. He thus announced that the people of 'respectable classes' would not be removed to the isolation wards or plague hospitals in the town. The Lieutenant Governor further declared that arrangements would be made for private hospitals for 'better class' people in their own compounds or in their garden houses. Beside that, the corporation would help rich people transform some of their houses into ward hospitals for family members. The members of the respectable classes were also allowed to house their sick relatives in private ward hospitals. It was decided that only family physicians would inspect these 'upper class' patients.[65] Soon the bhadralok press showered praises on the lieutenant governor, which indicated that the government, through these concessions, had won the approval of bhadralok public opinion. The bhadralok press heartily welcomed the news of the government decision to soften plague regulations for members of the respectable classes.[66]

However, the slum dwellers were condemned to be removed to the plague hospital. This discrimination against men of the 'coolie classes' was also reflected in plague notices, circulated for inspection by railway passengers, which particularly asked them to detain the 'pilgrims, gypsies, vagabonds and persons of coolie classes or people wearing dirty and torn clothes'. It was assumed that such people were the most likely carriers of plague;[67] thereby, these people were forcefully quarantined in the plague hospitals which aroused widespread opposition among workers.

The reasons for such opposition to segregation in hospital can be gleaned from the descriptions of the hospital by the health officer of the corporation who maintained that the mortality rate there was quite high. The main plague hospital of the city was located near Golghata in Maniktollah, the largest 'graveyard' of Calcutta in the nineteenth century. Dr Cook observed in his report:

to say of a man he is gone to Maniktollah was almost equivalent to saying "He is gone to the last resting place." As a result, to suggest sending a patient to Maniktollah was almost enough to frighten him to death if he was conscious, and the ignorant people did all in their power in the way of concealing cases and mobbing ambulance parties to prevent sending their friends and relatives to what they considered so undesirable a place.[68]

The most sustained resistance to this policy came from the scavengers of the town who made it plain that they would not work if their relatives were sent to the hospitals. From 4 to 20 May there occurred numerous strikes among municipal scavengers in different wards of the corporation. From 20 May this became a general strike of the scavengers in the city.[69]

The governor soon gave concessions to the workers and announced that no 'members of the poorer classes' would be taken to the hospital. The Plague Manual declared specifically that no person would be removed to a public hospital without his consent.[70] Workers of Calcutta achieved a victory on their own against the discriminatory policies of the government which favoured only affluent Indians.

The social distinctions made by the government between poor and rich reinforced among workers a consciousness of being an oppressed social group—different from affluent Indians. This was reflected in a new agitation against the 'plague inoculation' drive which gained notoriety for killing perfectly healthy people.[71] Dr Cook also noted that poorer people believed that *sahibs* would not die from inoculation because the latter 'were ticcaed with different stuff,'[72] and poor people assumed that affluent Indians were being offered a different medicine. When Raja Binoy Krishna of Shovabazaar was inoculated along with his family by Dr Cook, 'the lower class people are still giving out', noted an Indian newspaper, 'that the raja and his family have been inoculated with rose water, whereas they (poorer people) will be inoculated with poison.'[73] These statements reflect the deep distrust of government measures and the social awareness among workers of belonging to oppressed social groups who could be discriminated against by officials as well as by propertied Indians.

Thus, a large number of workers again took to the streets to oppose the plague inoculation drive in Calcutta. On 4 May 1898 workers from Calcutta port, the jute presses, and mills assembled at various centres of the city—'behaving in a threatening and defiant way'. The agitating workers stopped hackney carriage drivers, cut the traces of the horses and warned drivers not to carry patients to hospitals. In Chitpur the railway employees and workers in adjacent jute mills struck work. They ripped tramway lines and placed municipal carts across the road to block the traffic. At the same time, two smallpox vaccinators who went out to conduct the annual vaccination drive in a slum near the medical college were stopped and beaten up mercilessly, and attacks were also made on Europeans travelling in the town.[74]

In these mill towns, workers particularly resisted all measures perceived by them as inoculation attempts. On 3 May strikes spread across Howrah in the jute mills and railway concerns. Railway workers went on strike, believing that arrangements for forcible inoculation were taking place inside the workshop. Also, due to the inoculation scare, the conservancy superintendent of the municipality was not allowed to enter slums in the mill areas for sanitary supervision. All hackney carriage drivers stopped plying their trade and cart drivers and railway coolies also deserted their work. According to a rough estimate made by the district magistrate of

Howrah, nearly twenty thousand workers went on strike there and in the adjoining jute mill towns.[75] In Calcutta, peons of different concerns, hackney carriage drivers, and carters went on strike fearing that they would be forcefully inoculated. On 4 May jute mill workers started roaming around the town in large groups.[76] At about 8 a.m. the local inspector and the district superintendent of police found that a large number of people armed with *lathis* had gathered in the *maidan* at the centre of the town. The district superintendent assured them that there would be no inoculation in Howrah, at which point the crowd gradually dispersed. One of the police inspectors then proceeded to the Shibpur jute mill area and soon discovered a large crowd of nearly four thousand jute workers, proceeding towards the town with lathis. The police inspector, however, persuaded them to turn back.[77]

In some areas, however, violence was widespread. For example, at the centre of Howrah it was found that Burn and Company's workers struck work and came out of the mill as the men in another workshop raised an alarm that there was an inoculator outside. Some workers immediately attacked the public pleader Narsinga Dutta, forcing him to take shelter in the civil court compound. These people disappeared when they saw a large number of armed police approaching them.[78] In the Shibpur mill area of Howrah, a doctor assisted by an Indian sergeant and two Indian constables allegedly 'commenced [on] inoculating women of a slum'. The women assaulted the doctor and called their men from work who then began looking for the doctor and policemen.[79] Two persons, one European and a Bengali, were beaten up in Howrah for attempting to stop mill boys from throwing stones at tramcars. In the evening, some workers chased one unfortunate European sailor who was walking alone on the streets of Howrah. He jumped into the river to escape the wrath of the crowd and was drowned.[80]

These events created the fear of widespread disturbances in European business circles. The Bengal Chamber of Commerce wrote in a letter to the government for an urgent communication to be sent out to the workers: 'by the beat of drum, that there is no intention on the part of the authorities to make inoculation compulsory.' 'It is especially necessary', observed the Bengal Chamber of Commerce, 'that the notice should be conveyed in such a manner as to be plain to the most ignorant people as there is still a widespread idea, erroneous of course, that the government is intending to introduce compulsory inoculation.' The Chamber also noted:

[a] strike of considerable magnitude took place yesterday among the coolies employed by the different importing houses to remove goods to the bazaar, and considerable

obstruction resulted to business in consequence. The committee are informed that both railway and ship coolies are also abandoning their work in large numbers, and we have no doubt that you will realise the great importance of prompt action being taken in the matter.[81]

The government soon responded by introducing the Risley ticket which was issued in English and the vernacular and largely circulated by business firms amongst their employees. It ran as follows:

This is to certify that no one shall be inoculated unless he expressly desires it.[82]

This declaration gradually calmed down the city.

Interestingly, the plague riots unnerved the Bengali bhadralok politicians who feared a 'lower class upsurge' against the government. The 'lower class'—organized plague riots caught both the bhadralok politicians and colonial officials by surprise. The bhadralok-controlled journals expressed anger at the 'lower classes' for their opposition to plague regulations. The *Hitavadi*, for instance, declared:

Badmashes, wanting to have a splendid time of it, league themselves with ignorant people blinded by the prejudice and got up riot after riot, but did not in the least riffle the temper or [a]ffect the policy of the government.[83]

The *Charumihir* went a step further to prove bhadralok loyalty to the government by stating that 'the educated Indian community have no hand in these riots. They are got up entirely by the lower-classes. This ... should go a good way towards changing the unfavourable attitude of certain high officials towards the educated native community.'[84]

As a matter of fact, these riots exposed the absence of linkages between the bhadralok politicians and workers. Surprised at the workers' agitation against the government, the *Hitavadi* appealed that 'every educated person in the country should try to convince the illiterate masses if the latter got excited, not to assault any one and every one without reason'. It reminded the 'illiterate masses' that the latter 'will severely be dealt with if they resort to violence'.[85] The gulf between the bhadralok elites of Calcutta and the workers was further exposed by the statements of the *Dainik o Samachar Chandrika* who maintained that 'it is very difficult to convince the bustee population of the efficacy of sanitary measures, for the lower classes do not generally listen to the advice of their superiors.'[86] Finally, the radical *Sulabh Samachar* expressed their surprise at the fact that '... the educated classes cannot convince the illiterate and rowdy people of the town that unlawful assemblies or opposition to the authorities can offend the latter.'[87] These statements indicate that the bhadralok were drawn closer to the government by the concessions offered to them and they abandoned the workers who still felt threatened by government policies.

Similarly Muslim elites failed to control their poorer co-religionists. For example, *Darussultanat and Urdu Guide,* an influential Urdu journal of Calcutta, accused the Bengali babus of fomenting discontent among the 'ignorant Muslims' against the government, but also lamented that poor Muslims believed in 'bazaar gops' [gossips] and were ready to fall out with the government.[88] Elite Muslims, thus, stood helpless before the widespread unrest among Muslim workers in the city and in the mill towns.

By the end of the 1898, the plague scare which gripped the city came to an end.[89] The collective resistance of workers and other oppressed social groups in the city against the plague measures revealed their strength in organising protests against the discriminatory policies of the government. They forced the government to withdraw all regulations which they perceived to be against their interests. Both the government and their educated Indian allies failed to convince 'the lower classes of Calcutta' of the efficacy of such measures. In the late nineteenth century, the repeated confrontation between workers on the one hand, and police and other administrative institutions on the other, during strikes, riots, and agitations created among workers an anti-government mentality. However, the bhadralok-led nationalist movement failed to draw upon this constituency in the anti-government campaign.

Bhadralok-led Nationalist Politics and the Labour Movement: 1890–1910

In the late nineteenth century, the political activities of the Bengali bhadralok in Calcutta evolved around various associations. The growth of political associations in Bengal was accompanied by the establishment of Indian-owned newspapers. The Bengali newspapers of Calcutta represented factions and interest groups among the educated Indians. In spite of constant factional bickering, these groups as a whole gradually became critical of government policies and in their perception they represented the 'nascent Indian nation'. Yet, in the last decade of the nineteenth century, the leaders of the 'respectable sections' of Indian society had failed to establish any contact with the city's working masses.

The memorandum of the British Indian Association to the Royal Commission on Labour in 1892 reflected, to a certain extent, the bhadralok attitude towards workers. Its 1890 memorandum on the living conditions of the jute workers wrote of 'judicious distribution' of working hours between men, women, and children in spite of their observation that workers had no weekly holidays.[90] The memorandum clearly stated their interest in the matter:

[The] British Indian Association is a political association but several of its members are large landholders whose tenants work in different jute and cotton and other mills for the manufacture of textile fabrics.[91]

This letter indicates the bhadralok understanding of the living conditions of jute mill workers. The British Indian Association simply approved the existing industrial situation by stating that 'there is usually the greatest good feeling between the labourers and masters'.[92] They, however, failed to mention the numerous strikes at the end of the 1880s.

In Bengal, the nationalists saw government attempts to improve living conditions of workers as a conspiracy to undermine the interests of Indian entrepreneurs.[93] Indian newspapers were vocal in their criticism of government legislation which limited working hours of child labourers employed in factories. All the newspapers characterized the act as a conspiracy by Manchester to destroy Indian industries.[94] Interestingly, the editorials of these newspapers exhibited a complete ignorance of the working conditions in factories.[95]

The bhadralok intelligentsia firmly believed that India's economic development lay only in industrialization under the stewardship of Indian entrepreneurs. However, the Indian mercantile community in Bengal had as yet not made a sufficient headway in industry. The intelligentsia thus looked towards the Bombay-based Indian textile industry as a source of hope. Their defence of rising Indian industries compelled them to oppose a restriction of working hours in factories which, they thought, would adversely affect the interest of the Bombay industrialists. This generated a kind of indifference among the nationalists towards the workers. The *Amrita Bazar Patrika*, one of the proponents of the nationalist view, wrote:

[a] larger death rate among our operatives is far more preferable to the collapse of this rising industry ... We can, after the manufacturers are truly established, seek to protect the operators.[96]

Nevertheless, a small minority among the bhadralok engaged themselves in philanthropic activities among industrial workers. In the second half of the nineteenth century, Keshab Chandra Sen, a leading social reformer, established a technical school for workers which imparted training in trades like carpentry, weaving, watch repairing, lithography, printing, and carving. A night school for adult workers was started with his encouragement.

Sasipada Bannerjee, one of the most widely known social reformers, was a disciple of Keshab Sen. From 1865 to 1887, he set up eight organizations which were involved in reformist activities among workers.[97] Sasipada was also a Victorian liberal who drew inspiration from the Hindu concept of *Lokheeta* and the Christian concept of charity. Bannerjee ardently supported the cause of limited working hours and advocated legislation in this regard. He believed that education was the only way to improve the living conditions of the workers. The idea of organizing reformist activities among workers in a mill town in the late nineteenth century—against the dominant grain of bhadralok ideologies of the period—was a courageous act.

By the end of the nineteenth century, radicals within the Bramho Samaj broke away from the Nababidhan Samaj controlled by Keshab Sen and started a new Bramho association—the Sadharan Bramho Samaj. Members of the new association campaigned for improvement of the conditions of tea garden workers.[98] They also launched a movement for rent law reforms.[99] Sibnath Sastri, one of the most brilliant representatives of the new Samaj, emphasized socialism and secularism as alternatives to the revivalist Hindu politics of the period. He established a '*samadarshi*' society to propagate his ideas. However, the group never attempted to develop any mass support. Its members took patriotic oaths and discussed pressing political problems of the time but never developed a coherent plan of action.[100] It became a secret society practising empty rituals which in many ways was a prototype of later revolutionary terrorist groups. The late-nineteenth century bhadralok radicals believed in the effectiveness of an elite band of dedicated nationalists. This contradicted their desire to work within, and with the help of, the masses which was exemplified in the inability of bhadralok politicians to mobilize industrial workers during the swadeshi period. They could not transcend the social distance between themselves and the ordinary workers.

The first decade of the twentieth century witnessed an increase in the number of strikes in the jute mills. The increasing racial bitterness in the factories between Indian workers and European supervisors[101] created a potential support base for the nationalists. Furthermore, immediate dismissal of striking workers made it extremely difficult for jute mill workers to organize openly, which created room for outside negotiators to mediate during labour disputes.[102]

In 1905, the partition of Bengal led to the rise of a powerful nationalist agitation. In this period bhadralok nationalists tried to challenge the supremacy of European capital in Bengal by setting up swadeshi business enterprises. Labour unrest in British-dominated commercial concerns of Calcutta provided the nationalists with an opportunity to challenge British capital more effectively. The swadeshi leaders did not utilize the opportunity and their support for strikes in European mills was usually more of an accident than the result of a well-thought-out strategy. For instance, when on 4 September 1905 after marching through different parts of Calcutta, nationalist processions assembled at the college square, the news of a strike of Howrah clerks in an 'European industrial concern' suddenly became a symbol for bhadralok revolt against colonial domination.[103] The emotion of the crowd reached a crescendo when 'a professor of the city college burst into tears as he harangued [on] the audience which equally reciprocated his feelings by honest tears.'[104] These emotional outbursts marked the beginning of swadeshi intervention in labour politics. A.C. Bannerjee, a swadeshi leader, soon planned a defence association for the Bengali burrababus in European firms.[105]

Bhadralok leaders could not move beyond their immediate support base of mill clerks who were extremely conscious of their superior social position vis a vis that of the mill workers. For example, the strike by clerks in Burn and Company of Howrah typically reflected these concerns. In September 1905, Bengali clerks in Burn company struck work in protest against the installation of Rochester machines 'for accurate registration of attendance at the offices'. The clerks told the management that the new machine was derogatory to their upper caste social status[106] which suggests that bhadralok clerks were chiefly concerned with their social superiority over ordinary workers. These clerks, however, constituted only 6 per cent[107] of the total work-force and thus the success of the strike required the cooperation of manual workers. But the bhadralok clerks' claim to higher social status in this case earned little sympathy from ordinary workers.

The *hartal* (strike) of 16 October 1905 against the partition drew workers in large numbers.[108] In the initial stages of the movement, workers independently utilized nationalist symbols and slogans to press forward their demands. For example, a long strike started in November 1905 in the

Fort Gloster Jute Mill near Howrah against harsh working conditions and the arrogant behaviour of the factory manager.[109] The strike escalated when a European overseer objected to a clerk wearing a *rakhi* (a Hindu ornament handmade of thread) to work. When two of the swadeshi slogan-shouting clerks were stopped by the European assistants, other workers came forward to help these clerks as they felt they were 'all brothers in the mill and all brothers in Bengal.'[110] Thus, workers in their actions combined a new nationalist consciousness with their work-place grievances.

Nevertheless, the direct involvement of Swadeshi leaders in these strikes was limited to mediation. Within a year the same mill witnessed another strike against the wage cut of the operatives, and on this occasion workers objected to a new system of working hours which led to the loss of the night bonus. A strike started in the Fort Gloster Jute Mill on 1 March 1906 for the restoration of the night bonus. The manager promptly dismissed four sardars and seven clerks[111] and police suppressed this strike by indiscriminately arresting striking workers. The local influential bhadralok, sympathetic to the swadeshi cause, negotiated on behalf of the workers but few influential swadeshi nationalist leaders took interest in organizing help for the striking workers.

The most notable exception to this general reluctance of swadeshi leaders to mobilize workers was A.C. Bannerjee, who helped in establishing the first trade union in Bengal—the 'Indian Mill Hands Association'. Yet Bannerjee also viewed the problems of organizing industrial workers from a bhadralok perspective. In the first public meeting of the union at Budgebudge on 19 August 1906, Bannerjee, the President of the Union, warned against hasty and injudicious strikes. The object of the union, he stated, should be to bring about a healthier understanding between the 'master' and 'servant'.[112] The very use of the terms 'master-servant' relationship by A.C. Bannerjee indicates that he failed to go beyond the limitations of an inegalitarian perception of the social relationships. This union, as a consequence, attained little success in mobilizing common workers.[113]

The union depended upon head clerks or burrababus in organizing the workers. The role of the burrababus in the union became evident in a letter from the head clerk of the Delta Jute Mill at Sankrail which informed him about the 'withdrawal of a strike' in accordance with the proposal of Bannerjee. The letter emphasized that 'workers expect much of your help to form their "union"' as 'they are quite ignorant about this', and typically appealed to the bhadralok sentiment of patronizing the poor workers' demands. But polite Bengali usage like '*upkar*', or help in the charitable sense of the term, masked the reality where the burrababu himself was the most important organizer.[114]

However, clerks or other intermediaries like the sardars did not always enjoy popularity among ordinary workers. In Budgebudge, which was the centre of swadeshi labour politics, workers protested against the oppression of a sardar in the mill. The workers of the beam department of Budgebudge sent a letter to A.C. Bannerjee, drawing his attention to the oppression of a sardar and a clerk in the mill. This clerk and the sardar coerced common workers to pay bribes for new jobs and sanctions for leave. When the workers tried to lower the amount of puja subscriptions to be paid to these men, they were unduly harassed.[115]

The weakness of the swadeshi unions also became apparent in their failure to control recalcitrant burrababus, some of whom had an influence over large groups of workers. For example, Krishna Pada Haldar, a clerk of the Rajganj Jute Mill engine shop, had pointed out to A.C. Bannerjee on the eve of a major political rally:

We would be much obliged, if you kindly confirm your coming to the rally for the mill; could we be informed about it in advance. Also kindly do not mention my impression on our burrababu which I have told you in a secret discussion. It can hamper my position in the factory. I have a feeling that the criticism you made on the burrababu in the last session of our *Samity* might have an adverse effect on the Samity as he commands support of a large section of non-Bengali workers. If we antagonize the burrababu he might mobilize his supporters against the Samity. So I suggest we collaborate with the burrababu for the time being in order to maintain workers' unity. The burrababu apparently felt bad for not being able to attend the last meeting.[116]

The letter shows that swadeshi leaders had little direct contact with the workers and were completely dependent on the organizational skills and capacity of the burrababus.[117]

In this period, strikes swept across the mill belt.[118] The nationalist presence in these strikes was limited.[119] The workers organized these strikes and deployed their strategy of negotiation with the managers independently. They demanded shorter working hours and improvement in the living conditions in the mill towns.[120] An eye witness account of a jute mill labourer before the Indian Factory and Labour Commission provides us with a story of the mobilization pattern of workers. Muhammad Zulfiqar, a mill worker, informed the commission that both Hindu and Muslim workers met in the Hazinagar bazaar in Naihati and discussed the problem of working hours. In a similar meeting at Kankinarah bazaar in Bhatpara, workers decided to demand shorter working hours. In the meeting at the bazaar, Hindu workers wanted holidays for a week during Durgapuja and the Muslim workers two days each for Id ul Fitr, Bakr Id and Muharram. Both these meetings were widely attended.[121] The grievances among the labourers were so well-entrenched that a Muslim workers' organization like the Kankinara Mohammedan Association had to champion their demands from a common platform.[122]

Colonial officials often maintained that workers were incapable of being united; hence working-class protests were sporadic and spontaneous.[123] It is true that strikes were often abrupt and sudden in jute mills. The reasons for such sporadic strikes, however, lay not in the incapability of the workers to combine but rather the roots of the problem were to be located in the pattern of the managerial control over the workers. The predominance of temporary workers in the jute industry, absence of job security, and rapid dismissals of strike leaders acted as constraints on open coordination among different groups of workers. Moreover, police assistance to the mill managers through indiscriminate arrests of workers also prevented the growth of an open trade union organization. Mill managers, through their control over local municipalities and the judiciary, could strangle any protest of the workers in anticipation. In such a situation, strikes were likely to be sudden to catch the management unawares which was perhaps an effective strategy of negotiation with the managers. Workers thus defended their interests independent of help from nationalist leaders.

Conclusion

The direct control of the managers over the administration of the mill towns transformed strikes immediately into confrontations with local law-enforcing agencies of the state. This contributed to the distrust among workers of the administrative machinery of the colonial state which was further reinforced by their confrontations with the police during communal riots. The repeated confrontation between European factory officials and industrial workers created an anti-government attitude among various sections of the workers in Calcutta and provided bhadralok nationalist politicians with a crucial opportunity to build up an alliance with the labour movement against the colonial state. However, during the anti-plague regulation agitations, various sections of workers confronted the police despite bhadralok collaboration with the policies of the colonial state. The swadeshi leaders also could not reach out to the workers and failed to build up an alliance with the latter during the movement against the partition of Bengal between 1903 and 1908. The period after 1909 till 1918 witnessed a temporary lull in the labour movement and the nationalist agitations.[124]

. Thus in the pre-War political context workers retained a degree of independence in deploying their strategy of confrontation with mill managers. What came to be termed as 'riots' also appeared to be multifaceted events whereby workers' relationship with the law enforcement agencies of the colonial state played a crucial role in defining their targets of attack. Religious and regional loyalties did influence and inform workers' activities but such loyalties were more pronounced on certain occasions than others and did not reveal a broad parameter of political consciousness along religio-communal lines. Rather workers' politics was characterized by several forms of horizontal solidarities in the context of their relationship with mill management and the colonial state at different levels. Workers' interaction with the colonial state was structured through the newly emerging managers' raj in the mill towns and the political strategies of bhadralok elites drawn from white-collar employees of the mill management within this manager raj. However, increasingly such complex relationships among workers, managers, and the local level of the colonial state were reshaped by the growing intensity of mass nationalist movements and their complex diverse strands. More importantly, when workers confronted colonial capitalism and its immediate political form of the manager raj at the level of mill towns, complex dynamics of labour movements at the international level within global capitalism intervened in workers' politics in Bengal through different agencies. The full play of such diverse political forces could be clearly analysed in the post-War years in Bengal. Workers' protest reached its peak again during the post-war Khilafat and non-cooperation movements. The next chapter will explore the interaction between the labour politics and the nationalist movements in that period.

Appendix 4.1

The texts of Bengali letters and a petition drafted by workers are reproduced
here to indicate the nature of the relationship among nationalist leaders,
Bengali clerks, and workers themselves. Original Bengali versions of these
letters are preserved in the A.C. Bannerjee Private Papers, Nehru Memorial
Museum and Library, New Delhi.

1. Copy of the letter from Benod Behari Mookherjee to A.C. Bannerjee written on 12 Septemeber 1907

Manickpur
12 September
1907

Dear Sir,

I am glad to   ow joined to their work
according to   xpect much of your
help to fo   his. Please let us
know w'   r the next
meeti

Yo

I beg to acknowledge the receipt of your post-card and telegram. This
Saturday being the pay-day of month and hours too it will not be convenient.

Dear Mr Bannerjee,

convention in the month of January. Hence we would be much obliged if you let us know when it is convenient for you and we all promise to be present in that gathering. We the undersigned persons work in the Beam department of the Budgebudge jute mill. We are extremely grateful to you for your service in forming our union and we are its members. Hence we would like to apprise you of the oppression of our superiors and seek your able advice to remedy it. We hope you will protect us from this oppression perpetuated by them. We give you a brief sketch of the ways we are being oppressed and hope to narrate the whole story in person. We are forced to bribe the sardars and the babus to get our leave sanctioned by the *saheb* and we are harassed or even sacked from the job. So we had to reluctantly satisfy the whims of the superior. Last year due to the rising prices we decided to reduce the *Durgapuja* subscription. However Head Sardar Haricharan Khara instigated the Assistant babu Atul Chandra Chatterjee so that the subscription is raised. When they adviced the in-charge babu, Purna Chandra Ghosh, to collect more subscriptions, we decided not to pay any amount. As a revenge, they have now started to project us as guilty of various faults thus forcing us to contribute to the 'Whiteman's' company. After your writing to Purna Babu and Haricharan Khara, they have increased their misdeeds. Therefore, kindly suggest means of combating these elements and advice us on how to deal with the situation. Please protect us from this oppression.

Yours sincerely.

Budgebudge Jute Mill
Dated 11 Paush 1313.

3.   *Copy of the letter from Gurupada Mukherjee of*
     Rajganj Jute Mill to A.C. Bannerjee written o
     12 February 1908

Rajganj
12.2.08

to hold a meeting that day. The date and time for holding a meeting will be duly intimated to you. Please note.

Yours faithfully

Gurupada Mukherjee

Notes

1. In the 1890s the Indian Factory Commission reported: 'It is the rule for nearly all Indian factories to work from day light to dusk, that is taking extreme limits in summer from 5 a.m. to 7 p.m. or 14 hours with half an hour's interval. *IFC Report*, 1890, para 13. Also see Home Judicial progs. India, February, 1896, IOL.

2. General Miscellaneous Nos 21–25 of July 1896; Nos 24–25 of September 1896; Nos 26–27, 30–31 for 1898, 25–26 of August 1898, WBSA. According to the crude statistics provided by the K.L. Datta series, the prices of wheat and rice in this period in the industrial district of 24 Parganas increased from 97 in 1881 to 139 (the base being 1871–75=100). *Prices and Wages of India 21st issue*, Table No. 23, pp. 129, 134.

3. *Report of IFC, 1890*, pp. 66–77.

4. *Report on condition of lower classes in India*, Famine Nos 1–24, December 1888, Para 25, NAI. Describing the early years of jute mills, Samaresh Basu in his novel on Jagatdal has shown how factories remained closed for days as workers went out to celebrate festivals in nearby villages. Samaresh Basu, *Jagatdal*, Calcutta, 1945.

5. See R. Dasgupta, 'Material conditions and behavioural aspects of Calcutta working-class 1876–99', Centre for Studies in Social Sciences, Occasional Paper No 22, Calcutta, January, 1979.

6. Two novels throw light on various aspects of the lives of Jute workers: Saroj Bandapadhaya, *Biki kinir Hat*, Calcutta, 1975 and Samaresh Basu, *Jagatdal*, Calcutta, 1945.

7. *AARBM*, 1907, p. 8.

8. The old employees often 'educated' new workers about the supposed rights of workers. See for details Bengal Judicial progs; police dept; Jan. to March 1896, A Nos 8–10, p. 4961, IOL.

9. Judicial Dept Police Branch, January 1896, Nos A 7–12, Report on Police Supervision in Riverine Municipalities, WBSA.

10. General Dept Miscellaneous Branch 1895, Nos 21–22, Annual Report on the working of the Indian Factories Act XV of 1881 as amended by Act XI of 1891 in Bengal during 1895, p. 4935, IOL.

11. See 9 and 10 above.

12. See 9 above.

13. Ibid.

14. See for details quoted in Ranajit Dasgupta, 'Material Conditions and Behavioural Aspects of Calcutta Working Class 1875–1899' pp. 30–1.

15. Ibid.

16. See 9 and 10 above.

17. See 9 above. However, the factory inspector wrote in his annual report that 'in this case European employees had recourse to firearms, but with no serious results.' General Dept Miscellaneous Branch 1895 21–22, WBSA. See 10 above.

18. See 9 above.

19. In fact, in this period the India Jute Mill was the only concern which escaped the strikes. Mr Cockrane, who was manager of the India Jute Mill for 28 years told Pratt that he experienced no trouble in his mill due to the fact that he gave holidays liberally and opposed keeping 'wages of workers in hands'.

20. Ibid.

21. Ibid.

22. See Chapter 3 for details of such measures.

23. See Chapter 3 for details. For example in 1895 the local bhadralok population in Naihati petitioned to the police that European supervisory staff terrorized the neighbourhood; they also added that workers were under no control after distribution of wages on Saturdays. A high-level police officer while enquiring in the matter, dryly commented on the petition that 'as regards the latter part [sic] a great deal of truth in it' but ignored completely the first part of the complaint. Judicial Dept; Police Branch January 1896, Report on police supervision in the riverine municipalities, No A 7–12, WBSA.

24. Ibid.

25. For example, the manager of the Chapdani Jute Mill told Pratt that he did not like Muslim weavers 'because they always cause trouble in the mill'. Pratt also wrote to his superiors that Muslim weavers were the chief trouble makers though Pratt's own report indicated little about particularly Muslim workers' involvement in strikes and riots. Judicial Dept Police; Branch January 1896, 'Report on police supervision in the riverine municipalities', No A 7–12, WBSA.

26. See G. Pandey, 'The Bigoted Julaha' in The Construction of Communalism in colonial North India pp. 66–108.

27. Judicial dept; Police branch, July 1896, A 29–38, Lower Hoogly Jute Mill Riot Case, WBSA.

28. Ibid.

29. Interestingly, the District Magistrate found that 'There was nothing definite to show that they [the Hindus] had premeditated this slaughter'. Ibid.

30. Ibid.

31. There was no indication of any excitement and the manager told him that he had even forgotten that 24 May was the festival of the Bakr Id. The Id prayer passed off peacefully and Muslims sacrificed a cow in a nearby village. Information came to the manager at around 4–30 p.m. that low caste Hindus killed a pig in the mill compound. In fact, the low caste Hindus reported that they would have a festival (porab) as well as the Mohammedans ... It was clear, the district magistrate concluded from his enquiries that, they [low caste Hindus] did not wish to parade the carcass of the pig to wound the feelings of the Mohammedans ..., rather they were hiding it under a cloth and they fled away once they were caught which indicates a sense of guilt.

32. The leading Muslim employees told a police inspector that 'they stayed away from work as they feared that if work was resumed with the durwans still in the mill, they might not be able to restrain their members from using violence.'

33. The district magistrate in his later enquiry found that 'some Hindus' stayed back in the lines even after the so-called alarm and they experienced no disturbance. In fact, a Hindu head constable reported to the D.M, that he found Muslims in the lines extremely nervous when the alarm was raised and it was they who collected near a tank. The constable also added that there was a crowd waiting in the distance but they appeared to be mere 'spectators'. This story was corroborated by a Muslim head-constable who found the Muslim workers 'cooking and eating their meal' in the lines at the time of the alarm. The district magistrate finally came to the conclusion that the alarm was 'due to misunderstanding' and maintained that all newspaper reports of gun-carrying Muslims attacking the mill were highly exaggerated accounts.

34. Ibid.

35. Judicial Branch; Police department, A Nos 119–121, Kine sacrifice at Rishra on the Bakr Id, WBSA.

36. Ibid.

37. Judicial dept, Police branch, July 1896, A Nos 52–57, Rishra Cow Killing Case, WBSA.

38. Ibid.

39. Ibid.

40. Judicial dept, Police branch, August 1896, A Nos 1–13, Titagarh Riot case, WBSA. All three riot cases are discussed in detail by Dipesh Chakrabarty in his 'Communal Riots and Labour: Bengal's Jute Mill Hands in the 1890s', *Past and Present*, No. 91, May 1981. However, my understanding of 'communal' riots differs completely from that of Dipesh Chakrabarty.

41. Judicial dept, Police branch, August 1896, A Nos 1–13, Titagarh Riot case, WBSA.

42. This story is based on Judicial Dept, Police Branch, November 1897, A 39–43, WBSA and Reports on Indian Native Papers (RINP[B]) 17 and 31, July 1897.

43. Judicial Dept, Police Branch, September 1896, A 101–113,1896, WBSA.

44. Ibid.

45. Judicial Dept, Police Branch, September 1897, A 101–113, WBSA.

46. *The Samay*, 3 September 1897, quoted in RINP(B), 11 September 1897.

47. Ibid.

48. *The Samay* wrote in January 1897: 'To live among a people who consider it a religious act to kill kafers is more dangerous than living among ferocious animals. Of the ferocious animals the tiger alone kills a prey even when it is not hungry. But other beasts do not kill except when they are driven by hunger to do so. But the Musalman's religious thirst is so much that it is not quenched even if the kafer's blood deluges the earth.' RINP(B), week ending 8 January 1897.

49. Judicial Dept, Police Branch, September 1897, A nos 101–113, WBSA.

50. In fact a new act called the Calcutta Police Act 1897 was drafted after the riot to empower the district magistrate of 24 Parganas to improve draconian measures. Judicial Department, Police Branch, June 1898, A Nos 52–54, WBSA.

51. *The Englishman*, 21 April 1896.

52. The *Dainik o Samachar Chandrika*, 11 July 1897, RINP(B), 17 July 1897.

53. Judicial Dept, Police Branch, November 1897 A 39–43, WBSA.

54. Judicial Dept, Police Branch, November 1897 A 44, WBSA.

55. Judicial Dept, Police Branch, July 1896, A Nos 52–57, Rishra Cow Killing Case, WBSA.

56. *The General and Gauhari Ashrafi*, 31 July 1897 and RINP(B), week ending on 11 September 1897.

57. See RINP(B) week ending 27 March 1897 and RINP(B) week ending 17 April, 1897.

58. 'We are versed neither in politics nor in hygiene, still we have recommendation to make. Let the inhabitants of an infected town be shot down,' commented the *Burdwan Sanjivani* on these measures, RINP(B) week ending 3 April 1896.

59. *Indian Plague Commission 1898–99* Vol. I, Evidence taken from 29 November 1898 to 5 January 1899; Appendix No. XX, J.N. Cook *Report on plague in Calcutta*, p. 464 (Hereafter *Report on plague in Calcutta*).

60. *Hitavadi* of 6 May 1898. RINP(B) week ending on 14 May 1898. *The Hitavadi* 10 June 1898. RINP(B) week ending 18 June 1898. And also see *Bengal a plague manual Being a collection of the extant Regulations and Executive orders in*

Appendix 4.1

The texts of Bengali letters and a petition drafted by workers are reproduced here to indicate the nature of the relationship among nationalist leaders, Bengali clerks, and workers themselves. Original Bengali versions of these letters are preserved in the A.C. Bannerjee Private Papers, Nehru Memorial Museum and Library, New Delhi.

1. Copy of the letter from Benod Behari Mookherjee to A.C. Bannerjee written on 12 Septemeber 1907

Manickpur
12 September
1907

Dear Sir,

I am glad to inform you that the workers have now joined to their work according to your proposal of the last meeting. They expect much of your help to form their 'union' as they are quite ignorant about this. Please let us know when you will kindly manage your time to visit here for the next meeting. They solely depend upon you for this present matter.

Yours faithfully,

Benod Behari Mookherjee
Hd. Clerk. Delta Jute Mills
Sankrail R.D., Howrah.

2. Copy of the letter from Budgebudge Workers to A.C. Bannerjee written on 12 Septemeber 1907

Bande Mataram
Sri Aswini Coomer Bandopadhya,
President, Indian Mill hands Union

Respected Sir,

We are sorry that we were unable to join the last conversation of the union due to some unavoidable reasons. We feel the need of having a special convention in the month of January. Hence we would be much obliged if you let us know when it is convenient for you and we all promise to be present in that gathering. We the undersigned persons work in the Beam department of the Budgebudge jute mill. We are extremely grateful to you for your service in forming our union and we are its members. Hence we would like to apprise you of the oppression of our superiors and seek your able advice to remedy it. We hope you will protect us from this oppression perpetuated by them. We give you a brief sketch of the ways we are being oppressed and hope to narrate the whole story in person. We are forced to bribe the sardars and the babus to get our leave sanctioned by the *saheb* and we are harassed or even sacked from the job. So we had to reluctantly satisfy the whims of the superior. Last year due to the rising prices we decided to reduce the *Durgapuja* subscription. However Head Sardar Haricharan Khara instigated the Assistant babu Atul Chandra Chatterjee so that the subscription is raised. When they adviced the in-charge babu, Purna Chandra Ghosh, to collect more subscriptions, we decided not to pay any amount. As a revenge, they have now started to project us as guilty of various faults thus forcing us to contribute to the 'Whiteman's' company. After your writing to Purna Babu and Haricharan Khara, they have increased their misdeeds. Therefore, kindly suggest means of combating these elements and advice us on how to deal with the situation. Please protect us from this oppression.

Yours sincerely.

Budgebudge Jute Mill
Dated 11 Paush 1313.

3. *Copy of the letter from Gurupada Mukherjee of Rajganj Jute Mill to A.C. Bannerjee written on 12 February 1908*

Rajganj
12.2.08

Dear Mr Bannerjee,

I beg to acknowledge the receipt of your post-card and telegram. This Saturday being the pay-day of month and hours too it will not be convenient connection with plague issued by the Government of India and the Government of Bengal, Calcutta, 1903, p. 48.

61. Bangabasi, 30 April 1898, RINP(B), week ending 7 May 1898.

62. Bangabasi, 7 May 1898. RINP(B), 14 May 1898. Some residents claimed that they heard the European soldiers saying 'We shall have plenty of fun and plenty of money.' Hitavadi, 6 May 1898, RINP(B) week ending on 14 May 1898.

63. The Bengal government observed that nearly 150,000 persons out of a total population of 800,000 fled from the capital of the British empire in fear of the government's anti plague regulations. Report on plague in Calcutta, pp. 464–5.

64. The Englishman, 30 April 1898.

65. Report on plague in Calcutta, pp. 469–70.

66. See Sanjivani, 6 May 1898, RINP(B) week ending 14 May 1898.

67. Plague Manual, pp. 7–10.

68. See 60 above.

69. Ibid.

70. See 67 above, p. 4.

71. See The Englishman, 4 May 1898.

72. See 60 above, p. 476.

73. The Bangabasi, 14 May, RINP(B) week ending 21 May 1898.

74. Ibid., and The Englishman, 4 May 1898.

75. Judicial dept, Police branch, August 1898, A 14–16, Disturbances at Howrah with the plague inoculation scare, WBSA.

76. The Englishman, 3 May and 4 May 1898.

77. Ibid.

78. See 75 above.

79. The Englishman, 4 May 1898.

80. See 75 above.

81. See 60 above, p. 475.

82. Ibid.

83. The Sanjivani, 7 May 1898, RINB(B), week ending 14 May 1898.

84. The Charu Mihir of 9 May 1898, RINP(B), week ending 21 May 1898.

85. Hitavadi, 13 May 1898, RINP(B), week ending 21 May 1898.

86. The Dainik o Samachar Chandrika, 14 May 1898, RINP(B), week ending 21 May 1898.

87. The Sulabh Samachar, 14 May 1898, RINP(B), week ending 21 May 1898.

88. The Darussultanat and Urdu Guide. Similarly the Bengali Muslim journal the Mihir-O-Sudhakar talked about 'badmashes' inciting the illiterates. 16 May 1898

RINP(B) week ending on 21 May 1898. The *Mihir-O-Sudhakar*, 27 May 1898. RINP(B), week ending on 4 June 1898.

89. *Report on plague in Calcutta*, p. 468. See also *Indian Plague Commission 1898–99*, Vol. I. Evidence taken from 29 November 1898 to 5 January 1899, Appendix No. XXI Indian *Plague Commission 1898–99*, Vol. I. Evidence taken from 29 November 1898 to 5 January 1899 Appendix No. XXIV. See Statement of Hem Chunder Raychowdhury.

90. *Royal Commission on Labour (English). Foreign Report*, 1892, Vol. II, p. 146. *Report on the Labour Question in India*, Calcutta, 8 July 1892,. From Babu Raj Kumar Subadhikari, Secretary. British Indian Association, to the Government of Bengal, General, Department, WBSA. This was in stark contrast to their concern with those agrarian issues which had a bearing on their interests.

91. Ibid.

92. Ibid.

93. Bipan Chandra has made a detailed analysis of the nationalists' attitude towards the labour problem in his book *Rise and Growth of Economic Nationalism in India*, Chapter VIII: Labour, New Delhi, 1982.

94. *The Factories Act 1881* limited the working hours of children (7–12 years) to 9 hours per day. Ibid., p. 325. See RINP(B) week ending 19 April 1881. Indeed, the *Bharat Mihir* was not alone in this regard, RINP(B) week ending 19 April 1881 was full of such comments collected from Indian newspapers.

95. An apt example is the reporting in newspapers like *Sulabh Samachar and Kushdaha* which claimed with much confidence that English law would not be suited to India primarily for climatic reasons. *Sulabh Samachar and Kushdaha*, 18 January 1889. RINP (B), week ending 26 January 1889.

96. *Amrita Bazar Patrika*, 25 September 1875.

97. Dipesh Chakrabarty, 'Sasipada Bannerjee: A study in the nature of the first contact of the Bengali Bhadralok with the working classes of Bengal', *Indian Historical Review*, 1976, Vol. II, p. 344.

98. See Chinmohan Snehanabis, 'Bramho Samaj and toiling people', *Mainstream*, Vol. 127, Nos 1–26 Annual 1978 (hereafter 'Bramho Samaj'), p. 122.

99. Krishna Kumar Mitra's (Autobiography) *Atmacharit*, Calcutta, 1937, p. 94. Chinmohan Snehanobis, 'Bramho Samaj', p. 118.

100. C. Snehanabis, 'Bramho Samaj', p. 120.

101. See *The Administration of Bengal under Sir Andrew Fraser 1903–08*, published by the Government of Bengal, Calcutta, 1909, pp. 206–7.

102. For example, in 1900, the manager of the Kamarhatty Jute Mill dismissed five workers when they tried to raise money to help a strike in Kankinarah. General Department, Miscellaneous branch, July, 1901, A 20, WBSA.

103. The *Amrita Bazar Partika*, 4 September 1905.

104. Ibid.

105. Ibid.

106. Ibid., 9 September 1905.

107. Ibid.

108. Ibid., 16 October 1905.

109. *The Bengalee*, 10 January 1906.

110. S.N. Gourlay, 'Trade Unionism in Bengal before 1922: Historical Origins, Development and Characteristics', Unpublished thesis, University of London, London, 1983 (hereafter 'Trade Unionism in Bengal') p. 105.

111. Three of these sardars were Muslims. Sumit Sarkar, *Swadeshi Movement*, p. 229.

112. *The Bengalee*, 21 August 1906.

113. Sumit Sarkar provided a detailed analysis of the labour politics in this period in Bengal. See Sumit Sarkar, *Swadeshi Movement in Bengal*, p. 123.

114. Benod Behari Mookherjee to A.C. Bannerjee, 12 September 1907. A.C. Bannerjee Private Papers, Nehru Memorial Museum and Library. See Appendix for details of the letter.

115. Budgebudge Jute Workers to A.C. Bannerjee 11 Paush 1313. A.C. Bannerjee Private Papers, Nehru Memorial Museum and Library. See Appendix for details of the letter.

116. Krishnapada Haldar to A.C. Bannerjee date unknown. A.C. Bannerjee Private Papers.

117. In fact, the same burrababu could stop A.C. Bannerjee's meeting in the Rajganj Jute Mill. Gurupada Mukherjee to A.C. Bannerjee 12 February 1908. A.C. Bannerjee Private Papers. See Appendix for details of the letter.

118. *Report on the Anti-partition and Swadeshi movement in Bengal*, para. 12, Also *The Bengalee*, 2 August and 18 December 1906. *The Bengalee*, 1, 5, and 6 December 1906, *Administration of Bengal under Andrews Fraser, 1903–1908*, Calcutta, 1908, p. 8. For details see Sumit Sarkar, *Swadeshi Movement*, p. 230.

119 Only in the Delta Jute Mill (Sankrail) after two months of strike, the swadeshi activist Premtosh Basu came forward to help the workers. Letter from head clerk Benod Behari Mukherjee, to A.C. Banerjee, 12 September 1907. A.C. Bannerjee Private papers.

120. General department Miscellaneous branch, January 1907, B41–44,WBSA.

121. *See Report of IFLC, 1908, Vol. 2, Evidence*, witness No. 181.

122. See Bhatpara municipality proceedings 7 August 1908; *IFLC, 1908, Vol. 2*, witness No. 176, p. 263–5. *AARBM*, 1903, p. 4 and *AARBM*, 1918, p. 2.

123. *Report of IFLC, 1908*, Vol. 1, p. 14.

124. There occurred minor confrontations between Police and Muslim workers in 1909. Home Dept, political Branch, No 30B–69B, January 1909, WBSA. In March 1914 a similar agitation against the demolition of the Naskarpara mosque in Khiddirpur dock area spread all over the mill belt which again had manifestly anti-police attitude. Home Dept political Branch, File No 155/(SL-3), March 1914, WBSA.

5

Price Rises, Protest, and Nationalist Mobilization

The Khilafat and Non-cooperation Movements, 1918–1922

Introduction

This chapter investigates the relationship between the Khilafat and Congress strategies of mass mobilization and the rising labour militancy in Calcutta and the surrounding mill towns during the years immediately after the First World War. In this period, rising prices and the non-availability of essential goods led to widespread popular discontent. In the heavily urbanized environs of Calcutta, the continuing labour movement, bolstered by new hope and confidence, provided the main strength of the mass nationalist non-cooperation movement. This chapter argues that in the process the leaders of non-cooperation realized the potential political and economic threat of such direct involvement of the labouring classes in the nationalist movement. To demonstrate this, I compare and contrast the attitude of different segments of the leadership—the Khilafatists, the Gandhians, and the Das camp on the issue of working-class participation in nationalist politics.

For the workers, political propaganda, whether Khilafatist, or nationalist, was never separate from their economic grievances against traders, employers, and the government. Faced with social discrimination, both through communal stereotyping and economic deprivation, the working-classes found in the growing anti-colonial propaganda a means of enabling them to articulate their grievances into direct resistance. For the first time it gave them a sense of hope and confidence in their ability to effectively challenge what had seemed earlier an unassailable alliance of the colonial state, the European employers, and the indigenous elites.

It was in the post-war period that the elite-led nationalist organizations, for the first time, attempted to lead an all-India mass movement against the colonial state. A section of the Bengal Congress leaders became interested in mobilizing the working masses. Their interest was limited to drawing the participation of workers into the boycott of foreign goods, while they were quite clear that this specific purpose was not to be swamped by a more extended participation of the workers in the wider political programme of non-cooperation. The workers, however, defied these limits set by the nationalist leadership. They attempted to combine their work-place agitations with the anti-colonial struggle during the different phases of the non-cooperation movement. Those trade unions, sponsored by Gandhian nationalists and Khilafatists, which aimed to restrain rather than support strikes against employers dwindled as the workers lost confidence in their 'harmonizing' rhetoric. This transformation in worker militancy could be observed through several stages starting from economic grievances against price rises to organising political protests against colonial rulers.

The Economic Crisis and the Influenza Epidemic 1918–21: Social Context of Labour Militancy

From 1918 onwards Bengal experienced economic crisis marked by drought, poor harvests, and wartime dislocations in railway and shipping lines which led to a massive shrinkage in international trade. As a consequence, prices continued to increase throughout the war years, reaching a peak in 1920. In Bengal prices of essential commodities like kerosene, cloth, and salt rose sharply.[1] The price rise was not marked by any corresponding increase in workers' wages which led to a deterioration in the living conditions of the urban working-classes in and around Calcutta.[2] Moreover, in Calcutta in early 1918 prices had risen by approximately 70 per cent since 1914 while wages witnessed only a marginal increase of 15 per cent.[3] Similarly in rural areas, agricultural labourers and marginal peasants suffered due to price rises.[4] The high price of cloth almost paralysed everyday life. A letter to a newspaper from a suburban town observed that

beggars were unable to go out for alms for want of clothes ... schools practically empty because the students had no clothes and so could not stir out of their houses.

There has been a case of man committing suicide because he could not provide his wife with a piece of cloth. More than one respectable woman has had to wear straw mats.[5]

This letter reflects the social concern over the cloth crisis. The gap between rising prices and almost stagnant wages increased political and social unrest in the urban and rural areas.[6] Theft and burglary became common in Calcutta and suburban mill towns.[7] In the interior of Bengal numerous *haats* or rural markets were looted.[8]

Indian politicians of various political persuasions also took up the issue of 'cloth famine' in the Bengal Legislative Council, forcing the government to take some steps to deal with the situation. For example, on 5 March 1918, Amir Ali Khan, a member of the council, questioned the government in the Bengal Legislative Council: 'Are you aware that the prices of cloth has risen abnormally high?' 'If so', he said, 'is the government taking any step to regulate its prices?'[9] A.K. Fazlul Huq, the president of the Bengal Muslim League, while addressing the Bengal Legislative Council on 18 September 1918, spoke of a deep-rooted crisis in the rural economy, particularly due to the high prices of cloth.[10]

In June 1918, under pressure from Indian members of the Legislative Council, the Bengal Government sent circulars to district officials to keep an eye on middlemen who were supposed to be engaged in profiteering.[11] One desperate bureaucrat Secretary in the Commerce Department of the Bengal Government, wrote to Delhi that 'I again desire to draw [the] attention of the Government of India that [the] crisis is becoming more acute and signs of troubles are not wanting.'[12] On 13 July 1918 the Bengal government finally appointed a committee to inquire into the cloth crisis.[13]

These efforts had no impact on the crisis whatsoever and the growing mass unrest alarmed the Bengal Government. In August, the Government wired Simla that 'the prices of the imported piece goods had risen very rapidly during the last fortnight and stocks were being withheld from markets with a view to further rise in the prices. The position is of acute crisis and recrudescence of lawlessness is not impossible unless measures are taken.'[14] It demanded immediate remedial measures and asked for promulgation of the Defence of India Act to deal with the situation.[15]

The living conditions of the urban poor in Calcutta plunged further when an influenza epidemic broke out in the city. It struck Calcutta and the mill districts in the month of June 1918.[16] By July it assumed alarming proportions and spread all over the city with 'lightening rapidity'. In the city proper, offices were paralysed as it struck nearly one-third of the staff. The postal and conservancy services of the city and the mill towns suffered owing to the number of 'coolies' infected with the disease.[17] According to a calculation, the number of deaths in Calcutta increased by nearly 50 per cent in 1918 and further swelled by 20 per cent in December 1919.[18] Influenza apart, there was a sudden increase in death rates in greater Calcutta due to other serious diseases.[19] The areas in Calcutta with heavy concentration of slums experienced a higher number of deaths.[20] Young men between the ages of 20 and 40 suffered most in this epidemic.[21] It is they who constituted the core of the factory population and in 1919 they became more active in the strikes.[22]

The indifferent attitude of the municipal administration in Calcutta and in the mill towns to the sufferings of slum dwellers during the influenza epidemic contributed further to the growing discontent among workers. The municipal administration of mill towns remained in the hands of mill managers, thus multiplying workers' grievances against them. In Calcutta the worst affected slums became politically the most volatile districts of the city in the later part of the year.[23] Moreover, during the epidemic large numbers of workers gave up their jobs and left for their villages in Bihar. This led to temporary labour shortages in a period when the jute industry was expanding and created a favourable environment for collective bargaining by workers.[24] The post-War economic crisis generated widespread discontent among various sections of industrial workers which was gradually transformed into a political movement against the colonial state through interaction with the growing nationalist and pan-Islamist political trends.

The Making of a Protest Mentality: 1918–22

The Bengal Administration Report of 1919–20 observed that the extraordinary prices of foodstuffs, which reached a peak in September 1919, started declining in the province from 1920 onwards and the import of Burma rice 'put a stop to any crisis in local supply'. According to the report the economic condition of the wage-earning classes also stabilized in 1920. There were even signs, it was claimed, that the cultivators had benefited by the rise in the prices of agricultural products.[25] It would be wrong to accept the enthusiasm of this report regarding the improvement in living conditions as several other government records demonstrate that real wages of workers plummeted again in the mid-twenties. However, it is true that economic conditions improved in Bengal from the 1920s onwards in comparison to earlier post-War years. Yet this improvement in economic condition did not lead to political tranquility. On the contrary, from the 1920s strikes swept across the jute industry in Calcutta and the labour movement gained momentum. This shows that although the declining living conditions played a crucial role in creating widespread unrest, the strikes of this period were not simply a product of the economic crisis alone. Changes in the political environment of Bengal in the closing years of the War influenced workers' attitudes to the economic crisis and helped in the formation of a mentality of collective protest against employers, the colonial state, and sometimes Indian traders.

The War exposed the Indian people to world events. The participation of Turkey, for example, in the War against the British led to a widespread campaign organized by pan-Islamic groups against the colonial state. The Pan-Islamists had made concerted attempts to build a support base among Muslim workers since 1910 as the latter constituted a vast majority of the Muslims in the city.[26] According to a 1914 police report, the Pan-Islamists employed an agent called Hyder to preach *jehad* (holy war) among Muslim mill employees. Police also alleged that extremist Hindus in Chandannagar and Telinipara aided the Pan-Islamists in such campaigns.[27] In 1918, the Pan-Islamists stepped up their activities among Muslim workers to enhance their support base. The news of the growing labour movements in Europe and the Russian revolution made these politicians aware of the potentialities of a collective and organized labour movement in Bengal; hence they devoted their attention to the Calcutta workers. The *Risalat,* an Urdu newspaper of Calcutta sympathetic to the Pan-Islamic cause, claimed soon after the Russian revolution, that its main task was to educate the opinion of 'lower class' Muslims in the art of politics 'so that Moslem labourers become more powerful than the labourers of Europe.'[28]

In their attempts to mobilize Muslim workers, these Pan-Islamic newspapers adopted a rhetoric of deprivation, arguing that Indian Muslims were persecuted by the British government.[29] This propaganda sometimes combined an anti-government campaign with hysterical outbursts against Christians and Jews and was pregnant with messages of religious revivalism. For example, on 28 February 1920, Abdul Bari at the Khilafat Conference at Calcutta, reciting a verse from the Koran declared, 'this holy book has said that they (Muslims) should never think of friendship with the Jews and the Christians' and also added that 'if they (Moslems) give up their lives in the cause of religion, thousands of Moslems would grow up out of each drop of blood they would shed.'[30] No doubt, the extreme tone of the speech created a hysteria among the crowd and according to an intelligence report, 'as the speaker finished the speech and proceeded to take the seat, a large number of audience who were seating on either side of the passage leading to the dais approached the Maulana and kissed his hands.'[31]

In February 1920, leaflets of the Khilafat committee appealed for political *hartal* in the name of religion and described contacts with the government a sin for the faithful.[32] The Khilafat pledges were based on religious vows called *Ekrar nama* which declared unambiguously that '[w]e the undersigned are taking this vow that if the question of Khilafat is decided against the views of the Indian Mussalmans, then from the date, which will be fixed by the central Khilafat committee, we shall cut off all ties with the government according to the decision of the committee.'[33]

This clear use of religion appeared to have given a moral legitimacy to the political struggle of various groups of Muslim workers who had waged many protest movements against European factory officials and the police on various issues ranging from work-place grievances to municipal policies. This was evident in the way workers justified their participation in the contemporary political movement. From November 1921, under the leadership of C.R. Das, workers in large numbers started courting arrests along with volunteers of the Bengal Congress.[34] They were also joined by boatmen of the Hooghly river. The *Amrita Bazar*'s description of a trial scene of volunteers of working-class background at Jorabagan *thana* (police station) on Tuesday morning on 21 December 1921 reveals a deep influence of religion on them:

All the accused being asked by the magistrate said they were volunteers and were asking shopkeepers to close their shops on 24th. One of the mill hands, Jamuna Kaur, stated that he was a volunteer and would go to jail gladly for the country because he knew that there would be swaraj on 28th.

Another mill coolie Golam Jarhat of Rishra said that he came to Calcutta to request his countrymen to observe hartal on 24th.

Court: Do you know why shops will be closed on that day?

—I don't know.

—Do you wish to give any undertaking?

—No, I have taken up this work in the name of God and country.

Many Muslim workers tended to justify political strikes as a religious obligation and thus a matter of conscience. In the court, an elderly mill coolie could not explain the objective of hartal but stated that 'his conscience told him to organize strikes and so he was preaching this among his countrymen.'[35]

The post-war years also witnessed a new interest in the labour movement among politicians other than the Pan-Islamists which contributed to the strengthening of the labour movement in Bengal. The Director of the Industry and Labour Department in 1921 noted in an article that the process of organizing strikes was 'lubricated by the public discussion in the newspapers and by the active interest which was taken in some strikes by publicists not belonging to the working class, who began to express on behalf of the working men arguments regarding labour which had hitherto been heard [more] often in western countries than in India.'[36] Many Indian politicians also anticipated that workers would be enfranchised by the Montague-Chelmsford Reforms that were in the offing and tried to build up connections among various sections of workers. These political debates, discussions, and campaigns informed and influenced workers' politics.

The constant newspaper propaganda against the government's failure to tackle the cloth crisis also influenced political opinion among the poorer classes. Though very few workers were literate, stories published in the newspapers in periods of economic crisis and high political drama were often discussed in tea shops and roadside eating places in suburban towns. Thus newspapers had few readers but a larger audience among the urban poor. Newspaper reports made various sections of the working poor aware of the misery faced by the people across the country due to the economic crisis and used it to campaign against the 'inefficiency' of the government in tackling everyday problems of the ordinary people. The Bengali and Urdu press accused the government of complete inaction to deal with the cloth crisis.[37] The disappearance of salt and clothes created widespread political discontent cutting across all social divisions. Demands were also raised for abolition of salt duties.[38] Finally, the issue of boycott of foreign clothes returned to the front lines of Bengali newspapers. The *Nayak* called for a revival of the indigenous textile handloom industry and boycott of foreign clothes which to a large extent anticipated Gandhian propaganda during the non-cooperation movement:

The people of Bengal, both Hindu and Mussalmans, should also swear by God and their motherland never to use foreign made clothes, however fine they may be. [emphasis mine][39]

This line of argument was picked up by various other Bengali newspapers who started a campaign for revival of indigenous industry and the boycott of foreign clothes.[40]

Haat and bazaar looting by [the] lower classes again led to confrontation with the police and created a widespread anger against police action.[41] Police brutalities heightened the poor people's anger. On such occasions, the police were manifestly anti-poor and this created a mentality of non-cooperation with the police among the lower classes. The *Nayak,* a widely circulated newspaper of Calcutta, described the situation in dramatic language:

The policy of terrorism on which the British system of rule is based finds its fullest expression in the hands of police ... The *pahara wallahs* rarely know how to address civilly the illiterate rustic. Because of this prevailing spirit of dread of the police on their part, the public generally give the former as wide a berth as possible and never voluntarily render them any assistance.[42]

Stories of illegal confinement of coolies in mill town lockups were published in the Bengali press and this generated widespread discontent.[43] According to a newspaper report, anger against speculation and hoarding made looting—in the perception of peasants and workers—a legitimate form of protest against the 'cloth famine'.[44]

In this rebellious political situation, the contrast between low and almost stagnant wages and high profit and unprecedented boom in the jute industry generated widespread discontent among workers. In the war period the jute industry experienced rapid growth. The demand for sand bags had led to an artificial increase in the production of jute cloth while raw jute prices collapsed due to disruption in world trade.[45] The gap between low expenditure on raw materials and the swelling prices of gunny bags produced an unprecedented rise in profits for jute industrialists.[46] New factories were opened and [the] number of looms in old factories increased rapidly.[47] This led to massive expansion in the industry's workforce from 158,261 in 1913 to 242,652 in 1923 (or nearly 34.77 per cent increase) which was never experienced in the history of the jute industry in the entire colonial period.[48] In such circumstances stagnant wages were regarded by workers as evidence of blatant discrimination by the European employers and the government. In a note to the Home Secretary, Government of India, the

Chief Secretary to [the] Bengal government observed that 'the high cost of living has caused suffering and discontent and the sufferers ... are inclined vaguely to attribute their misfortunes to Government or their employers, who in the case of the concerns employing large bodies of industrial labour, are mainly European firms.'[49] In a period of rising prices a situation of stagnant wages helped turn workers against their immediate bosses like the burrababus. Popular anecdotes appearing in the columns of the trade union journal *Karmi* reflect this mentality clearly. The following dialogue is illustrative of such an attitude:

An employee in an European concern asked his colleague about their monthly salary 'Did you hear news of any increase Bipin?' The colleague answered, 'Yes, an increase in the rent of houses, in the prices of the cloth, rice and the other daily expenses.' The indignant colleague again intervened, 'I want to know about increase in pay.' The other person replied, 'well the burrababu actually pleaded with the sahib for an increase in the salary of all the employees. The sahib became very angry with the request but he increased only the salary of the burrababu and not ours!'[50]

Thus the price rise and the ensuing economic crisis created the conditions for the formation of a protest mentality among workers, a consciousness forged by a variety of political movements and campaigns and one which found expression in strikes and widespread anti-trader riots.

The Politics of Protest: Riots and Strikes in Mill Towns of Bengal

From 1918 onwards different sections of urban workers organized strikes demanding increase in wages. In this period, workers organized a series of strikes independent of any direct nationalist influence. They sustained their effort through their connections in the slums and neighbourhood and extended it all over the mill belt. Through these strategies jute workers emerged as an independent political force who were capable of challenging the powerful combination of employers and the colonial state.

The first strike wave began in the mill towns from April 1918. In March 1918 the Hooghly Jute Mill workers went on strike demanding a wage increase.[51] On 9 April, weavers of Kankinarah Jute Mill in Bhatpara 'petitioned' for an increase in wages to meet the rising cost of living. Without a satisfactory answer from the management they left work on the morning of the 9th and immediately the mill manager called for police help. A military detachment arrived from Barrackpore who dispersed the striking workers. The manager of the mill, however, later promised to consider the workers' case.[52] On 8 May 1918, again, the weavers of South Baranagore Jute Mill went on strike demanding a pay increase.[53] In September 1918 coachmen in the city stopped plying their trade, demanding higher rents. Jute bailers at the Sealdah Mills stopped work in October demanding a wage increase. Workers at the Khidderpur Dock and railway workers at Kharagpur also put down their tools in December 1918 for the same reason.[54] Strikes for pay increase also cut across racial barriers. European pilots of Calcutta port went on strike in August 1918, demanding a wage increase.[55] In January 1919 disaffection spread among workers in Kharagpur railway workshop and a strike situation prevailed there for nearly a month.

In most cases workers failed to realize their demands through strikes, which increased their frustration. At a period when the possibilities of collective bargaining declined, workers directed their attacks on traders and thus tried to establish a 'popular' control over inflationary tendencies. In this situation the campaign of the Bengali press against alleged 'profiteering' by Marwari traders created an environment of anger against them in Calcutta.[56] Popular unrest against Marwaris and the government reached its height in September 1918 when rumours were afloat about government reluctance to take action against the Marwari traders despite large stocks of clothes being piled by them in Calcutta.[57] With the gradual deepening of the economic crisis all over Bengal these grievances increased further.[58]

As a result of a powerful campaign organized by the Pan-Islamists, discontent among the Calcutta proletariat reached a point of outburst against Marwari traders and the government in September 1918. In Calcutta city the mobilization for this campaign began as an opposition to the publication of a derogatory remark on Prophet Muhammad in the *Indian Daily News*.[59] On 4 August the Bengal Muslim League passed a resolution condemning the news item. On 11 August the Anjuman i Mainul Islam, at a meeting in the Indian Association Hall in Calcutta resolved to hold an all-India Muslim conference on 8 and 9 September on Muslim grievances. On 13 August the Bengal Provincial Muslim League wrote a letter to the *Indian Daily News* demanding an immediate apology. By the middle of August, Fazlul Huq, who remained aloof from the agitation, sent a set of questions to the Bengal Legislative Council demanding a discussion on the subject. On 21 August the *Indian Daily News* added fuel to the fire by publishing a rejoinder to counter 'calumny engineered by vernacular newspapers' against it.[60] Pan-Islamic newspapers transformed the issue into a general crusade of the Muslims against the government.

Interestingly, workers interpreted this militant rhetoric against the government as an opportunity to settle their grievances with the Marwari traders. For long, Muslim workers and even poorer Hindus blamed Marwaris for their eviction from central Calcutta and subsequent loss of livelihood.[61] Most of the evicted Muslim workers migrated towards Muslim-dominated mill suburbs like Garden Reach.[62] Furthermore, Marwari enthusiasm for contribution to the war loan fund was viewed as a bribe to the government to prevent action against hoarding.[63] Thus, in the context of the postwar economic crisis anti-government Pan-Islamic rhetoric stimulated many Muslim workers to organize radical action against the Marwari trading classes. In fact, Pan-Islamists declared the forthcoming convention as an all-India meeting of the Muslims to redress all wrongs inflicted on the community.[64] While the leaflets of the Pan-Islamic leaders described the coming convention as a 'meeting for the protection of Islam', the organizers emphasized on the resolution of the economic hardships of the people, including the cloth crisis.[65]

Despite pan-Islamic appeals for unity, the propertied Muslim leaders who had always been interested in constitutional bargaining felt threatened by the Khilafatist campaign.[66] Their representatives quickly sought to demonstrate their loyalty to the government through a meeting with the governor.[67] The governor expressed concern about the potential for violence following any meeting convened by Pan-Islamists in Calcutta where the Muslim poor were already tense owing to a range of economic grievances. Some of these Muslim notables were attempting to explain to the president of the reception committee of the All India Conference that such a meeting would precipitate a situation worse than the Mutiny.[68] These fears led them to seek police protection on the night of 9 September when mobs of the poor of both communities threatened to overrun the city.[69]

The attempt to stop the meeting escalated political tension in the city. While the organizers were resisting the government's attempt to scuttle the conference, Muslim workers joined the fray when rumours about a Marwari conspiracy to deprive them of clothing were floated.[70] Bakr Id and Durgapuja were appoaching, and the cloth crisis assumed a new significance since new clothing—a ritual requirement—on these festive occasions, was by now beyond the reach of both poor Muslims and Hindus.[71] There were also rumours about Marwari designs to evict the poor from central Calcutta slums.[72] These rumours played upon the fears of economic insecurity among Muslim workers and created a bitter animosity towards Marwari traders, the loyalist Muslims, and the government.

As a result, when groups of poor Muslims gathered at the Nakhoda mosque for the conference, heard that the leaders of the reception committee were to meet the governor to try to remove the bar on the Conference, they bitterly opposed the deputation. Believing it to be a futile exercise, they shouted that 'there was no use [to] going to the treacherous governor, as he would not hear anything after having taken 14 lakh of rupees' from the Marwaris. 'In the opinion of the *badmashes*,' according to one daily newspaper, 'Keshoram Poddar [a rich Marwari cloth merchant] is reported to have advanced a crore of rupees to the war loan fund, out of which Rs 66 lakh have gone towards the war loan and the balance has been divided between the governor and the police.'[73] In other words, the crowd shouted slogans which were related more to their economic grievances and directed against the Marwari traders and the government. However, no strong anti-Hindu feelings were displayed by the protesters. During the march, Muslim workers neither mentioned the paragraph in the *Indian Daily News*, nor did they talk about the Sultan of Turkey. When shouting slogans against the Marwaris, workers accused the traders of adulteration—an accusation without any communal content whatsoever.[74] In other words, workers interpreted the Pan-Islamic programme as an opportunity to protest against the city's traders.

The trouble in the city started when the police prevented the procession from advancing towards the governor's house at the Lalbazar crossing. Kalami, a leading Urdu journalist, requested them to return back to the mosque. While returning to the mosque, a large section of the protesters gathered on Halliday street and a conflict ensued between the guards of the rich Marwari houses and the Muslims. One Sikh guard of the Birla family allegedly fired upon the Muslims on the street.[75] This started the riot which continued for two days when the lower classes of both communities looted shops and houses of the rich people indiscriminately.

The Muslim jute mill workers of Calcutta played an active role in this unrest and attempted to close the mills. Muslim workers in the Ganges Jute Mill of Howrah struck work to join the meeting in Calcutta. The European manager of Lansdowne Jute Mill was mercilessly beaten by workers and the

Beliaghata Jute Mill workers looted nearby houses.[76] On 10 September a large procession of mill workers from the Gardenreach area tried to enter the town, allegedly made up of fanatics whose bare bodies were smeared with ashes. But as the procession came near a bridge, the military forces fired upon the workers and the accompanying children. According to eyewitness accounts, the workers were peaceful and were proceeding towards the Nakhoda mosque in central Calcutta.[77] This unprovoked military firing into large numbers of unarmed workers probably created an even deeper mistrust of the *sarkar* (government) among the jute mill hands.

However, despite official anticipation, the so-called 'communal riot' did not lead to clashes between Hindu and Muslim mill workers in industrial towns. Rather, the violent events of September 1918 represented a conflict between Marwari traders and police on the one hand and Muslim workers on the other. Even contemporary newspapers portrayed the riot not as a religious conflict, but as an outcome of the economic crisis which angered various sections of the urban poor against Marwari traders and the government.[78] This became particularly evident in the selective attacks by rioters on European police and Marwari traders. It is important to note that Bengali Hindu police officers on duty were not attacked; often stray violence against them turned out to be 'the work of upcountry Hindu rioters'.[79]

Thus, the campaign of the Pan-Islamist leaders generated tensions which went beyond their control. The Pan-Islamist leaders became helpless before such widespread mass violence. The riot started in the city when the leaders of the movement were negotiating with the governor. As the news of the riot reached these leaders, they were reluctant to leave the safety of the governor's palace in order to avoid hostile attacks from their followers.[80] Finally, after police suppressed the violence, Nazamuddin signed a government leaflet calling off the agitation.[81] It is thus impossible to view the riot as an evidence of the growing ability of Muslim leaders to exploit religious grievances in their favour. The September riot had a long-term impact on the political strategies of the Congress and the Muslim League in Calcutta. The riot of 1918 made the nationalist leaders aware of the fact that if the nationalists organized a mass movement that included urban workers to press for more political reforms, it would possibly go beyond their control. Yet, the leaders also could not ignore the simmering discontent among the working-classes which was gradually leading towards confrontation with the government.

By the middle of 1919 the dissatisfaction among workers in the mill towns around Calcutta was gathering strength and found expression in strikes and anti-trader violence. In 1919, a four day working week was introduced in the jute industry which reduced the earning of jute workers while the cost of living increased by 11.7 per cent over the previous year. Fearing widespread discontent, some mill managers granted 20 per cent increase in bonuses to their workers.[82] However, soon after, a long strike was organized in the Lawrence Jute Mill which ended in failure. In this period employers were trying to reach short-term working agreements among themselves and long strikes only served their purpose. Realizing the futility of collective bargaining at a period when the mills were working 'short time', workers resorted to bazaar looting. The government immediately took measures to control the price rise.[83] In a way they successfully deployed their strategies to direct government attention to their plight.

By the autumn of 1920, the real wages of jute workers plummeted again.[84] Strikes swept across the industry from June 1920 onwards.[85] From September onwards the intensity of these strikes, in terms of loss of man-days and number of striking workers, increased dramatically.[86] The government was struck by the suddenness of this upsurge[87], though actually these strikes were a culmination of a six-month period of labour unrest in the industry.[88] In fact, in January 1920 a large number of jute mill workers had ceased work demanding a wage hike. Some workers demanded an allowance to compensate wage loss for the decrease in number of weekly workdays from 5 to 4 and in general workers demanded a 50 per cent wage increase. They actually achieved a 20 per cent, wage rise through collective bargaining. In mid 1920 the industry went back to a five day week because employers desired to increase production. Consequently the workers organized lightning strikes to realize their demand for a wage increase. In September 1920, workers of the Hooghly Jute Mill struck work demanding a 10 per cent wage increase, which the management conceded. Inspired by these successes workers ventured on new strikes at the end of October.[89]

In this period strikes were organized by the workers themselves without the intervention of the nationalist leadership and were ended when they failed to reach an agreement among themselves. At the beginning of November 1920, the Hoogly Jute Mill workers in the Shibpur–Howrah area inspired their neighbours in the slums, mainly weavers of the nearby Fort William Jute Mill, to go on strike for a pay increase.[90] On 20 November 1920, the weavers of this mill went on strike and demanded a 25 per cent wage hike. This particular strike continued for 13 days and soon gripped the entire Howrah mill district. On 25 November, Fort William workers influenced their neighbouring Ganges Jute Mill workers of Shibpur, to cease work. under the leadership of weavers and on the same day, nearby Howrah Jute Mill workers struck work with similar demands. Thus, in the last week of November nearly 27,000 workers ceased work in various mills.[91] On 2 December 1920, a large assembly of jute workers met in Shibpur bazaar in Howrah to discuss their future activities. Moulvis from Calcutta also attended. However, no nationalist leader was present in the meeting. This meeting remained inconclusive and consensus among the workers showed cracks due to lack of resources to sustain the strike. On 3 December a section of the workers of the Ganges Jute Mill attempted to return to work. By 4 December the old mill started working when nearly 700 workers reported at the factory gate.[92] Finally, on 5 December, in a meeting in the same bazaar, the workers decided to return to work.

The pattern of social organization of the workers in relation to the production system of the mills influenced and informed the dynamism of this strike movement. In the jute industry weavers constituted the main backbone of the strikes. Their longer tenure of work in the factory gave them enough manoeuvring space in labour politics. As skilled and better paid workers, they advanced loans to other workers at a period of crisis and assisted them in getting jobs and housing and even employed extra hands on daily basis. Thus, weavers were in a position to organize strikes more effectively than other workers. Furthermore, general workers, who were mostly *badlis* (temporary), did not stay in one factory for long and had little stake in long-term collective bargaining. Often during strikes, the badlis left the work-place in search of new jobs to compensate immediate wage losses. For example, between July 1920 and February 1921, during these strikes, workers lost wages to the tune of Rs 9 lakh in immediate terms and Rs 36 lakh in prospective terms.[93] Despite a long-term gain like a bonus or short working hours, this was a terrible loss for badli workers who were always on the margins of subsistence. Strikes thus started in weaving departments where skilled workers were employed, who could sustain immediate wage losses for a long-term gain, but the latter also knew that they had to resolve their demands in a short time. They could not afford to embark on long strikes which might adversely effect the unity of the weavers and other workers. In a way, competition for jobs and resources in a scarce situation ruled out any long-term combination across various departments in individual factories. The short and lightning nature of the strikes in this context was in fact a better strategy for collective bargaining. Moreover, the management in the jute industry had always viewed the expression of grievances by workers as 'insubordination' and imposed violent punishments, culminating in dismissal from jobs.[94] The lightning strikes also caught them unawares.

In 1920 workers tried to overcome these internal constraints by extending strikes to different factories, thus extending the arena of confrontation with the mill management and local propertied elites. Striking jute workers tried to take advantage of the contacts within slums in expanding conflicts to other factories. Sometimes the same person worked as a part-time worker in various factories and spread the news of the strikes. Cohabitation in slums and bazaars by workers employed in different industries also helped in spreading strikes in different factories. Workers from the same localities offered help in picketing other industrial concerns.[95] These networks helped workers to quickly spread strikes across the mill towns through concerted actions. For example, on 25 November workers in the South Union Jute Mill at Metiaburz went on strike for better yarn and demanded a 25 per cent rise in wages.[96] Receiving this information, in the same month the Gouripore Jute Mill weavers struck work demanding more wages and better yarn. Immediately, strikes spread to the neighbouring Reliance Jute Mill at Bhatpara.[97] Weavers in the Baranagore Jute Mill ceased work again on 8 December 1920. They returned to work when the weavers were convinced that the Howrah workers were not granted any wage increase.[98] On 14 December, strikes started in the North Union Jute Mill in Sealdah when European assistants took action against weavers for bad yarn.[99] This incident immediately provoked violence and the manager was assaulted by the weavers. Soon the news spread across the industrial belt and the alleged supply of bad yarn caused strikes in the South Union Jute Mills at Metiaburz.[100] When news of this strike reached the Chapdani Jute Mill, weavers struck work, demanding better yarn.[101] These strikes, despite being limited to different departments, spread across various factories and as a consequence had an impact on the entire industry. For example, within a week after the strike in Howrah Mills in November, industrial conflicts spread across all the mill towns around Calcutta, involving nearly 40,000 jute workers.[102]

In the mill towns, bazaars became the centre of working-class strike activities. During these strikes, workers also attempted to mobilize resources in the bazaars by coercing shopkeepers to keep prices low during these periods. Workers looted bazaars mainly owned by zamindars to ensure low prices of food items during strikes.[103] Shopkeepers, who were perceived as hoarders and held responsible for soaring prices, became a target of attack. Meetings were frequently held in bazaars and through discussions in these meetings, strikers decided their course of action.[104] These locality-based mobilizations, through the network of slums and bazaars, surprised the government officials who always suspected the existence of a secret political organization among the workers.

The threat of widespread strikes at the end of 1920 led mill managers to grant concessions immediately to avoid long-drawn-out conflicts.[105] For example, in 1920 nearly all strikes were short-lived and the percentage of success was remarkably high. Out of 97 strikes that took place in Bengal in the last six months of 1920, only 31 ended in complete failure for the strikers. Even in the case of strikes extending over a little longer period between 1 July 1920 and 26 February 1921, 12 per cent of the demands of the workers were met in full, 66 per cent were settled by meeting the demands of the strikers partially, and the remaining 22 per cent ended in failure.[106]

Labour strikes in the jute mills opened up new aspects of Bengal politics. In 1890, workers developed resistance to the combination of the government and the mill owners at the local level. Strikes in this period remained confined to the individual mills. In 1890, despite some attempts made by the workers, they failed to extend the strikes all over the mill belt, while in 1921 they were able to do so. Successful strikes transformed workers into a 'formidable' and 'conscious political force' in the eyes of the commission appointed by the Bengal government.[107] In fact, on their own, workers set a new agenda in Bengal politics in this period through their strike actions. It was the success of the strikes that drew the attention of the militant nationalists to the potentialities of workers as an important political force capable of waging a struggle on their own and throwing a challenge to the combination of the employers and the state. It was these possibilities which C.R. Das referred to later in his speech at the Gaya Congress.

These strikes created a particular alarm among colonial officials who feared a complete breakdown of law and order in the jute mill towns. The administration feared a repetition of the 1918 riots in Calcutta. As Lord Ronaldshay wrote to King George V: 'the Muslim worker if aroused is capable of serious rioting as our experience in September 1918 showed.[108] Police officials in the 1920s started implementing defence schemes for the protection of mills. On 3 August 1920, the deputy inspector general of police, Burdwan range, the superintendent of police at Hooghly, and the district magistrates of Howrah and Burdwan met to plan the defence of the mill areas. The deputy inspector general of police suggested that the 'most effective and simple' form of defence would be 'to provide each mill a machine gun for use in the situation of extreme gravity.'[109] The conference recommended strengthening of the military police at Chinsura by stationing a permanent reserve force at Howrah. The deputy inspector general of police concluded: 'Having regard to the acuteness of the present situation brought about by economic and political causes, it is for consideration whether the government will not be justified in taking power for employment of a larger police force permanently stationed to cope with the strike situation, which must be admitted to be chronic at present time'.[110]

With an increase in the number of strikes, alarmed police officials considered implementing more effective policing of the workers. On 5 February 1921, the inspector general of police wrote to the chief secretary to the Bengal government that 'on examining the strength of the auxiliary force at each mill as contained in the list supplied to me, I am not at all impressed that this small force will have any deterrent effect. Crowds in Bengal have had very little experience of machine guns and the sight of a gun manned by 2 or 3 men will, I am afraid, have very little deterrent effect in the first instance at any rate.'[111] After a tour of the mill towns along the Ganges, he again wrote to the acting secretary to the Bengal government that 'I have just motored through the mill area. What we shall have to be prepared for is a general strike of mill hands in the mill area, this I think is bound to come sooner or later.'[112]

The Bengal government's fear of unrest among jute workers became so deep that they took elaborate steps not only in preventing strikes, but also planned in advance a civil evacuation. In July 1921 the Bengal government proposed a rallying post at Barrackpore where 'all the European inhabitants would assemble in the event of necessity arising, and from which the community as a whole could be moved to Ichapore—a place of strategic importance, if possible under escort.' In an elaborate scheme of European civil evacuation, the proposal said that 'it is anticipated that at least 24 hours before notice would be given before the necessity of collecting refugees at the post would arise.' The SDO and the cantonment magistrate were entrusted with the proposed task of supervising the entire evacuation. At the end, they planned to transfer the treasury to a safe place.[113] In other words, the powerful movement of unarmed jute workers could cause considerable panic among colonial officials.

Thus various sections of workers, through strikes, successfully increased their wages and also proved that they could paralyse the activities of the state at the local level. They organized their agitations independent of nationalist help. The Pan-Islamic movement in 1918 played a significant role in stimulating agitation among workers, but the latter interpreted the Pan-Islamist movement in terms of their own needs and attacked Marwari traders instead of displaying any particular communal sentiments against the Hindus. Moreover, these incidents show that a movement articulating its demands in the rhetoric of religious nationalism could stimulate the growth of class-based political action which indicates that there did not exist any barrier between unity based on class or community.

Nationalist Strategy and the Formation of Trade Unions

The leaders of the Bengal Congress had no definite political strategy even at the beginning of 1919. C.R. Das, who was perhaps the most far-sighted and secular representative of Indian nationalism in Bengal, still believed that legislative councils were a safer arena for the Congress to confront the government. In the Calcutta session of the AICC, exasperated Gandhi finally threatened to go it alone. The cloth crisis and inflationary trends, along with the Khilafatist propaganda and strike waves in the mills, created an environment of political unrest in Calcutta. Under these circumstances in December 1920, after an initial duel between Gandhi and C.R. Das at Nagpur, the Congress witnessed a pact between the two leaders. Gandhi gave his historic slogan 'swaraj within a year' in this session. Soon the Bengal Khilafat and the Congress provincial committees adopted mass non-cooperation as their goal. Yet the organizers of these movements did not agree on a common strategy for mass mobilization.

The Congress activists in Bengal continued to be divided among Gandhians, Khilafatists, and C.R. Das supporters, each pursuing their own forms of agitation. C.R. Das was keen on mobilizing workers in the non-cooperation movement through strikes in European concerns to promote the nationalist cause among them. In contrast, the Khilafatists and Gandhians opposed direct involvement of workers in the political movement and tried to restrain the strike wave in the jute mills. This was in consonance with their all-India policies as framed by Gandhi.[114]

It was the Gandhians who took the initial steps towards organizing jute workers in trade unions. Pandit Krishna Kumar Sastri, a disciple of Gandhi, travelled through the mill towns of Titagarh and Bhatpara preaching the message of the boycott movement among the workers. Muhammad Mahsin and Swami Iswar Das also preached non-cooperation in the mill towns.[115] These leaders advised workers to abandon their drinking habits and encouraged them to boycott the British courts.

From January 1921 onwards, Khilafatists like Muhammad Mahsin started building unions among jute workers. In January 1921, a union called the Bengal Central Labour Federation (hereafter BCLF) came into existence on the initiative of Muhammad Mahsin and a few sardars employed in different jute mills.[116] K.C. Raychowdhuri[117], a liberal trade unionist, was elected as the chairman of this union and Muhammad Mahsin became its general secretary. Between January 1921 and April 1922 these two trade unionists helped to set up unions in various jute mills in the Calcutta—Howrah industrial belt.[118]

The Khilafatists and Bengal Gandhians scrupulously adhered to the official Congress programme of not involving workers in the political struggle but they had little direct control over strikes. [119] In fact, Khilafatists and liberals together tried to organize trade unions to resist strike waves in the industrial belt. Between March and January 1921, the BCLF made an attempt to settle strikes and resolve the grievances of workers through negotiation with the managers. They offered to settle a strike in Saxby and Farmer's engineering works in Howrah—an offer rejected by the management. In March 1921 they intervened in the Lilooah railway workshop strike and finally did settle it through the mediation of C.F. Andrews.[120] These events show that the BCLF leaders, true to their Gandhian ideology, tried to end industrial disputes and strikes in the mills through negotiation. In fact, the 'sufferings of workers' during the Lilooah strike convinced these trade unionists of the 'human wastage involved in long-drawn strikes'.[121]

Muhammad Mahsin, like earlier swadeshi trade-unionists, depended upon intermediaries in the mills to build up unions. They succeeded in establishing contact with sardars in the mills and expanded the network of the union among the latter. By April 1921 the BCLF called for a constitutional conference of affiliated unions. On 17 April 1921, seventeen affiliated unions of the BCLF attended the conference in the Federation Hall of Calcutta. Nearly all the mills on the banks of the Hooghly sent their representatives. According to a newspaper report, most of these delegates were jute mill sardars who represented jute factories located at Cossipore, Barrackpore, Ghusri, Konnagar, Jagatdal, Ichapore, Bally, and Chapdani.[122] The presence of these factory sardars at the conference suggested a close correlation between the sardars and the activities of the BCLF office-bearers.

Mahsin, the general secretary of the Federation, clearly indicated his inclination to establish sardari control over workers which appeared to him as the only institution capable of preventing sudden strikes in the jute mills. In his speech at the conference, Mahsin declared that 'sardars exercised the influence of benefactor within the mills and outside; they were the de-facto judges.' He deplored the fact that sardars now exercised very little control over common workers 'who have found them to be instruments of their capitalistic masters.' He claimed that workers were confused and this led to strikes in the jute mills. In essence, the federation of unions which emerged in the wake of the strikes did not have roots among workers but was controlled by intermediaries like the sardars.

The BCLF aimed at creating a better industrial relationship in the jute industry through conciliation between employees and employers and emphasised on its commitment to oppose strikes in the mills. The social and political motive behind the formation of the union was explained in a message by Andrews which was read in the conference where he mentioned:

I was very anxious to take part in it (the conference) because I had recently seen of the condition of the poor workers during the Lilooah strike which has made me realise more than ever the immediate need of a labour federation to help the labouring classes to obtain what is just, without the terrible human waste and suffering of a great strike.[123]

However, the conference did not reach a consensus on the pattern of functioning. C.R. Das challenged several articles of the proposed constitution of the union. He urged that affiliated unions of the federation must be purely Indian bodies and wanted more financial autonomy for the affiliated unions at least. However, Maulana Akbar and Mahsin explained the situation in Urdu to the mill sardars who supported Mahsin's proposal. Hence Das did not carry much weight in the union. This became evident in the functioning of the union in the latter part of the year.[124]

The BCLF throughout its brief career opposed strikes and supported mutually-agreed industrial conciliation between workers and the management. The BCLF leaders opposed C.R. Das when he supported the steamer strike in East Bengal to protest against atrocities committed on tea garden workers at Chandpur railway station. In a meeting convened by the BCLF, Shyamsunder Chakrabarty, J.L. Bannerjee, and Mahsin condemned both the police *lathi* charge on tea garden workers and the strike aided by C.R. Das and his supporters in East Bengal Railways and Steamer Company. They even bribed a *serang* of the East Bengal Steamer Company to oppose the strike.[125] Yet the BCLF was in a delicate situation in 1921 when popular protest against jute mill managers was escalating.

Despite attempts by the BCLF to persuade workers not to press for sudden industrial action, strikes continued in the first half of 1921 as inflation eroded the gains from the 1920 wage hike.[126] The majority of the strikes had purely economic causes, but the most serious strikes of this year were caused by racial distrust and political feelings prevalent at the time.[127] For example, in April 1921 a jute mill manager in Howrah was beaten up by workers when he tried to deduct a fine from their bonus for observing a political hartal. In May 1921 a rumour spread in Howrah that boys from slums were kidnapped by the managers for sacrifice at the foundation of the Ludlow Jute Mill. Soon workers in the Lawrence and Fort Gloster Mills in nearby areas went on strike and a serious riot started in the area.[128]

Ironically, it was the campaign of the Khilafatists and the Gandhians that helped in creating an environment which made non-cooperation possible. The constant campaigning by them against the government, marked by an appeal to religion, created among workers a mentality of protest against any perceived exploitative relationship and helped in the growth of a powerful labour movement. With the increasing momentum of the labour movement, prominent sardars found that they had less scope to effect compromises between management and workers. Sardars became unpopular among workers when they went against the popular political feelings among the operatives. In the Hastings Jute Factory, in April 1922, strikes broke out against a sardar who allegedly misbehaved with a woman employee of the mill. Strikers demanded the dismissal of the sardar.[129] Soon the strike spread to the nearby Wellington Mill where 300 women workers left work as they were not satisfied with their pay and demanded dismissal of a sardar who was allegedly oppressive.[130]

These strikes against sardars were not based upon work-place grievances alone. For example, the main target of strikers in the Wellington Mill was a Muslim sardar called Jaher Ali. Jaher Ali had for long been powerful in local politics which was evident from the fact that he had been a trustee of the local mosque for 42 years. He had opposed workers joining the meeting of Gandhi in April 1921. Soon his position was openly challenged in a Khilafat meeting in the slum and he was socially ostracized, a decision rescinded in another Khilafat meeting the following week. But after this incident, when five workers were dismissed for allegedly assaulting an European assistant, workers suspected that Jaher Ali had a hand in the dismissal and started agitating against him. Finally, grievances of the women workers strengthened the demand for his dismissal from the factory. By the end of 1922 Jaher Ali left the area due to widespread opposition from workers.[131] The gradual erosion in the hold of sardars over workers obviously led to a weakening of the BCLF which depended upon sardars to settle industrial conflicts.

The BCLF however protested against the involvement of workers in the political struggle. In a meeting in June 1921, leading non-cooperators like Padamraj Jain and Shyamsunder Chakrabarty declared that strikes were not part of the Gandhian political programme.[132] The Employees' Association of white collar clerical staff connected with the BCLF declared in its monthly mouthpiece that class struggle was a European phenomenon and that it had no place in India's spiritual tradition.[133] True to the Gandhian political ideology, the BCLF more than once displayed hostility not towards capitalism or domination of European capital but towards 'industrial civilization' which they believed polluted workers who were simple-minded villagers. Gandhians thus regarded these 'polluted rural folk' 'unfit' for the non-violent political struggle for swaraj. A letter to the *Karmi* by Gandhian leader Shyamsunder Chakrabarty brought out the position of the union clearly:

The high priest of the cult of Ahimsa parama dharma has fully realised that industrial workers away from ... the charm of free simple pastoral life working under brutalised conditions in mills and factories where passions and prejudices find full play are unfit for non violent political work.[134]

The Gandhian leaders, thus, not only wanted to restrain violence during strike waves in the jute mills but also regarded workers as unfit for non-violent political work. Workers, however, exerted pressure on the BCLF leaders to support their strikes. This was more evident in the final phase of the tramway strikes in Calcutta in the November of 1921. During this strike, along with Morneo, an influential Anglo-Indian labour leader, the

BCLF secretary, Muhammad Mahsin, and the president of the Employees' Federation, Mr K.C. Raychowdhury, addressed a series of meetings of tramway workers. On 29 October at a meeting of the tramway workers K.C. Raychowdhury defended the strike on the ground that it was an economic strike and not a political one.[135] He repeated his position again at a meeting at Halliday park on 3 November 1921 which was echoed by the general secretary of the BCLF-affiliated taxi drivers union also.[136] However, it appears that K.C. Raychowdhury supported the strike under pressure from workers. It became obvious that they would go on strike without waiting for the leaders to support them as happened in earlier tramway strikes.[137] The workers' perception of the relationship between their own struggle and the swaraj movement can be gauged from the speech of a tramway employee. A tramway worker, Ali Ahmed, accused the leaders of the swaraj movement, as well as office bearers of the union, of ignoring the demand of poor workers and warned them that swaraj could not be achieved without support from them.[138] Such speeches reflect the workers' expectation that nationalist politicians should support the labour movement on issues important to the workers. They regarded their strike as part of the movement towards swaraj despite vigorous denial from the official leadership.

The growing participation of workers in the non-cooperation movement was marked by an increasing attempt by them to integrate work-place grievances with nationalist politics. For example, tramway workers on their own adopted nationalist slogans and volunteered to organize political hartal with the help of workers in nearby jute mills. The report on picketing in the Belgachia tram depot in north Calcutta on 16 November brings out clearly the influence of the nationalist movements on workers:

About five hundred up-countrymen composed of some strikers and mill-hands assembled in front of the depot. They loitered around ... for about an hour with flags and drums and shouted 'Gandhi Maharaj ki jai.' and then dispersed when they definitely heard that the authorities of the company would not run cars yesterday.

The striking workers assembled at Halliday park that evening and then paraded the northern parts of the city requesting shopkeepers to close their shops on Thursday for a general hartal to protest against the coming of the Prince of Wales to India.[139] In fact, the city experienced a widespread disruption from the evening of 15 November as some militant taxi drivers tried to stop taxis and buses in north Calcutta.[140] The political strike which took place on 17 November 1921 in Calcutta to protest against the arrival of the Prince was successful due to the intervention of the workers. L.F. Rushbrook Williams, while writing the official history of the Prince's tour observed that:

The presence in the city of large numbers of upcountry men ill-educated and prone to violence, facilitated the employment of terrorism against the peaceful Bengali mercantile classes.[141]

However, such political mass upsurges among industrial workers created a distance between them and the Gandhian trade unionists. The increasing participation of workers in political movements alarmed Gandhian labour activists like Mahsin. On 2 December he held a series of meetings in Rishra, Hastings, and Wellington Jute Mills in the Hooghly district, advising workers not to participate in political strikes. Ironically, a fervent Khilafatist like Mahsin also appealed to the government to protect workers from political propaganda. Finally on 21 December Mahsin sent a telegram to Gandhi seeking his advice on the increasing involvement of jute workers in political strikes. Gandhi replied in a brief sentence: 'Labourers need not join hartal.'[142] Mahsin was swimming against the current as millenarian expectations of swaraj now combined with a new self-confidence among workers in their ability to wrest concessions from mill owners. The *Amrita Bazar Patrika* reported on 24 December 1921 that:

mill workers of some of the jute mills near Calcutta are demanding from their employers full payment of their wages this week and not part payment as is the practice in the jute mills to keep three days wages in hand while paying a week's wages. The reason for such demand is, we are told, that workers are in the belief that there will be swaraj on 29th. It is stated that authorities in one or two mills had a conference among themselves on Wednesday night but their decision is not known.

Rumours of an ensuing 'Gandhi raj' also led workers to go on strike. The 'presence of elephants' in one locality was imagined to be the 'vanguard of a Gandhi army'.[143]

Moreover, a section of the Bengal Congress leaders, who were closely aligned with C.R. Das, encouraged the workers to join the political movement. He gave a call for wider mass opposition to the use of European goods in Bengal. Das wanted to organize workers within the fold of the Congress to prevent mass upsurge outside it. He argued for the establishment of organizations representing workers and peasants interests to reconcile 'class conflict'. He argued:

the Congress should lose no time in appointing a committee, a strong workable committee to organise labour and peasantry in India. *If the Congress fails to do its duty, you may expect to find organizations set up in the country by labourers and peasants detached from you, disassociated from the cause of swaraj, which will inevitably bring within the arena of peaceful revolution class struggle.* [Emphasis mine][144]

C.R. Das here clearly addressed the educated elites, representatives of the propertied classes. Das wanted to organize 'peasants and workers' from the political perspective of the propertied elites, without allowing workers to define swaraj from their perspectives. Even the 'special interest of the workers and peasants' were to be defined by the bhadralok nationalists. Like his opponents in the colonial bureaucracy, Das wanted workers to be represented by their prosperous countrymen, denying the workers any independent role in politics. Though Gandhi and Das differed radically on the need to mobilize workers for the purposes of the nationalist movement, in terms of their nationalist commitment towards avoiding all forms of class conflict they were not far apart.

Das had for long wanted to use workers as a political base to enter institutional politics. However, the Montague–Chelmsford reforms made it clear that the government would nominate workers' representatives to the assembly. This led towards an initial setback for Das who wanted to build up a powerful political base for entering the assembly rather than simply to form a trade union. However, in the course of the non-cooperation movement, Das could build up bases in industrial pockets through independent labour leaders.

Das's followers gained support among workers in December 1921 when the expectation of swaraj—however vaguely understood—soared. By the middle of December 1921, a large number of jute mill workers started courting arrest under the leadership of C.R. Das. Lord Ronaldshay, the governor, was alarmed. He noted in his diary on 20 December 1921 that: 'We have to make arrests daily varying in numbers from 40 to 50 to over 200 and our jails are overflowing. Up to Saturday 17th most of those arrested were students; but since then nearly the whole has been mill hands; paid for the purpose.'[145] Subsequent events proved that 'bribes' alone did not inspire workers living on the border of starvation to risk their jobs and get arrested.

The government unleashed its full administrative power to defeat the Congress-Khilafat volunteers when the latter called for a hartal on the day the Prince of Wales was due to arrive in Calcutta. The government devoted its attention particularly to the industrial belt around Calcutta. Police banned 'seditious meetings' in industrial areas and imposed restrictions on the activities of major leaders. They raised a force of civil guards and compelled the factory sardars to join these civil guards, making them responsible for law and order in the industrial belt.[146] Even then on 23 December according to the governor, 'rowdy mill hands tried to terrorise the people.' The police arrested nearly one thousand workers to foil the attempt.[147] This finally led to a partial failure of the hartal in Calcutta on 24 December. The governor claimed a victory over the non-cooperators as Indians gathered in large number on the racecourse to cheer the Prince.[148] However, this optimism turned out to be unfounded.

In fact, from December 1921, despite the absence of the major leaders there were daily 'battles' between the forces of law and order and Congress activists in Calcutta and the industrial belt. [149] The police often were so demoralized by the widespread opposition to their activities that they were sometimes withdrawn from the spot of conflict.[150] The police commissioner also observed that ordinary policemen were not free from sympathies for the swaraj movement.[151]

Workers and the ordinary policemen in Calcutta were from the same social background. The latter increasingly exhibited their discontent against the government. They combined economic grievances with 'patriotic duties'. Again, religion was utilized by the agitators to build up consensus among ordinary police constables. In the month of March a postcard written in Hindi was circulated among the police asking

All police constables of Calcutta police force including Hindus and Mussalmans are hereby informed that we already submitted a petition for the increment of our pay but government did take no notice. We are serving as police constables to be full at our bellies. Now we must submit another petition and will be united together and strike our works from the 15th June 1921 at 10 a.m. ... Hindus will take beef and Muslims take pig if they do not agree with the proposals. You must vow the same and after reading this card hand it over to others.

The Calcutta Police formed their own association and pressed for a redressal of their economic grievances. A few even resigned from their posts and left for Bihar, shouting slogans of non-cooperation.[152] Common policemen like workers pushed forward their economic demands and religion became a source of their inspiration.

In January 1922, the number of working-class volunteers available for courting arrests declined temporarily bringing respite to the embattled commissioner of police.[153] But strikes were hardly over. At the end of January the nationalist leader Swami Dinananda, in a meeting of the Titagarh Congress Committee, spoke of organizing union branches in every factory to sustain the agitation. In the Titagarh Jute Mill in March 1922, two workers attacked the manager when one popular British supervisor was dismissed. Some days after this incident police tried to arrest these workers. Immediately other workers rushed out of the factory shouting 'Gandhi Maharaj ki jai'. They requested the police to release the two men. When their requests failed, the police were attacked. In retaliation the police opened fire, killing two workers and injuring forty more.[154] The key factor in this strike was the slogan 'Gandhi Maharaj ki jai' which became the rallying cry of workers indicating how they adopted nationalist slogans and utilized them to press their demands. The strike also indicated that despite racial ill-feeling between workers and the management, workers were ready to take up the cause of those British whom they regarded as their friends.[155]

The new confidence of the workers irked mill managers who could not accept the new organized opposition of workers to managerial dictates. For example, in March 1922, a strike occurred in the Titagarh Paper Mill over workers' objection to the introduction of tickets to control their working hours which allegedly increased their work load but reduced their earning. They also demanded compensation for a worker who died in an accident while working in the mill. Mr Bookley the manager of the factory complained to Mr K.C. Raychowdhury, who came to mediate the strike, that the arrogance of the workers was getting out of hand.[156]

Working-class participation in the nationalist agitation eroded the influence of the BCLF. In this period of intense nationalist agitation the BCLF collapsed and faded into oblivion. In April 1922 the BCLF treasurer resigned, accusing Mahsin of accepting money from the Congress thus establishing an undesirable link between political parties and the BCLF.[157] However, the collapse of the BCLF did not have much impact on labour politics. With its repeated opposition to popular strikes the organization had already lost its base among workers. It came to be identified with the institution of sardari in the jute mills but soon the influential sardars also realized that the popular tide of the nationalist movement would wipe out their personal influence if they opposed such strikes. As a consequence they might have made a silent retreat from the BCLF, causing the organization to collapse.

In the first three months of 1922, leaders of the Congress in Calcutta presided over a movement over which they had little control. In rural areas, violating the dictum of the Congress leaders, peasants in many places resorted to a 'no rent' campaign. The fear of a peasant uprising posed a perennial threat to the Bengali bhadralok. The rise of a militant working-class movement only added to the burdens of the Congress leaders. The situation seemed grim to the followers of C.R. Das as well, who also had no definite political goal in their attempt to mobilize jute workers, except for using them in courting arrests. The Bengal Congress leaders realized that the non-cooperation movement had now gone beyond the control of the elites. They also felt that a politically assertive peasant population who lived under the direct economic domination of the Hindu propertied bhadralok would threaten their control over the rural economy. Gandhi's withdrawal at the final hour provided a way out for their dilemma.

Despite the formal withdrawal of the Congress-sponsored non-cooperation, political strikes continued in various factories in order to avert the dismissal of their colleagues arrested during the non-cooperation movement. In March 1922, workers in the Northbrooke Mill demanded the dismissal of a sardar who allegedly opposed re-employment of those employees who were arrested on the charge of organizing a political hartal.[158] Strikes on issues of work-place grievances continued undisturbed. In July 1922, 8,000 workers in India Jute Mill at Sreerampur struck work demanding better supply of raw jute and 25 per cent increase in wages. Nearly 2,000 boatmen employed in Bali Engineering Works also observed strike action, demanding a wage increase.[159] Gradually, in the post-non-cooperation period, independent labour leaders developed new trade unions which paved the way for the rise of socialist and communist groups in labour politics.

Conclusion

The large-scale participation of workers in the Khilafat and non-cooperation movements was a response to their heightened awareness of their political and economic grievances. This awareness emerged in the wake of inflationary conditions and a strike wave in the jute mills. The mass strikes organised on the eve of the non-cooperation movement alarmed colonial officials who feared a collapse of law and order in the industrial belt. The Congress leaders had little to do with these strikes. The strikes also exposed both the weaknesses and the strengths of the labour movement. In the jute mills, strikes were organized by skilled workers and did not always reflect the needs of the vast majority of casual workers who supported them only in the short term. As a result it became necessary to workers to settle strikes quickly. At the same time the strike wave reflected the growing intensity of labour resistance to employers' policies and it was now clear that workers were capable of organizing strikes independent of outside support.

In the 1890s, workers responded to the oppressive measures of European employers and the colonial state by confronting police and municipal administrations. Though sometimes they won a few concessions, it was a defensive strategy. In the post-war period, they were more able to go on the offensive—to take on the alliance of the employers and the state on their own terms. Even when the Gandhian trade union leaders intervened to restrain labour militancy, workers were able to set and adhere to their own resistance agenda. In fact, the mass strikes organized by the jute mill workers during this period helped create the political environment in which other popular anti government agitations took place.

However, attracted by the religious message of the Khilafat and non-cooperation movements, workers joined the nationalist agitations on their own. Workers, through their participation in politics, sought to address their immediate social and economic grievances. Religion also played an important role in providing a moral legitimacy to their movement. Through the interplay of political, economic, and religious factors, workers developed a sense of belonging to a persecuted 'social group'.

The politics of any social class or group is not simply the function of the putative features of the class itself, but are influenced and informed by the structure of the field of action in which that class is located. This became evident in industrial workers' politics in the non-cooperation era and it would become more so clearer in post-non-cooperation politics in Bengal. In this context, the changing structure of politics informed and influenced workers' political activities. In the post-non-cooperation era, the nature of labour politics changes further.

As new links were established between the organized world of institutional politics and disenfranchised workers through nationalist organizations, the bitterness of communal conflicts and notion of shared political space between different communities that evolved through the non-cooperation movement would decline rapidly because of communal competition for positions in the political institutions of the Raj. Congress involvement in the legislative council and the Calcutta corporation in the post-non-cooperation period led to a rapid collapse in Hindu and Muslim unity at the level of elite leadership. Yet, despite the increasing communal clashes in the 1920s, the jute workers mounted a sustained defense of their interests with the help of the rising socialist and communist political movements in Bengal.

Notes

1. *Annual Administrative Report 1919–20,* pp. 1–7. Salt, which was inevitable for cooking, became particularly expensive in Calcutta and the adjoining mill towns. Source: *Prices and Wages in India*, Calcutta, 1920, pp. 140–1, The *Nayak* of 27 April 1918 reported that high price of kereosene oil was causing tremendous grievances among people. RINP(B) week ending 20 April 1918.

2. A relatively well-paid jute mill worker in 1918, such as rovers, earned only Rs 3 in a week. Apart from expenditure on food, fuel, and remittances back home, he had to spend Rs 4 or Rs 4–8 annas for a single pair of dhuti or saree. This was an obvious indication of the lack of purchasing power of the Calcutta workers. Salary of rovers is taken from *Prices and Wages in India,* Issue 37, Calcutta, 1923, p. 223. The price of the cloth was taken from *Mussalman,* 29 March 1918.

3. However, trade unionists in 1921 gave a far higher figure for price rise than the official statistics. Mr K.C. Raychowdhury, President of the Employees Association in a speech in the Bengal Legislative Council on 20 June 1921 asserted that his own inquiry shows that 'the cost has actually gone up 110 per cent, including the necessaries of life ...'. *Karmi,* the monthly bilingual journal of 'Employees Association', First Year, Vol. 1, August 1921, p. 8. From the estimates given in the prices and wages series, it appears that the wages of the jute workers also remained stagnant. *Prices and Wages in India,* Issue 37, Calcutta, 1923, p. 223.

4. The *Mussalman,* 29 March 1918.

5. *The Bengalee,* 23 April 1918, RINP(B), 27 April 1918.

6. *The Bengalee* of 20 January wrote that 'people who have not revolted during famine were revolting now, disappearance of salt, clothing and coal driving people mad.'

7. *The Bengalee,* 26 December 1917.

8. Nearly eighty-two cases of *haat* looting were reported during 1918–19. *Annual Report on Administration of Bengal, 1918–19,* p. 15.

9. Com Dept Com Branch A1 File 1-Q/6 April 1918, WBSA.

10. Com Dept Com Branch A no 2 File No Q 1/18 September 1918, WBSA.

11. Com Dept Com Branch A, 7 July 1818, From McDonald Secy to GOB to all the district officials, 10 June 1918, WBSA.

12. Com Dept Com Branch A 3 File No 10 c-1 June 1918, WBSA.

13. Com Dept Com Branch A File No 10 c-1/7 July 1918, WBSA.

14. Com Dept Com Branch A1 File No 10 c-1/7 July 1918, WBSA.

15. Com Dept Com Branch A1 File No C/7 July 1918, WBSA.

16. *Annual Administrative Report of Bengal, 1918–1919*, p. 123.

17. *Report on Municipal Administration of Calcutta Vol. I for the year 1918–19*, pp. 81–2.

18. *Census of India 1921, Vol. vi Pt. 1*, p. 63.

19. See 17 above, pp. 69–70.

20. Ibid., p. 83.

21. Ibid., p. 82.

22. See evidence of the Manager of the Belliaghata Jute Mill in Curjel Report. Com Dept Com Branch, April 1923, B77 Appendix B, WBSA.

23. The areas with high death rates from influenza and other diseases were Khidirpur, Entally, Colubagan, and Jorabagan. Predominantly Muslim in composition, these areas constituted the core of the Khilafat movement in the city. *Report on Municipal Administration of Calcutta Vol. I for the year 1918–19*, p. 80.

24. *Bulletin of Indian Industries and Labour: Industrial Disputes in India 1921–28*, Calcutta, 1930, pp. 2–3.

25. *The Report on the Adminstration of Bengal 1919–1920*, p. iii.

26. Majority of Muslims in Calcutta and the surrounding mill towns belonged to various segments of working-classes but not in materially rewarding professions. *Census of India 1921, Vol. VI City of Calcutta*, p. 107.

27. Confidential Political Dept Political Branch Files 290,1912 and 66,1913, WBSA. See also Rajat Ray, 'Revolutionaries, Pan Islamists and Bolsheviks: Maulana Abul Kalam Azad and the political underworld of Calcutta 1905–1925' in Mushirul Hasan (ed.), *Communal and Pan Islamic trends in Colonial India* (2nd edition) New Delhi, 1985, pp. 101–24; and also Gail Minault, *The Khilafat Movement Religious Symbolism and Political Mobilization in India*, p. 39. For details regarding pan-Islamist leadership and manifestly anti-police attitude in the mill towns see Home Dept political Branch File No 155/(sl-3) March 1914, WBSA.

28. The *Resalat*, 23 December 1917, RINP(B) for the week ending 5 January 1918.

29. The *Sadaqat* on 3 February 1918, RINP(B) for the week ending 9 February 1918; *Resalat* on 21 February 1918, RINP(B) 2 March 1918.

30. Home Political confidential file no 106, 1920 February, WBSA.

31. Ibid.

32. Ibid.

33. Home Political confidential file no 247, August 1920, WBSA.

34. See Sumit Sarkar, 'The Conditions and Nature of Subaltern Militancy: Bengal from Swadeshi to Non-cooperation c. 1905–22', *Subaltern Studies Vol. III*, p. 223.

35. The *Amrita Bazar Patrika*, 22 December 1921.

36. The director of the department of the industries and labour in Bengal 'Trade disputes in Bengal' *The Journal of Indian industries and Labour Vol. 1, Pt. 1*, Feb 1921, p. 71.

37. *The Bengalee*, 19 February 1918, also see RINP(B) week ending 16 February 1918, comments of *Nayak*, the *Dainik Bharat Mitra*, and the *Mohammadi*. RINP(B) week ending 2 March 1918.

38. *The Bengalee*, 3 January 1918, RINP(B) week ending 5 January 1918, the *Nayak* 24 January 1918, RINP(B) week ending 2 Feb 1918.

39. The *Nayak*, 7 August 1918, RINP(B) week ending 17 August 1918.

40. *The Bengalee* of 8 August gave a similar call for boycott of foreign clothes, the *Hitavadi* of 9 August repeated the same call, RINP(B) week ending 17 August 1918.

41. Tales of torture on a pregnant 'Muslim woman' by police filled newspapers of the day. See the *Bangabasi* 12 January, RINP(B) week ending 19 January.

42. The *Nayak* 31 January, RINP(B) week ending 9th February, 1918. See also for details of such events the *Mohammadi* 1 February, RINP(B) week ending 2 February 1918; *The Bangali* 20 January 1918, RINP(B) week ending 26 January 1918. For instances of large-scale police repression see the *Mohammadi* 18 January RINP(B) week ending 26 January 1918. The journal complained of arrests of 13,000 people in Rangpur. See also the *Nayak* 31 January 1918, RINP(B) week ending 9 February 1918.

43. The *Mohammadi*, 5 April 1918, RINP(B) week ending 13 April 1918.

44. The *Nayak*, 13 March 1918, RINP(B) week ending 23 March 1918.

45. See To the secretary of GOI Dept of Commerce and Industry From G Findlay Shirras *Index number of Indian prices 1861–1918*, Calcutta, 1919, pp. 1–2.

46. Out of forty-four jute mill companies whose dividends were reported in 1918, thirteen paid dividend of 200 per cent or more, and only nine (including two new concerns) paid less than 7 per cent. *Bulletin of Indian industries and Labour Industrial disputes in India 1921–28*, Calcutta, 1930, Also see WBSA Commerce Department Commerce Branch File 2J-I, pp. 87–134B, September 1932. Appendix II Confidential p. ii. Gillchrist's note to Govt. of Bengal.

47. *AARBM*, 1913, p. 21; *AARBM*, 1919, p. 14; and S.R. *Deshpande Report on an Enquiry into Conditions of Labour in the jute Mill Industry in India*, Delhi 1946, p. 6.

48. Ibid., p. 6 See for the impact on the demography of the individual mill towns in the first chapter.

49. WBSA Chief Secretary, Bengal to GOI Homes, D.O.2087 P,Political Confidential FN 39(1–2) 1921.

50. The *Karmi*, August 1st year 1921, Vol. 1, p. 5.

51. S.N. Gourlay, 'Trade Unionism in Bengal' Unpublished PhD thesis London, 1983, pp. 191–2.

52. *The Statesman*, 13 April 1918.

53. Ibid., 8 May 1918.

54. K. McPherson, *The Muslim Microcosm: Calcutta 1918 to 1935*, Weisbaden, 1974, pp. 36–37 (hereafter *The Muslim Microcosm*).

55. Lord Ronaldshay, My Bengal Diary, 30 August 1918, p. 153, IOL MSS Eur D 609/1.

56. The *Mohammadi* all along argued that Marwaris were responsible for the hoarding. See RINP(B) week ending 12 January, 19 January, 26 January 1918. The *Nayak* which earlier was accused by the *Mohammadi* on 25 January 1918 (RINP(B) week ending 2 February 1918) of propagating anti-Muslim feelings during *hat* looting also held the Marwaris responsible for the 'artificial crisis in cloth supply'. 13 March RINP(B) week ending 23 March 1918. The *Bangabasi* 26 April 1918, RINP(B) week ending 4 May 1918, The *Dainik Basumati*, 29 July 1918, 3 August 1918.

57. The *Amrita Bazar Patrika* of 3 September 1918.

58. *Nayak* on 18 April 1918 complained against the high prices of kerosene when the market in Calcutta was well stocked. RINP(B) week ending 27 April 1918. Salt prices also increased. *Mohammadi* 5 April RINP(B) week ending 13 April; the *Bengali* of August 1918 wrote about new high price of cloth.

59. Actual lines were 'Not far away the wayfarer describes an Arab with clear-cut features and a world of mysticism in his eyes gazing into gutter as reverently as it were his Prophet's tomb.' *Report of Non Official Commission*, p. 3.

60. *Report of the Non Official Commission*, pp. 4–6.

61. The *Nayak* 10 September 1918, RINP(B) week ending 21 September 1918. Also see *Report of the Non-official commission on the Calcutta Disturbances*, Calcutta, 1918, p. 24; The *Hitabadi* 20 September in RINP(B) week ending 28 September.

62. The proportion of the Muslims in the city proper decreased continuously from 1891 onwards. Between 1891 and 1901 the number of Muslims was reduced by 1.5 per cent, which further decreased by a rate of 3.5 per cent in the next decade. Between 1911 and 1921, there took place a further decay in the number of Muslims by nearly 8.6 per cent. *Census of India 1921 Vol. VI*, Calcutta, p. 34.

63. *The Statesman*, 29 May 1918.

64. Lord Ronaldshay, My Bengal Diary, 22 August 1918 (though the date was given 22 August it seems to be a late entree), p. 160, IOL MSS Eur D 609/1.

65. *The Bengalee*, 11 September 1918.

66. This indicates that it is not easy to depict this riot as a movement towards the development of a Muslim identity as opposed to the other communities which K. McPherson seems to argue. See *The Muslim Microcosm*, pp. 36–7.

67. Lord Ronaldshay, My Bengal Diary, 30 August 1918, pp. 156–7, IOL MSS Eur D 609/1.

68. Lord Ronaldshay, My Bengal Diary, 3 September 1918, p. 159, IOL MSS Eur D 609/1.

69. Lord Ronaldshay, My Bengal Diary, 9 September 1918, p. 174, IOL MSS Eur D 609/1

70. The *Amrita Bazar Patrika*, 3 September 1918.

71. *The Bengalee* on 10 September and The *Nayak* on 10 September RINP(B) week ending 21 September 1918.

72. The *Nayak* 10 September, RINP(B) week ending 21 September 1918.

73. The *Dainik Bharat Mitra*, RINP(B) week ending 21 September 1918.

74. *The Bengalee*, 11 September 1918.

75. *Report of the Non Official Commission*, p. 56.

76. See Suranjan Das, *Communal Riots in Bengal 1905–47*, Delhi, 1991, p. 70.

77. Ibid., p. 64.

78. *The Bengalee* of 11 September 1918; The *Dainik Basumati* on 11 September 1918; RINP(B) for week ending 21 September 1918; *The Nayak* clearly stated on 10 September 1918 in RINP(B) for week ending 21 September 1918.

79. The *Nayak* 16 September 1918, RINP(B) for week ending 21 September 1918.

80. Lord Ronaldshay, My Bengal Diary, 9 September 1918, p. 174, IOL MSS Eur D 609/1. Kenneth McPherson sees this riot as one of the stepping stones towards the establishment of a communal identity in Muslim politics of Calcutta. See *The Muslim Microcosm*, pp. 40–7.

81. Lord Ronaldshay, see 80 above.

82. See for details S.N. Gourlay, 'Trade Unionism in Bengal', p. 171.

83. The *Amrita Bazar Patrika* 10, 12, 19 September 1919, Please also see S.N. Gourlay, 'Trade Unionism in Bengal', p. 174.

84. *Bulletins of Indian Industries and Labour Industrial Disputes in India 1921–28*, Calcutta, 1930, pp. 2–3.

85. J. Sime, Letters to India, Dundee Jute Flux Workers Union, 27 April 1926. Unpublished letter to *The Statesman*. Also see *Report of the Committee on the Industrial Unrest in Bengal Calcutta 1921*, p. 1. See The Director of Industry and Labour department 'Trade Disputes in Bengal', *The Journal of Industry and Labour, Vol. 1, Pt. 1*, February 1921, p. 76.

86. For details see *The Journal of Industry and Labour Vol. 1, Pt. 1*, February, 1921, pp. 76, 79.

87. *Report of the Committee on the Industrial Unrest in Bengal Calcutta*, 1921, p. 12.

88. See 24 and 29 May 1919 and 7 June 1919, The *Amrita Bazar Patrika*; and 28 October 1919, *The Statesman*.

89. *Report of the Committee on the Industrial Unrest in Bengal Calcutta*, 1921, p. 12.

90. Ibid., p. xxxv.

91. Ibid.

92. Ibid., p. xxxv.

93. The *Karmi*, 1st year, Vol. 1, 1st issue, p. 5.

94. Managerial violence was an essential component of every day factory life. This is particularly evident from the fact that even at the height of the non-cooperation movements Curjel wrote: 'I noticed as we went around the mill he (the manager) did not hesitate to hit workers lightly with his cane.' WBSA Com dept. Com Branch, April 1923, B no. 77.

95. See 92 above, p. xxvii.

96. Ibid.

97. Ibid., p. xxxvi.

98. Ibid.

99. Ibid., p. xl.

100. Ibid., p. xliii.

101. Ibid., p. xlviii.

102. Calculated on the basis of the statistics provided in the *Report of the committee on industrial unrest*, pp. xl–xlviii.

103. For example, in Howrah on 27 November 1920, looting in bazaars were started by the striking Fort William workers. They were soon joined by striking workers from other mills. Ibid., p. xxxv.

104. Ibid.

105. The director of the department of industries and labour, 'Trade disputes in Bengal', *The Journal of Indian industries and labour Vol. 1, Pt. 1*, February 1921, pp. 71–80.

106. The *Karmi 1st year, Vol. 1*, 1st issue, p. 5.

107. The Committee which was set up to enquire into the industrial unrest, wrote in 1921: 'At all events, labour is developing a new consciousness of its own solidarity and role. We have been told on the highest authority that the development of Indian nationhood cannot be achieved without disturbing the placid pathetic contentment of masses of the people, and so far as industrial world in Bengal is concerned this requisite to political progress has already been achieved.' *Report of the committee on the Industrial Unrest*, p. 3.

108. Lord Ronaldshay to George V, 12 May 1920, The Zetland collection, IOL MSS Eur D 609/1; also quoted in Sumit Sarkar 'Subaltern Militancy', *Subaltern Studies, Vol. III*, p. 296.

109. Home Pol Confidential File no. 189 August 1920, WBSA.

110. Ibid.

111. Home Pol Confidential File no. 1 Feb 1921, WBSA.

112. Ibid., Letter no. 5IG/F 63–21.

113. Home Pol Confidential File no 152(1–2A), July 1921, WBSA.

114. See Sumit Sarkar, *Modern India*, p. 208.

115. For details of their activities see Rajat Ray *Social Conflict and Political Unrest in Bengal 1875–1927*, p. 275 and S.N. Gourlay 'Trade Unionism in Bengal', pp. 222–33.

116. Muhammad Mahsin was himself an ardent Gandhian and secretary to the Bengal Khilafat Committee for brief period in 1920. The *Amrita Bazar Patrika* 20 August 1920.

117. K.C. Raychowdhury was a liberal trade unionist who during his stay in England joined the Labour Party. After the introduction of the Montford reforms he was nominated as the Labour member in the Bengal legislative assembly in 1920. See for a brief biographical note Hiren Mukhopadhaya *Tori Hote Tire*, Calcutta, 1974, pp. 88.

118. S.N. Gourlay, 'Trade Unionism in Bengal', pp. 222–33.

119. Thus Khilafatists during the 19 March hartal in 1920 did not involve workers who were advised to take leave only for midday prayer. McPherson, *Muslim Microcosm*, p. 61.

120. Ibid.

121. The *Amrita Bazar Patrika*, 23 April 1921.

122. Ibid.

123. This account of the BCLF conference is based on two reports made by the *Amrita Bazar Patrika* on 19 April 1921 and 23 April 1921.

124. Ibid.

125. See 118 above.

126. For details of these strikes see *Report of the Committee on the Industrial Unrest in Bengal*, Calcutta 1921, p. 1A (hereafter Industrial Unrest).

127. *The Bulletin of Indian Industries and Labour Industrial Disputes in India 1921–28*, p. 5.

128. Rajat Ray, *Social Conflict and Political Unrest in Bengal 1875–1927*, p. 275.

129. The *Karmi*, 1st year, 9th issue, Jaisthya 1922, p. 198.

130. The *Karmi*, 1st year, 11th issue, Vol. 1, p. 212.

131. This story is borrowed from S.N. Gourlay, 'Trade Unionism in Bengal', p. 181.

132. *The Statesman*, 31 May 1921.

133. The *Karmi*, 1st year, 1st issue, August 1921, p. 1.

134. The *Karmi*, (English version) 1st year, March 1922, Vol. 1, No. 7, p. 85.

135. The *Amrita Bazar Patrika*, 29 October 1921.

136. Ibid., 4 November 1921.

137. In January 1921, tramway workers first went on strike and then forced the leaders to support their action. See for details S.N. Gourlay, 'Nationalists, Outsiders and the Labour Movement in Bengal during the Non-cooperation Movement' in Kapil Kumar (ed.), *Congress and Classes: Nationalism, Workers and Peasants*, Delhi, 1988, pp. 34–57.

138. The *Amrita Bazar Patrika*, 5 November 1921.

139. Ibid., 16 November 1921. Also see Hiren Mukherji, *Tori Hote Tire*, p. 91.

140. Ibid., 15 November 1921.

141. L.F. Rushbrook Williams, *The History of the Indian Tour of HRH the Prince of Wales*, Calcutta, 1922, p. 56. Reading Collection IOL.

142. This section is based upon *The Statesman* 24 December 1921 and S.N. Gourlay, 'Trade Unionism in Bengal', pp. 222–31.

143. *RCLI, Vol. V. Pt. I*, (Bengal Evidence), p. 128.

144. Presidential Address, Gaya Congress, 1922. Quoted in Sanat Basu, 'Labour Journalism in the Early 1920s: A Case study of Bengali labour journals', *Social Scientist*, Vol. II, No. I, January 1983, p. 35.

145. The diary of Lord Ronaldshay, The Zetland collection, IOL MSS Eur D 609/1.

146. Home political Confidential File 395/24, WBSA.

147. The diary of Lord Ronaldsay, 25 December 1921, The Zetland collection, IOL, MSS Eur D 609/1.

148. Hiren Mukhopadhyay, a later Communist MP from Calcutta, observed in his autobiography that on the day the prince arrived in Calcutta the city was decorated with lights which attracted thousands. But many abstained from observing

the show. Calcutta was rather ripe with rumours of the attainment of swaraj. One established doctor approached Mukhopadhyay's father to enquire whether his bank notes and company's share would become redundant after the coming of swaraj at the end of December. Hiren Mukhopadhaya, *Tori Hote Tire*, pp. 91–100.

149. Home Political Confidential File no. 14, Serial No. 17, 25 January 1925, WBSA.

150. Ibid.

151. Lord Ronaldsay' diary on 11 December 21, The Zetland collection, IOL MSS Eur D 609/1.

152. Home Political Confidential, File No. 39/13, 7 November 1921, WBSA.

153. Home Political Confidential File 14, January 1922, WBSA.

154. The *Karmi*, 1st year, Vol. 1, No. 8, Falgun 1328, March 1922, p. 20.

155. Ibid.

156. The *Karmi*, 1st year, Vol. 1, 7th issue, Magh 1328, February, 1922, p. 30.

157. S.N. Gourley, 'Trade Unionism in Bengal', pp. 222–33.

158. See 156 above, p. 8.

159. Ibid., p. 10.

6

Labour Politics and the Rise of the Socialist Movement in Bengal, 1923–29

Introduction

This chapter seeks to understand developments in the labour movement in the 1920s, especially those related to the general strike of 1929 organized in the Calcutta–Howrah industrial belt and the rising influence of the Workers' and Peasants' Party among jute mill workers. This, however, was not a unilinear development since workers also participated in widespread sectarian violence, a growing feature of the intensification of communal politics in this decade.

The chapter takes note of both of these trends and attempts to analyse the differing contexts in which workers were attracted to either. Through an investigation of the politics of legislative assembly, communal mobilizations, attempts at unionization, and the rise of socialist politics, it demonstrates that the process of the unfolding of class-based politics and communal clashes among workers in Calcutta in the 1920s was influenced and informed by changes in both national and international political and economic structures of global capitalism. It is within these divergent structural contexts that political mobilization of different sorts led to the development of differing types of workers' movements in Calcutta.

Institutional Politics and Communal Tension in Bengal: 1923–9

The sudden withdrawal of the non-cooperation movement in February 1922 by Gandhi caused a loss of confidence among the Bengali Muslim

Khilafatists in the Hindu leadership of the Congress. It now became imperative for the Congress to maintain its alliance with powerful Muslim politicians from rural East Bengal. But clashes in their social and economic interests complicated the possibility of such an alliance. On the one hand, Muslim politicians began to campaign for the rights of tenants whom they increasingly saw as a potential political constituency—a belief that had been strengthened by their experience of peasant mobilization during the Khilafat agitation. On the other hand, Bengali Hindu zamindars, who constituted an important political constituency of the Congress, re-emphasized their opposition to this land reforms. These contradictions led to considerable vacillation and infighting within the Congress and consequently the party took ambiguous positions on issues related to the political mobilization of peasants.

C.R. Das, the leader of the Bengal Congress, at the Gaya session of the Congress in December 1922, sought to resolve the issue by arguing for a return to the legislative councils. Though the Congress rejected his proposals, Das and Motilal Nehru organized a separate party in February 1923 with the purpose of organizing continuous and consistent obstruction to the government within the legislative councils.[1] Das tried to give his strategy of council entry a wider mass appeal by creating a new populist political rhetoric 'swaraj for 98 per cent'.

He explained this new political rhetoric in detail in his presidential address at the 1923 All India Trade Union Congress (AITUC) conference in Lahore.[2] Das gave 'labour' a new meaning by pointing out that 'labour represents 98 per cent of the population of India when we consider that labour also includes the peasants.'[3] Emphasizing the revolutionary potential of the labouring classes, he quoted from the Communist manifesto calling upon workers to unite as 'they had nothing to lose but their chains'.[4] Das, however, gave his arguments for socialism an ethical twist by concluding that:

The right of holding private property is useless and unjust unless it leads to higher national interests—I do not object to private property but I object to the evil in it. The selfish man will give up being selfish if he thinks less of himself and more of humanity. It is the same with the nation. Let property be so pursued, that each man will of his own accord dedicate it to the country. When people say private property be done away with, do not be misled. It is in short the evil inherent in private property that should be done away with. This is true socialism.[5]

Das thus declared his faith in charity and voluntary renunciation of wealth but not abolition of private property and was opposed to the notion of 'class struggle'.[6] Though Das repeatedly emphasized organizing workers and peasants within the Congress organization, in reality, however, he depended upon pacts and alliances among elite politicians. With an eye on forming a majority in the assembly and also to end the bitter Hindu-Muslim quarrel, Das entered into the famous 'Bengal pact' with the Muslim elite leadership in 1923. The pact conceded the Muslims of Bengal a statutory majority share in the administration and government of the province after *swaraj*. It provided for a voluntary banning of playing of music before mosques, the freedom of Muslims to perform *Korbani*, and the promise of a greater percentage of Muslim employees in a swarajist-controlled Calcutta corporation.[7] Through this pact C.R. Das also recruited new Muslim politicians to the swarajist cause, including Saheed Suhrawardy, the future Prime Minister of Pakistan.[8]

The pact generated a new hope for the solution of the Hindu-Muslim problem among many, yet it had serious limitations. It emphasized that Hindus and Muslims had separate interests and only Muslims could champion the cause of their co-religionists. This ideological premise of the Congress also might have caused the party to ignore broader issues like protection of the tenancy rights of peasants who constituted the vast majority of the Muslim population in Bengal. Such an understanding of the situation contributed, in turn, to further communal tensions.

The newspapers controlled by Hindus criticized the pact vehemently. It was represented as having betrayed 'national interests'.[9] Prominent politicians like Sir Surendranath organized a public meeting against the pact for its alleged 'anti-Hindu middle class' nature.[10] A substantial section of the *bhadralok* community felt threatened by Das' pact with the Muslims. The Hindu zamindars were afraid of the increasingly assertive Muslim peasants, and the Hindu petty bourgeoisie became alarmed by the possibilities of increased Muslim hold over official appointments.[11]

Notwithstanding these protests, Das swept the council poll in 1923, including those constituencies where white collar workers predominated. The spectacular victory of the Swarajya party candidate, Dr Bidhan Chandra Roy, against Sir Surendranath Bannerjee in the industrial seat of Barrackpur, was the glaring evidence of it.[12] The electorate included a significant number of mill employees like *sardars* and mill clerks. Through personal contacts and skilful propaganda, Das roped in labour reformers like Santosh Kumari in the Naihati–Barrackpur industrial belt[13] whose campaign helped Dr Roy win the election. In fact, among all non-Mohammedan constituencies this victory elicited the largest margin.[14]

The Swarajya party, however, could not effectively expand its base among workers in industrial centres after its victory in the legislative council and the Calcutta corporation. In the 1920s, the Bengal Congress gradually came under the control of a powerful coterie of Calcutta-based politicians, the 'big five' of Bengal, who remained lukewarm to the organization of workers under the Congress aegis.[15] The Congress instead concentrated on continuing their opposition to the government within the legislative council.

In the new legislative council, the Hindu swarajists soon developed differences with their Muslim counterparts. In the beginning the Swarajists impeded every successive move of the Government to set up a responsible ministry in Bengal. Government's budgets were refused, salaries of the ministers were not granted, and dyarchy was seriously crippled.[16] Facing these limitations, the Government immediately resorted to the age-old tactic of 'divide and rule'. In a legislative assembly elected by a separate electorate, non-swarajist Muslims were now encouraged by the government to assert their independence from the control of the 'Hindu Swarajist party'. A resolution for immediate implementation of the Bengal pact moved by loyalist Muslims was avoided by Das through an adjournment motion.[17] Muslims became suspicious of the sincerity of Hindu leaders in executing the pact. The idea gained further ground when in August 1924 Swarajists succeeded in removing a predominantly Muslim ministry.[18] The threat of communal division loomed large on the horizon.

In these circumstances the Hindu Mahasabha, backed by Marwari traders, took initiative in organizing communal propaganda from 1923 onwards. Isolated incidents of communal violence were used for this purpose. In January 1924, a small affray over a religious procession at Howrah created a tremendous reaction among the Hindu-controlled newspapers.[19] In January 1924, rumour spread in Calcutta that certain leading Hindu merchants, like Deviprasad Khaitan and Madanmohan Burman, were preparing for a show of strength against the Muslims. Swami Viswananda, a prominent labour activist, wanted to lead a procession of Hindu wrestlers who had come to Calcutta for an exhibition of martial arts. He told the city police commissioner of his plans to counter the 'anti-Hindu conspiracy' of the government and the Muslims. He wanted to induce wrestlers (now in Calcutta) to tour the country, organizing *akharas* (training centres) in the vicinity of Hindu temples where Hindus would be trained in the art of wrestling.[20]

The Swami planned to raise a 'Mahavir Dal' on the model of the Akali Dal. This *dal* (group) would be utilized to seize certain Hindu temples in Bengal from the hands of the *Mahants* and also to avenge 'the Muslim attacks on Hindus'. He recruited Krishna Tirtha Jagatguru Sankaracharya into the project. The dal's nucleus was formed in mill towns near Barrackpur where twenty-five factory *durwans* (guards) volunteered 'to give their lives for religion'. In order to recruit more people, the Swamiji approached the secretary of the Oriya Labour Association to select some strong men for the purpose. In a meeting at the Maheswari Bhavana, the Marwari-controlled community centre in central Calcutta, he complained 'no one cared to take up the agitation on behalf of the Hindu community' and argued that 'talk of Swaraj, talk of independence all is sham unless we are united and can protect our own religion ...'. He finally sent his message: 'You are strong and Hanumanji wants you in this critical juncture to come forward to purge the Hindu community of all sins and to see that the Hindu community can play its own part—glorious part which she has been playing in world's history.'[21] Such meetings further increased communal tensions. In 1924, on the day of Bakr Id a riot broke out among the jute mill hands at Garden Reach. In Kankinarah thousands of Hindu workers marched to a local mosque and kept up a barrage of music throughout the day.[22]

Hindu–Muslim tensions at the local level sharpened with the growing tensions at the institutional level. In October 1924, the Calcutta corporation ordered the removal of the remains of an arguably Muslim saint (*pir*) from New Market in central Calcutta and the decision angered local Muslim petty traders.[23] Notwithstanding Muslim opposition, in August 1925, the Advocate General of the Bengal Government ordered the body to be exhumed.[24] On 23 August 1925, the Indian Seamen's Union organized a meeting where Muhammad Daud, a veteran Muslim trade unionist, warned that 'if the body was exhumed the authorities would take the risk on their shoulders and ... no Mohammedan would tolerate the action in any case.'[25] Muslim trade union campaigning on communal issues was matched by the counter propaganda organized by Lala Lajpat Rai and Pandit Madan Mohan Malaviya among the up-country Hindus who were against the Bengal pact, Korbani, and the pir burial in central Calcutta.[26] Again Marwari traders took the most aggressive stand on the issue. In Calcutta, G.D. Birla, a prominent Marwari industrialist, argued strongly for the forcible conversion of Muslims to Hinduism through the *suddhi* movement.[27]

In 1925, as communal tensions increased, Muslims began to see the Sikh guards of Marwari houses as allies of the Hindus. So deep was the distrust of Sikhs among the Muslims that many even believed that the Sikhs were kidnapping children for sacrifice at the construction site of the new docks in Khiddirpur. In June 1925, eight Sikhs perished in a communal riot.[28] Das' death in the same year deprived Bengal of a leader who commanded respect from both Hindus and Muslims. Indeed, on 3 July 1925 during the Bakr Id festival when the Congress was holding a condolence meeting in Calcutta, the up-country Hindu and Sikh workers employed in the dock attacked Bengali Muslims for the alleged sacrifice of a cow and killed a Muslim worker on the spot. Despite the severe admonishment of Hindus by J.M. Sengupta, Gandhi, and Maulana Azad[29], an underlying tension in the area caused workers in the nearby jute mills to stop work. The situation worsened on 4 July when rumours of riots spread across the city.[30] Soon after this in Titagarh, on the day of Ganesh Chaturthi, Muslims attacked a procession of Hindus who were playing music before a mosque.[31] In Shyamnagar, another mill town, Muslims objected to loud arati (prayer) on the day of *Janmashtami*.[32] In Kankinarah, Muslim workers fought their Hindu counterparts as the latter tried to pass a local mosque in a procession, playing music. Hindu newspapers paraded these incidents as evidence of Muslim 'high-handedness'.[33]

By the middle of 1925 there emerged various communal organizations in the city. The Arya Samaj, the Mahabir Dal, and the Hindu Mahasabha became active in preaching against cow sacrifice on the day of Bakr Id.[34] In April 1925, Muslims formed their own organizations—the Tanzeem and the Tabligh.[35] Sir Abdur Rahim floated a separate Muslim party.[36] Bengali Muslim radicals lost faith in the Congress as the latter abandoned the rural improvement schemes mentioned in the manifesto of the Swarajya Party. Fazlul Haq and Mujibur Rahman organized a Muslim Council Party.[37] Both aimed at protecting and advancing the cause of the Muslims in Calcutta and in Bengal.

The constant communal propaganda and formation of parties representing exclusively Hindu and Muslim interests created an environment of communal animosity in Calcutta. On 2 April riots swept across Calcutta. An Arya Samaj procession playing music while passing before a mosque in Central Calcutta at the time of *Azan* triggered off massive communal violence.[38] Riots continued sporadically for three months. The Muslim rioters singled out Marwari merchants,[39] but the Hindus were effectively organized by Hindu communal bodies. The Hindu Mahasabha leader Madan Mohan Burman was reported to have provided shelter to Hindu rioters.[40] Hindus also distributed leaflets to boycott Muslim taxi drivers. Arya Samajists dressed as Muslims attacked Hindus in order to provoke riots.[41]

The post-riot situation witnessed a continuation of bitter communal tussles in the city. After the riots, Hindu politicians demanded that the mosques that obstructed the path of processions be removed from the main roads instead of imposing restrictions on the processions.[42] The Congress also annulled the Bengal pact.[43] The press played an active role in encouraging communal sentiments in the town.[44] In 1928, the final rupture between radical Muslim leaders and the Congress took place when the latter voted with the Europeans and the non-Congress zamindars for the government-sponsored Bengal Tenancy Protection (Amendment) Bill. The Bill was opposed by a large number of Muslim members from east Bengal and a lone Congress nationalist, J.L. Bannerjee.[45] This episode marked the final disillusionment of the radical Muslims with Congress politics. At the end of the 1920s, after the formation of the Simon Commission for new reforms, the position of the legislative assembly was marginalized in Bengal politics. A new surge of mass movements created an environment for the politics of protest.

By now the communal political competition in the corporation and the legislative council had prompted politicians to curve out a constituency among the labouring masses of the city. In this period Muslim politicians like Suhrawardy tried abortively to build a trade union base among Calcutta workers.[46] Despite the intensification of communal politics due to the political bickering in institutional politics, the labour movement experienced intensification of industrial action under the influence of the left. Apart from the Congress isolation from mass politics, the emergence of a language of class emanating from both revolutionary movements in the world and social imperialists operating within the imperial political establishment contributed to this process.

The British Imperial Establishment and Indian Labour

In the 1920s, in sharp contrast to the late nineteenth century,[47] the colonial state at various levels evinced a direct interest in labour affairs. In the late nineteenth century, despite pressures from domestic textile industries to restrict working hours in the Indian factories and strikes in the mills, few attempts were made by the state to fundamentally reform conditions of work. It was only in the post-Great War era that radical changes in international and domestic politics altered the colonial state's views regarding labour.

The most important impetus in rethinking strategies concerning labour in India came from the growing variety of labour movements in Europe and India. The Russian revolution in 1917 and the failed German revolution led by the Spartakusbund in December 1918, had a critical impact upon the imperial establishment in Britain. Moreover, the new Post-War imperial administration in Britain already included within its fold labour reformers, and the ascendant Labour Party soon replaced the Liberal imperialists as a major political force in the country. In this unsettled political climate in post-War Europe, it was regarded as absolutely necessary to establish an international organization to monitor and promote reforms in industrial relations. The new vision was to ensure the hegemony of capital through a partnership among moderate unions, captains of industry, and the managers of the state in an advanced capitalist society. This was the beginning of an experiment in establishing a corporatist form of governance.

The establishment of the International Labour Organization (ILO) in 1919, at the time of the Peace Conference, convened first in Paris and then at Versailles, marked the beginning of this experiment with new corporatist alliances. Its ideological roots may be located in the writings of two industrialists, Robert Owen (1771–1853) of Wales and Daniel Legrand (1783–1859) of France, while the real efforts began with the foundation of the International Association for Labour Legislation in Basel in 1901.[48] However, there was an immediate political aim in founding this organization. The preamble of the ILO's constitution noted that without an improvement in their condition, the workers, whose numbers were ever increasing as a result of industrialization, would create a revolution—an 'unrest so great that the peace and harmony of the world' would be 'imperiled'.[49]

To overcome these revolutionary challenges to capitalist industrial society, the ILO prescribed a tripartite alliance between labour unions, employers' organizations, and the government. This idea of alliance among representatives of capital, state, and labour unions was further reflected in the composition of the governing body of the ILO, half of whose members were government representatives of member states, one-fourth workers' representatives, and one-fourth employers' representatives. The prominent role assigned to moderate trade unions was reflected in the fact that the first chairman of the ILO conference in Washington was Samuel Gompers, head of the American Federation of Labour (AFL).[50] Britain and France were crucial players in the ILO from the beginning, but the United States became a member of the ILO only in 1934 under the Presidency of her possibly first social democratic President, Roosevelt.

The prominence of Britain in this new international organization also compelled the Government of India into rethinking its industrial development strategies. In the immediate post-War years, labour militancy nearly paralysed the functioning of the two most crucial industrial centres of Bombay and Calcutta. The emergence of the All India Trade Union Congress (AITUC) in 1920 and the active interest taken by some nationalists in labour obviously alarmed them. The idea of a corporatist alliance among moderate unions, the colonial state, and employers appeared to many in the White Hall as well as in Delhi as a perfect antidote to communists and nationalists. Hence a search began for an ideal trade unionist who could fit the bill for such corporatist alliance in colonial India.

The pressure for reform in India increased rapidly when the ILO in the first six International Labour Conventions dealt with hours of work in industry, unemployment, maternity protection, night work for women, minimum age, and night work for young persons in industry. The British government in England also faced queries from local trade unions. For example, on 22 January 1924, following the defeat of the Conservative ministry in parliament, the Labour party, for the first time in its history, formed the government in the United Kingdom. The new government sanctioned the arrest of leading Communists in India and initiated the Kanpur Conspiracy Case on 23 April 1924. A few months later the British TUC sent a delegation to the Secretary of State, Lord Oliver, to protest against the arrest of the Communists in India. Lansbury, a leading member of the TUC delegation, also pressed Lord Oliver to extend voting rights to at least the educated members of the working classes. Lord Oliver promptly blamed the British bureaucrats in India for their failure to press for further reforms in the administration. It was not only in the United Kingdom where British trade unionists voiced their concern. They also sought to expand their activities in India. In 1925, a deputation comprising a labour member of parliament and a Dundee trade unionist reached Calcutta. John Sime the leader of the Dundee Flax and Jute Union, continuously wrote in the newspaper against the exploitation of Calcutta workers.[51] Soon the new idea of social imperialism—the notion of commonwealth of primary producers in the empire—gained currency.[52]

A crucial consequence of these trends was the enactment of a series of labour laws. Between 1919 and 1929 the colonial state enacted legislations to create a rudimentary structure of industrial relations machinery. The amendment of the Factory Act in 1922, the Workmen's Compensation Act in 1923, the Trade Unions Act in 1926, the Trade Disputes Act 1928, the Maternity Benefits Bill in 1929, and the Payment of Wages Act in 1933 were products of these ideas of a rudimentary structure of a corporatist state. As legal intervention provided workers with certain legal rights, it also restricted her/his activity as trade union organizer. At the centre of these debates was a concern to create an efficient producer and a healthy trade union movement to protect the interests of workers. However, most colonial officials agreed that Indian workers were unable to represent themselves, hence they had to be represented.[53] In a similar vein, they argued that unions had to be protected from the evil influence of political agitators.[54]

A more sophisticated critique of this new act obviously highlighted the difference in the situation in the advanced industrialized countries of Europe and India. While the necessity of trade unions in Europe was readily accepted, the author argued that in India:

Industrial enterprises are still in their infancy, such organization of labour is not conducive to its welfare. Specially industrial concerns with small and limited capital can very ill afford to be met with a strong labour organization controlling and sometime dictating wages including hours of labour, housing accommodation, old age, and invalid pension etc.[55]

Thus, stringent clauses were included regarding the monitoring of funds of the union. The Trade Union Act of 1926 made the registration of a union compulsory. The government appointed auditors to supervise the funds of these unions.[56] This Act forbade outsiders from the membership of the executive bodies of the unions. The Trade Disputes Act of 1929 prohibited lightning strikes in Public Utility Services and restricted strikes in the general industries.[57] The right to picket, a crucial clause in British trade disputes legislation, was not included in the Indian Trade Disputes Act on the ground that 'it would be very difficult in India to prevent peaceful picketing ... from degenerating into undesirable form of intimidation.'[58] The government's firm decision not to pay wages to workers for the period of a strike also handicapped the unions.[59] The Public Safety Ordinances of 1929 imposed restrictions on funds being sent to India from abroad.

The government also firmly opted for selection rather than the election of union representatives to various legislative boards. The government sought to reward moderate loyalist trade unionists by nominating them to prominent positions. Yet the process of selection often defeated the government's purpose. For example, when the Secretary of State at London nominated Shiva Rao to represent Indian workers at the Round Table Conference, the Viceroy's Office telegrammed that Shiva Rao was not suitable because as a Brahmin he could not be accepted as the true representative of Indian labour. The government rejected V.V. Giri's nomination for his 'bad political record'. Instead, Lord Irwin argued that Ernest Kirk, who had been working for labour for a long time at Coimbatore, would be an ideal representative. Wedgewood Benn, the Secretary of State, dryly wrote back to Lord Irwin: 'surely, it would be incongruous to select an Englishman, however excellent his qualities, as the representative of Indian labour.'[60] The last instance demonstrated that by the end of the 1920s the government of India had lost the ability to recruit new collaborators, not tainted by nationalism or labour radicalism, to run the industrial relations machinery effectively. Nor were the upper echelons of the Indian administration, such as Lord Irwin, enthusiastic about the new idea of social imperialism.

Despite its limited impact, this legislation recognized the Indian worker as an industrial person with putative rights to engage in collective bargaining. The government reforms produced a new political language of class in the field of industrial relations and created a new arena of trade union politics. The new legal rights, initiated to strengthen the bargaining power of the working class, enabled Communist and socialist trade unionists to intervene more and more in labour politics. These unionists took advantage of the legislation offered to secure workers' rights and also exposed their limitation when the Government failed to uphold their own legislation in the field of industrial relationship. Thus the irony of the search for a colonial variant of the corporatist state was that it strengthened labour radicals rather than moderates.

Thus the nature of colonial capitalism, particularly the colonial ideological discourse of the Indian labour as peasant migrants incapable of looking after their welfare, undermined the corporatist alliance conceived by the colonial state. Paradoxically, the spasmodic colonial attempt at social engineering created the institutional context for the rise of labour radicalism. It would, however, be wrong to interpret the rise of left wing labour movement in terms of a failed colonial attempt at social engineering. The organic roots of the socialist and communist variants of the labour movement could be traced to the disillusionment of radicals with Swarajist politics and their search for an alternative path for the organization of a popular movement.

The Emergence of the Socialists: The Peasant and Workers Party of Bengal

The emergence of the communist movement in Bengal has often been attributed to the Comintern and Soviet encouragement.[61] This argument tends to gloss over the local political situation and ignore the role played by labour and peasant movements in Bengal in the development of the socialistic organizations. Rather, the roots of the left wing tilt could be traced back to the continuation of strikes in mill towns even after the withdrawal of the Khilafat–Non-cooperation movement.

In 1922, after the withdrawal of the Non-cooperation movement, as strikes in the mills continued, different groups of labour activists sought to mobilize workers. Moderate labour leaders like Moulavi Latafat Hossain and K.C. Roychowdhury,[62] with powerful connections among bureaucrats and employers, sought 'to educate workers' in trade unionism and established the Kankinarah Labour Union in Bhatpara which, however, remained modest in size.[63]

More successful than moderates was the militant woman nationalist Santosh Kumari Devi, who, inspired by C.R. Das' radical speech at the Gaya session of the Congress, started her activities among workers in the Gouripur jute mill during a strike in May 1923. At Gouripur, workers demanded the removal of an oppressive sardar. Santosh Kumari met these workers, helped them draft a demand charter, and supplied the strikers with food at her home. With her support, the workers built up an effective organization and marched nearly 32 miles to the headquarters of the Company compelling them to accept their demands.

The victory of the strikers encouraged Sanstosh Kumari to establish a labour union at Gouripur and several night schools for workers and their children at Salkea, Bhatpara, Garifa, Halishahar, and Sodepur. On 6 April 1924, she started a journal called *Sramik* (worker)[64] which published socialist articles.[65] Kalidas Bhattacharya of Bhatpara, a former nationalist revolutionary, and Bankim Mukherjee, a socialist labour activist, joined Santosh Kumari in organising the union. The union gained additional strength from the support of the British trade unionists from Dundee[66] and became the nucleus of socialist activities in the mill towns.

As the process of unionization progressed, labour activists published new journals to debate issues pertaining to labour movement. For example, press employees brought out a journal called *Samhati* which, in its first issue, appealed to the workers to unite in the name of God and declared that 'to be poor was no sin'.[67] While informing its readers about the formation of various unions, the journal criticized the Soviet political system as well as western capitalism.[68] Increasingly *Samhati* adopted a pro-socialist stance, as in a series of articles on the living conditions of jute workers Santosh Kumari emphasized the need for class-based political organizations. R.C. Mazumdar, a well-known historian, introduced the Sanskrit word '*sreni*' as a Bengali substitute for the word 'class' and traced the history of 'class' organizations in India from the ancient period. Left wing nationalists thus began examining the class organization of society in the 'Indian tradition'.[69]

While the labour movement witnessed a left wing turn, the leading nationalist labour union, the Bengal Provincial Trade Union Congress (BPTUC), influenced by the Swarajya Party, remained extremely moderate. The BPTUC was established in 1922 as a federation of unions of clerks. To Bengali clerks, it was self-evident that 'European' companies were mercilessly exploiting them. They adopted a political language of 'class awareness'[70] but there existed a contradiction between their 'working-class' political rhetoric and their social position. One of the leaders of these unions, Mukundalal Sarkar, writing in *Karmi* reminded his 'brother workers' not to forget their own 'domestic servants', 'cooks', and 'cleaners', who 'contribute daily to the smooth functioning of their life'.[71] The so called 'brother workers' who employed domestic servants and cooks were obviously bhadralok. Claiming social superiority over manual labourers, the leaders of these unions vehemently opposed the inclusion of factory workers in their federation.[72]

The nationalist silence on class issues now came under attack from two radical Swarajists—Hemanta Kumar Sarkar and Syed Shamsuddin, who became active in organizing peasant meetings in eastern Bengal demanding social and economic emancipation of the peasantry.[73] Soon many zamindars in the Congress branded these programmes as Bolshevik, and in the same breath accused peasant leader Hemanta Kumar Sarkar of spying on behalf of the police.[74]

Hemanta Kumar, however, successfully mobilized the radical section of the Swarajist party. A conference of peasant representatives was held in Bogora in eastern Bengal which gave birth to a new party called the Labour Swaraj Party of Bengal.[75] This party elected the old labour activist and barrister N.C. Sen as its president. Nazrul Islam, a radical Bengali poet, edited the new party mouthpiece called *Langal* (plough). *Langal* was to witness a change when Nazrul Islam called in his friend Muzaffar Ahmed, a former prisoner of the Kanpur Communist Conspiracy case, to assist him in the task. Ahmed slowly introduced Marxist ideas in the party.[76]

Since 1922 Muzaffar Ahmed had been making relentless efforts to build up a communist political group in Bengal. In the Gaya Congress he circulated the communist document 'A new programme for national liberation struggle' calling for the election of a national assembly on the basis of universal suffrage and the establishment of a republic in India. The emphasis was on the abolition of landlordism and nationalization of public utilities under the control of democratically elected workers' committees.[77] After the Gaya Congress, communists looked towards C.R. Das as the emerging 'revolutionary leader of class struggle' and requested him to organize a 'real revolutionary party'.[78] This hope soon evaporated and finally in 1925 the Indian communists in a conference at Kanpur established a party of their own. The new party assigned Muzaffar Ahmed the task of organising a branch in Bengal.

Aware of their lack of strength to organize an independent political struggle, Ahmed attempted to transform the Labour Swaraj Party into a 'revolutionary party of the working-class'. However, the Labour Swaraj Party had a left-wing nationalist agenda of combating the Swarajist surrender to the interests of the landed aristocracy in Bengal. This became evident in 1926 during the second praja conference—a gathering of delegates of prosperous tenants of zamindars—in Krishnanagar in Nadia district of Bengal. The conference changed the name of the Labour Swaraj Party to Bengal Peasants and Workers' Party. In this conference again, Muzaffar Ahmad tried in vain to name the new party Workers' and Peasant Party, privileging, according to Marxist ideology, workers over peasants. However, his proposal was rejected outright and the party came to be known as the Peasant and Workers Party.[79] Even the politicians who returned from the Soviet Union to India refused to side with communists.[80] Thus, despite accepting the validity of a class-based political party, Bengal radicals had rejected the idea of a vanguard organization of the working-class and rather constituted a united platform of radical nationalists. However, Ahmed was elected the editor of party's new journal *Ganavani*, and his house at 37 Harrison Road became the central office of the party. Soon many radical political activists, including communists and left nationalists, joined the PWP.

The PWP and the Development of a Militant Labour Movement in Bengal: 1926–8

In 1926 Muzaffar Ahmad wrote in *Langal* that, 'intoxicated by religion, Indian workers and peasants showed no propensity to protest against their exploitation.' He appealed to educated Indians to provide them with a 'new meaning of life.' This comfortable myth that their ideologically-informed goodwill would offset their ignorance of the realities of working-class life was rudely shaken when bhadralok PWP volunteers started organizing workers into unions. It was brought home to the organizers that they were complete outsiders and that the workers resented their intrusions. Gopen Chakraborty, the well known communist organizer realized that in order to establish a close rapport with the workers he had to share their life and work.[81] Only by taking up employment in factories could bhadralok organizers gain acceptability among workers.

Yet even then in cases of strikes and protests, it was workers who developed their own strike action. Often bhadralok organizers were not able to grasp the technicalities of the situation. For example, in 1928 workers from Keshoram Cotton Mill contacted the Peasant and Workers Party leaders to help them in their strike against the management's decision to switch over from payment by the pound to payment by the yard. Moni Singh, a bhadralok trade union activist, deputed to assist workers failed to understand why the workers were aggrieved.[82] Finally, Moni Singh met a weaver master who explained the workers' demands to him. The cotton mills in this period switched over from pound payment to yard payment, causing a decline in the salary of the weavers. Though it became clear to Moni Singh that the payment by pound could not be kept, he had no alternative but to support workers demands.[83]

The bhadralok leaders, however, proved to be effective in negotiating strikes. During the strike in Keshoram Cotton Mill, Moni Singh arranged a meeting with 'Dutta Sahib', a friend of his uncle, and district magistrate of

24 Parganas. Due to the mediation of the district magistrate, Ghanashayam Das Birla, the owner of the mill, accepted a deputation of ten workers and conceded their demands. He even paid their salary during the strike period.[84] Thus the bhadralok social connections, tinged with radical nationalist colour, sometimes helped in enhancing the bargaining power of the workers.

From 1925, the Indian economy slowly entered a period of recession leading to the systematic retrenchment of workers by railway workshops and jute factories. Since 1923, many jute mills had switched over from a multiple-shift system to a single-shift system, rendering a large number of workers unemployed. Workers resisted the curtailment of their jobs and wages through strikes. The PWP sought to transform these strikes into a concerted movement against the employers and the colonial state. They were now successful in recruiting new members and establishing new branches.

Kalidas Bhattacharya, an associate of Santosh Kumari Devi, established a powerful labour union at Bhatpara.[85] The PWP activists from Bhatpara union often intervened in different local strikes to help the strikers and built up a network of support bases.[86] For example, Gopen Chakraborty, a successful PWP trade-unionist, described how he moved around in mill towns:

my usual dress was a drum (*dholok*) swung across my waist, a ladder on my shoulder, a bucketful of glue in hand to stick posters ... I used to hit the drum, gather workers and hold meetings from factory to factory.[87]

Moni Singh, the other PWP activist, also built up a base in Metiaburz through his successful intervention in the strike at the Keshoram Cotton Mill. Describing his popularity among local workers, Singh later recalls in his autobiography that when he was arrested from a picket line nearly a thousand workers encircled the police station. Panic-stricken police officers requested him to tell the workers that 'he is not under arrest'. Singh was also active in the Clive Jute Mills of Metiaburz. In January 1929, the Clive Jute Mill witnessed a strike when a worker named Shovan was fined and physically assaulted by an European assistant. Moni Singh immediately intervened in the strike and drafted a petition to the managing director of the mill.[88]

By helping workers to organize strikes, the PWP activists marginalized the Congress in the labour movement. The Congress commitment to the cause of the united front against the Raj stood in the way of their supporting industrial action among workers, particularly against Indian employers. In

1928 during the strike in the Keshoram Cotton Mill, Subhas Bose, a prominent Congress leader, in a meeting organized by the Birla family in Garden Reach, appealed to workers to withdraw the strike. Moni Singh, the PWP activist, opposed Subhas Bose in the same meeting and requested the workers to continue the strike.[89] The immediate response of the workers was that they wanted to continue the strike. The meeting broke up and the Congress lost face among the workers.

The Peasant and Workers Party made a breakthrough in the labour movement during a strike in the Lilooah railway workshop in 1928. In September 1927, when two thousand workers were retrenched in the nearby Kharagpur railway workshop, strike became inevitable. On 5 March 1928, when four employees were dismissed in the Lilooah railway workshop in Howrah, workers immediately went on strike demanding reinstatement of the dismissed workers, a minimum salary of Rs 30, provision of living quarters, and recognition of the union. The management declared a lock out. Soon the labour leaders from PWP intervened at Lilooah.

The PWP tried to transform the strike into a political battle against the employers and the state. The party started a new weekly journal called *Lal Paltan* (red brigade) to spread the message of 'socialism' among workers. With the symbol of hammer and sickle as its logo, a cartoon at the centre of the front page depicted a healthy and strong worker clad in scanty clothes firing a cannon at a well-dressed dhoti-wearing rich man.[90] The caption below the cartoon declared:

We want to live like human beings. We need proper food, good health, leisure after work, medicine and health care and a place to live after retirement. We demand security for our children. We do not like to die of starvation. In the troubled path of life, humanism, honest labour and solidarity among ourselves will save us. Our rise has caused fear in the hearts of selfishness and our demands were striking it like cannon balls.[91]

This distinctly humanitarian message marked by an appeal to workers to unite and struggle against capitalism gave its argument a moral sanction. It carried articles on 'the fall of the most powerful emperor of the world, the Czar of Russia before the might of the working masses.'[92] Apart from stories focusing on the Russian Revolution, there were news items dealing with the success of strikes elsewhere and appeals for funds. Though the language of the journal remained distinctly sanskritized Bengali, it might have had wide circulation among the workers. Sibnath Bannerjee, a labour leader at

Lilooah, wrote to another labour activist that they will soon flood the mill belt with *Lal Paltan*. 'The need of the hour,' wrote Bannerjee, 'is not a highbrow theoretical journal like *Ganavani*, but a magazine like *Lal Paltan* telling stories of exploitation and struggle of workers in simple language.'[93]

The PWP organized spectacular marches in the industrial belt to spread the message of the strike among workers. Waving festoons and red flags, workers marched through the mill towns to Calcutta on numerous occasions, impressing upon other workers the strength of organized labour movement. In March 1928, the PWP held their second conference at Bhatpara and changed the name of the party to Workers and Peasants Party (WPP), indicating a new confidence that they had derived from organized labour movement. Thus the evolution of the WPP had little to do with the dictates of the Comintern, which later criticized Indian Communists for setting up a two-class party of workers and peasants. Indeed, if the imperial establishment's search for a colonial variant of corporatist state resulted in strengthening left wing workers' politics, the Comintern's supposedly failed attempt to create a powerful, ideologically pure revolutionary workers' movement led to the establishment of a popular front for workers' struggle. In other words, the global context informed the perspective of workers' politics in Calcutta but the complexity of local struggles gave the global movement a different twist. Workers' autonomy remained a crucial and integral part of this political context and the redefining of the movement. This again was manifested in the organization of the Lilooah strike which provided the WPP with a powerful mass base.

The strike in Lilooah dragged on and workers also reached the limits of their resources despite an occasional flow of help from the international labour movement. As radicals could not provide a meaningful resolution, the railway workers at Lilooah, in August 1928, negotiated the end of the strike through the moderate leader C.F. Andrews. The radicals, realizing the danger of being marginalized, unconditionally withdrew the strike.[94] In other words, despite actively supporting the WPP's activities, the workers were aware of the limits of their resources and displayed the independence and flexibility to initiate and negotiate strikes even in opposition to the strategies of their political leaders.

The WPP, however, emerged as a powerful force and drew the attention of militant workers elsewhere. In March 1928, the Ludlow Jute Mill workers in Chengail struck work, demanding an increase of pay and formation of a union. Facing stubborn repression of the authorities, Mahadeo, a leader of the workers, then approached Kishorilal Ghosh, the general secretary of BPTUC, to help them in organizing the struggle, who in turn, approached the WPP for assistance. The WPP sent two new volunteers, Radharaman Mitra and Bankim Mukherji, who formed a new union, called the Ludlow Jute Mill Union, to conduct the struggle in the area.

Concerned with the presence of WPP activists in the area, the managers warned Bankim Mukherjee not to enter the mill premises. On 22 April 1928, a day after the warning, the BPTUC sent a letter to the manager asserting the rights of the trade unionists to go to the 'coolie lines' of the factory. The infuriated manager trampled the letter under his feet and dismissed the worker who had carried it.[95] The workers declared a strike in the evening of the same day. Soon Philip Spratt, a British WPP activist, arrived on the spot to help Bankim Mukherji and Radharaman Mitra. On 24 April 1928, nearly three thousand workers assembled near the mill. Philip Spratt asked the strikers to form 'an army of [workers] wearing union badges, thoroughly drilled and disciplined who were to carry on the picket peacefully at important places so that the [black-legs] could not be brought in.' Spratt emphasized the formation of a strike committee and requested workers to involve women in the strike to expand the mass base of the union. Imbued by the notion of collective strength, workers informed the local sub-divisional officer that they would function through the union and would not need his offer to mediate the issue through sardars. By next morning the strikers not only enforced the picketing but also forced domestic servants of British factory officials to go on strike. They ensured the boycott of the factory officials in the local bazaar through picketing. The strike suffered a jolt when women workers accepted the authorities' favourable terms and decided to join work. Finally, on 11 May 1928, after negotiation with the manager, the workers withdrew the strike.[96]

Inspired by the strike, the WPP activists campaigned for a month to organize a labour union at the Fort Gloster Jute Mills at Bauria in Howarh district, and on 15 July 1928 a union was established. The next day the manager dismissed the leading union workers. When workers gathered to protest against the dismissal, the police opened fire and arrested many workers. A few workers who could not bear the cost of legal procedure and faced starvation, surrendered their bail and accepted jail sentences. Yet the strike continued for six months demanding the right to form a trade union.[97]

By the end of 1928 the WPP emerged as a powerful political force in the mill towns with a large network of unions in the Calcutta–Howrah industrial belt. The WPP in this period also developed a small but dedicated cadre to support their action among workers. Even the Bengal Congress approached the WPP for help when it established a labour cell in 1928 to coordinate the trade union movement with the Congress activities.

The WPP in this period tried to build up an organized movement among industrial workers along radical nationalist political lines. In December 1928, addressing the workers in Bauria before their demonstration at the Congress annual Conference in Calcutta, Bankim Mukherji said that the 'ultimate object of the labour agitation was not to gain increased rates for workers but to attain freedom of the country. The object of the Congress was to liberate the country by demolishing the existing government, to promulgate new laws, to introduce new police, and to improve the economic condition of the country.' In other words, the WPP's message to workers was that of a nationalist struggle sensitive to the aspirations of the working classes.[98]

These attempts to build up a constituency among workers, however, also led the WPP to confront the Swarajist-dominated Calcutta corporation. The WPP helped the scavengers of the Calcutta corporation to organize a struggle against the insensitive administration of the Swarajists for better wages.[99] The struggle of the scavengers in the mill town of Howarh in 1928 antagonized the local bhadralok population so much that they started attacking scavengers.[100] So uncomfortable were the Bengal Congress leaders that Subhas Bose refused the workers' procession, led by the WPP leaders, entry to the venue of the Calcutta session of the Congress in 1928.[101] Workers forced their entry into the Congress enclosure even after the Congress volunteers resisted them with lathis. The WPP's demand for the declaration of the full independence at the Congress session also went against the spirit of the official Congress call for dominion status for India.

Yet, the WPP's relationship with the workers was not free of tension. The party's ideology placed faith in revolutionary class struggle as the panacea for all ills. The strikes by workers in the jute mills were perhaps more a reflection of the mutuality of interests among them on shared grievances than their desire to organize a political revolution. In fact, workers were reported to have regarded the WPP leaders as 'union-babus' indicating that WPP leaders were still outsiders in the workers' perception.

The police repression of ordinary workers further impeded the growth of trade unions. Attempts to organize strikes were treated by local government officers as a criminal offence. The government not only arrested

Sitaram Mondal, a militant worker of the Lilooah work shop, but pleaded that Sitaram Mondal should remain in custody because 'he had been organizing meetings of workmen and in one meeting, particularly, he addressed the audience urging them to go on strike.'[102] During the Bauria Jute Mill strike the management bore the cost of bringing workers to trial on behalf of the police. The workers had little resources to combat the collaboration between the state and the employers.

Mill managers often victimized the leading organizers after the strikes. In most cases, trade unionists failed to prevent the dismissal of workers from the factories. Many workers ended up in jail without adequate legal support.[103] As a consequence, mill-hands distrusted the ability of the trade unionists to realize their demands. The inability of the trade union to live up to workers' expectations probably accounted for its limited influence in the mill towns. The WPP activists were thus unable to sustain their organizations in the mill belt in long term. All stringent provisions of the Trade Disputes Act were applied against them. At the local level the police and management remained far more active against them.

During strikes, the militant strategies of the WPP earned immediate support from workers. But the workers were not ready to sacrifice their immediate gains for political aims, which still remained distant to them. As a consequence, the government attempt to suppress the WPP in March 1929 was met with little protest in the mill towns.[104] The removal of the WPP leaders did not destroy the militant labour movement. In spite of tensions between the WPP and ordinary workers, sustained propaganda by the former strengthened the spirit of resistance among the latter. The long struggle of workers against inhuman living conditions in the jute mills received widespread attention due to the WPP propaganda. In 1921 the workers' attempt to spread the strike all over the jute belt failed to spark off a general strike, but in 1929 the general strike materialized largely due to the support of the WPP. Ironically in 1929 employers' attempts to coordinate their strategies throughout the industry produced solidarity among workers in their determination to resist retrenchment and wage losses on account of the general strike.

Business Restructuring and the General Strike of 1929

In the interwar years the IJMA, the cartel of jute producers, experienced a bitter trade feud within the industry. At the end of the First World War, expatriate control over the industry was seriously challenged by the rising groups of Indian traders—popularly known as Marwaris, who emigrated from their native regions in Rajasthan—all over north India in the early part of the nineteenth century. These traders set up wide commercial networks all over India and accumulated substantial amounts of capital which enabled them to establish financial foothold in major industries in the north and eastern regions of the country.

Since the first decade of the twentieth century, the IJMA leaders increasingly depended upon Marwari capital for timely cash injection in the business. It is thus not surprising that in return for their investments Marwaris were keen on entering the board of control of the companies. This was intensely disliked by British traders who were not ready to surrender their exclusive preserve to Marwari merchants.[105] The discomfort of British industrialists increased further when in the 1920s several Marwari businessmen established their own mills and refused to join the IJMA. To the irritation of British leaders of industry, these outside mills profited from the IJMA's short-term working hours. The IJMA's policies, like all cartels in the world, were to match output with demand though the policy did not always produce the desired results.[106] From 1921, the IJMA tackled the issue of overproduction in jute commodities through a short-term agreement for 54 hours of work in the mills. The attempt by outside mills, primarily controlled by Marwari traders, to ignore these rules seriously challenged the efficacy of the cartel.

Initially, the IJMA contained the threat of Indian competition by bringing these 'errant Indian mills' within the fold of the cartel. Yet by 1928, many small Indian firms were keen on leaving the IJMA as they believed that they would be able to produce jute clothes at lower prices and thus could make profit by undercutting the price offered by the IJMA.[107] The anger and frustration of the British industrialists could be gauged from the chief of Bird and Company, one of the largest managing agency houses in Calcutta, E.C. Benthall's famous comment on the margin of a letter from Mokandlal—a jute share holder: 'Indians are determined to get into the industry which will mean survival of the fittest in due course ....'[108] Benthall did not confine his views to the margin of a letter only, he stated in a letter to his colleague Sir George Godfrey:

I do not think that we are by any means through our worst troubles in the trade nor shall we get on to a really sound basis until a period of stress has eliminated some of the new comers.[109]

Benthall reiterated these views again to a colleague as he asserted:

we should not get on to a really sound basis until we go on full time with the survival of the fittest. If it comes to good management we can always defeat such people as have recently come into the trade.[110]

Though alarmed by such competition, the IJMA did not declare an all-out war against them. Prominent figures within the cartel feared that such a war could lead to a drastic fall in profit for shareholders and would gradually squeeze investments at a time when the international market was not favourable to jute products.[111] More importantly, the smell of profit became too tempting for many IJMA members who cheated on the self-imposed working hour restrictions.[112] By the late 1920s and early 1930s so pervasive became the problem of preserving the discipline concerning working hours that the IJMA had to maintain a widespread establishment to police its own mills.[113] Yet many IJMA mills continued to evade the working hours agreement.[114] The presence of Indian firms only fuelled the competition among the IJMA mills and further eroded the control of the cartel. The IJMA members made frantic efforts to preserve the control of the cartel over production and strengthen their position in the international market.

This led to a series of experimentations with working hours to maintain unity among IJMA members. From 1926 onwards a number of the IJMA mills switched over from multiple shift to single shift mills. This provoked a wider labour unrest. Workers regarded this as the beginning of a systematic retrenchment to reduce costs and the introduction of the single shift system was the first step in that direction. Trade feud and the gradual shrinkage of the international market no doubt accelerated the process. However, the new 60 hour working week agreement across the industry in 1928, which was to be implemented from 1 July 1929, further undermined workers' earnings. This was again related to the complex policies followed by the IJMA regarding working hours and bonuses paid to workers.

After the First World War, the IJMA introduced a 54 hour working week in the mills. The mills decided to work for 4 days a week with 13.5 hours a day. The two idle days in a week were kept to meet sudden spurts in demand. To compensate the loss of wages to workers, mill-owners sanctioned an allowance known as *khoraki* which was less than a day's normal wage. In 1929, the IJMA tried to simultaneously curtail production costs by stopping the payment of khoraki across the industry following the new agreement on a 60 hour working week. The new arrangement thus caused an increase in working hours but wages declined.[115] The new policy also affected bonuses of the weavers working in the single shift mills. The prevailing method of payment of salary for weavers in jute mills was a basic rate per cut of 100 yards. There was a system of bonuses based on the number of cuts. Under the new 60 hour working agreement the management also increased the number of cuts needed for bonuses which, according to a labour union, made it impossible for the weavers to earn the higher bonus. Thus the trade feud among mill-owners and their attempt to find a solution to this trade feud through the industry-wide agreement on working hours provoked reaction among workers all across the industry.

From its inception, the nature of operation of the jute industry allowed individual mills to make regional and local adjustments with workers on the issue of salary, but trade feuds increasingly compelled the management to take decisions across the industry that had adverse impacts on the earnings of workers, irrespective of their local peculiarities. As a consequence, workers' responses to such measures increasingly assumed an industry-wide form. The presence of the WPP and radical labour movement, in this context, assisted workers in organizing such industry-wide protests. This became evident in the industrial dispute that emerged in 1929 in the wake of the 60 hour working week adjustment.

Within a week of the introduction of these new working hours, labourers in the jute mills of Bhatpara started an agitation. They refused to work for more than 54 hours or to take their salary. The local moderate trade unionists of the Kankinarah labour union intervened in the dispute and asked for a conference between the workers and the managers. Ignoring the advice of the local moderate labour leaders, the workers used their neighbourhood networks to approach a local lawyer.[116] In other words, the workers independently rejected established trade-union leaders in favour of confrontation with the employers. More interestingly, the weavers developed a new form of political agitation. The weavers in the Bhatpara mills attended their work but did not take more than one cut causing a glut of yarn and subsequent closure of the factories.

A large number of the workers now had the freedom to pursue their own modes of action. From the mill town of Bhatpara, they marched on to other mill towns and started picketing in order to persuade local workers to come out of their mills. By 5 August the strike had spread to Titagarh, the other important mill town located on the east bank of Ganges. In Titagarh, even the workers of the local shoe factory and engineering works observed a sympathetic strike. On 29 July, workers of the jute mills located in the Sealdah region of Calcutta came out in protest against the new working hours. On 5 August the trouble spread to the south of Calcutta where two mills in the Metiaburz area—the Clive and the Union Jute Mills—ceased working. By 8 August, nearly all the mills on the east bank of the Hooghly came to a standstill. In some cases, strikers operated through their neighbourhood networks. For example, the Kankinarah labour union in its memorial to the RCLI mentioned that

six weeks of intense agitation and propaganda in favour of the sympathetic strike failed to create any impression on the workers employed in other industries but they came out with jute workers, who lived with those in the same basti and enjoyed their fellowship.[117]

The strike spread rapidly in spite of police presence in the mill areas to contain trouble.[118] It is not suggested here that this strike was an expression of natural solidarity among workers. Supporters of the strike also used coercion to force the non-strikers to join it. Shopkeepers were warned, for instance, that if they supplied non-strikers with food, their shops would be looted. Women, who were mostly employed in low skilled jobs without a rural support network, suffered more than other workers during the strikes. Male workers feared that women might return to work causing the strike to collapse. The government reports mentioned many attacks on women workers forcing the latter to abstain from work. The 'time workers', who constituted a vast majority of the workforce, were also said to have showed some reluctance in joining the strike in the initial stages. Lack of resources among workers also constrained the strike. On 6 August in Gouripur, the strikers clashed with Kabuli moneylenders who might have tried to collect their dues from the workers in a period when they were without salary. Many workers left for homes declaring that they would come back only after the settlement of the strike. The trade union stepped in to cushion the effect of the workers' lack of resources.

The WPP-affiliated Bengal Jute Workers Union made an effort to sustain and spread the strike. They established a central office at Harrison Road in Calcutta, obtained a telephone to keep contact with the mill belt, and hired a car to conduct the propaganda. The union leaders collected funds for workers to sustain the strike. On requests from the union, the Congress Swarajya party leader J.M. Sengupta appealed to the people for donations for the labourers. The government report also mentioned that even Marwari speculators donated large sums of money to the Bengal Jute Workers Union.

The BJWU could rope in politicians of different views to support the general strike and pressurize the government to mediate between the workers and the IJMA. Even Swami Viswananda, the militant Hindu politician went to the Titagarh Mills to picket. At the same time, Saheed Suhrawardy spoke in the legislative council for government intervention to settle the strike. The BJWU contacted Bidhan Roy, the member of the legislative council from the Barrackpur mill area. On 6 August 1928, Roy moved an adjournment motion in the legislative council requesting the government to help end the strike. J.C. Gupta, Subhas Bose, and Suhrawardy also supported him. This discussion within the legislative councils, according to a government report, paved the way for government intervention in the strike. Indeed, the strike created a political context whereby politicians generally renowned for their marked internal differences joined hands. The common issue of class grievance marked by the independent action of workers compelled politicians to close their ranks, particularly as the politicians knew that in the ensuing battle with the colonial state on the issue of constitutional reforms they needed the support of the workers.

More interestingly, labour politics produced a new kind of populist politician with nationalist connections. These politicians had no identifiable trade union organization but depended upon a popular strike wave to curve out a mass base among workers. In reality, grass roots level militant workers utilized the support of such politicians to negotiate with the management. The most prominent among them was Prabhabati Dasgupta—a highly educated lady of immense free will. Not only had Dasgupta violated strict caste rules by selecting as her partner a prominent Muslim nationalist leader, Bakhar Ali Mirza, whom she later married, she also worked among poor toilet cleaners who were regarded as the most polluted social outcastes in Hindu society. A chain *bidi* smoker—a habit which she picked up while working among cleaners in mill municipalities, further suggests her unconventional way of life. Indeed, industrial action organized by workers enabled individuals such as Prabhabati to search for an alternative avenue of politics. Prabhabati was an individualist and regarded herself as a social worker and philanthropist. Though she thought that she had an iron grip over workers, they possibly viewed her more as a negotiator. Hence her popularity was contingent upon her ability to negotiate and deliver a satisfactory solution to the problem. The IJMA was reluctant to negotiate with Prabhabati or her unregistered union where the WPP activists were till then her allies. Yet circumstances forced the IJMA to commence negotiations with the BJWU through government mediation.

By 13 August the general strike led to a stoppage of work in all the mills north of Calcutta.[119] The IJMA also started negotiations with Prabhabati Dasgupta through the government at the same time. On 14 August, Prabahabati decided to withdraw the strike when the IJMA agreed to pay the correct proportionate increase in the total earnings for the extra hours worked, reintroduce khoraki, and also maintain the old systems of bonuses in the mills.

The settlement led to a new development in the strike situation. The mills on the west bank of the Hooghly which hitherto had remained unaffected by the strike, witnessed tremendous unrest. Workers in these mills demanded assurances from the managers that they would also receive the benefits of the new settlement. However, the management refused to give any written undertaking in this regard. Workers' distrust of the managers led them to strike. In Howrah, workers at the Fort Gloster Mill offered the most resolute opposition to the managers. The constant harassment of workers by the managers during the long strike a year before, particularly strengthened the opposition of workers. The news of retrenchment in the other mills could also have fuelled the strikes. The leaders of the Bengal Jute Workers Union, who were given permission by the police to enter the region, soon became identified with the management and were even abused by the workers. In many mills workers expected more favourable concessions from the management. In two factories workers observed strikes in sympathy with other workers. These events showed that the WPP was powerful only when they enjoyed the support of the workers but they did not dictate the terms of the labour movement in the jute mills.

Soon after the strike the BJWU was besieged with complaints from workers about victimization. The large number of workers who went back to their villages during the strike, were refused jobs in the mills once they came back. The IJMA also started massive retrenchment of workers. Many disputes over wages between mill managers and workers took place after the strike was officially withdrawn by the BJWU. The discontent simmered in the jute mill belt and a strike was about to break out in Bhatpara. The BJWU leaders, in many cases, were unable to understand the complications of the situation, and Prabhabati was caught in the technicalities of wage calculation. In this situation bitter fighting within the union developed.

The old activists of the WPP broke relations with Prabhabati. The constant inner bickering gradually led to the decline in the support base of the BJWU. As organized resistance petered out under the pressure of internal conflicts within the ranks of unionists, the management mounted its most effective form of repression through retrenchment. The onslaught of depression further restricted the possibility of collective bargaining.

In 1930 workers retreated into a defensive position. They sustained a tremendous wage loss during the strike which might have put them under financial strain. In a dire economic situation jute mill workers might have tried to consolidate their jobs rather than risking strike action. The IJMA took the opportunity to implement its policy of retrenchment, and the factories retrenched large number of workers over a period of two months. The BJWU made some effort to resist the retrenchment but failed to organize effective protests.

Though the WPP-affiliated BJWU played an important role in spreading strikes, they too had their limitations. In this period the WPP was crippled by the arrest of experienced trade union leaders. Within the union there was no unanimity of opinion regarding the general strike. According to Moni Singh, even Prabhabati Dasgupta, who became the most important leader of the strike, opposed the decision of the second general strike because of financial difficulties. The leaders often could not establish contact with workers during the strike as the police used the Ordinance No. 144 to prevent the outside organizers from reaching the mills. The bhadralok WPP volunteers who arrived from Calcutta did not know Hindi or Urdu—the languages spoken by the workers. The union tried to establish contact with workers through leaflets where most of the workers were illiterate.[120] Thus, while the BJWU provided political support from outside, the motivation for the strikes came from the workers themselves. The changing structure of business in the wake of trade feuds and intensification of internal conflicts constituted the immediate contexts of the strike.

Conclusion

This chapter has explored the process of the making of differing contexts within labour politics that influenced and informed the making of workers' politics in Bengal. These differing contexts could explain the reasons behind the sharp rise in riots and strikes in the 1920s that came to signify labour politics. Historians often presume the dichotomy between communal riots between Hindus and Muslims and class-based political action. This investigation clearly indicates that the sharp increase in communal riots did not restrict the intensification of class conflicts in the factories in the 1920s. Rather, there was an increase in both communal and class conflicts in the same period.

The reason for the increase in conflicts could be located in the way organized politics expanded its hold on the labour movement in particular and politics in general in Bengal. Communal riots did not simply reflect the transpositions of rural communal conflicts in urban contexts; rather they reflected an ongoing all-India phenomenon whereby several forces operating within national politics articulated narrow sectarian interests and transformed each localized conflict into a national political issue and transformed riots into highly organized political events supported by the political and economic resources of a community. Relations between the Hindu and Muslim communities were imagined in a new fashion in the light of the developments in high politics that rendered differing local details irrelevant. Issues, motives, and contexts were pressed into an uniform political structure in which collective memories of riots were registered. Thus, workers' participation in riots became routine events of national politics which gained its own dynamics and left behind its own political legacy.

Similarly, there evolved a language of class for identifying workers' collective interests as producers in an emerging industrial economy. The policies of the colonial state and their attempt to accommodate labour in the structure of institutional politics played a crucial role in defining this language of class. The attempt to accommodate labour in the domain of the institutional structure of governance was the consequence of changes in the global political economy. First, the emergence of labour as an international political force, brought about by the changes in the political power equation between labour and capital in metropolitan economies, informed and influenced the policies of the colonial state. The rise of both social democratic and communist movements, as well as their related international institutions—in the form of the ILO and Comintern—impinged on the pattern of functioning of the colonial state. The pressure generated by these institutions compelled the colonial state to create a legal definition of the working person and her/his right to form trade unions and engage in collective bargaining. Bounded by the pressure of several interest groups and its own autocratic/bureaucratic political tradition, the colonial state was unwilling, as well as unable, to progress much in the direction of reforms. Indeed, the end result of these reforms created a legal infrastructure for an industrial relationship that opened up a new political territory for radical labour activists to reclaim workers' interests.

Similarly, the dynamics of nationalist movements and the inherent contradiction in nationalist mobilization sharpened the communalization of politics, as well as facilitated the emergence of class-based political movements and a political party purporting to represent working classes both at a discursive plain and in every-day politics. Indeed, so sharp was the contradiction between the rhetoric and practice of mainstream nationalist formations that radicals within the nationalist fold departed to form a separate political platform for workers and peasants. Finally, as the bhadralok organizers of the WPP attempted to link the labour movement with their self-defined radical political struggles, they were compelled to address the immediate concerns of the workers. Soon diverse segments of workers reversed the agenda of bhadralok political activists and re-negotiated it towards every-day bread-and-butter struggles. This encounter in workers' politics turned out to be an important event of political re-education of bhadralok political activists as well as worker militants.

In a similar way, the postwar politics of business were marked by a prolonged crisis of cartels related to a vicious trade feud against the background of shrinkage in the international market and depression in the global economy. Yet again, as capital in Calcutta industry groped for a resolution of a conflict through readjustment in working hours agreement, it also inadvertently assisted in the intensification of workers' resistance across the industry.

Thus there existed differing contexts through which workers politics evolved. These situations were informed by internal contradictions and were marked by dialectical transformations. The dialectics of these transformations in the context of the historical evolution of events provide us with clues to understand the oscillation between strikes and riots, class-based action and communal riots. Indeed it brings forth the salience of the interrelated structure of politics as a manifestation of global-level operations of the capitalist economy. Such clear transformations at various levels of the capitalist economy in the post-war years transformed labour politics in Bengal. Yet these transformations were not definitive, derivative processes of development in which events in the metropole dictated events at the periphery. Rather, at each level the exigencies of political situations, marked by its own contradictions, shaped the changes in labour politics. The next chapter will further investigate the transformation of workers' politics in the post-depression years when institutional politics embraced and provided a particular structure to labour movement and further intensified both communal polarization and organization of class-based action.

Notes

1. Iqbal Singh, *The Indian National Congress: A Reconstruction Vol. II 1919–1923*, Delhi, 1988, p. 451.

2. *Documents of the History of the Communist Party of India, Vol. II 1923–25*, Edited with introductory and explanatory notes by G. Adhikari, New Delhi, 1974, p. 72 (hereafter *Documents of the History of Communist Party, 1923–1925*).

3. Ibid.

4. C.R. Das quoted in E. Roy, 'Where are the masses', *Inprecor*, Vol. 3, No. 36, 9 May 1923, *Documents of the History of Communist Party, 1923–1925*, p. 90.

5. Ibid., p. 93.

6. Referring to the Russian revolution, Das in his presidential address at the Gaya Congress declared that '[t]he soul of Russia must free herself from the socialism of Carl [sic] Marx' and predicted a victory for the counter-revolution. *The Encyclopaedia of the Indian National Congress, 1921–1924 India at the crossroads* Vol. VIII, Delhi, 1980, pp. 119–21.

7. For details on the Bengal pact see Shila Sen, *Muslim Politics in Bengal*, New Delhi, 1976, p. 53.

8. For details concerning Suhrawardy's role in Calcutta politics in this period see K. McPherson, *The Muslim Microcosm*, pp. 78–80.

9. *Amrita Bazar Patrika*, 23 December, 1923.

10. Ibid., 25 December 1923.

11. See for details R. Ray, *Urban roots of Indian Nationalism Pressure groups and Conflicts of Interests in Calcutta city politics, 1875–1939*, New Delhi, 1979, p. 116.

12. S.N. Roy, *Report on the General Election of 1923 in Bengal*, Calcutta, 1923, p. 16.

13. See Manju Bandhapadhya, *Sramik Netri Santosh Kumari*, Calcutta,1984, pp. 10–11.

14. Nearly 8,030 votes were polled and Dr Roy secured 5,689 votes, defeating his rival by a margin of 3,406 votes. See 12 above.

15. The 'big five' comprised the rising Bengali entrepreneur—N.R. Sarkar, a zamindar called Tulsi Goswami, a highly successful physician—Bidhan Roy, an

influential barrister Nirmal Chunder Chanda, and Sarat Bose, the elder brother of Subhas Bose. See for details Bidyut Chakrabarty, *Subhas Chandra Bose and Middle-Class radicalism: A Study in Indian Nationalism 1928–1940*, London, 1990.

16. *The Bengal Administration Report, 1924–25*, p. iii; N.N. Mitra (ed.), *Indian Annual Register 1924–25*, pp. 415–8.

17. *The Indian Annual Register April–June*, pp. 415–7.

18. *The Bengal Administration Report, 1923–24*, p. ii.

19. *Amrita Bazar Patrika*, 1 January 1924. See also RINP(B) Week ending 14 January 1924.

20. Home Political Confidential File No. 69 January 1924, WBSA.

21. Ibid.

22. *The Indian Annual Registrar 1924, July–December*, p. 75.

23. For a detailed and interesting explanation of why and how a mendicant of completely unknown religious affiliation was claimed by local Muslim petty traders as their patron saint after his death, see P.K. Datta, *Carving blocs: communal ideology in early twentieth century Bengal*, New Delhi, Oxford University Press, 1999.

24. *The Bengal Administration Report, 1925–26*, p. xvi.

25. *Amrita Bazar Patrika*, 25 August 1925.

26. *Mussalman*, 14 April 1925.

27. G.D. Birla to Gandhi; letter written on 11 June, G.D. Birla, *In the shadow of Mahatma*, Bombay 1968, pp. 4–5.

28. See 16 above, p. 64.

29. *Amrita Bazar Patrika*, 3 July 1925.

30. Ibid., 4 July 1925.

31. Ibid., 25 August 1925.

32. Ibid., 7 September 1925.

33. For such accusation see above.

34. *The Statesman*, 12 April 1925.

35. *The Statesman*, 23 April 1925. See also article of Muzaffar Ahmad, 'Kothay Pratikar?', *Langal*, 28 January 1926, in Goutam Chattapadhya (ed.), *Samhati, Langal, Ganavani*, p. 101.

36. *Indian Annual Register*, July–December 1926, Vol. II, No. III and IV, pp. 97–98.

37. *Proceedings, Bengal Legislative Council*, 10 December 1925, pp. 312–32.

38. *Indian Annual Register*, Vol. I, No. I and II, January–June 1926, pp. 70–1.

39. *Amrita Bazar Patrika* 1 and 2 May 1926.

40. *Report of the Commissioner of the Police on Calcutta riots in April 1926*, see 38 above, p. 70.

41. Suranjan Das, *Communal riots in Bengal*, pp. 82–88.

42. *Indian Annual Register* Vol. I and II, No. III, July–December 1926, pp. 85–7.

43. See 38 above, p. 85 and *Bengal Administration Report 1925–26*, p. x.

44. According to the *Bengal Administration Report*, '[t]he exchange of abuse between Hindu and Moslem papers was violent in the extreme. No accusation was too low, no suggestion too mean if the object was to vilify the opposite party.' *Bengal Administration Report, 1926–27*, pp. 240–5.

45. Ibid., p. 11.

46. K. Mcpherson *The Muslim Microcosm*, p. 118.

47. Please refer to the debates regarding *Indian Factories Act 1881*; *Report of the Indian Factory Commission 1890*; *Royal Commission on Labour (English), Foreign Report, 1892 Vol. II*. See section entitled *Report on the Labour Question in India*.

48. 'About the ILO who we are -ILO History', ILO document available on ILO website *http://www.ilo.org/public/english/about/history.htm*.

49. Ibid.

50. For details of his life see *http://www.kentlaw.edu/ilhs/gompers.html*, a website maintained by the Illinois Labour History Society.

51. See District Jute and Flax Workers' Union Book, series entitled 'Letters to India', John Sime, 10 March 1926.

52. For an interesting description of British socialist views on the empire see P. Cain (ed.), R. Macdonald, *Labour and Empire*, London, 1998, Series title: The empire and its critics 1899–1939: Classics of Imperialism. Compare this with documents produced by the Labour government on the end of empire. R. Hyam (ed.), *The Labour government and the end of empire 1945–1951*, London, 1992. For a detailed historical analysis of the idea of the empire and the British Labour party, see P.S. Gupta, *Imperialism and the British Labour Movement 1914–1964*, London, 1975.

53. See for details of this debate A.R. Cox, 'Paternal Despotism and Workers' Resistance in the Bengal Jute Industry 1920-1940'. Unpublished PhD thesis, October 1999, pp. 194–214.

54. Commerce Department Commerce Branch Progs, File No 1A-14(16) of 1924; Serial No. 144, WBSA. From J.N. Gupta, commissioner of the Burdwan Division to the Secretary to Government of Bengal.

55. Commerce Department Commerce Branch Progs, File no 1-A-14(18) of 1924, Serial No. 146, WBSA. Views of government pleader quoted in the report from the commissioner of the Presidency Division to Secretary to the Government of Bengal, Commerce Department.

56. Notes on Trade Union Congress Deputation to the Secretary of State, 23 July 1924, Private Office Paper, Secretary of State, L/PO/1/14, IOL.

57. Ibid., IOL.

58. Private Office Papers, Secretary of State for India, L/PO/1/14 July 1924, IOL.

59. See Private letter from Lord Birkenhead to Lord Irwin, dated 8 December 1927. Private Office Papers of the Secretary of State L/PO/1/16.

60. Private Office Papers of the Secretary of the State for India, L/PO/1/26(1), IOL.

61. See for details of this argument J.P. Patrick, *Communism and Nationalism in India M N Roy and Comintern Policy 1920–1939*, Princeton, 1971.

62. For the close relationship between Roychowdhury and his employers, see letter from K.C. Roychowdhury to Edward Benthal on 13 May 1933 K.C. Roychowdhury requested Benthal to intervene on his behalf to put his name as witness before the Joint Select Committee in Parliament. Benthal Papers Box II.

63. The union never had a membership of more than a thousand workers. *RCLI, Vol. V, Part. I,* Evidence of K.C. Roychowdhury.

64. The first issue of this paper sold 600 copies among the workers. One issue of the paper which survived had mainly focused on the organization of the women workers. *Sramik Netri Santosh Kumari,* Calcutta, 1984, pp. 33.

65. *Sramik,* first year 25th issue, 26 February 1925, in Manju Bandopadhyay, *Sramik Netri Santosh Kumari,* p. 66.

66. John Sime, the Labour leader from Dundee, intervened on behalf of the union when a worker in Gouripur Jute Mill died because of the physical assault by an European assistant. District Jute and Flax Workers' Union Book entitled 'Letters to India', John Sime, 8 April 1926, Dundee district Archives Dundee. Ibid., 10 March 1926. The Dundee union also sent financial help to this union regularly. David Patrie, *Communism in India 1924–1927,* Calcutta, 1972, p. 130.

67. *Samhati* 1st year, 2nd issue, 1330, Goutam Chattapadhya (ed.) *Samhati, Langal, Ganavani,* Calcutta 1992, p. 4.

68. 'Amra Ki Chai' ('What do we want') see above, pp. 10–13.

69. R.C. Mazumdar, 'Prachin Bharate Sramik Sangha' ('Workers' Association in Ancient India') see above, pp. 15–20.

70. See the *Karmi* 1st year, January 1922, Vol. I, No. 5, pp. 63–4.

71. The *Karmi,* (Bengali Edition), Pratham Varsa, Astam Sankhya, Chaitra 1328 (April 1922) p. 68.

72. The *Karmi,* Vol. II, Issue III, October 1922.

73. Goutam Chattapadhaya *Rus Biplab o Banglar Mukti Andolan,* Calcutta, 1967, pp. 72–3.

74. Muzaffar Ahmad, *Amar Jiban O Bharater Communist Party,* Calcutta, 1989, p. 338.

75. Ibid.

76. Ibid.

77. 'A Programme For the Indian National Congress', quoted in full in Muzaffar Ahmad's *Amar Jiban O Bharater Communist Party*, pp. 421–34.

78. M.N. Roy and Evelyn Roy, 'Open Letter to C.R. Das' One Year of Non-cooperation,' Chapter xiii, quoted in *Documents of History of Communist Party, 1923–1925*, pp. 6–16.

79. See 77 above, pp. 339–40. See also *Documents of the History of the Communist Party of India Vol. III A 1926*, pp. 155–62.

80. For example, Sibnath Bannerjee, who joined the Labour Swaraj Party after his return from the Soviet Union, had little sympathy for the communists. For details of his view see Home Political Confidential File No. 121, Sibnath's Letter to C.R. Das, 5 September 1924, WBSA.

81. Goutam Chattapadhaya, *Communism and Bengal's Freedom movement. Vol. I, 1917–1929*, New Delhi, 1974. Appendix: Interview with the Gopen Chakraborty, pp. 135–9.

82. Moni Singh, *Life is a struggle*, Delhi, 1988, pp. 21–2.

83. Ibid., p. 23.

84. Ibid., pp. 25–8.

85. Report on the Royal Commission of Labour in India, Vol. V, Part II, pp. 145.

86. See 82 above, pp. 25–8.

87. Goutam Chattapadhaya, *Communism and Bengal's Freedom movement. Vol. I, 1917–1929*, pp. 136–9.

88. Meerut Conspiracy Case proceedings, SL. 3234.

89. Ibid., pp. 23–4.

90. See 88 above, SL. 3107, *Lal Paltan*, 1st year, 3rd issue, 13 October 1928, NAI.

91. Ibid.

92. Ibid.

93. Sibnath Bannerji to Kalidas Bhattacharya, 18 September 1928, Meerut Conspiracy Case proceedings, SL. 3157, NAI.

94. Philip Spratt, 'EIR Dispute', *Documents of the History of the Communist Party, 1923–1925*, pp. 335–40 and Dharani Goswami, 'On Lilooah Strike', *Documents of the History of the Communist Party, 1923–1925*, pp. 332–4; 'Lilooah', *Ganavani*, Vol. II, No. X, issue 26, July 1928, in *Samhati, Langal, Ganavani*, Calcutta, 1992, p. 193–4.

95. See 88 above, SL. 2741, Strike Report of Ludlow Jute Mills, Chengail, 24 April 1928, NAI.

96. Ibid.

97. Muzaffar Ahmad, *Amar Jiban O Bharater Communist Party*, pp. 485–6 and Radharaman Mitra 'Baruria Jute Mill Strike', *Documents of History of Communist Party, 1923–1925*, pp. 350–3.

98. See 88 above, SL. 2739, 4 January 1929.

99. Ibid.

100. Muzaffar Ahmad, *Amar Jiban O Bharater Communist Party*, pp. 471–9.

101. Ibid., pp. 479–85.

102. *Amrita Bazar Patrika*, 21 August 1928.

103. See 100 above, p. 490. Also see Meerut Conspiracy Case proceedings SL. 3160, NAI.

104. Panchanan Saha, *History of the Working-Class Movement in Bengal*, p. 109.

105. For details on the issue from a different perspective, see O. Goswami, *Industry Trade, and Peasant Society: The Jute Economy of Eastern India 1900–1947*, pp. 100–15; D. Chakrabarty, *Rethinking Working-Class History: Bengal 1890–1940*, pp. 14–64; G.T. Stewart, *Jute and Empire: The Calcutta Jute Wallahs and the Landscape of Empire*, Manchester, 1998, pp. 93–147.

106. For a detailed analysis of the IJMA's policies, please look at O. Goswami, *Industry Trade, and Peasant Society*.

107. Speech by C.G. Cooper at the Debate on Short Time Agreement, 6 November 1928, IJMA Report of the Committee 1928, pp. 66–8. Quoted in G.T. Stewart *Jute and Empire: The Calcutta Jute Wallahs and the Landscape of Empire*, pp. 102–3.

108. Centre of South Asian Studies (hereafter CSAS) Benthall Papers (hereafter B.P.) Box 1, Letter from Mokandlall dated 13 Decmber 1928.

109. CSAS, B.P. Box 1, Benthall to Godfrey 31 December 1928.

110. Ibid., Benthall to Monty, 31 December 1928.

111. For detailed analysis of the crisis see G.T. Stewart *Jute and Empire*, pp. 93–146; O. Goswami, *Industry Trade, and Peasant Society*, pp. 100–15; D. Chakrabarty, *Rethinking Working-Class History Bengal*, pp. 50–63.

112. See for details O. Goswami, as in 111 above.

113. Thomas Duff and Company Archives (hereafter TDA), Dundee University Archives (hereafter DUA), Managers' Report to Directors, Victoria Jute Mill, 1930, pp. 5–7.

114. CSAS, BP Box 1, P. Thomas to Edward Benthall, 4 December 1928.

115. Ajit Dasgupta, 'Jute Industry in India', in V.B. Singh, (ed.), *Economic History of India*, Bombay, 1956, p. 226.

116. *RCL1, Vol. V, Pt. 1*, pp. 129–61.

117. Ibid., p. 159.
118. Ibid., p. 139.
119. Ibid., pp. 130–2.
120. Ibid., p. 144.

7

The Coming of
Provincial Autonomy
Labour Militancy and
Changes in Bengal Politics

Introduction

The general strike of the jute workers in 1937 was the culminating point of
labour resistance to the process of rationalization introduced by the jute
industrialists during the Great Depression. As the depression unleashed
economic devastation in the province, Bengal politics in the 1930s witnessed
the intensification of peasants' and workers' movements demanding changes
in agrarian property structure and industrial relations. At the same time,
the collapse of various forms of traditional social ties between Hindu moneylenders, traders, and landlords on the one hand, and the predominantly
Muslim peasants in East Bengal on the other, escalated communal tensions.
The intense competition between the Hindu and Muslim petty bourgeoisie
for increasingly scarce government jobs further increased these tensions. In
these circumstances, communal tension was also sharpened by constitutional
reforms enshrined in the communal award of 1932 and the Government of
India Act of 1935 which transformed economically powerful Hindus into
a statutory minority in the newly-constituted provincial assemblies.

This chapter examines how and why forms of intense class confrontations between labour and expatriate capital, represented by the general strike
in the jute industry in 1937, got transformed into communal polarization
and internal violence among workers along Hindu–Muslim lines. It argues
that the transition from political action based on horizontal alliances among
workers to a fragmented communal, vertical alliance between propertied

elites and workers has to be located in specific historical contexts against the background of the changing political and economic configuration in the society and its articulation through the institutional structure of the state. It stresses that this transformation could be understood in terms of the dialectics of late colonial politics whereby radical political action from below led to the consolidation of a rickety political coalition of propertied elites who were themselves engaged in a crucial intra-class fractional political contest for hegemony over the political and economic structure in Bengal.

While workers organized alliances among themselves and initiated their movement for changes in industrial relations against the background of new political democracy, frightened by labour militancy the colonial capitalists cobbled together a new political coalition among propertied elites including Muslim landholders, Hindu businessmen, and non-Congress Hindu landed magnates. The new provincial government unleashed massive repressive strategies against labour militants and actively promoted Muslim League Unions and Hindu–Muslim tensions to counter labour militancy. In this circumstance, many workers tried to reach a compromise with employers through moderate pro-government unions. This signalled a momentous shift in workers' politics at the grass roots level, marking the making and unmaking of class-based political action. Yet such intra-class political contests did not diminish the significance of class conflicts in Bengal; rather, it made them bitter and contentious. The nature of state-sponsored communal division among workers remained a crucial aspect of this intra-class fractional manoeuvering and strategies of a fraction of the ruling political coalition of propertied elites to establish political hegemony in Bengal and at the same time such attention to labour militancy signified the political importance of organized labour in the predominantly agrarian society of Bengal.

The Strategies of Capital in the Jute Industry: The Emergence of a Conservative Political Coalition

By the end of the 1920s expatriate British traders who managed the jute industry in Bengal were keen to establish an effective political presence in elected constitutional bodies ranging from municipalities and provincial assemblies to the imperial legislative council. Its main purpose was to strengthen the bargaining position of the IJMA within the political structure of the Indian state. This became manifest in the early 1930s when the IJMA sought state assistance in reinforcing shorter working hours in their mills, thus enabling the cartel to adjust its production to the international market.

The failure to reach an agreement with the mills outside the IJMA concerning working hours convinced many within the cartel of the necessity of seeking state intervention. In 1932 the IJMA appealed to the government to enact legislation restricting working hours. The reason for such a demand was to secure for jute workers a shorter working day. However, the British colonial officials in Bengal were not sympathetic to the IJMA's cause and some were outspoken critics of the cartel.[1] In 1932, after prolonged whining, the IJMA was able to secure the intervention of the governor who brokered a peace deal between them and mills outside the Association, based on a new working hours agreement.[2] The agreement, however, soon faced a crisis with the outside mills threatening to withdraw; in July 1935 it became acute. Many IJMA members complained against the highly restricted working hours and argued that 'the mills in the last quinquennium have turned out only 20 per cent more goods than they were turning out 25 years ago with 90 per cent more looms at work. This position turned out to be more uneconomic'.[3] Soon Scott, the IJMA chairman for the year, started complaining of the relatively stronger position of non-IJMA mills.[4] Government legislation to prevent further expansion in the industry appeared crucial to many members of the IJMA, and the reason for such clamour for government intervention is apparent:

We have endeavoured to restrict our trade without being willing to fight the pirates. In leaving ourselves vulnerable we have encouraged the present unsatisfactory position. If we are prepared to continue any form of short time agreement it can only be provided if we have adequate protection either in the form of a guarantee amongst ourselves to break prices at the first threat of building or extension by outsiders. Whether we do this by government assistance or by fighting is the only issue. Doing it with suitable government protection means that we shall be able to achieve our desires without heavy losses.[5]

The Bengal government, in a letter to the IJMA on 12 August, clarified that it was not willing to accommodate their demands. It maintained that since the jute industry in Bengal was a vital economic institution, raw jute purchased by the industry constituted a crucial channel for the flow of ready cash to peasant households. Cultivators would hardly benefit from restricted working hours which would limit the demand for their product. At a time when depression wrought havoc in the countryside and the lower peasantry remained trapped in a situation of escalating debt and falling prices for their products, the government did not welcome IJMA's proposal to squeeze the peasantry further through a short-term working hours legislation. It also feared that limited working hours would restrict employment opportunities for workers who were already suffering from job losses.[6]

The government's missive caused a new wave of panic among the IJMA members. Non-IJMA mills also expressed their dissatisfaction with the existing working hours' agreement,[7] and soon almost all members formulated schemes to stave off the crisis in the industry.[8] A prominent IJMA member proposed the establishment of a Jute Fabrics Licensing Committee to regulate the export sector of the trade.[9] While excess capacity of mills created hurdles in the way of establishing control of the cartel, rumours regarding the collapse of an agreement with the non-IJMA members forced many companies to operate a 'hand to mouth policy'.[10] Many members came forward with the idea that there should be a new scheme for the development of a quota system to restrict the trade and a new 54-hour working week be introduced. By the middle of September the agreement with outside mills did not materialize, and exasperated Indian members of the IJMA (under Birla's leadership) threatened to resign. Such polarization between Indian and British members threatened the very existence of the IJMA.[11] This situation alarmed the government so deeply that Governor Woodhead himself proposed to enact a legislation for a 54-hour working week and volunteered to lobby for the IJMA with the central government.[12] However, Benthall put the final seal by arguing for a voluntary quota system agreed upon with government support, rather than direct intervention. Benthall, who was apparently calling for a full-fledged war against outside mills, was reminded of the grim situation in the international market by his colleagues in other firms who had consulted the accountants of a Dundee-based firm.[13]

Benthall and his associates became more and more aware of the danger of competing with forces outside India. The increasing shrinkage of the international market and the possibility of the invention of a cheap substitute to jute entered their calculation.[14] Thus, ironically, the crisis of the IJMA brought home the point that the future of the industry depended on cooperation among diverse sections of industrialists including Indians, and required the assistance of a friendly government.[15] Expatriate capitalists realized the need for a broader and wider coalition among propertied elites in Bengal.[16] They also realized that the solution to the crisis in their industry depended on changes in local politics. In this context, the reluctance of the Bengal government encouraged British traders to stand on their own and to embark on an ambitious project of building a coalition with Indian business groups and landed magnates. Thus the trade dispute, instead of dissolving unities among expatriate industrial interests in the sphere of politics, consolidated it further.

As a first step towards direct intervention in Bengal politics, British industrialists decided to strengthen their political position through a competent and cohesive independent European political lobby in provincial and central legislative assemblies. Benthall, who was a prominent figure in both the colonial business circle and British bureaucratic elites in India,[17] articulated the need for such political organization in no uncertain terms. In a letter to Hubert, a business colleague, he put forward an idea of united representation of the Chambers of Commerce in the central legislature.[18] He consulted various European firms to contribute to the fund of such a central political organization. The main aim behind floating such an organization was to establish an effective political machinery comprising trained parliamentarians to safeguard British interests in legislative bodies. This position also gained currency among his colleagues.[19]

The real problem for expatriate traders was the absence of a steady supply of political recruits.[20] However, the urgent need for the establishment of a political lobby also caught the attention of other members of the British business lobby in Bengal. European members closely monitored the functioning of the Imperial legislative assembly at Simla and pondered about their future strategy concerning the Bengal legislative assembly. T.C. Mortimer, a prominent member of the Bengal jute lobby, wrote to his colleague in Calcutta regarding the necessity of setting up a secretariat to serve provincial European representatives in the assembly.[21] By 1937–8, with the introduction of provincial autonomy, an elaborate organizational structure was created to strengthen the European group in legislative politics and to develop a cohesive and effective lobby.[22]

While arrangements continued for creating a powerful legislative lobby representing British business, British businessmen became involved in securing an 'adequate' representation in the new provincial assembly through constitutional reforms. The Bengal Chamber of Commerce upheld the idea of safeguarding British business interests by demanding the allocation of assembly seats on the basis of the volume of British capital invested in the province.[23] In Bengal, the idea of European representation on the basis of volume of investment was put forward by Henderson, President of the Bengal Chamber of Commerce. He wrote:

In dealing with this matter it is necessary to make it plain (a) that the representation of British commercial interests cannot properly be examined apart from the question of the representation of the non-official European community in India as a whole, and (b) that the importance of the position of the British non-official community in India derives not much from its numbers as from the trading interests that it represents. It is therefore necessary to take into consideration the seats allotted to special commercial institutions.[24]

In terms of constitutional arrangements in Bengal, Benthall favoured an upper council exercising restrictions on the lower council in the legislative assembly. He feared that an outright Muslim majority would be detrimental to propertied interests as the latter lagged behind Hindus in terms of education and wealth. In such circumstances, his idea was to assign both near-equal numbers of seats and to give Europeans the balancing role.[25] It would be wrong to assume that British business in Bengal was united under a single banner. Often there arose bitter differences among British expatriate trading organizations. While Benthall favoured a clear political liaison with Indian business, other British businessmen emphasized the strengthening of a powerful European political party.[26] Yet, despite such internal differences, their political agenda remained clear. They demanded that the police system should remain under the Governor's control; the provision of adequate representation in terms of allocation of seats in provincial legislative assemblies; and the introduction of commercial safeguards to prevent 'discrimination' by Indian-controlled provincial governments.[27] This agenda was based on a clear understanding that it was only at the provincial level that British business, through back-room wheeling and dealing, could exercise more effective political influence. At the all-India level, British trading influence could be outweighed by the Congress and the powerful Indian capitalist organizations.[28]

Based on these calculations, and led by veteran political negotiator Sir Hubert Carr, British business vigorously lobbied with the London government and Parliament for more political say at the provincial level. These efforts of British businessmen were handsomely rewarded in the Communal Award of Bengal. The bitterness of Indian politicians over the communal distribution of seats in Bengal could be located in a note prepared by A.H. Gaznavi. Speaking from the perspective of the Muslims of Bengal, he noted that while Europeans, who were not entitled to 1 per cent of the seats in terms of their demographic presence, were provided with 10 per cent of the seats while Muslims, who should have more than 51 per cent of the seats in terms of demographic composition of the province, had only 47 per cent of the seats.[29]

The award not only provided British business with a substantial number of seats but also reduced the Hindu community to a position of statutory minority. In the new legislative assembly of 250 seats, Hindus were provided with 80 seats, Muslims gained 119 seats, Europeans 11 seats, and European Commerce 14 seats.[30] Moreover, in accordance with the suggestion put forward by the European Association and the Bengal Chamber of Commerce, the governor enjoyed the power to dismiss the ministry and to prevent any radical legislation aiming at redistribution. In a concession to Indian trade and commerce, the government reserved more seats for Indian businessmen and landed aristocrats.[31] In practice, these commercial constituencies became pocket boroughs of various politicians.

The British business lobby was not satisfied with their victory; their real task still lay ahead. They needed to form a political coalition which would be sympathetic to their interests in Calcutta. Here Benthall's views provide interesting insights into British business politics. Soon after the announcement of the communal award, Benthall cautioned fellow British traders in a memorandum on terrorism that it would be wrong to place hopes on Muslims to prevent the rise of the Congress in the province. He wrote unequivocally:

There are some who place great reliance on the fact that the Moslems have hitherto not only refrained from civil disobedience and terrorism but have opposed it and they hope that the heavy representation of Moslems in Bengal will enable a Moslem first minister to take office with the aid of the Europeans and certain sections of the Hindus. While this is a possibility, past records indicate that no reliance can be placed upon the Moslems as a whole, even if the existence of a Moslem ministry is at stake. Those who share these fears believe that the example of the Calcutta Corporation is likely to be repeated, in which the steadying influence of the Moslems has been negligible as the rank and file proved that they cannot resist inducements to support the Congress Party.[32]

No doubt, to Benthall, the best possible scenario would be the formation of a predominantly anti-Congress ministry comprising conservative Muslim leaders and 'moderate Hindu elements', which in turn would depend upon the British business lobby for its survival. Yet who could steady the wayward pro-Congress Muslim forces? British business found an answer to this problem. They focussed their attention on a prominent Muslim personality, Sir Khwaja Nazimuddin. Nazimuddin had the right pedigree and appropriate political inclination.[33] Fiercely anti-Congress, unwavering in his loyalty to the British crown and a firm supporter of conservative, propertied, interest groups, this representative of the Urdu-speaking landed aristocracy in Bengal appeared to British business as a man capable of looking after their interests. Nazimuddin appeared an attractive political investment to British industrialists because of his singular incapacity to build up a popular mass base and thus his vulnerability to behind-the-curtain manipulation by powerful pressure groups.

The British trading lobby's confidence in Nazimuddin's ability became clear when he floated an English evening daily *Star of India*, to rally educated Muslim public opinion on his side. On Nazimuddin's request Benthall mounted a considerable campaign to secure advertisements for the paper. In a letter to Sir Richard Chevenix French, a member of the Viceroy's revenue board, on 13 August 1933 Benthall asked for advertisements from different sections of Muslim ruling elites in India. He described the *Star of India* as a good paper and the only organ which holds together the Moslems of Bengal.[34] At the end Benthall was also ecstatic about Nazimuddin, whom he described as the 'most trustworthy man—a chap in who I place utmost confidence'.[35] His concern for the paper reveals the nature and extent of British business support for Nazimuddin. Even a cursory glance at the paper reveals that the *Star of India* was able to secure a sizeable amount of European patronage. In 1934, the centre-page of the newspaper carried advertisements from Bathgate Castor Oil, The Chartered Bank of India, Central Bank of India, Calcutta Wine Merchants and Titagarh Paper Mill—all British concerns—while most other Indian newspapers of the day were satisfied with advertisements from Hrishikesh Oil Mill or Kalimata Flour Mill or some obscure astrologers of Bowbazar street in Calcutta.[36] The *Star of India* was edited by a British journalist called H.G. Franks who was for long associated with British business in India.[37]

The significance of British support for the *Star of India* could hardly be underestimated. In the 1930s, Muslim politics in Bengal remained in a flux. While 'nationalist' Muslims were increasingly disillusioned by the Congress, particularly because of its callous insensitivity to the interests of Muslim peasants in East Bengal, Calcutta's north Indian Muslim business lobby, along with the Urdu-speaking landed aristocracy, became active in forming an exclusive Muslim political organization. They played a crucial role in establishing the *Star of India* and promoting the Independent Muslim Political Party in Bengal. Eventually, they joined hands with Jinnah and established the Muslim League organization in Bengal. In the 1930s, the *Star of India* became the mouthpiece of the rising Muslim professionals in Bengal and played a crucial role in mobilizing the support of this small but politically significant community around the newly-constituted Muslim League. The significance of the financial support from British business became apparent in July 1937 when the *Star of India* faced financial insolvency. Advising on continuing their financial support to the *Star of India*, Edward Benthall wrote to his brother Paul:

I think it would be a great pity if the paper ceased to function just at this stage. ... Remember so far as we are concerned we have made a good profit out of it in the past and if we don't incur a loss we shall have done well because unquestionably the paper has played a valuable role in building up Mohameddan ideas and thereby a stable ministry to be formed. Have a frank talk with Nazimuddin and give him the limits to which you are prepared to go, he will understand.[38]

In the late 1930s, the conservative Muslim landed aristocracy and British business needed each other to safeguard their interests from radical nationalists. Conflicts between Muslim firms and European business remained at a rather nebulous stage as Muslim business remained too weak to mount a crucial challenge to the entrenched hold of European business in Bengal. However, it would be wrong to presume that expatriate traders relied upon Muslim political opinion alone to organize their support.

British business also had supporters among Hindu landed magnates. Most prominent among them was Sir B.P. Singh Roy. He was, like Nazimuddin, a loyal supporter of the crown and expressed his anti-Congress views quite candidly. His main fear was from 'left wingers' in the Congress. Deeply opposed to any move towards India's independence, Singh Roy proudly wrote to Benthall in June 1933:

The Congress ... leaders are being held by these left wingers who want to secure the constitution only to wrench more powers with the ultimate object of the severance of the British connection as in Ireland. I hope the Government at home will also realise all these facts and will not give the Congress a chance to capture the legislature to further its mischievous ends. People with stake in the country, whose interests are identified with the stability of Government should be given an effective voice in the Upper Houses both in the Centre as well as in the Provinces.[39]

Not surprisingly, this gallant knight of the empire was trusted by British business as the authentic representative of the moderate Hindu elements in the province, a partner in their coalition against radical nationalists. The biggest catch for British capital was, however, Nalini Sarkar.[40] Sarkar's claim to fame came from his crucial position as a financial magnate. He was a powerful player in Bengal politics.[41] His success in business brought him the leadership of the Bengal National Chamber of Commerce, the organization of Calcutta's Bengali traders dealing mainly in piece goods. As the head of Bengal National Chamber of Commerce, he sat on the Calcutta Port Trust which in turn elected him to the Calcutta corporation. With the help of the Congress, he became the mayor of this nationalist-dominated body in 1934. He had a long and impeccable record of service to Indian traders in Calcutta and was also a formidable opponent of European business interests there.[42] Sarkar represented conservative propertied interests within the Congress and was close to the B.C. Roy faction and the Congress high command. From 1934 onwards the relationship between Sarkar and the European business lobby warmed up when the latter supported him in the Calcutta Corporation mayoral election against Fazlul Haque.[43] Even then, it was a surprise for the British trading lobby in 1935, when this high-ranking Congress leader approached them for their opinion regarding electoral arrangements and the formation of a pro-business political organization.[44]

Sarkar's attempt to extend cooperation with European business was a significant political move. The reasons for such a move could ostensibly be found in the factional fighting within the Congress where Sarkar's lobby was gradually losing out to the Bose brothers. However, it would be wrong to over-emphasize factional considerations in understanding Sarkar's moves. While it had the tacit approval of the Hindu trading lobby in Calcutta, it can be explained more adequately by focusing on the political and economic circumstances in Bengal in the 1930s.

In these years, the Great Depression sharpened the process of communal polarization and class antagonisms in Bengal politics. The restriction in the working hours of jute mills contributed significantly to the collapse of raw jute prices, the main cash crop in Bengal, in a period of a general plunge in the prices of agricultural products. As the agrarian crisis deepened, money lenders who provided loans to peasants for cultivation made attempts to recover their capital from their debtors as early as possible. This had a communal ramification in eastern Bengal where activities of Hindu moneylenders provoked discontent among a predominantly Muslim peasantry. In East Bengal, radical peasant and tenant organizations gained popularity through their demands for radical agrarian reforms, and on many occasions peasant action was initiated from below by the poorest sections of rural society—the share croppers.[45] Mostly recruited from lower orders of Hindus or Muslims, these peasant activists were unwilling to accept the high-caste Congress leadership in Bengal politics.[46] In urban areas, rising urban unemployment also brought into existence radical youth organizations who had little faith in Congress politics. Women's movements also gained prominence with various forms of women's organizations coming into existence.[47] With revolutionary terrorism losing its dynamism, many youths felt attracted to Marxism.[48] The All India Student Federation, a radical student body, came into existence in this period.[49] Unemployment also contributed to growing communal bitterness as it stiffened the competition between the Hindu and Muslim petty bourgeoisie for government jobs and official patronage. Hindu–Muslim conflicts during religious festivals or on the issue of the consumption of animal flesh (suspected to be beef) by Muslims in mill areas became common.[50] Thus, the depression created dual possibilities in Bengal politics. On the one hand, radical organizations were clamouring for sweeping changes in the colonial social order through reforms in agrarian and industrial relations; on the other, communal bitterness started surfacing in every aspect of political life. Alarmed by the growing political insecurity and economic chaos, politicians with strong trading connections such as Sarkar, became keen on forming a business-friendly provincial ministry to safeguard their own economic interests.[51] It was clear that they might forfeit their chances of preserving their economic position by opposing Muslim politicians who were already granted a statutory majority in the provincial assembly. Rather, dialogue with Muslim politicians with an eye on a political coalition of propertied elites would be politically more beneficial in such an unsettled environment. The political alliance between the propertied elites of Bengal and the European business lobby started taking shape in this context. The hope for such coalition matured when the electorate gave an inconclusive verdict in the 1937 elections.[52]

The results of the 1937 election exposed the limitations of the Congress. Apart from movements directed against the colonial state on peasant issues[53], it remained insensitive to any suggestion for land reforms.[54] In the 1930s, the Hindu middle classes, who constituted the main support base of the

Congress, were not yet sufficiently detached from the land. Like the Congress, the newly formed Muslim League could not win the trust of Muslim peasant activists because of the presence of the large numbers of Muslim landed aristocracy in the party. Many of these peasant organizers joined the Peasants and Tenants Party (Krishak Proja Party) of Fazlul Haque, an organization which was committed to land reforms and sympathetic to broad pan-Indian nationalist aspirations. This had provided the Congress with the opportunity to form an alliance with radical Muslims but the alliance collapsed due to the Congress's failure to prioritize land reforms.[55] The Muslim League now stepped into this power vacuum. Nalini Ranjan Sarkar became a crucial player in forming the alliance between the Peasant and Tenant Party and the Muslim League; the meeting took place at his residence in Calcutta.[56] Nalini Sarkar was not alone in his venture. He remained in close touch with Gandhi and even took Birla into confidence. Hindu landed elites and business organizations shrewdly realized that without representation in the government, they would be unable to prevent any organized onslaught on their economic positions.[57]

The coalition that emerged out of these negotiations appeared to be a formidable combination of propertied interests in Bengal. While among new ministers Khwaja Nazimuddin, Mussharraf Hossain, B.P. Singh Roy, Srish Chandra Nandi, and Prasanna Kumar Raikut came from the landed aristocracy, Nalini Sarkar represented the Hindu business community in Calcutta, and Suhrawardy was close to the Urdu-speaking Muslim traders. The sole exception was Nausher Ali who was soon hounded out of the ministry by the Muslim League.[58] The main actors in this ministerial drama were well known: Nalini Sarkar, Nazimuddin, Suhrawardy, and B.P Singh Roy. Most ministers were not elected by any popular territorial constituencies but entered the assembly through special constituencies for landlords and chambers of commerce. Thus the ministry, from the time of its formation, was highly unrepresentative in character, and very soon radical elements of the KPP revolted against the Muslim League leadership. As a consequence, the ministry remained dependent on the support of the European lobby.

It would, however, be erroneous to believe that such a coalition became a cohesive political block on its own. For example, although British business provided their support to this ministry, many European members complained about its alleged communal nature.[59] Benthall, who was a keen supporter of the government, blamed the Congress for causing such communal trouble and asked British members to throw their weight behind the government. More importantly, Benthall stated that he did not even fear the possibility of the Congress's coming to power. What he objected to was the

outside activities of Congress in the shape of a large communist subversive movement which will be timed, as Nehru has said in his book, for the next economic crisis.[60]

Interestingly, British trading organizations observed that the Congress party was divided between two sections, capitalist and labour.[61] British industrialist lobbies felt insecure and threatened by the growing strike wave in the jute industry in February 1937. The doubts of expatriate traders concerning the coalition ministry's role in preventing labour radicalism were put aside when, at a dinner in the Bengal Club before the budget session in August 1937 the finance minister Nalini Sarkar assured the Europeans that the present government '[is] out to protect British Capital'. He further said that 'candidly in doing so I believe that I am protecting my own business and I will do all in my power to prevent anything which would tend to the flight of British capital from Calcutta.'[62] Nazimuddin warned Europeans of the communist menace and 'the determination of the government to suppress any such difficulties'.[63] Thus the coalition partners of the Bengal government acted to convince British capital that they needed to stick together in order to counter the red menace in Bengal. The visible symbol of such a red menace was the general strike of industrial workers. The only thing that bothered the Europeans were the radical promises of the KPP.[64] However, Fazlul Haque, fondly called by the East Bengal peasantry as 'the tiger of Bengal', was then firmly caged by vested propertied interests represented by Nazimuddin, B.P. Singh Roy, and British industrialists. Benthall was quick to see the advantage of the new situation for British business:

... [W]hat a powerful position we have got with the government if we care to use it constructively in the right way. In fact, if we work things rightly I believe they would adopt any policy that we liked to press upon them, provided that we have definite constructive approach.[65]

In other words, expatriate traders became part of the new propertied political coalition in Bengal from this period onwards. It was the ascendancy of this coalition of propertied interests that presided over the suppression of the general strike of jute workers in 1937 and institutionalized the communalization of labour politics through government-sponsored trade unions for Muslim workers. Communalization of labour politics thus constituted a crucial aspect of the strategies of propertied elites as a whole. A segment of Hindu propertied elites accepted the situation as very few alternatives were available within the institutional structure of politics to which the Congress also committed its support.

Retrenchment, Rationalization, and Workers' Grievances: Changing Industrial Relations in the Jute Industry during the Great Depression

The depression years in the jute industry were marked by spiralling unemployment resulting from the organized retrenchment of workers, increasing intensity of work, and a decline in real wages. Alarmed by the decline in their profit margins industrialists in the early 1930s adopted a policy of sweeping retrenchment. In 1930, ninety jute mills in and around Calcutta employed nearly 264,417 workers. In 1933 it had declined to 208,246. [66] By 1934 the number of retrenched workers increased to 84,000. Along with retrenchment, the curtailment of working hours also helped the industrialist to attenuate the wage bills. The reduction in the wages of industrial workers in the largest industrial centre of Bhatpara in this period amply testified to this.

TABLE 7.1

Number of workers employed in the jute industry in
Bhatpara and their wages between 1930–34

Year	Number of working looms	Daily consumption of jute in maunds	Number of labourers engaged	Amount of wages paid monthly
1930–31	9,657	21,429	50,990	10,28,607
1931–32	8,210	19,050	43,518	7,68,408
1932–33	8,584	18,518	43,093	7,72,206
1933–34	8,484	18,357	42,329	7,48,310

Source: Annual Administrative Report on Bhatpara Municipality (AARBM) 1930, 1931, 1932, 1933, 1934.

The average monthly wages of the labourers engaged in Bhatpara decreased from Rs 20.20 in 1930 to Rs 17.70 in 1933.[67] Though such figures only indicate gross decline in the wages without revealing much details about its impact on different sections of workers, it definitely suggests a fall in the earnings of average workers. Many managers supervised retrenchment and wage cuts in a way that they could economize on the resources of the factories without undermining what they regarded as productive capacity of the mills. Thus a mill manager of Shyamnagar North Mill wrote back home in 1933:

During the year reductions in labour and wages were carried out from time to time in order to economize as much as possible and in the various departments; hands were paid off wherever it was found possible to do so without effecting [sic] the working efficiency.[68]

Moreover, despite no general overhauling of machinery, many companies introduced new machines in this period in order to further reduce the number of workers. T.G. Morrow, who was appointed by the Victoria Jute Mill to investigate possibilities of mechanization, candidly wrote to his superiors that these machines

are mainly labour-saving devices, and if [sic] incidentally they help to make a better yarn (as they certainly do) this is not their chief recommendation. Mills, fitted with one another of the above devices, are working with one quarter to one third of the labour previously employed.[69]

Many managers claimed that the shorter 40-hour working period allowed workers to obtain much more free time. Yet they obscured the fact that the intensity of work in the factories increased substantially. Managers, in fact, tried to extract more labour within the limited time period under the new working hours of agreement. This was possible due to the introduction of the single-shift system in many factories in place of long, cumbersome, and complicated multiple-shift system of work. For example, a manager of the Shyamnagar North Jute Mill wrote back home:

as regards labour on the single shift system this is proving plentiful and a better class of worker is available. A higher standard of work can be got from the operatives as they realise there is a plentiful supply of labour in Bazaar to replace them if their work prove unsatisfactory ... accurate check can be kept on the number of roll attendance and each worker can be identified, there being no remaining shift to cause confusion. More time could be devoted to the actual supervision of work by the overseer, babus and sardars as only two roll calls per day have to be taken, whereas previously, on the multiple shift sometimes as many as five had to be taken.[70]

Writing on the new labour situation, the manager of Titagarh expressed his satisfaction in the following terms:

The new arrangement is a great improvement as each worker is now confined to his/ her machine throughout the day instead of previously having the relieving shift and moving all over the department.[71]

The new system enabled supervisors to come into direct contact with workers which enabled them to identify more efficiently the number of actual employees in the mills. This also lessened the possibilities of having an informal working arrangement among weavers, particularly to do each other's work, whereby a worker could obtain leave from work without formal permission.[72] In order to further enforce and tighten discipline in the mill, the management adopted measures to restrict the movement of workers during working hours. The manager of Shyamnagar Jute Mill wrote quite candidly to his directors that:

It was found necessary during the year to close all means of exit from the compounds during the hours [the] mill was working, to stop the practice of workers going out for tea etc. Consequently gates were erected against the wall of the compound ....[73]

These developments unsettled the workers, who raised objections against what they perceived as gross violation of customary practices within factories.[74] With the growing unemployment and steadily increasing supply of workers, managers could suppress any sign of protest through summary dismissals.[75] Workers' resistance to the new industrial regime petered out due to fear of retrenchment. Retrenchment also had a profound effect on the employment pattern in factories in terms of age and gender. The services of young boys, who were employed in the mills to assist elderly workers, were terminated permanently during the Depression era. Women workers were also increasingly replaced by men.[76] This further contributed to the increasing pressure of work which was reflected in the rising number of accidents in the jute mills.[77] Such systematic retrenchment profoundly altered the nature of labour politics in the mills and had serious repercussions on community-level power equations.

The newly-changed work situation, for example, put even more pressure on the spinners as the introduction of new machinery and the reduction in the number of workers occurred on a larger scale in the spinning departments. These changes also fostered better-organized opposition among spinners to industrial discipline. Indeed, it became difficult for the management to pacify spinners during sudden strikes. A story of labour unrest in the Titagarh Jute Mill of Thomas Duff Company may be seen as representative of such cases where the persistent resistance from spinners was evident. In 1931 a new wage rate was introduced in this mill. Soon workers of the spinning, beaming, and calendeering departments refused to accept the new rates; they were also joined by the weavers. After such a display of solidarity among the workers from different departments, a vast majority of them, including weavers and beamers, accepted the new wages the next day. Dissatisfaction remained only in the spinning department.[78]

The increasing pressure on the spinning departments had different social implications as well. The weavers were mostly upcountry Muslims recruited from Bihar and east UP, while the spinners were predominantly Hindus drawn from different corners of the subcontinent. In major industrial centres such as Titagarh, Telegu-speaking south Indian migrants, commonly known as Madrasis, were mainly employed in the spinning departments. The predominance of Telegu workers in the 1937 general strike also reflected the impact of the reorganization of work at the shop-floor level and the militant opposition such reorganization encountered from spinners. Thus during the 1937 strike, Telegu workers increasingly came to the forefront of the struggle in the mills.[79] This however did not imply that weavers were not involved in the strike at all. Rather, they played a crucial role in organizing strikes[80] and grass roots-level factory committees. But the militant participation of spinners further widened and intensified the nature of opposition from the workers. Indeed, when the Muslim League organizers in the last phase of the general strike of 1937 contacted many Muslim weavers, the latter became reluctant to push the strike further. However, the Telegu spinners still remained in the forefront of the strike. Thus the alteration of the industrial regime, along with changes in the political circumstances in Bengal, influenced community-level social mechanisms of the politics of protest in the jute mills.

In order to reinforce this work discipline, management regarded the services of sardars and babus as vital for the maintenance of industrial discipline. Hence it introduced several measures to benefit these workers. For example, in 1930 for the first time the Thomas Duff Company introduced new benefits such as provident fund for clerical employees.[81] The residential quarters of the babus and sardars were provided with electricity by many companies.[82] The new municipality act of 1932 empowered the rate-payers to exercise franchise in industrial municipalities. These rate-payers were mainly composed of relatively affluent sardars, traders, mill clerks, and other bhadralok residents.[83] Such measures undoubtedly strengthened the hands of these intermediaries but increasingly isolated them from ordinary workers. The petty tyrannies of these men which were earlier regarded as customary by ordinary workers now increasingly came to be considered as *julums* (repression) by them.

Managers tried to promote recreation among workers to divert their attention from politics and to resist possible outbursts of political unrest against this harsh industrial regime. The manager of the Victoria Jute Mill observed that sports was 'the finest way to keep the minds of the people healthy and free from communal strife and extremist political views.'[84] Sports departments of the factories were extremely active in promoting football among workers. Mill managers also sponsored football shields and competitions and pompously presided over the distribution of prizes.[85] Management also opened new schools for the children of babus and sardars; these children were encouraged to join scouts movements. The manager of the Angus Jute Mill observed that the scouts movements appeared to be quite popular with such students.[86] In many factories tea-shops were opened and vendors were allowed to sell sweetmeats during intervals. Welfare, in this context, could hardly be divorced from the desire to maintain industrial discipline. In fact, a manager reported to his supervisors that such measures 'would help to confine the workers inside the compound during the working period.'[87]

Despite such piecemeal welfare measures, departmental strikes and communal riots were recurrent events in mill towns. Hindu–Muslim fracas became increasingly common during religious festivals. Minor stoppages of work became common in everyday industrial life as the jute trade recovered from the Depression in 1936. Workers demanded an end to retrenchments and also less heavy work. While these efforts of the workers escalated tensions in the mills, the approaching elections and granting of provincial autonomy added a new dimension to the renewed battle within the industry.

The General Strike of 1937: Labour on the Offensive

The prospective election in January 1937 attracted the attention of various sections of labour leaders to the necessity of organizing a common platform to fight the election from. Indeed, throughout the early 1930s trade unions were notoriously divided by their factional infightings and broad ideological divide. In the aftermath of the Shanghai crisis in 1928, Indian communists, under the influence of the sixth Comintern Congress, vehemently opposed the moderate trade unions causing two subsequent splits in the AITUC in 1929 and 1930. The Communists themselves were involved in bitter internal squabbles.[88] Despite internecine conflicts among unions and labour activists, in October 1936 they established a United Front Parliamentary Board to fight the 1937 election.[89] Eight different left wing groups, including communists came together and prepared a list of candidates for the provincial election. The forum clashed with the NTUF, an organization of conservative mould, which promoted a far less radical political programme.[90] The election campaign of the United Front paved the way for radical action throughout the industry. In the stronghold of the Congress Socialist Party in Howrah, regular study-circles were organized in the slums and training was provided for developing branches of trade unions. Election meetings everywhere attracted crowds of workers. In meeting after meeting speakers demanded security of employment, pensions and gratuities, the termination of illegal exactions and bribes by sardars and babus. In Howrah, the leading socialist (but avowedly non-communist) trade unionist Sibnath Banerjee, unfolded a new ten-point charter of demands which included: (1) Permanency of services; (2) Lowest salary being fixed at Rs 30 per month; (3) Free quarters; (4) Provision for old age; (5) Leave with pay for a month and one month's sick leave annually; (6) Free medical help; (7) Unemployment benefit; (8) Jobs for relations; and (9) Free education for children of workers.[91] Such campaigns linked everyday struggle at the shop-floor level with a wider political battle for representation of workers' interests in the legislative assembly. The election campaigns created an environment for wider confrontation between capital and labour.[92] Workers hoped for at least the restoration of the pre-Depression situation in the mills. In the ensuing election, the Left candidates defeated their rivals by substantial margins.

As the campaign against dismissals and retrenchment gained ground during the electioneering, industrial conflicts became rife in the factories. Unions, however, remained divided in their attitude towards the extension of industrial action. Gandhians, socialists, and communists became involved in a bitter quarrel over the necessity of a general strike.[93] The campaign against retrenchment and corruption of sardars and babus evoked enthusiastic response from the workers.[94] As the trade recovered in 1936 and the political climate became more favourable for collective bargaining, workers began to protest against arbitrary dismissals and the ongoing process of retrenchment. In August 1936, at the conference of the All-Bengal Jute Workers' Union the Congress Socialist Party already raised a slogan in favour of a general strike.[95] Thus, conflicts among unions over the strategy of confrontation with employers became insignificant as workers engaged themselves in spreading the strike.

The 1937 general strike started as a protest against the arbitrary dismissals of weavers. On 1 February 1937, weavers at the Fort William Jute Mill stopped work in protest against the dismissal of spinners and weavers for bad work. The strike spread to the neighbouring Ganges Mill on the issue of the dismissal of three weavers. Soon the strike took the form of general protests against retrenchment, wage cuts, and ill treatment of workers. While the strike in Howrah was about to fizzle out, workers in the south of Calcutta, in the Budgebudge Mills struck work on similar issues. On 23 February 1937, when the management dismissed four weavers in the Budgebudge Mills, nearly 3,000 workers walked out in protest. The strike spread to five other mills when a local trade union official was arrested allegedly for fomenting trouble. As industrial action escalated, the managements were able to persuade local officials to arrest the 'ring leaders'. Large assemblies were banned in the troubled mill belt. These repressive measures, the government hoped, would restrict outside intervention. However, repression often strengthens opposition, and the workers marched in a large body to the nearby Birla Jute Mills. Here they were joined by local employees who assaulted the security staff when they tried to prevent workers from leaving the factory.[96] Outside leaders had little role to play in such mobilization of workers as they were often refused entry to the mill areas by the police.

The general strike slowly expanded northwards and by the end of March it embraced the entire mill belt which remained unsettled from 1 February to 10 May 1937. As the strike progressed, mill areas witnessed a fierce contest between the strikers and the management. While mill owners held meetings with sardars and burrababus, distributed leaflets and pasted posters printed by the IJMA in the slums and mill lines, strikers organized their counter meetings, held marches in the bazaars, and clashed with loyal workers, police, and security officials.[97] In places where loyal sardars and burrababus enjoyed the support of workers, a vast majority of workers refrained from joining the strike. This provoked fierce physical fights among loyal workers and striking employees from other mills.[98]

Violence and intimidation by the police, security staff, and loyal sardars on the one hand, and counter-violence by militant strikers on the other also influenced the outcome of the contest at the local level. On most occasions, symbolic violence and gestures of intimidation by striking workers from other factories provided employees the excuse to leave work. For example, in the afternoon of 3 May 1937, as the Angus Jute Mill resumed its second shift of the day, workers returned to their work in full strength and displayed no signs of unrest. But an uneasy calm descended as rumours about a strike in the nearby Chapdani area reached the mill. At around 2 o'clock, striking workers from neighbouring mills began to gather outside the walled compound. Soon they started showering stones on the building. The police rushed to the spot and dispersed the crowd. A section of the crowd then proceeded to the residences of the clerical employees, popularly known as babus' quarters. After struggling for an hour, they eventually broke down the gate adjacent to the bales godown, but were prevented from entering the compound and were almost immediately dispersed. Such intimidating behaviour and violent gestures outside the mill compound triggered commotion among workers inside. As soon as stones hit the window panes, women in the sewing department panicked and rushed for shelter in the well-protected weaving section. This, combined with rumours that the strikers were creating a disturbance in the 'lines' or dwelling places of workers, caused the weavers to leave their looms. The other departments were similarly affected and at 3 p.m. the engines were stopped. No one was injured, but approximately 300 glass panes were broken as a result of the stone-throwing. For nearly two weeks after this incident, the Angus Jute Mill, along with other mills of the area remained out of operation.[99] However, it would be wrong to interpret such incidents as the absence of support among workers for the strike. On the contrary, in August 1937, soon after the general strike, the Angus Jute Mill became the most important centre for popular trade union movements and series of strikes.

Indeed, as the Angus case demonstrates, the general body of workers of a mill were anxious to evade direct confrontation with the management. Negotiation was left to the central body of the strikers, a coalition of union activists, members of legislative assemblies from labour constituencies, and sympathetic leaders of political parties. As the strike progressed to an end, the demands became known. Workers asked for: (1) restoration of wages prevalent prior to 1931–2, (2) security of service, (3) proper service rules, (4) introduction of pension, gratuity and maternity benefits, (5) Interval for refreshment, (6) consultation with unions regarding the settlement of grievances and appointments, (7) reinstatement of dismissed workers, (8) stoppage of bribery and fines, and (9) reappointment of those workers who lost jobs during the Depression. Many of these demands aimed at reversing the changes introduced during the 1930s.

As the strike escalated, the battle was extended to the assembly floor and at the end of March the Congress leader Sarat Bose called for the extension of the strike. Finally, Chief Minister Fazlul Haque intervened and a compromise was reached with the Central Jute Strike Committee comprising representatives of all sections of the trade union organizers. The settlement between the management and the Strike Committee was ambivalent in nature. It was made clear that: (1) there would be no victimization in the factories, (2) trade unions would be recognized, (3) there would be a thorough investigation into questions concerning wages and powers of sardars and overseers in the matter of appointment and dismissals, and (4) prohibitory orders under Section 144 would be withdrawn. Under this agreement, workers returned to work on 10 May 1937. The rituals that marked the ending of the strike confirmed among the officials the suspicion of communist influence over the strike. As the director of the Thomas Duff Company recorded:

On the 10th May we resumed work after the last strike. The workers were told that although they were to resume work that day they must not enter the factory until their leader Mr Zaman came along and waved a red flag and they were to wait for him even although it would be an hour or two. This actually happened and Mr Zaman made a triumphant tour, visiting each mill in turn from Serampore to Angus, waved his red flag and each mill then resumed work. We were the last on the list and while some workers were inside, the majority waited patiently until he came along which was about 8.40 a.m. He got a rousing cheer when he waved his red flag and the workers without another word or gesture actually ran from the gates to their machines and in five minutes were working as if nothing had happened.[100]

The rhetoric of the coming of *Mazdur Raj* (workers' rule), and slogans like *Mazdur ki Jai* (Victory to Workers), in a period of steady erosion of employment and increasing workload generated a millenarian hope throughout the mill belt. The industrial action marked by slogan-shouting, waving of red flags as a ritual, clandestine meetings, and night marches impinged upon the workers' consciousness. Many of the organizational techniques preached by socialist leaders were adopted by the workers and used in organizing strikes at the grass roots level. The emergence of factory committees in the Titagarh mill belt, where socialist unionist Mohammed Zaman was active, was an useful instance. These factory committees comprised representatives of different departments in the factories. As grass roots-level organizations, these committees tried to redress the grievances of their constituents in the factories to further their hold. Soon after the end of the general strike, the managers discovered that sardars and burrababus, who traditionally acted as intermediaries between workers and managers, had lost their hold over the workers. The director of Thomas Duff Company vividly described in a private memorandum how he was

amazed to find a crowd gathered into groups of four, representing, not departments, but sections of departments throughout the mill. More amazing still, included were four lots of women representatives and not a sirdar or babu to be seen anywhere. It took 2 1/2 hours to interview all the groups and listen to all their grievances. Most of their grievances concern treatment meted out to them by sirdars and others in charge.[101]

Interestingly enough, not only had the intermediaries like sardars and burrababus no say in these factory committees, but 'union babus' also had minimal influence in deciding their everyday functioning. Workers decided to put forward their grievances on their own and had enough confidence to negotiate with the managers directly. This was even appreciated by the director of Thomas Duff Company who observed:

The doctrines preached have been very cleverly put to the worker and he has now thrown aside any influence Sirdars and babus may have had over him and thinks he is standing on his own .... The outcome of this, curiously enough, is that the management, instead of being more estranged from the workers, is actually in closer touch with them.

He further noted that:

The workers themselves now come to give their points of view which may sound very real to them. Lots of the grievances brought up show that the workers are realising their value in the scheme of things and wish to be treated as well as and in the same manner as ourselves.[102]

Yet the growing strength of the factory committee did not herald an age of cooperation between labour and capital. On the contrary, the factory committee was pressurized by common workers to end the process of arbitrary dismissals as practised by the management. This led to a protracted confrontation between management and workers.

The management of the Angus Jute Mill ran into trouble in May 1937 when they tried to discipline workers through the time-tested practice of dismissing errant employees. Since a vast majority of workers had no security of jobs, managers could easily terminate the services of those whom they perceived as surplus employees. But the newly-formed departmental working committees challenged the managerial authority on such issues. When the management tried to dismiss some weavers for their low-quality production, departmental committees immediately raised their objections. A deputation of the weavers expressed their grievances to the manager regarding such treatment but with no effect. Management not only disregarded the warnings of the weavers but also dismissed some spinners the next day, allegedly for not carrying out orders properly. Soon the departmental working committees intervened and expressed their dissatisfaction with the proceedings.[103]

Subsequent events on that day demonstrated the extent of hold the factory committee had on common workers. Immediately after the dismissal of the spinners, several of the committee members signalled the workers to stop work as a mark of protest and work in all departments came to standstill for about 1 1/2 hours. The members of the working committee assured the manager that if he reinstated the dismissed spinners, work would be carried on normally and the manager, realizing the danger of a prolonged conflict, reinstated the dismissed spinner. But the truce lasted for three hours only. The factory committee again intervened when the manager decided on the same day to terminate the services of six women workers; possibly women members of the working committee raised their objections to these dismissals. The committee soon disrupted the functioning of the factory for a brief period of 15 minutes while demanding proper rules and service conditions.[104]

Tension in the factories continued unabated. When the local labour leader Zaman was arrested and was sentenced to rigorous imprisonment for six months, the factory committee promptly called a strike. The defiant mood of the workers could be observed in their violation of the most mundane instructions given by the management. This could be noticed, for example, in the spinners' decision to wear *dhoti*, the traditional Indian dress, instead of shorts which the management had earlier introduced as working dress.[105] This defiance was more symbolic, but it reflected their confidence in their ability to defy the management. It also sent unmistakable signals to the authority that their rules were losing meaning for ordinary workers.

The factory committee emerged as the most powerful political body in the workplace that enjoyed unprecedented popularity among workers. Departmental representation allowed the factory committee to arrive at any consensus very quickly. As the factory committee asserted its control over the production process, lower level 'overseers in charge had practically no say in the running of their departments'.[106] The management took the challenge very seriously. As the trouble in Angus continued unabated, the director of Thomas Duff Company grimly noted in a letter to his superiors:

If labour has reached the stage of practically demanding control of the industry, in my opinion there can be only one course open to employers, and that is to fight to the last ditch regardless of cost.[107]

The factory committee further aggravated the confrontation with management through orchestrating attacks on those sardars who had opposed the general strike in the jute mills. When attempts were being made to arrest the 'culprits', the factory committee declared a strike in the mill. The management on 16 July, in a desperate gamble, decided to terminate the services of nearly 104 workers who were active in the factory committee and ordered them to collect their outstanding wages and leave the quarters. In order to throw the workers out of the mill line, the management sought the help of the district magistrate. The latter instructed the police to launch a combing operation to search for the dismissed workers in the 'Coolie Lines'. Most of those workers, however, had already disappeared as only 14 of them were found in the lines. They were brought to the office, paid their due wages, and sent out of the district.[108] The dismissal of the active trade unionists in the Angus Jute Mill was not an isolated example; the managing director of Thomas Duff Company noted in his description of the IJMA meeting that all over the mill belt workers were dismissed from their jobs.[109] This further intensified industrial action as the government report recorded numerous strikes in different mills across the jute mill belt in the post-settlement period.[110]

The rapid unfolding of the confrontation in the Angus Jute Mill caught even the communist leaders unprepared, who searched for an amicable resolution of the conflict. The trade union organizers arranged a meeting between the representatives of the Angus Jute Mill workers and the premier of Bengal, Mr Fazlul Haque, for a settlement. But the Haque ministry did not come to the aid of the workers. On the contrary, it placed more restrictions on the activities of the radical labour leaders and tried to promote unions which were friendly to the management of the jute mills. The factory committees were frowned upon by many trade unionists who regarded personally-supervised, loose, amorphous organizations as more suitable to their designs. Thus in many instances, workers listened to the suggestions made by trade union leaders, but developed and deployed their own strategies against the management. Such autonomy, ironically, also undermined the hold of many trade unionists themselves. Factory committees constituted the radical moment of departure in the field of trade union politics, when workers developed their own organizations to create instruments for the democratic running of industry.

The entire strike organization remained in an amorphous state due to the internecine conflicts among trade unionists over the control of the strike movement. There emerged a central strike committee led mainly by members of the legislative assembly elected from the labour constituencies.[111] These leaders operated through their contacts with intermediate level labour leaders much closer to workers themselves. Most prominent among these groups of leaders was M.A. Zaman, a former communist and member of the Congress Socialist Party. Below these groups there existed the most crucial leaders of the strike movement—the militant workers, mainly drawn from the weavers and spinners. They led the movement at the grass roots-level and organized new forms of democratic trade union organizations, namely the factory committees. Collectively, the strike movement was called the Red Union Movement. However, there existed little coordination amongs its leaders and most of these rival groups vied with each other for political hegemony over the movement, but with little success. All official documents generated by the trade union movement indicated a lack of communication between party leaders and labour militants.[112] Workers were not promoted in the organization of the political parties and thus had little direct contact with the party organization. On their part, labour militants were more concerned with changing the structure of the industrial regime rather than promoting any specifically-designed political agenda of the party.

The challenge provided by the grass roots-level labour militants to the existing industrial regime actually transformed the labour question into a central plank of political coalition-making among the propertied elite groups. As the workers' movement came to challenge the provincial government, it became apparent that there would be attempts by the Congress party to use the strike to put pressure on the government. Thus it became imperative that the unstable coalition of the propertied elites establish industrial peace. The strike movement had initiated the process of radicalization of the youth and student movements.[113] For a far-reaching impact, it also needed to make connections with other segments of workers employed in the British-controlled tea plantations and mining industry in the province.[114] More importantly, the strike movement had to establish ties with jute cultivators in eastern Bengal in order to put effective pressure on the leadership.[115] Hence, the movement had the crucial potential of bringing about a counter coalition of workers and peasant groups that could accelerate the movement for democratization of the economic and political structure of the province. This view of the situation was actually confirmed by the rather nervous jute barons in their private correspondence. M.P. Thomas, a close confidant of Benthall, wrote to him in early June—almost a month after the general strike:

I have never seen anything like these strikes- not for lawless [sic]and rioting, as there has been comparatively little of this, but for the way the excellent intelligence service and organization of the agitators, both Congress and Communists showed up. At the moment I understand they are ... are proposing to concentrate on the real masses the agriculturalists—with a view to getting them worked up to the required pitch to pull off a whole, hearted [sic] red showing in conjunction with industrial labour whenever they consider the time ripe.[116]

Offensive of the State and Capital: Reform, Repression, and Riots

The strikes in the jute industry shook the confidence of expatriate capital. They recognized the need to organize a new form of labour management. As workers started organizing departmental factory committees, Edward Benthall, the master strategist for British capital in Bengal, advocated the setting up of work committees comprising workers' representatives and British supervisory staff in order to maintain direct communication between themselves.[117] However, the hierarchical culture in the mills prevented any meaningful discussion between workers and supervisory staff members. The environment of such meetings, in the words of Paul Benthall, was frosty and concentrated only on the progress of the Mohamedan Sporting Club in the league.[118]

The management was also reluctant to constitute work committees as they feared that such moves could strengthen the hands of the militant workers involved in the strike. Paul reminded Edward Benthall of the serious change in the consciousness of average workers as he pointed out that '[t]he average coolly [sic] has his own point of view and thinks that we are exploiting him all the time ...'.[119] There was clear reluctance among British industrialists to consider the establishment of work committees in the wake of the strike movement. Indeed, so furious was M.P. Thomas, a confidant of Benthall, that he described workers as 'ungrateful lot of sods' who did not appreciate the continuous welfare work of the firm.[120] What was the real nature of the welfare of the labour that the IJMA bosses had in their minds? The attitude of the IJMA bosses towards labour welfare was evident from their plans of reforms of labour management to prevent future strikes among workers. This was clearly revealed in a letter by Paul Benthall to his brother Edward:

The IJMA have also in view the establishment of an Intelligence Service worked by one Intelligence Officer with four assistants each responsible for a district. They will establish Intelligence organizations in each mill which will give the officers warning of developments and of the general trend of the opinion .... Of course, ... the Intelligence Officer will have to have some official designation other than 'Intelligence Officer', which will justify their existence and will give them access to the mill areas without undue comment. Possibly they will be designated 'Welfare Officers' and will nominally be in charge of the welfare of labour e.g. quarters, lights drains ....[121]

For the captains of the IJMA, labour welfare could not be distilled out of the question of industrial discipline. Indeed, the establishment of the post of labour officer became so confusing to the IJMA that Paul Benthall admitted to his brother 'neither do they, I think, have any clear idea as to what their Labour Officers' work will be'.[122] For Paul the idea of labour officer was clearly related to the preservation of discipline among workers as he recommended the appointment of a military officer as labour officer.[123] Edward Benthall accepted the suggestion with a mild warning that a military officer who was accustomed to the disciplined 'fighting caste' would find it difficult to cope with an unruly heterogeneous workforce.[124] Benthall did not dismiss the idea of an organized intelligence-gathering machinery. He advised his brother to approach CID's anti-terrorist cell to recruit such an officer.[125] Indeed this appeared to be a primary consideration regarding labour welfare among the most enlightened representatives of British business in Bengal.

However, men like senior Benthall were adamant about direct contact with workers through such work committees.[126] Facing a storm of protests from his colleagues, Benthall thought that the best way forward would be the formation of a work *panchayat* which he believed would be much more in tune with the workers' social background.[127] He argued for the training of several British assistants in Indian languages and even recommended the recruitment of local Europeans, Anglo-Indians, and even Indians at the supervisory level to maintain channels of contacts with workers.[128] After a round of discussions with his colleagues, Benthall unfolded his plan for future reorganization of labour departments comprising both local company-level officials who would be in touch with local workers and the IJMA which would appoint a labour officer to coordinate 'all labour problems affecting mills as a whole and when a grievance arose such as regularization of pay rights, he will have at his finger-tips, knowledge of the circumstances of all mills.'[129]

The underlying philosophy of Benthall's labour management scheme appears to be simple:

We shall never have any labour trouble of really dangerous nature so long our labour are fairly treated and get a square deal including a rise in pay if food prices rise. Organized troubles there may be, but labour will never get very nasty so long as they have no real grievance.[130]

What was remarkable in Benthall's advice was his recognition of workers as economic persons who would respond to economic incentives and sensitive labour administration. The paternalism of factory managers had to be tuned in with the economic welfare of labour through direct contact with ordinary workers. Not that Benthall's advice was accepted without a debate. Indeed, many of his arguments were criticized. The Employers' Federation was kept out of the scheme of labour officers because of the fear that Indian business interests would become involved in labour affairs. New talk of the establishment of a labour bureau was raised and shelved due to the lack of clarity of proposals.[131] However, there was no doubt that the IJMA awoke from a long slumber as far as labour was concerned. No longer was the hiring and firing of workers left in the hands of sardars and burrababus. British supervisory staff recruited workers directly. Every decision of dismissal was taken after consultation with managers and a written notice was served.

Scrupulous care was taken to end physical punishment to workers. The management tried to keep bribes and other forms of extractions made by sardars and burrababus under check.[132] Soon the IJMA moved towards the establishment of an employment bureau to systematize recruitment processes. In other words, labour was no longer taken for granted.

This did not imply that the IJMA had overnight become tolerant, enlightened industrial employers following modern corporate notions of partnership in industrial management. Indeed, this was far from the truth. Mr Burn, the chairman of the IJMA, in a secret meeting with Mr Suhrawardy, the newly appointed Muslim League labour minister, did not contradict when Mr Suhrawardy tacitly stated that he knew that recently there had been a number of dismissals. But he appreciated that it was due to the drastic steps taken by the mills in question to get rid of those employees who were definitely known to be the cause of disturbances among the workers.[133] In other words, political victimization was not only tolerated but actually used as a means to ensure industrial peace. Moreover, the notion of labour officer functioning as the enforcer of discipline among workers remained unaltered. When one Colonel Spain was appointed labour officer by the Bird and Co., Paul Benthall wrote to his elder sibling about the elaborate arrangements of escape which had been planned for this official in case of labour militancy.[134] The irony of the situation was not lost on the elder Benthal who wrote back: 'I am amused at your providing offices with a bolthole at the back in case labour controls him instead of the reverse'.[135] The key operative word here is 'control'. Labour officers should control labour rather than acting as impartial adjudicator of labour disputes from a labour welfare perspective. This scheme of labour control was refined over the years through the introduction of service cards containing detailed information regarding a worker's employment record.[136] Some mills even planned to introduce a photo-identity card of workers.

Behind this comic drama of hiring military strongmen to control and discipline labour, there was a desire to modernize the labour-management relationship. The entire scheme of introducing layers of labour officers establishing direct contact with workers through a work council and slowly replacing the services of sardars and babus in favour of formal rules of recruitment of workers through labour offices indicated a departure from the colonial ideology of peasant workers requiring paternalist administration. Most managers regarded and justified the sardari system of recruitment and associated abuses in the name of Indian customs and rural cultural traditions. In 1937, the challenge from workers to the entire industrial management system through egalitarian factory committees rudely awoke the colonial capital to the need of modernization of labour management. Benthall talked about work panchayat as a rudimentary structure of workers' organization that could act as an alternative to trade unions since 'proper trade unions' were not existing in India.[137] He would soon find that some of his colleagues were not hostile to the idea of a loose cluster of local trade unions opposed to a 'red flag' union. As the British industrialists debated and discussed reforms in labour management system in the industry, they also tried to sound the first Indian provincial government for their ideas concerning management of the labour problem.

As the strike movement intensified, it became clear to British industrialists that industrial peace hinged crucially on the policies of the maverick labour minister of the Muslim League government, H.S. Suhrawardy. British captains of the jute industry were not sure of the ability and commitment of the new labour minister to stem the tide of the strike movement. They remained in touch with pro-British ministers such as Nazimuddin who regularly informed them of the cabinet position on the issue.[138] Suhrawardy had more far-reaching plans for labour reform.[139] His ambition was to build up a trade union organization as an affiliate body of the Muslim League. He also planned to use communal propaganda to break the hold of the red flag union and then replacing it with a broad coalition of conservative union activists, including Hindu politicians within the fold of the hegemonic influence of the Muslim League. He also made it clear that such unions would remain dependent on him for financial patronage. This federalized union would make him valuable to both his party which lacked a mass base in and around Calcutta and the British industrialists who needed an ally in the world of unsettled labour.

Suhrawardy announced broad outlines of his policies at the 3rd session of the Bengal Labour Conference in Calcutta. He made it clear that he would wait for the employers and workers to settle trade disputes on their own. He streamlined his scheme of organizing a federalized trade union organization with a number of labour welfare programmes such as schools for children, centres of recreational activities for workers, setting up of cooperative credit societies, insurance schemes, cooperative stores for essential commodities, and providing assistance to workers in obtaining the benefits of factory acts. The aim was clear: the establishment of a Muslim League-led union with Suhrawardy as its leader and complementing the union with welfare work. Suhrawardy's hands were further strengthened by the British industrialist lobby's suspicion of Fazlul Haq who was regarded as vulnerable to pressures from the Congress, particularly when he was not surrounded by British bureaucrats and Muslim League members. This unease on the part of British capital became evident in the frosty attitude of Mr Burn, the chairman of the IJMA, towards the ministry. Alarmed by the prospect that ministers would play into the hands of 'agitators', McKerrow and Campbell, leaders of the European group, contracted Nalini Sarkar to sooth the hurt ego of ministers.[140]

In this politically unsettled environment, Suhrawardy made his point brutally clear to the representative of British commerce. In a conversation during a business lunch with Mr Chapman Mortimer, Suhrawardy told him that the only way to combat 'red flag' unionism was to organize a centrally cohesive trade organization that would control the representative unions at each mill. Since Suhrawardy was unable to use government funds to finance such unions, he demanded that mills should provide funds for such organizations. Chapman Mortimer obviously protested against the notion of employers funding unions as it would raise the accusation of employers' manipulating the union organizations. Suhrawardy persisted in his point and maintained that it would be a secret deal. He subtly used the threat that if this was not done the communists and opposition would become dominant. When Chapman Mortimer suggested that Suhrawardy should do something to end the Bengal and Nagpur Railway strike at Kharagpur, the labour minister said that the government would foment communal trouble there to end the strike. Alarmed by the minister's response, Mortimer warned in a note that Suhrawardy's scheme contained seeds of future communal trouble.[141] On his part, Suhrawardy sent his message loud and clear that if the British capital needed his support then they had to provide assistance to his scheme.

Suhrawardy's insistence on the support of the mills to form trade unions increased further as time passed. In a meeting with Mr Burn, the chairman of the IJMA, he made it clear that contact between employer and employees should be made through the medium of elected representatives of organized labour. For that purpose alone, the existence of trade unions was absolutely necessary. He argued that employers failed in realizing their duties towards labour in this respect. To undermine the communist hold over labour, Suhrawardy maintained that employers should be prepared to do everything in their power to help labour to organize itself on sound, proper lines and always included the giving of financial assistance for the formation and running of the unions. He claimed that he publicly laid down the principles on which he thought trade unions should be formed and worked and certain people had followed his advice and had made it known that their unions were modelled on the lines approved by him.[142]

The IJMA chairman contested Suhrawardy's ideas by claiming that the employers would be happy to consult and accept guidance from the labour commissioner who, however, should get in touch with the IJMA before going to the mills. Indeed, there occurred a clash of ideas over the reforms of labour-management relationship whereby the IJMA demanded that the government should introduce a legislation along the lines of the Bombay Trade Disputes Act, enabling a set of specialized labour commissioners to act as adjudicators. Mr Burn maintained that the IJMA did not wish to find themselves trapped into supporting trade unions which were pawns on the political board.[143] However, despite Burn's opposition to the ideas of 'genuine trade unions', a euphemism for trade unions loyal to the company, Suhrawardy's scheme was not totally dismissed by influential members of the British industrial circles. M.P. Thomas of Bird and Co. believed for long that mills should finance local unions to foster 'genuine trade union' movement.[144] More forthcoming in support of Mr Suhrawardy was the visiting director of Thomas Duff Company who wrote to his colleagues that Suhrawardy

was doing his utmost to get properly constituted Trade Unions going into the mill areas but was receiving little actual support from the mills themselves ....[145]

The implication was apparent that mills should support Suhrawardy in his endeavour. It was not that support of the mills was totally withheld from him. Suhrawardy was advised that he should privately consult the organization's mill owners before taking up any case for getting grievances among workers redressed.[146] Benthall also appreciated Suhrawardy's work in settling labour disputes and also his plan to emerge as trade union boss.[147]

Why and how did Suhrawardy come to enjoy the confidence of British capital for his schemes? His programme was based on three 'R's: repression, rewards, and riots. In October 1937 he made it clear in a public statement that he did not consider 'the so-called unions of red flag unions as genuine unions'.[148] The government arrested radical labour leaders, prevented elected members of the legislative assembly from holding meetings in their own constituencies, and tolerated the dismissal of radical factory committee members. When protests flared up against these dismissals, the labour minister unleashed police machinery on them. Under his instruction, even the trade union tribunal refused to recognize unions suspected to be of radical orientation.[149]

Suhrawardy knew that repression alone was not going to succeed. He judiciously combined repression with reforms and rewards. He was instrumental in organizing the Bengal National Chamber of Labour. Throughout the later part of 1937 this union opened its branches in various mills. Suhrawardy sanctioned money to these unions through his new ministerial scheme, the Bengal Provincial Workers' Welfare League. The White Union, as the Muslim League union came to be known, also emphasized their connections with the ruling party and their ability to influence the state machinery to support their positions.[150] The lure of funds attracted many. Liberal dispersal of grants to promote *madrasas* and *maqtabs* and various forms of community organizations by the labour ministry consolidated Suhrawardy's position among ordinary Muslim workers. Many of these grants were also used for the improvement of bastis, dilapidated school buildings and mosques in mill areas, and promotion of fan clubs of the Mohameddan Sporting Club among workers.[151] The political language of Muslim League unions evolved around a patron-client relationship. The White Union projected the government as the patron of workers and employers as the custodian of their interests. There was a scrupulous emphasis on amicable, peaceful settlement of industrial disputes. All these enhanced the union's prestige among workers.

Suhrawardy was not entirely opposed to the idea of including Hindu workers within his union. His strategy was to reinforce the authority of mill managers. He did not mind using sardars and burrababus to consolidate his union though his official pronouncements were to the contrary. His measures started bearing fruit at the grass roots level as the manager of the Shyamnagar South Jute Mill reported that the Bengal National Workers' Union of the 'Mohameddan fraternity' opened a branch in his mill and comprised 976 members of which 40 per cent were Muslims and 60 per cent Hindus.[152] It might appear surprising that a Muslim League-sponsored trade union was able to recruit Hindu workers. This demands a careful survey of the response of Hindu sardars. The Hindu sardars and burrababus possibly realized that the rise of the popular factory committees would put an end to the hold of the sardars and burrababus over the workers. Even at the top level, the Bengal National Chamber of Labour included prominent but moderate Hindu trade unionists such as K.C. Roychowdhury, Singheswar Parsad of Kankinarah, Nanak Chand Dusya of Budgebudge and Rammohan Upadhya of Rishra.[153] Thus Suhrawardy's strategy was to establish the hegemony of the Muslim League over labour politics, though communal hooliganism constituted an important ingredient of his overall scheme.

As industrial conflicts escalated in the post-strike period, Suhrawardy's union made more strident appeals to Muslim sentiment, particularly in those regions where Muslim workers supported 'red flag' unions. Thus they decried union leaders such as M.A. Zaman of 'red flag' union as false Mussalmans. Maulanas loyal to the Muslim League in several mills invoked religious sanctions against financial help being provided to *kaffir* strikers.[154] The result of such propaganda soon became evident. Zaman's followers branded Suhrawardy's followers as agents of the company and violently thrashed them.[155] But the fall out of these clashes was the growing tension between Hindus and Muslims. In 1938, as a second wave of strikes escalated in the Titagarh region on the issue of dismissal of a few spinners who assaulted a mill manager, communal polarization became evident. With the opening of Muslim League unions, the Arya Samaj stepped up its activities in Titagarh. Cases of stray assaults between Hindu and Muslim workers became increasingly common. The district administration held a peace meeting of the two communities. When Niharendu Dutta Mazumdar and Zaman intervened to prevent the slow deterioration in the situation, Muslim workers clearly stated that they were not getting their wages because of a strike to reinstate Hindu workers. Soon the Hindu and Muslim communities boycotted each other in Titagarh. So fierce was the rioting that the Eastern Frontier Rifles had to be deployed in addition to local police forces.[156] Meanwhile, Moulana Mohiuddin, the leader of the Muslim League trade union, stepped up his campaign in the entire mill belt against Zaman, alleging the latter of being the agent of Hindus.[157]

The escalation in communal tension further enabled the labour minister to consolidate his position among Muslim workers. The polarization between Hindu and Muslim workers appeared to be complete in the eyes of managers and police officers in the 'upcountry workers'-dominated regions such as Titagarh and Bhatpara.[158] Thus Suharawardy's strategies were a judicious combination of reforms, rewards, repression, and riots. The minister was partially successful because of his ability to tap some of these sentiments and provide an institutionalized form to these sentiments through the White Union over an attempt to establish Muslim League hegemony.

It would be wrong to credit Suhrawardy however, with the entire responsibility of curtailing the influence of the 'red flag' union. The White Union would not have succeeded in organizing its mass base among workers had the diverse socialist groups been able to proletarianize their party organs. The real problem that the red flag unions faced was the absence of an organic link between grass roots-level labour activists and trade union leaders who could counsel a proper course of action. Factory committees initiated confrontations with the mill management and challenged the authority of the mill administration. As industrial conflicts escalated, the 'red flag' union found it difficult to sustain strikes. This was particularly evident in the collapse of the red support base in Angus where grass roots-level factory committees constantly confronted the industrial management. For example, in Angus Jute Mill a massive strike for the appointment of new spinners provided little peace of mind to Zaman. Zaman could not arrange resources to sustain the strike and even advised workers to go back to their villages in order to avoid starvation. This proposal evoked a poor response among the workers.[159] Zaman finally tried to settle the issue by approaching the management directly. The director of the Thomas Duff Company wrote back home:

Late on Monday afternoon, I had a call from Zaman requesting us to reconsider our decision particularly in regard to the demand of the spinners for an additional spinner per pass for the Hessian and Sacking Warp frames, and also that of the weavers that there should be no dismissals unless production falls to 25 per cent below [sic]. Management refused to accept the demands but accepted that 20 additional spinners were to be appointed and dismissed weavers would be appointed after two weeks.[160]

Zaman went to Angus that night, informed the workers of the intransigent attitude of the management, and advised them to return to work. At the same time he suggested that they themselves should hold a meeting early in the morning, and that later in the forenoon he would return and again address them. This meeting witnessed furious debates among the workers as a large body of weavers did not relish the idea of going back on the old terms. Zaman then promised to obtain at least two concessions for the workers. He promised them that the management would provide opportunities for those who went back home to join later in the week. Moreover, the dismissed workers would be appointed again if there were vacancies. With these assurances Zaman and Rajani Mookherjee, a communist activist, eventually persuaded the general body of workers to return to work and informed them that the management had agreed to start up the mill and factory on Thursday morning, 10 August.[161]

The strike gained some advantages for workers as fines were imposed now with restraint and managing agents instructed mill officials that dismissals could only be made by the managers after a worker had received two warnings from the European assistant and after the case had been thoroughly investigated by the manager himself. This partial victory did not sustain the mass base of 'red flag' union. With the collapse of the strike, the 'red flag' union could make little progress in the factory. For example, when trouble flared up on 11 January 1938 after the dismissal of a woman worker, Zaman failed to initiate another strike. Zaman held two meetings in the bazaar and led parades of his followers who marched round the boundaries of the mill lines shouting slogans but with little effect on the general body of workers. The management gained a new confidence and dismissed another worker for insubordination on 21 January. The manager happily noted that the incident provoked little protests from the spinners.[162]

The popularity of unions was now physically mapped out at a symbolic level. When tensions among workers increased, supporters of the 'red flag' union wore red badges to demonstrate their defiance of the management. But soon the Muslim League-led rival union introduced green badges. In a report to his superior, the manager of the mill quite frankly identified the Muslim League Union as a body loyal to the company:

About this time an opposition badge was introduced by the party loyal to the company and after a few days, the number of their badges seemed to be in excess of the red badges.[163]

This symbolic victory of the Muslim League marked the end of the hold of the 'red flag' union in the Angus Jute Mill. Workers launched a democratic trade union organization under the influence of the 'red flag' union but the failure of the leadership of the movement to establish an organic link with workers and to prepare them for a careful strategy of collective bargaining ended in a prolonged strike with no tangible gain. The coy moves made by the management in alliance with the Muslim League union finally ended the battle in their favour. The failure of the 'red flag' union to gain any tangible results even after a prolonged strike sapped the morale of workers who gradually switched sides from the 'red' union to the pro-company

Muslim League union. It would be wrong to visualise such transfer of loyalty as a simple manifestation of the triumph of natal religious ties over class alliances. Both these processes were actually a reflection of the failure of the 'red flag' union to evolve a correct political strategy in the face of Suhrawardy's extremely clever movement of reward, repression, and riots. In a battle for survival in the twilight years of colonial rule, the propertied classes in Bengal and their representatives seemed to be remarkably liberated from pangs of conscience and appeared less bothered to look beyond their immediate tactics of fomenting communal trouble to gain strategic victory in order to safeguard their propertied interests.

Conclusion

The general strike of 1937 was a crucial landmark in Bengal politics. Many historians have neglected the role of industrial conflicts in defining politics in predominantly agrarian countries. However, in late colonial Bengal the jute industry was located at the commanding height of the economy connecting local economies in the agrarian hinterland of Bengal with global capitalism. The crisis in the industry thus had a profound impact on local politics. The strategic political maneuvering of expatriate capital to safeguard their interests crucially informed and influenced political processes in Bengal. The success of British capital to extract concessions from the colonial state in the form of a high level of statutory representation in the legislative assembly further consolidated their influence and played an important role in developing the broadest possible coalition of propertied interests. However, economic and social havoc unleashed by the Depression of 1937 also escalated the degree of class and communal conflicts in Bengal. Industrial action in the mill belt witnessed the sharpening of class confrontation. In the face of escalating industrial action and growing demands for reforms of the industrial regime in Bengal, a judicious combination of reform, repression, rewards, and riots appeared to be the only way out to the propertied alliances comprising the representatives of expatriate capital. It would be obviously wrong to attribute the escalation of class conflicts and communal tensions entirely to strategies of capital and local state, yet it would be a serious error to neglect their role in defining political and material conditions for such conflicts.

Many Marxian narratives of working-class history have in the past led us to believe that deformed by the structural constraint of colonialism

Calcutta workers were unable to develop a political consciousness to confront colonial capital. To challenge this poor theoretical formulation, historians inspired by the subaltern school discarded the centrality of class in the historical narrative. But the importance of class as a political category could be realized if we look at it not simply as a structural phenomena but also as a product of political action and thus could be made, formulated, and collapsed. To explain the industrial action of workers, we have to refer to the purposive behaviour of members of a social formation as agents of social change in particular material and political contexts. The particular instance provided in this chapter indicates how various forms of political mobilization fostered both class-based industrial action and communal conflicts within the mills, and why many workers switched over their strategies of political action from supporting radical factory committees to sectarian Muslim League unions in response to a particular turn in the material context of the movement. Finally, this chapter questions the tendency to treat communal riots as a reflection of pre-bourgeoisie community consciousness of workers. In the context of labour history, we could argue that communal riots were not inevitable products of workers' loyalties to religion, kinship ties, or language. Rather, the nature of a political movement among workers depended on how such loyalties were activated in a particular historical context in a particular form of political action.

In the context of Bengal politics, the general strike was significant from two different perspectives. First, the Muslim League experimented with a particular form of politics that combined institutional reforms which addressed some of the aspirations of popular forces with a communal twist that enabled it to consolidate its sectarian support base. In that sense they provided particular direction to the pressure for reforms from popular movements that emanated from the depression period. This very form of politics proved to be extremely rewarding to the Muslim League in the late colonial era. Secondly, communalism is often posited as the other of nationalism. However, the political alternative to communalism, as this story demonstrates, came not from nationalism but from a redistributive radical politics based on class-based alliances of popular social forces. Indeed, the inchoate and possibly ill-defined concept of Mazdur Raj infused by millenarian hopes for a just social order as articulated by Calcutta workers during the strike still remains a source of inspiration in the struggle against communalism and sectarian nationalism of all varieties, particularly its recent virulent Hindu form.

Notes

1. See R.N. Gilchrist's note of 7 April 1932, Com Dept Com Branch, September 1932, B87–134, WBSA.

2. *IJMA Report of the Committee for 1932*, Calcutta, 1933, p. 16.

3. CSAS, B.P. Box X, Memorandum of E.C. Benthall to S.K. Scott and Cambell of Inchcape group, 2 July 1935.

4. CSAS, B.P. Box X, Discussion between G.B. Morton and S.K. Scott, 22 August 1935.

5. CSAS, B.P. Box X, From G.B. Morgan to Benthall. Calcutta, 16 September 1935.

6. CSAS, B.P. Box X, R.L. Walker, Additional Deputy Secretary to the Govt of Bengal, Commerce and Marine Dept to the Secretary, IJMA, Calcutta, 12 August 1935.

7. CSAS, B.P. Box X, G.B. Morton to H.P. Bernet, 28 August 1935.

8. Indeed G.B Morton, a leading figure in Bird and Co, wryly noted in a letter to his colleague: 'Here everybody has a scheme of sorts and if we agree with any one scheme, it is used as propaganda, and if we do not agree with every scheme we are regarded as enemies of the trade! We are, however, managing to steer a middle course.' CSAS, B.P. Box X, G.B. Morton to Tom, 16 September 1935.

9. CSAS, B.P. Box X, Memorandum by Aikman, 26 August 1935; Memorandum by B.M. Birla enclosed under cover of his letter of 14 March 1935.

10. CSAS, B.P. Box X, G.B. Morton to E.C. Benthall 18 September 1935.

11. CSAS, B.P. Box X, Cable received from Scott, Calcutta, 20 September 1935.

12. CSAS, B.P. Box X, G.B. Morton to Edward Benthall, 13 September 1935.

13. CSAS, B.P. Box X, Edward Benthall to G.B Morton, 20 September 1935.

14. See *IJMA Report 1934* pp. 282–6.

15. In a letter to Benthall, G.B. Morton clearly observed that 'The view is definitely held in many quarters here that the present challenge to the Jute Mills association is partly political, especially since the negotiations with outside mills are almost certainly doomed to failure.' CSAS, B.P. Box X, G.B. Morton to E.C. Benthall, 13 Sept 1935. The political nature of the threat to the IJMA became more manifest when Birla threatened to walk out with Indian members. Scott, who was the Chairman of the IJMA in 1935, cabled Benthall that Birla's exit would make 'the passage of any subsequent legislation [concerning working hours] difficult owing to Birla's powerful influence' in the assembly. CSAS, B.P. Box X, Cable received from Calcutta 20 September 1935.

16. Indeed, as early as 1929 while passing through the Gulf of Suez on a voyage to England, Benthall noted in his diary that there were three paths open to him to survive as a businessman and politician: (a) to join hands with rich Indian groups while retaining the master hand for himself or, (b) to merge with Indian interests. CSAS, B.P. Box VII, Diary entry, 24 January 1929, Gulf of Suez.

17. For details regarding Sir Edward Charles Benthall's career, see J.F. Riddick, *Who was Who in British India*, Connecticut, 1948.

18. CSAS, B.P. Box III, Benthall to Hubert, June 13, 1933.

19. CSAS, B.P. Box III, Birley to Henderson, 22 April 1933.

20. CSAS, B.P. Box III, E.C. Benthall to Birley, 25 April 1934.

21. CSAS, B.P. Box X, J.A. McKerrow to A. Lockhart, 23 September 1935.

22. CSAS, B.P. Box X, Memorandum on Political Organization of the Europeans in Bengal, J.A. McKerrow to E.C. Benthall, 19 July 1937. However, it is wrong to argue that the British organized in an orderly manner an effective political lobby in Bengal as members of the British assembly team bitterly fought with each other on the issue of the election of a leader. CSAS, B.P. Box X, T.C. Mortimer to Benthall, 15 July 1937; CSAS, B.P. Box X, Telegram of J.A. McKerrow to E.C. Benthall, 10 July 1937.

23. CSAS, B.P. Box III, Notes on Commercial Representation and Franchise by the Committee of the Bengal Chamber of Commerce.

24. CSAS B.P. Box III, Henderson to Barlett, 8 June 1933.

25. CSAS, B.P. Box 1, Diary entry for 21 January 1931. Also see Bidyut Chakrabarty, 'The Communal Award of 1932 and its Implications in Bengal', *Modern Asian Studies*, 23, 3, 1989, pp. 493–523.

26. See 'Open Warfare on White paper', *The Englishman*, 22 May 1933. Henderson, the chairman of the Bengal Chamber of Commerce, also discussed the issue in detail in a letter to Barlett, a Madras-based trader. CSAS, B.P. Box X, Henderson to Barlet, 8 June 1933.

27. These demands were clearly evident in several negotiations that representatives of British interests in Bengal entered into with Indian industrialists, politicians, and British government representatives. See letter to *The Times*, 30 June 1933, by the Royal Empire Society, London. Also see Benthall's letter to Henderson on the same date. CSAS, B.P. Box III, Benthall to Henderson, 28 June 1933. For detailed documentation of negotiations with Indian politicians and industrialists, see CSAS, B.P. Box II, Memorandum of Conversation with Mr Birla on 4 October 1931; summary of discussions between Sir Hubert Carr, Mr E. Benthall, Mr Gandhi, Sir P. Thakurdas and Mr Birla between 29 September and 14 October 1931; Letter from Sir Maurice Gwyer to E. Benthall, 17 October 1931; CSAS, B.P. Box III, Memorandum of a discussion with Sir Purushottam Dass Thakurdas, 14 June 1933 at Grosvenor House.

28. See Maria Misra, *Business, Race and Politics in British India c. 1850–1960*, Oxford, 1999, p. 173. However, Misra is wrong in suggesting that these businessmen were close to F.H. Khan, the first premier of Bengal and she omits the name of the person who was the closest to the expatriate traders, Nazimuddin.

29. CSAS, B.P. Box III, Note by Mr A.H. Gaznavi on Sir N.N. Sircar's Memorandum.

30. IOLR, L/PO/48(ii), 16 August 1932.

31. The members of the Bengal Legislative Assembly were not elected by one general electorate as is the case in all true parliamentary systems but different groups of members who were elected by twelve separate franchises. See IOLR, L/PO/48(ii), Communal Decision,16 August 1932.

32. CSAS, B.P. Box XII, Memorandum on Terrorism in Bengal.

33. For details of Nazimuddin's early career see N.K. Jain, *Muslims in India (Vol. II)*, New Delhi, 1983, pp. 87–8.

34. CSAS, B.P. Box III, Benthall to Sir Richard Chevevnix French, 13 August 1933. Benthall was involved in the political project behind the *Star of India* from the beginning. Nazimuddin wrote to Benthall about their joint project for providing a stable government for Bengal by educating Muslim public opinion of the need for such an alliance, and sought his help to collect the necessary funds for the newspaper from European businessmen as well as Aga Khan and the Nizam's government. CSAS, B.P. Box III, Nazimuddin to Benthall, 25 April 1933

35. CSAS, B.P. Box III, Benthall to Sir Richard Chevevnix French, 13 August 1933.

36. This is not surprising as the European Association's Bengal Provincial Committee clearly endorsed Benthall's line of providing support to the paper. European Association Bengal Provincial Committee, Minutes of Meetings, 20 July 1928 to 28 January 1933. Also see minutes of meeting on 21 February 1933. Quoted in Rajat Ray, *Urban Roots of Indian Nationalism*, p. 175.

37. For details regarding how Benthall mobilized the European Association to support the *Star of India*, see Rajat Ray, *Urban Roots of Indian Nationalism*, pp. 171–7. Apparently, *Star of India* enjoyed the blessings of the government of Bengal. On 6 January 1933 in a meeting at the Governor's house, top officials of the Bengal government decided to extend their support to the project. NAI Home Political File No 45/1, 1933. For details see Bidyut Chakrabarty, *Subhas Chandra Bose and Indian Middle Class: A Study in Indian Nationalism 1928–1940*, London, 1990, p. 185, fn 48.

38. CSAS, B.P. Box X, Edward Benthall to Paul Benthall, 13 July 1937.

39. CSAS, B.P. Box XII, B.P. Singh Roy to Edward Benthall, June 1933.

40. For details of Sarkar's career see S.P. Sen (ed.), *Dictionary of National Biography Vol. IV, (s-z)*, Calcutta, 1974.

41. See B. Chakrabarty, *Subhas Chandra Bose and Indian Middle Class,* Appendix 1, pp. 176–7.

42. See R. Ray, *Urban Roots of Indian Nationalism,* p. 137.

43. Ibid., pp. 177–82.

44. J. McKerrow, a colleague of Benthall in Bird and Co., wrote about Sarkar's repeated queries about the possibilities of the formation of a constitutional party with the British business groups. CSAS, B.P. Box X, J. McKerrow to E.C. Benthall, 12 November 1935.

45. Review of events in Bengal for second half of December 1937, 5 January 1938, IOL/L/P and J/5/141.

46. See S. Bose, *Agrarian Bengal: Economy, Social Struicture and Politics, 1919–1947,* pp. 181–232.

47. Review of the event of the second half of May 1937, IOL/L/P and J/5/141.

48. IOL, Hallet Collection, MSS Eur 251, 33. *India and Communism* Confidential Report of H. Wilson, Intelligence Bureau, 1933. Also see Muzaffar Ahmed, *Amar Jiban o Bharater Communist Party,* Calcutta, 1989, Fourth Print, p. 28.

49. See R. Sen, *Bharater Communist Partyr Itibritta,* Calcutta, 1996, pp. 20–21. Also see Saroj Mukhopadhyaya, *Bharater Communist Party o Amra. [Pratham Khanda],* Kolikata, 1989, p. 58; 122. The widespread impact of the establishment of this organization may be seen in a pamphlet issued by *Sahityka,* a non-political literary organization patronized by Tagore in Santiniketan Ashram. Rabindra Bhavana Archives, Vishva Bharati University.

50. For details of such confrontation in Naihati and Budgbudge in 1934 see Home Political Confidential, no. 117/1934, WBSA.

51. Sarkar's main concern was to form a constitutional party with the assistance of European traders in order to include all segments of business into a single political body. See for details CASA, B.P. Box X, J.A. McKerrow to Benthall, 12 November 1935.

52. In the 1937 election, in the Muslim constituencies the Muslim league had won thirty-nine seats, and the KPP captured thirty-six seats and independents bagged another 36. Tripura Krishak Samity which maintained a distance from the KPP won five seats. However, the KPP polled 31.78 per cent of total votes in rural areas and the Muslim League 26.52 per cent. In the general constituencies, the Congress secured fifty-four seats. For details see Sugata Bose, *Agrarian Bengal: Economy, Social Structure and Politics 1919–4,* Cambridge, 1986, p. 205.

53. See S. Mukhopadhyaya, *Bharater Communist Party o Amra,* p. 52.

54. Indeed, a sizeable majority of the members of Congress legislative party was composed of Hindu landed gentry. See for a description, N.C. Chaudhuri, *Thy Hand, Great Anarch! India 1921–1952,* New Delhi, 1987, p. 470.

55. For details of the negotiation between the Congress and Tenants and Peasants Party, see Abul Mansur Ahmed, *Amar Dekha Rajnitir Ponchas Batsar*, Dacca, 1970, pp. 134–9. N.C. Chaudhuri, who was then the personal secretary of Sarat Bose, the Congress leader of Bengal, argued differently. According to Chaudhuri, the KPP's proposal to form an alliance was not accepted 'owing to the decision of the All-India Congress not to accept office even in the provinces where it had obtained absolute majorities. It was also unwilling to let the Congress parties in such provinces where they had no majoirty to cooperate with any other party.' N.C. Chaudhuri, *Thy Hand, Great Anarch!*, p. 465.

56. S. Sen, *Muslim Politics in Bengal 1937–1947*, New Delhi, 1976, p. 95.

57. According to Chaudhuri, Birla and Azad had played a crucial role in saving the ministry by persuading Gandhi not to allow N.C. Sarkar, who was the only prominent Hindu minister, to resign from the ministry. *Thy Hand, Great Anarch!*, pp. 478–86.

58. S. Sen, *Muslim Politics in Bengal*, p. 119.

59. CSAS, B.P. Box XII. Chapman Mortimer to E.C. Benthall, 29 July 1937.

60. Ibid., E.C. Benthall to Mortimer Chapman, 11 August 1937.

61. Ibid., Strictly Confidential Note for Partners only: An Assessment of Political Situation in Bengal.

62. Ibid., J.A. McKerrow to E.C. Benthall, 31 July 1937.

63. Ibid.

64. Ibid.

65. Ibid., E.C. Benthall to J.A. McKerrow, 11 August 1937.

66. See for details, Commerce Department Commerce Branch July, 1932, 3C-1, Progs B322, WBSA.

67. This calculation is based on *AARBM* statistics 1930–34, as shown in Table 7.1.

68. University of Dundee, TDA, Manager's Report to Directors, Shyamnagar North Jute Mill, 1932, p. 14.

69. Report entitled 'Labour saving Devices for Jute Mill Machineries', University of Dundee, TDA, Manager's Report to Directors, Shyamnagar North Jute Mill, 1932.

70. University of Dundee, TDA, Manager's Report to Directors, Titagarh Jute Mill No. I, 1932, p. 15.

71. Ibid., 1931, p. 17.

72. See 68 above, 1930, p. 12.

73. Ibid., 1933, p. 16.

74. See workers' petition to the district magistrate of 24 Parganas against the gates being closed during working hours and their being confined to factories. GOB Political Department, Political Branch d/o No. 126, WBSA.

75. As early as 1930, the manager of the Shyamnagar North Jute Mill reported about how the larger pool of supply of workers had helped him to suppress 'agitation' among weavers effectively. See 72 above, 1930, p. 14.

76. For details of the process of retrenchment of women workers see Samita Sen, *Women and Labour in Late Colonial India: The Bengal Jute Industry,* Cambridge, 1999, pp. 121–4.

77. See for details A. Cox, 'Paternal Despotism and Workers' Resistance in the Bengal Jute Industry 1920–1940'. Unpublished PhD dissertation, Cambridge University, 1999, pp. 182–3.

78. University of Dundee, TDA, Manager's Report to Directors, Titagarh Jute Mill No. 2, 1931, p. 14.

79. CSAS, B.P. Box X, M.P. Thomas to E.C. Benthall, 5 July 1937.

80. For a detailed and brilliant discussion of the impact of rationalization on weavers, see A. Cox, 'Paternal Despotism'.

81. University of Dundee, TDA, Manager's Report to Directors, Shyamnagar North Jute Mill 1932, p. 42.

82. University of Dundee, TDA, Manager's Report to Director, Victoria Jute Mill 1933, p. 41.

83. For example, in 1933 of those who were elected to the municipal board, five were either sardars or mill babus. *AARMB*, 1933, p. 2.

84. University of Dundee, TDA, Manager's Report to Directors, Victoria Jute Mill 1934, pp. 65.

85. University of Dundee, TDA, Manager's Report to Directors, Angus Jute Mill 1934, p. 36.

86. Ibid.

87. See 73 above.

88. For details, see Intelligence Branch 35/26 and Ranen Sen, *Banglay Communist Party Gathaner Pratham Yuga 1930–48*, Calcutta, 1981, quoted in Nirban Basu, *The Political Parties and Labour Politics 1937–47 (With Special Reference to Bengal)*, Calcutta, 1992, p. 75, fn 7.

89. Special Branch File No 302/38, Report dated 16 October 1936. Quoted in Nirban Basu, *The Political Parties and the Labour Politics in Bengal 1937–47*, p. 28.

90. Actually the NTUF came into existence during the split in the trade union movement in the 1930s between the Communist-dominated Red Trade Union Congress and the Moderate Union Leaders from non-Communist background. For details of NTUF, see Nirban Basu, ibid.

91. For details concerning electioneering, see TDA, University of Dundee Manager's Report to Directors, Shyamnagar No. 1 and 2 Mills, 1937, p. 4. Also see CSAS, B.P. Box XII, J.R. Walker (MLA, McLeod and Co. Ltd.) The note prepared for circulation to the IJMA members, 'Jute Strike Situation'.

92. CSAS, B.P. Box XII, J.R. Walker, 'Jute Strike Situation'. Also see, WBSA GOB Political Department Special Branch, Confidential File no. 72/37. Hartal on 1 April. Letter No. F 4/6/37 From R.M. Maxwell, Secretary to the GOI to the Chief Secretary to the GOB, 16 March 1937, p. 1. Also quoted in A. Cox 'Paternal Despotism', pp. 247, fn 5.

93. For details see A. Cox, 'Paternal Despotism', pp. 247–56.

94. Indeed, the workers' defiant mood became evident in the strike in the Hukumchand Jute Mill and the Anglo Indian Mill in April 1936. For details see A. Cox, p. 246.

95. GOB Special Branch Papers File SW521, 'All Bengal Jute Workers' Union Conference held on 29 August 1936.'

96. WBSA Com Dept Com. Branch No. 1191. Weekly Report on Industrial Disputes 6 February 1937, pp. 2–3 and also see WBSA Home Department Political Confidential File No. 72/37 April 1937.

97. TDA, DUA Private Official Letter McDonald to G.A. Mason, 29 April 1937, and also Private Official Letter C.M. Garrie to G.A. Mason, 26 April 1937 and 15 May 1937.

98. TDA, DUA, Manager's Report to Directors, Shyamnagar North Jute Mill 1937, p. 55.

99. TDA, DUA, Manager's Report to Directors, Angus Jute Mill 1937, p. 51.

100. TDA, DUA Private Official Letter, Reports from Managers as to how they kept in touch with labour during the recent strike, 10 June 1937, p. 13 (In the collections of letters from 13 May 1937 to May 1938).

101. Ibid., p. 14.

102. Ibid.

103. See 99 above.

104. See 100 above, p. 46.

105. Ibid.

106. Ibid.

107. Ibid.

108. Ibid.

109. Ibid.

110. Home Political Confidential File No: 484/37, Reports on Industrial Situation, WBSA. From R.H. Parker Joint Secretary to the GOB to the Secy, GOI Department of Industries and Labour.

111. For a detailed analysis of the ideological position of these leaders see N. Basu, *The Political Parties and Labour Politics 1937–47*.

112. See *The New Age*, August 1937. For the problems of the Congress Socialist Party see Devendranath Sen, Congress Socialist, 13 March 1937, No. 10, p.13. For a detailed review of the situation, see A. Cox 'Paternal Despotism', pp. 265–76.

113. During the strike, there took place several strikes in educational institutions in Calcutta on demands specific to students of these institutions. *Amrita Bazar Patrika* 23 April 1937, p. 7 and 2 May/April 1937. For an understanding of the impact of strike on Calcutta's avant garde intellectuals see Shyamal Krishna Ghosh, *Parichayer Adda*, Calcutta, 1990, pp. 29–30.

114. For details of the growing discontent among workers in railways, steamer companies, mining industry, cotton mills, tramways, and electricity corporation in Calcutta see Fortnightly Reports of April 1937 and Fortnightly Reports of May 1937. Also see CSAS, B.P. Box XIII, Paul Benthall to Edward Benthall 8 September 1937 and CSAS, B.P. Box XIII, S.B. to Edward Benthall, 9 September 1937. Leonard Gordon, *Bengal: The Nationalist Movement (1876–1940)*, New York, 1974, pp. 240–1.

115. For details concerning efforts of trade union leader establishing connections with jute cultivators see Fortnightly Reports for the second half of May 1937, p. 7.

116. CSAS, B.P. Box XII, M.P. Thomas to Edward Benthall, 3 June 1937.

117. CSAS, B.P. Box XI, E.C. Benthall to Paul Benthall, 27 July 1937.

118. CSAS, B.P. Box XI, Paul Benthall to E.C. Benthall, 19 July 1937.

119. CSAS, B.P. Box XII, Paul Benthall to Edward Benthall, 21 July 1937.

120. CSAS, B.P. Box XII, Monty (M.P. Thomas) to Edward Benthall, 5 July 1937.

121. CSAS, B.P. Box XII, Paul Benthall to Edward Benthall, 11 August 1937.

122. Ibid.

123. CSAS, B.P. Box XI, Paul Benthall to Edward Benthall, 11 August 1937.

124. CSAS, B.P. Box XI, Edward Benthall to Paul Benthall, 21 August 1937.

125. Ibid.

126. CSAS, B.P. Box XI, E.C. Benthall to Paul Benthall, 1 August 1937.

127. CSAS, B.P. Box XI, E.C. Benthall to M.P. Thomas, 15 July 1937.

128. CSAS, B.P. Box XII, E.C. Benthall to Paul Benthall, 5 August 1937.

129. Ibid., 14 July 1937.

130. Ibid.

131. CSAS, B.P. Box XII, Paul Benthall to Edward Benthall, 26 July 1937.

132. CSAS, B.P. Box XII, Monty (M.P. Thomas) to Edward Benthall, 5 July 1937

133. CSAS, B.P. Box XII, McKerrow to E.C. Benthall, 2 August 1937.

134. CSAS, B.P. Box XIII, Paul Benthall to Edward Benthall, 20 September 1937.

135. CSAS, B.P. Box XIII, Edward Benthall to Paul Benthall, 28 September 1937.

136. The IJMA Circular Files 1937–8, 'Suggestions for the betterment of the conditions of labour', letter from R.H. Parker, Joint Secretary to the GOB, to the Secretary of the IJMA, 15 September 1937. Quoted in A. Cox, 'Paternal Despotism', p. 294.

137. CSAS, B.P. Box XII, E.C. Benthall to Paul Benthall, 14 July 1937.

138. CSAS, B.P. Box XII, T. Chapman Mortimer to E.C. Benthall,19 April 1937.

139. Fornightly Review of Events in Bengal, 7 May 1937 John Anderson to the Marquess of Linlithgow, p. 2.

140. CSAS, B.P. Box XII, The IJMA Secretary A.C. Daniel to M.P. Thomas, 31 July. Report on the Burn's Interview with Suhrawardy in the Presence of Mr A. Hughes, ICS, Labour Commissioner on 28 July 1937 at Writers' Building.

141. CSAS, B.P. Box XII, Strictly Private and Confidential Synopsis of conversation between the Honourable Mr Suhrawardy and Mr Chapman Mortimer at Lunch on 5 June 1937. Report sent on 7 June 1937.

142. CSAS, B.P. Box XII, The IJMA Secretary A.C. Daniel to M.P. Thomas, 31 July Report on the Burn's Interview with Suhrawardy in the Presence of Mr A Hughes, ICS, Labour Commissioner on 28 July 1937 at Writers' Building.

143. CSAS, B.P. Box XII, The IJMA Secretary A.C. Daniel to M.P. Thomas, 31 July Report on the Burn's Interview with Suhrawardy in the Presence of Mr A Hughes, ICS, Labour Commissioner on 28 July 1937 at Writers' Building.

144. CSAS, B.P. Box XII, Monty (M.P. Thomas) to Edward Benthall, 5 July 1937

145. TDA, DUA, Private Official Letter, Sir Alexander Murray, 28 December 1937.

146. CSAS, B.P. Box XIX, Diary entry for 19 March 1940.

147. CSAS, B.P. Box XII, E.C. Benthall to J.A. McKerrow, 12 August 1937.

148. *Amrita Bazar Patrika* 19 October 1937.

149. In 1939, for example, the Trade Union Constitution Tribunal recognized only twenty-seven out of sixty-one unions which applied to it. N. Basu, *The Political Parties and Labour Politics 1937–47*, p. 119.

150. Home Political Confidential 326/1937, WBSA.

151. Interview with Abdul Latif of Kankinara on 22 February 1995. This claim was also corroborated by letters from workers to the Bengal Government to support

local madrasas in the name of Muslim national tradition. Commerce Department Commerce Branch B File 111/476, WBSA.

152. TDA, DUA, Manager's Report to Directors, Shyamnagar South Jute Mills,1937, pp. 44.

153. N. Basu, *The Political Parties*, p. 120.

154. Home Political Confidential, No 326/1937, WBSA.

155. Home Political Confidential, No 326/1937, WBSA.

156. Home Political Confidential, No 115/38, WBSA.

157. Home Political Confidential, No 326/1937, WBSA.

158. Commerce and Labour Department Commerce Branch, December 1938 4j-16, B45 and Special Branch File No. 516/38 Report dated 15.08.1938, WBSA.

159. TDA, DUA Report of the Manager, Angus Jute Mill to the Director, Thomas Duff Company, p. 37.

160. Ibid., p. 51.

161. Ibid.

162. Ibid.

163. Ibid.

Conclusion

'Farewell to the Working-Class'[1] has become a common refrain in Western social history from the 1980s. In the 1980s, the restructuring of advance capitalism, the rise of neo-liberal market-oriented political parties to power, the collapse of Keynesian economic orthodoxy, and subsequently the command economies of the East have eroded the appeal of class as an analytical tool in understanding history. At the social level, the decline of a supposedly homogenous male, manual working class in the United Kingdom and other parts of western Europe has further compelled many historians to 'Rethink Class' as a social entity. Prominent socialist and Marxist thinker, E.J. Hobsbawm, has termed this new trend as the halting of the forward march of labour.[2] The collapse of earlier certainties concerning labour history has thus compelled socialist historians in Britain to devote their attention to reworking the paradigm of the class.[3] Increasingly, class is viewed as a complex process of social formation that interacts with gender and racial identities. [4] The earlier vision of class as a monolithic construct that constitutes a master identity has now been exiled from history writing.

This rethinking regarding class has an echo in Indian history writing. In the 1980s, subaltern historians revolted against the formulaic national Marxist historiography and its supposed connections with Delhi's ruling court in post-colonial India. These historians have projected their efforts as a collective endeavour to write a history from below with a focus on subaltern initiative in reinterpreting their own politics. Rethinking working-class history by Dipesh Chakrabarty is a crucial instance of 'subaltern' intervention in labour history writing.[5] This rethinking has however, reinforced the old beliefs that Indian workers were actually peasant migrants trapped in their timeless rural communitarian structures based on primordial ties. In a way, such work reinforces the idea that there exists a monolithic ideal proletariat in metropolitan capitalism but Indian workers were not part of it.

This thesis has demonstrated that class is always in the process of making and unmaking itself. The notion of class is neither fixed nor given. Workers' awareness of belonging to a distinctive social category based on economic relationship and shared grievances at workplaces is contingent upon immediate political and social circumstances in which they evolved their strategies of negotiation among themselves on the one hand, and employers, colonial state, and politicians purporting to represent themselves, on the other. Central to such a process was the migrant workers' strategies of survival in an uncertain labour market.

This thesis has explained the migrant workers' politics in terms of their survival strategies in the mill towns of Bengal, and in order to do so has reviewed the rural society of Bihar and eastern UP which supplied the majority of workers to the jute mills in Bengal. In fact, the pattern of growth of the industrial work-force in Bengal was inseparably related to changes in the rural economy of Bihar and east UP. Trapped within declining rural resources and low wages, migrant workers depended upon their village bases to sustain themselves in urban areas. This was evident in the way workers survived in the hostile urban labour market in Bengal. In the late nineteenth century increasing population pressure on land, the expanding hold of zamindars on rural resources and commercialization of agriculture led to impoverishment of the peasantry in Bihar and eastern UP. A significant section of the rural poor migrated outside the region to supplement their meagre earning from agrarian resources. It was these migrants who sought jobs in the jute mills of Bengal.

The growth of the railways enabled these workers to leave their families in the rural areas to look after their meagre resources. A vast majority of workers from Bihar and east UP were single male migrants who wanted to supplement their family income from land by working in the jute mills. In a situation of constant flow of labour, mill managers utilized the sustained rural connection of the workers to keep their wages down. Workers thus had little economic incentive to bring their wives to the mill towns. Mills also minimized their labour cost by relegating the tasks of housing the workers to private hands. This led to the development of insanitary and overcrowded slums. The insanitary environment of mill slums often had a very adverse effect on women, particularly during pregnancy. The high infant mortality rate in the urban slums acted as a deterrent to migration of women to the towns. As a result, the number of women progressively declined in the mill towns. Such separation between the adult male workers and their wives made it imperative for the jute workers to visit their villages regularly.

These visits, in fact, were strategies of survival for urban workers which helped them sustain their urban jobs. The need for such visits was further necessitated by a complete absence of arrangements for workers to stay in the towns during periods of illness. The insanitary environment, inadequate food, and complete absence of social security measures had adverse effects on the general health of the workers. There was a marked deterioration in the health of those mill operatives who stayed for longer periods in the mill towns. The village bases thus became essential for the workers to retain their urban jobs. As explained by R.S. Chandavarkar in the context of Bombay, in Calcutta also, return migration to villages was a manifestation of rural loyalties but also a survival strategy in the urban labour market.[6]

In the mill towns workers developed networks based on intersecting loyalties to caste, religion, and region to enter and retain their foothold in the labour market. Often workers from the same village, caste, linguistic group, and religion stayed together. Yet such ties were fluid and were constantly being created and recreated. There did not exist any impermeable boundary among workers along caste, regional, and religious lines. The few workers who had a household establishment in the mill towns selected their partners from different caste backgrounds. Even within the same regional and religious group, workers who were highly paid could afford to confine their wives within *purdah* whereas whole families of low paid workers were forced to work in factories.

Workers also depended upon the services and help of various types of powerful social entrepreneurs like jobbers, grocers, neighbourhood bosses, and moneylenders to survive in the towns, groups who exercised a significant influence over working-class politics. In this context it is important to understand the role of the *sardars* in the social life of the workers. The burrababus or head-clerks ran the day-to-day administration of the mills and jobbers or sardars were entrusted with the task of disciplining labour. The managers expected sardars to recruit new workers for the factory, supervise their jobs, and even to provide workers with housing. Despite the important position of the sardars in the mill hierarchy, there were serious constraints on their power and influence among workers. To build up a base among workers, a sardar had to extend his influence outside the factory compound in the neighbourhood, and had to make arrangements not only for jobs of workers but also for housing and credit. In this he had to compete with grocers, money lenders, liquor sellers, and even local toughs. As such the sardar did not enjoy much power in the jute mills but often played the role of negotiator between workers and the managers. In a way, caste, linguistic, and religious ties were overlapping in nature and they did not constitute simply a manifestation of workers' longing for their ties based on natal origins but also reflect their social organizations and survival strategies in the urban labour market. The presumed, unlimited power of certain social entrepreneurs such as sardars and burrababus have been shown to be grossly exaggerated—instead, detailed studies of neighbourhoods reveal complex social organizations and various nodal points of power and patronages. The power of many of these elements was contingent upon their ability to offer patronage and represent workers. These ties, under no circumstances, reflect the primordial loyalties of workers. Indeed, historians' fascination with seeming primordial social divisions among workers have led them to neglect divisions among workers based within the workplace.

The jute mill workers were not only divided along lines of caste, region, and religion but also in terms of the regularity of employment, wages, and skill. The entire jute workforce was divided into three different segments of workers. A vast majority of workers were recruited on a daily basis and had no security of jobs. These workers gathered every day at the gates of the jute mills to obtain jobs in the factories. Apart from daily workers there were two different sections of workers in the jute mills. The temporary workers were recruited for a brief period and had a little more security of jobs than daily workers. Finally there were the weavers who had to be trained over a period of years and were therefore more difficult to replace in the short term. In such a situation, competition among workers was harsh and it was difficult for them to unite for collective bargaining, though certain grievances like long working hours, low wages, and unsafe working conditions in the factories were common to all sections of workers. In fact, common grievances and shared living conditions did not automatically lead towards solidarities across various sections of workers. Solidarities were products of the way workers were governed not only within their factories but also in their slums and neighbourhoods.

This study asserts that the social history of labour cannot be separated from the political history of institutions of governance, political parties, and trade unions. The issues of governance in everyday life in mill towns and the identity formation of workers as a collective entity is imbricated together in shaping specific events, individual lives, and workers' collective actions. The most crucial and hitherto neglected area in this regard is the pattern of governance of mill towns and their impact on the evolution of labour history. The mill towns were governed by the mill managers. The mill managers controlled municipalities, the local judiciary, and even local police forces. Mill managers depended upon the local bhadralok to assist them in administering mill municipalities. Many of these bhadraloks were local zamindars who opposed any development in the slums as a means to save their properties. The absence of a regular water supply and sanitation in overcrowded slums often led to epidemics in the mill towns. Mill managers blamed workers for their diseases and tried to control epidemics by removing insanitary slums and regulating the activities of workers which adversely affected their living conditions. This led to confrontation between various sections of workers and the managers. Since managers controlled the local judiciary and the police, they were effectively able to suppress discontent among workers.

This confrontation between the municipal administration and workers helped the latter to forge alliances among themselves against the police and the town administration. Moreover, it also contributed to a deterioration in the relationship between local propertied elites and the workers. Although local propertied elites were engaged in confrontations with the managers for control over the mill towns, they opposed workers' inclusion in the municipal boards and organized pressure on the Government to extend elected representation to the mill towns on the basis of property qualification. In such a situation, workers were forced to organize alliances among themselves if only to fight and realize some of their demands and grievances. Thus the manner in which institutional politics functioned influenced the creation of solidarities among workers.

This study has examined the impact of the intervention of the state machinery on the labour movement chronologically from the late nineteenth century in order to capture the complexity of political developments in Bengal. It has sought to investigate the high points in the labour movement and in nationalist politics when strikes, riots, and agitations led to increasing confrontations between workers on the one hand, and managers and law-enforcing agencies of the state, on the other. It has also explored the relationship between the bhadralok-led nationalist movement and workers' politics during periods of confrontation. By examining these situations, this volume has explained how workers deployed their strategies of negotiation with the managers and the state in changing political circumstances. The exploration of connections between workers' politics and nationalist movement prompted the author not only to review the stereotype that in the absence of trade unions workers were helpless, mute victims of nationalism, but also the idea that political alignments at the elite level were not influenced by workers' resistance. The particular forms of solidarities that workers' politics took in this period can also be explained and investigated by referring to the particular pattern of the governance of mill towns.

From the middle of the 1890s, mill towns in Bengal began to experience various kinds of confrontations between the workers and the colonial state. In the 1890s, the intervention of the local administration and the police in industrial disputes led to an escalation of strikes and thereby enhanced solidarities and alliances among several sections of workers. The repeated confrontations between the law-enforcing agencies of the colonial state and the workers led to the emergence of distrust among workers of the colonial state. Such distrust found expression not only in the collective bargaining strategies of the workers but also in the way they chose to confront the colonial state during riots.

The prejudices and biases of local officials in the mill municipalities against Muslim workers sometimes contributed to violent clashes between the police and the Muslim urban poor. Muslim workers felt threatened by the emphasis of the government on local practices in observing controversial religious rituals like cow slaughter. On these occasions they confronted not only the Hindus but also fought the police. Antipathy among the urban poor for the police was so strong that during many confrontations with them, Hindu workers also supported their Muslim colleagues. In these contexts workers confronted the police and developed unities against police action. The state's discrimination against workers during epidemics reinforced the anti-government mentality among them. This became particularly evident during the plague riots in Calcutta in the 1890s.

In this decade workers confronted various government agencies, including the police, without outside support. In the late nineteenth century, elite politicians had little interest in addressing themselves to workers' issues and grievances. Thus Muslim elite politicians opposed the anti-government riots by the Muslim workers. Similarly bhadralok nationalists, concerned with the growth of Indian industries, opposed working-class militancy. During the plague riots, bhadralok leaders secured concessions from the government for the rich, but tried to restrain workers' agitations over the segregation of people indiscriminately categorized as plague patients. Even at the height of the swadeshi movement, bhadralok politicians did not have any clear-cut policies towards industrial workers. A few swadeshi politicians established trade unions among workers but these unions were more dependent upon the support of the bhadralok clerks.

Workers deployed their strategies of negotiation with the combination of employers and the colonial state on their own. To avoid managerial repression they resorted to lightning strikes which caught the managers unawares. Moreover, the loss of wages during strikes often caused grievances among casual workers who had fewer economic resources. Thus lightning strikes also enabled workers to maintain solidarities. However, strikes in the pre-war years were often a response to the exploitative policies of the employers and the colonial state.

In the postwar years the economic crisis in Bengal affected workers adversely. While the prices of essential items increased unprecedentedly, wages did not rise correspondingly. Moreover, in the postwar years various forms of political propaganda drew workers' attention to the discrepancies between the high profits enjoyed by the owners of industry and their own low wages. The Khilafatist propaganda particularly emphasized the exploitative nature of the colonial government and appealed to the religious sentiment of workers. This propaganda generated a sense of self-respect and helped legitimize the working poor's struggle against the combination of employers and the colonial state. Although Khilafatists and Gandhian nationalists were opposed to the inclusion of workers in the official programme of nationalist agitations, workers interpreted the nationalist propaganda independently and initiated their own struggle for wage increase. The mass strike of 1920 created an environment for the rise of mass nationalist protest in Calcutta. A section of the nationalist leadership tried to control the labour movement by establishing trade unions, but they failed in their attempt. In fact it was the militant labour movement which made nationalist propaganda successful in Calcutta. During the non-cooperation agitation, the labour movement in Bengal moved into a stage of offensive attack on the combination of employers and the state. It was these changes in the mentality of the workers that paved the way for the rise of the socialist movement in Bengal. However, it would be wrong to project such a development as a manifestation of the maturity of the revolutionary consciousness of the proletariat.

The withdrawal of the non-cooperation movement led to fierce political debates in the Congress party over the best strategy for nationalist agitations. A large majority of Congress politicians joined the legislative assembly to oppose dyarchy from within. The Congress Swarajya Party organized a pact with the Muslim leaders to settle the Hindu-Muslim conflict. The pact stipulated that the Muslims would be allowed a majority of the seats in the assembly and would secure higher employment in government service under the swarajist regime. The pact provoked vehement opposition from the Hindu elites in Bengal. Soon a political movement started in Bengal against the Swarajya party. The post non-cooperation period in Bengal witnessed a slow polarization between the Hindu and Muslim politicians with exclusive communal agenda which was manifested in the formation of political groups like the Mahabir Dal and the Tabligh and Tanjim organizations. In this context communal riots among workers lost their earlier anti-police character.

However, labour politics in Bengal also became more organized under the impact of the growing socialist movement. The Congress' failure to implement their own political manifesto disillusioned many Congress men in Bengal and led to the formation of the Labour Swaraj Party which aimed at organizing workers and peasants to achieve their demands and to mobilize the labour movement within the nationalist struggle. The Labour Swaraj Party, renamed as the Workers' and Peasants' Party, soon became a united platform of socialist and communist political activists. The new party intervened in various strikes in the mill towns and built up a support base among the workers. In this process they also organized a number of strikes which prepared the ground for the first general strike in Bengal in 1929.

The general strike of 1929 indicated the impact of the WPP on the labour movement in Bengal. In 1921, workers tried to extend the conflicts in individual jute mills to the other neighbouring mills in Bengal but not to the degree of a general strike. In 1929, however, strikes spread all over the mill belt in Bengal due to the efforts made by the WPP. In this context it is necessary to point out that the WPP did not initiate or end the strike. Workers deployed their strategies of negotiation independently but their actions were increasingly influenced and informed by the organized political movement from outside. The political developments of the 1920s perhaps witnessed the beginning of long-term changes towards a more powerful labour movement under left organizations. This period also witnessed an intensification of communal politics which was to have a significant impact on later political developments.

This survey of the process of the emergence of the labour movement in Bengal also demonstrates that there were no impermeable boundaries between class-based collective action of workers and their sense of belonging to a religious community, whether Hindu or Muslim. Moments of confrontation with the colonial state on religious issues (like destruction of mosques) in the 1890s were characterized by a coalescing of their religious and class identities. In fact, on certain occasions workers of one religious community supported their colleagues of the other community in the latter's fight against the state. However, in the 1920s in a different political situation, workers accorded priority to their religious identity during communally-charged circumstances and confronted workers belonging to other religious communities.

The rise of a nationalist and socialist movement impinged upon the political perspectives of workers but they deployed their bargaining strategies with employers independently and thus the Khilafatists and communists were able to mobilize workers only on selective issues and failed when workers rejected parts of Khilafatist or communist political views which did not serve their own interests. This was particularly visible in the silence of the workers when communist leaders and leading socialist trade unionists were arrested during the Meerut trials. The long-term political developments towards communal riots and the growing socialist movement also reflected flexibilities in the attitudes of workers according to different political contexts. Thus the growth of the socialist movement in Bengal was not a reflection of the development of a monolithic class consciousness, nor were the communal riots evidence of a unilinear march towards complete communal polarization. In fact, workers, like all other urban social groups, selected their political strategy of negotiation with their employers and the state in an eclectic fashion and tried to exploit political parties to serve their own ends. Yet workers were in a position to influence not only their destinies but politics at the top. Indeed, the nature of organized and defused resistance from workers could change the nature of political combination at elite level politics as much elite level politics influenced the grass roots. Politics in the 1930s, and the emergence of a coalition of propertied elites, could not be divorced from the pressure generated from below by workers themselves, particularly through the second general strike in 1937.

Does class matter? Indeed, it matters, but not in a way many historians have imagined in the Indian context. As the idea of class as a master identity crucially related to the production relations in a society gives way to the complex pattern of identity formation in interaction with diverse forms of social and political processes, we can recover it as a defused form of social and political entity that can be made and remade depending on the contingency of immediate social and political circumstances. Historians have emphasized class as a monolithic construct that manifested itself through socialist parties and trade unions: they have also tried to fill the absence of class with other forms of monolithic constructs, such as communities based on primordial loyalties. This book argues for a complex and variable micro-history of the formation and reformation of class whereby workers have their own agency to make and remake class as a political category. To reject the idea of class totally, we are left with the danger of viewing workers as prisoners of diverse forms of primordial loyalties and as guided by predetermined destinies rather than making their own histories in adverse social, political and economic circumstances. Instead, we have revealed, in this study of a labour force in colonial Bengal, a picture of slow and incremental gains made by workers through their various forms of struggles.

Notes

1. André Gorz, *Farewell to the Working Class*, London, 1982.

2. See Eric Hobsbawm et al., *The Forward March of Labour Halted?*, London, 1981. For the general context of these debates, see Michael Schneider, 'In Search of a "New" Historical Subject: The End of Working-Class Culture, the Labour Movement, and the Proletariat', *International Labour and Working-Class History*, 32, 1987, pp. 46–58.

3. See James Curran, (ed.), *The Future of the Left*, London, 1984; Stuart Hall and Martin Jacques, (eds), *New Times: The Changing Face of Politics in the 1990s*, London, 1991; Eric Hobsbawm, *Politics for a Rational Left: Political Writing 1977– 1988*, London, 1989; Stuart Hall, *The Hard Road to Renewal*, London, 1988.

4. David Roediger, *The Wages of Whiteness: Race and the Making of the American Working Class*, London, 1991; Noel Ignatiev, *How the Irish became White*, New York, 1995; Matt Wray and Annalee Newitz, (ed.), *White Trash: Race and Class in America*, New York, 1997; also Laura Tabili, *We ask for British Justice: Workers and Racial Difference in Late Imperial Britain*, Ithaca, 1994; Ava Baron (ed.), *Work Engendered: Toward a New History of American Labour*, Ithaca, 1991; Lenard

R. Berlanstein, *Rethinking Labour History: Essays of Discourse and Class Analysis*, Urbana and Chicago, 1993.

5. Dipesh Chakrabarty, *Rethinking Working Class History Bengal 1890–1940*. Princeton, 1989.

6. R.S. Chandavarkar, *The Origins of Industrial Capitalism in India: Business Strategies and the Working Classes in Bombay, 1900–1940*, Cambridge, 1994.

Bibliography

A. GOVERNMENT RECORDS

1. Unpublished:

West Bengal State Archives, Calcutta
Commerce Department Commerce Branch.
General Department Emigration Branch.
General Department Miscellaneous Branch.
Home Department (Confidential) Police Branch.
Home Department (Confidential) Political Branch.
Home Political Proceedings.
Judicial Department Police Branch.
Land Revenue Department, Survey and Settlement Branch.
Local Self Government Department Municipality Branch.
Local Self Government Department. Local Self Government Branch.
Medical Department Medical Branch.

India Office Library and Records, London
General Department Miscellaneous Branch.
Judicial Department Police Branch.
Private Office Paper, Secretary of State.
Reports on Indian Native Papers (Bengal).

National Archives of India, New Delhi
Home Department Political Branch.
Meerut Conspiracy Case Proceedings.
Report on Condition of Lower Classes in India, Famine Nos 1–24,
    December, 1888.

A. GOVERNMENT RECORDS

2. Published:

Census of India

O'Donnel, C.J., *Census of India 1891, Vol. I*, Calcutta, 1893.

——, *Census of India 1891, Vol. III, The lower provinces of Bengal and their Feudatories*, Calcutta, 1893.

O'Malley, L.S.S., *Census of India 1911, Vol. V, (Part 1and 2)*, Calcutta, 1913.

Plowden, W.C., *Census of India, Vol. III, General Report and Statements, Census of North Western Province 1872*, Allahabad, 1878.

Thomson, W.H., *Census of India 1921, Vol. V, (Part 1and 2)*, Calcutta, 1923.

White, E., *Report on the census of North Western Province and Oudh and the native states of Rampur and native Garwal*, Allahabad, 1882 [Census of India 1881].

District Gazetteer

Drake, D.L., *Azamgarh District Gazetteer*, Allahabad, 1911.

Nevill, H.R., *Ghazipur District Gazetteer*, Allahabad, 1909.

O'Malley L.S.S., *24 Parganas District Gazetteer*, Calcutta, 1914.

——, (Revised by A. Middleton), *Saran District Gazetteer*, Patna, 1930.

——, (Revised by J.F.W. James) *Sahabad District Gazetteer*, Patna, 1924.

O'Malley, L.S.S. and Chakraborty, B.R., *District Gazetteer of Howrah*, Calcutta, 1909.

Settlement Reports

Hubback, J.A., *Report on the Survey and Settlement operations in the districts of Sahabad 1907–1916*, Patna, 1917.

Irvine, W., *Report on the Revisions of Records and Settlement in Ghazipur district 1880–1885*, Allahabad, 1886.

Roberts, D.T., *Report on the Revision of Records and Settlement in parts of Balia District 1882–1885 AD*, Allahabad, 1886.

Government Acts and Reports

Bengal a plague manual. Being a Collection of the extant Regulations and Executive orders in connection with plague issued by the Government of India and the Government of Bengal, Calcutta, 1903.

Cook, J.N., Report of the epidemics of plague in Calcutta during the years 1898–1899, 1899–1900 and to 30 June 1900, Indian Plague Commission 1898–99 Volume I, Appendix, Calcutta, 1900.

Datta, K.L., Report on an enquiry into the rise of prices in India, 4 vols, Calcutta, 1914.

Deshpande, S.R., Report on an Enquiry into Conditions of labour in jute mills in India, Delhi, 1946.

Foley, B., Report on Labour in Bengal, Calcutta, 1906.

Harrison, H.L., Report of the Committee appointed by the Government of Bengal to Prepare a Scheme for the Amalgamation of the Town of Calcutta with the Urban Portion of the suburb, Calcutta, 1887.

Kerr, Hem Chunder, Report on the Cultivation of, and Trade in Jute in Bengal: The Bengal Jute Commission 1873, 2 Vols., Calcutta, 1877.

Labour in the United Kingdom Dependencies, Central Office of Information, London, 1957.

McLeod, R., Annual Report on emigration from the port of Calcutta to British and Foreign colonies, 1890, Calcutta, 1891

Municipal Manual for Bengal, Calcutta, 1926.

Murry, A.R., Report of the Indian Industrial Commission, Vol. VI, (Confidential evidence), Calcutta, 1918.

Proceedings, Bengal Legislative Council debates, Calcutta 1912–1935.

Progress and Administrative Report on Railways in Bengal 1885, Calcutta, 1885.

Report of Excise Commission 1883–84, Calcutta, 1884.

Report of Indian Factory Commission, Calcutta, 1890.

Report of Indian Factory Labour Commission, Vol. I and II, London, 1909.

Report of Labour Investigation Committee, New Delhi, 1946.

Report of the Committee on the Industrial Unrest in Bengal, Calcutta. 1921.

Report on the Administration of Bengal, Calcutta, 1918–1936.

Report on the conditions of the Lower Classes of Population, Calcutta, 1888.

Report on the Consumption of Tari in Bengal, Calcutta, 1886.

Report on the Royal Commission of Labour in India, Vol. V (Part 1 and 2), Vol. IX, London, 1931.

Reports on Indian Constitutional Reforms, Calcutta, 1918.

Roy, S.N., *Report on the General Election of 1923 in Bengal*, Calcutta, 1923.

Royal Commission on Labour Foreign Reports, 1892, Vol. II, The Colonies and The Indian Empire, London, 1892.

Selection of Papers Relating to the Famine of 1896–97 in Bengal, Vol. I (October to November), Calcutta, 1897.

Shirras, G. Findlay, *Index number of Indian prices 1861–1918*, Calcutta, 1921.

The Bengal Administration Report, 1923–24, 1924–25.

The Bulletin of Indian Inddustries and Labour Industrial Disputes in India 1921–28.

Williams, Rushbrook L.F., *The History of the Indian Tour of HRH of the Prince of Wales*, Calcutta 1922.

B. PAPERS OF ORGANIZATIONS

Annual Administrative Report on Bhatpara Municipality.

Archives of Thomas Duff and Company Limited, Jute merchants, Dundee:

1. Minute Books of the Shyamnagar Jute Factory Company Limited 1874–1875.
2. Manager's Report to Directors, Angus Jute Mill.
3. Manager's Report to Directors, Titagarh Jute Factory Company Limited.
4. Manager's Report to Directors, Shyamnagar Jute Factory Company Limited.
5. Manager's Report to Directors, Victoria Jute Mill.
6. Private Official Letters from Calcutta agent to Managing Directors, Thomas Duff and Company.

Bhatpara Municipal Minute Book.

District Jute and Flax Workers' Union Book, series entitled 'Letters to India', John Sime, 10 March 1926.

Indian Jute Mill Association, Report of the Committee for 1895, Calcutta, 1895.

Preface to Badyabati Young Men Association Library Catalogue, Badyabati, 1990.

Preface to Catalogue of the Bhatpara library, Bhatpara, 1991.

Proceedings of Bhatpara Municipality, 1901–1937.

Report of the Indian Jute Mill Association.

Report of the non-official Commission on the Calcutta disturbances, Calcutta,1918.

Report on Municipal Administration of Calcutta, Vol. I, for the year 1918–19, Calcutta, 1919.

Sahityka, Rabindra Bhavana Archives, Vishva Bharati University.

C. Papers Relating to Individuals

Nehru Memorial Museum and Library, New Delhi
A.C. Bannerjee Private Papers.

National Library of Scotland, Edinburgh.

Personal and family papers of George Dott.

Transcript of an interview with Sibnath Bannerjee.

Centre of South Asian Studies, Cambridge
Benthall Papers, Boxes I–XII.

Tegart Papers, Boxes I, II, and III.

India Office Library, London
Collection of Letters of Lord Ronaldshay to King George V.

Reading Collection.

Transcript of an Interview of Griffith, Percival, Oral archives.

Transcript of an Interview of Melville, Stephen Ian, Oral archives.

Zetland Collection, Diary of Lord Ronaldshay, India Office Library.

2. Private Collections

Bhattacharya, Panchanan, *Cha bagan theke jail hajote,* Dr Arun Nag, Visva Bharati University, Santiniketan.

Nayacharya Madhusudan, *Bhatparar Smriti,* Unpublished handwritten manuscript, Subho Basu, Santiniketan.

D. Newspapers, Periodicals and Journals

Amrita Bazar Patrika.
Bulletins of Indian Industries and Labour.
Desh.
India Daily News.
Journal of Indian Industries and Labour.
Karmi.
Mihir-o-Sudhakar.
Mohammadi.
Mussalman.
Sramik.
Star of India.
The Bengalee.
The Englishman.
The Indian Annual Register 1924–25 (ed. N.N. Mitra).
The Statesman.

E. Interviews

George Harrison, Dundee, 7 August 1992.

F. Books, Articles, and Theses

Adhikari, G. (1974), (ed.), Documents of the History of the Communist Party of India, Vol. II, IIIA, III C, New Delhi.

Ahmad, Muzaffar (1989), *Amar Jibon O Bharater Communist Party*, Calcutta.

Ahmed, Abul Mansur (1970), *Amar Dekha Rajnitir Ponchas Batsar*, Dacca.

Anderson, D.M. and David Killingray (1991), *Policing the Empire: Government, Authority and Control, 1830–1946*, Manchester.

Arnold, David (1988), (ed.), *Imperial Medicine and Indigenous Society*, Manchester.

Bagchi, A.K. (1972), *Private Investment in India, 1900–1939*, Cambridge.

——, 'Working-Class Consciousness', *EPW*, Vol. XXV, No. 30, 28 July 1990, pp. PE 54–60.

Bandhapadhya, Manju (1984), *Sramik Netri Santosh Kumari*, Calcutta.

Bandopadhyay, Prabhat Mohan (1936), *Balir Itihaser Bhumika*, Bally.

Baron, A. (1991), (ed.), *Work Engendered: Toward a New History of American Labour*, Ithaca.

Basu, Nirban (1992), *The Political Parties and Labour Politics 1937–47 (With Special Reference to Bengal)*, Calcutta.

Basu, Samaresh (1946), *Jaggaddal*, Calcutta.

Basu, Sanat (1983), 'Labour Journalism in the Early 1920s: A Case Study of Bengali Labour Journals', *Social Scientist*, Vol. II, No. 1, January 1983.

Bayly, C.A. (2000), 'Rallying Around the Subaltern', in Vinayak Chaturvedi (ed.), *Mapping Subaltern Studies and the Postcolonial*.

Berlansteined, R. (1993), *Rethinking Labour History: Essays of Discourse and Class Anaysis*, Urbana and Chicago.

Bhattacharya, Debaprasad (1989), 'Bhatpara Swabhabe Swatantra', *Siladitya*.

Birla, G.D. (1989), *In the shadow of Mahatma*, Bombay.

Bose, Mrinal Kumar, 'Railways and Local Self Government: The Halisahar–Kanchrapara area of West Bengal, 1906–17', *Proceedings of the Indian History Congress, Golden Jubilee session, Gorakhpur, 1989–90*, pp. 479–89.

Bose, S. (1986), *Agrarian Bengal: Economy, Social Structure and Politics 1919–1947*, Cambridge.

Bramford, P.C. (1974), *Histories of the Non Co-operation and Khilafat Movements*, Delhi.

Brass, T., 'Moral Economists, Subalterns, New Social Movements and the Re-emergence of a (Post-) Modernised (Middle) Peasant', In V. Chaturvedi, *Mapping Subaltern Studies*.

Bremaan, J. (1985), *Of Peasants, Migrants and Paupers: Rural Labour Circulation and Capitalist Production in West India*, Oxford.

Broomfield, J.H. (1968), *Elite Conflict in Plural society: Twentieth Century Bengal*, Berkeley.

Buchanan, D.H. (1934), *Development of Capitalistic Enterprise in India*, New York.

Cain, P. (1998), (ed.), R. Macdonald, *Labour and Empire,* London. Series title: The empire and its critics 1899–1939: Classics of Imperialism.

Chakrabarty, Alok Kumar (1990), *Maharaja Krishna Chandra O Tatkalin Bangali Samaj,* Calcutta.

Chakrabarty, B. (1990), *Subhas Chandra Bose and Middle-Class radicalism A Study in Indian Nationalism 1928–1940,* London.

Chakrabarty, Dipesh (1976), 'Sasipada Banerjee: A Study in the Nature of the First Contact of the Bengali Bhadralok with the Working Classes of Bengal', *Indian Historical Review,* Vol. 2.

_____ (1981), 'Communal Riots and Labour, Bengal's Jute Mill Hands in the 1890s', *Past and Present,* No. 91, May.

_____ (1989), *Rethinking Working Class History: Bengal 1890–1940,* Princeton.

Chakrabarty, Nirod Mishra (1927), *Bangalar Jatya Itihas,* Howrah.

Chandavarkar, R.S. (1981), 'Mill Districts in Bombay Between Two Wars', *Modern Asian Studies,* Vol. XV.

_____ (1992), 'Plague Panic and Epidemic Politics in India, 1896–1914' in Terence Ranger and Paul Slack, (eds), *Epidemics and Ideas Essays on the Historical Perception of Pestilence,* Cambridge.

_____ (1994), *The Origins of Industrial Capitalism in India: Business Strategies and the Working Classes in Bombay, 1900–1940,* Cambridge.

Chandra, Bipan (1982), *Rise and Growth of Economic Nationalism in India,* New Delhi.

Chattapadhya, Goutam (1974), *Communism and Bengal's Freedom Movement, Vol. I, 1917–1929,* New Delhi.

_____ (1992), (ed.), *Samhati, Langal, Ganavani,* Calcutta.

Chatterjee, P. (1984), *Bengal 1920–47: The Land Question,* Calcutta.

Chattopadhaya, K.A. (1952), *Socio Economic Survey of Jute Labour,* University of Calcutta.

Chaturvedi, V. (2000), 'Introduction', in V. Chaturvedi (ed.), *Mapping Subaltern Studies and the Postcolonialism,* London.

Chaudhuri, N.C. (1987), *Thy Hand, Great Anarch! India 1921–1952,* New Delhi.

Chowdhury, B.B., 'The Process of Depeasantization in Bengal and Bihar, 1885–1947', *IHR,* Vol. II, No. 1.

_____ (1975), 'Land Market in Eastern India 1793–1940, Part I: The Movement of Land Prices', *IESHR Vol. XII, No. 1*, January–March.

_____ (1975), 'Land Market in Eastern India, 1793–1940, Part II: The Changing Composition of the Landed Society', *IESHR Vol. XII, No. 1*, April–June.

Chowdhury, Satyajit (1980), *Pramathanath Mitra Bardhapak*, Calcutta.

Cohen, A.P. (1989), *The Symbolic Construction of Community*, London.

Cohn, B.S. (1987), *An Anthropologist among the Historians and other essays*, Delhi.

_____ (1996), *Colonialism and its forms of knowledge: The British in India*, Princeton.

Cooper, F. (1987), *On the African Water Front*, New Haven.

Cox, A., 'The Calcutta General Strike of 1937', unpublished draft paper.

Curran, J. (1984), (ed.), *The Future of the Left*, London.

Das, A.N. (1983), *Agrarian Unrest and Socio-Economic Change in Bihar*, New Delhi.

Das, Suranjan (1991), *Communal Riots in Bengal 1905–47*, Delhi.

Das Gupta, R. (1987), *Migrant Workers, Rural Connexions and Capitalism: The Calcutta Jute Industrial Labour 1890s to 1940s*, Indian Institute of Management, Calcutta.

Dasgupta, A.K. (1956), 'The Jute Industry in India 1857–1956', in V.B. Singh (ed.), *Economic History of India 1857–1956*, Bombay.

Dasgupta, R. (1976), 'Factory Labour in Eastern India: Sources of Supply 1855–1946', *Indian Economic and Social History Review*, Vol. 8, No. 3.

_____ (1979), 'Material Conditions and behavioural aspects of Calcutta working class 1875–99', Occasional Paper No. 22, Centre for Studies in Social Sciences, Calcutta.

_____ (1981), 'Structure of Labour Market in Colonial India, *EPW*, Special Issue, Vol. XVI, No. 44–46, pp. 1781–1806.

_____ (1994), *Labour and Working Class in Eastern India: Studies in Colonial History*, Calcutta.

Datta, P.K. (1999), *Carving Blocs: Communal Ideology in Early Twentieth Century Bengal*, New Delhi: Oxford University Press.

de Haan, Arjan (1994), *Unsettled Settlers: Migrant Workers and Industrial Capitalism in Calcutta*, Rotterdam, p. 28.

Deb Roy, Munindra (1901), *Hugli Kahini*, Calcutta.

Duyker, E. (1987), *Tribal Guerrillas: The Santals of West Bengal and Naxalite Movements*, New Delhi.

Fernandes, L. (1997), *Producing Workers: The Politics of Gender, Class and Culture in the Calcutta Jute Mills*, Philadelphia.

Fetsher, I. (1991), 'Class Consciousness', in Tom Bottomore (ed.), *A Dictionary of Marxist Thought* (Second Revised Edition), Oxford.

Freitag, Sandria (1989), (ed.), *Culture and Power in Benaras, Community, Performance and Environment 1800–1980*, Berkeley.

Gangopadhaya, Mohanlal (1963), *Asamapta Chatabda*, Calcutta.

Ganguly, B.N. (1938), *Trends in Agriculture and Population in the Ganges Valley: A Study in the Agricultural Economics*, London.

Ghosh, A.K. and Mazumdar, S.K. (1985), (eds), *Garifa United Sporting Club Centenary Souvernir*, Naihati.

Ghosh, Parimal (1990), 'Communalism and Colonial Labour Experience of Calcutta Jute Mill Workers 1880–1930', *EPW*, Vol. XXV, No. 30, 28 July, pp. PE 61–74.

_____ (2000), *Colonialism, Class and a History of the Calcutta Jute Millhands 1880–1930*, Hyderabad.

Ghosh, Shyamal Krishna (1990), *Parichayer Adda*, Calcutta.

Gordon, L. (1974), *Bengal: The Nationalist Movement 1876–1940*, Delhi.

Gorz, A. (1982), *Farewell to the Working Class*, London.

Goswami, Omkar (1991), *Industry, Trade and Peasant Society: The Jute Economy of Eastern India 1900–47*, Delhi.

Gourley, S.N. (1988), 'Nationalists, Outsiders and Labour Movement in Bengal During the Non-cooperation Movement 1919–1921', in Kapil Kumar (ed.), *Congress and Classes: Nationalism, Workers and Peasants*, Delhi, pp.34–57.

Grierson, G.A (1893), *Notes on the District of Gaya*, Calcutta.

_____ (1926), *Bihar Peasant Life*, Patna.

Guha, R. (1983), *Elementary Aspects of Peasant Insurgency in Colonial India*, Delhi.

_____ (1989), (ed.), *Subaltern Studies, III*, New Delhi.

Gupta, P.S. (1975), *Imperialism and the British Labour Movement 1914–1964*, London.

Guy Standing (1985), 'Circulation and Labour Process', in Guy Standing (ed.), *Labour Circulation and Labour Process*, London.

Hall, S. (1988), *The Hard Road to Renewal: Thatcherism and the Crisis of the Left*, London.

_____ (1992), 'What is This "Black" in Black Popular Culture?', in Gina Dent, (ed.), *Black Popular Culture*, Seattle.

Hall, Stuart and Martin Jacques (1991), (eds), *New Times: The Changing Face of Politics in the 1990s*, London.

Hasan Mushirul (1981), (ed.), *Communal and Pan Islamic Trends in Colonial India*, Delhi.

Henry, Pelling (1963), *A History of British Trade Unionism*, Harmondsworth.

Hilton, R. (1974), 'Peasant Society, Peasant Movements and Feudalism in Medieval Europe', in H.A. Landsberger (ed.), *Rural Protest Peasant Movements and Social Change*, London.

Hobsbawm, E.J. (1971) (1984), Notes on Class Consciousness in *Worlds of Labour: Further Studies in the world of labour*, London, p. 27

_____ (1989), *Politics for a Rational Left: Political Writing 1977–1988*, London.

Hobsbawm, E.J. et al., (1981), *The Forward March of Labour Halted?*, London.

Humphrey, Caroline and Michael Carrithers (1991), (eds), *The Assembly of Listeners, Jains in Society*, Cambridge.

Hyam, R. (1992), (ed.), *The Labour government and the end of empire 1945–1951*, London.

Ignatiev, N. (1995), *How the Irish became White*, New York.

Jain, N.K. (1983), *Muslims in India (Vol. II)*, New Delhi, pp. 87–8.

Joyce, P. (1990), 'Work' in F.M.L. Thompson (ed.), *The Cambridge Social History of Great Britain 1750–1950*, II, Cambridge.

_____ (1991), *Visions of the People: Industrial England and the Question of Class*, Cambridge University Press, Ch. 1.

Katznelson, I. (1986), *Working-Class Formation: Nineteenth Century Patterns in Western Europe and the United States*, London, pp. 14–23.

King, Anthony (1976), *Colonial Urban Development, Culture, Social Power and Environment,* London.

Klein, Ira (1973), 'Death in India', *Journal of Asian Studies,* 32, 4.

_____ (1984), 'When the Rains Failed: Famine Relief, and Mortality in British India', *IESHR,* Vol. XXI, No. 2, April–June, pp. 139–52.

_____ (1989), 'Population Growth and Mortality, Part 1,—The Climatric of Death', *IESHR,* Vol. 26, No. 4, December, pp. 387–404.

Kumar, Kapil (1988), (ed.), *Congress and Classes: Nationalism, Workers and Peasants,* Delhi.

Lenin, V.I. (1988), *What is to be done?* (Originally published in 1902). Translated into English by Joe Fineberg and George Hanna. Introduction and Glossary by Robert Service, London.

MacPherson, V. (1974), *The Muslim Microcosm: Calcutta, 1918 to 1935,* Weisbaden.

Mahalanabis, P.C. (1963), 'Bengal Labour Enquiry: Jagatdal, 1941, 1942 and 1945', in *Experiments in Statistical Sampling in the Indian Statistical Institute,* Calcutta.

Marks, S. and R. Rathbone (1982), (ed.), *Industrialisation and Social Change in South Africa: African Class formation, Culture and Consciousness 1870–1930,* Harlow.

Marx, K. (1969), 'The Eighteenth Brumaire of Louis Bonaparte', in Marx and Engels, *Selected Works Vol. 3,* Moscow, pp. 479.

McGuire, John (1983), *The Making of a Colonial Mind: A Quantitative Study of the Bhadralok in Calcutta 1857–1885,* Canberra.

Metcalf, Thomas (1989), *An Imperial Vision: Indian Architecture and Britain's Raj,* London.

Milliband and J. Saville (1965), (eds), *Socialist Register,* Merlin Press, London.

Minault, Gail (1982), *The Khilafat Movement Religious Symbolism and Political Mobilisation in India,* New York.

Misra, M. (1999), *Business, Race and Politics in British India c. 1850–1960,* Oxford.

Mitra, Ira (1981), 'Growth of Trade Union Consciousness among the Jute Mill Workers', EPW, Special Number, November.

Mitra, Krishna Kumar (1937), *Atmacharit,* Calcutta.

Mukhaopadhaya, Hiren (1974), *Tori hote tire*, Calcutta.

Mukherji, S. (1982), 'Some Aspects of Commercialisation of Agriculture in India in Eastern India, 1891–1938', in Ashok Sen, P. Chatterjee, and S. Mukherji (eds), *Perspectives in Social Science, II: Three Studies on the Agrarian Structure of Bengal before Independence*, Delhi.

Mukhopadhaya, S. (1989), *Bharater Communist Party o Amra [Pratham Khanda]*, Kolikata.

Newitz, A. and Matt Wray (1997), (eds), *White Trash: Race and Class in America*, New York.

O'Donnel, C.J. (1880), *The Ruin of an Indian Province: An Indian Famine Explained, A Letter to the Marquis of Harlington, Secretary of State in A Liberal and Reforming Government*, London.

Pandey, G. (1990), *The Construction of Communalism in Colonial North India*, Delhi.

Patrick, J.P. (1971), *Communism and Nationalism in India: M N Roy and Commintern Policy 1920–1939*, Princeton.

Pelling, H. (1954), *The Origins of the Labour Party*, Oxford.

_____ (1963), *A History of British Trade Unionism*, Harmondsworth.

Pratt, Mary Louis (1992), *Imperial Eyes Travel Writings and Trans culturation*, London.

Ranger, Terence and Paul Slack (1992), (eds), *Epidemics and Ideas: Essays on the Historial Perception of Pestilence*, Cambridge.

Ray, Durgacharan (1984), *Debgoner Mortey Agaman*, Calcutta, First Published 1887, Reprinted, Calcutta.

Ray, R. (1976), *Urban Roots of Indian Nationalism: Pressure Groups and Conflicts and Interests in Calcutta City Politics, 1875–1939*, New Delhi.

_____ (1984), *Social Conflict and Political Unrest in Bengal, 1875–1927*, Delhi,

Riddick, J.F. (1948), *Who Was Who in British India*, Connecticut.

Roediger, D. (1991), *The Wages of Whiteness: Race and the Making of the American Working Class*, London.

Roy, S.N. (1923), *Report on the general election of 1923 in Bengal*, Calcutta, p. 16.

Saha, Panchanan (1978), *History of the Working Class Movement in Bengal*, Delhi.

Said, E. (1978), *Orientalism*, London.

Sarkar, Sumit (1973), *Swadeshi Movement in Bengal*, New Delhi.

_____ (1989), *Modern India, 1885–1947*, London.

_____ (1989), 'The Condition and Nature of Subaltern Militancy: Bengal from Swadeshi to Non Co-operation 1905–22', *Subaltern Studies III*, New Delhi, pp. 271–320.

Sarkar, T. (1987), *Bengal 1928–1934 Politics of Protests*, Delhi.

Schneider, M. (1987), 'In Search of a "New" Historical Subject: The End of Working-Class Culture, the Labor Movement, and the Proletariat', *International Labour and Working-Class History* 32, pp. 46–58.

Seal, Anil, et al. (1973), *Locality, Province and Nation, Essay on Indian Politics 1870–1940*, Cambridge.

Sen, M. (1978), *Sediner Katha*, Calcutta.

Sen, R. (1996), *Bharater Communist Partyr Itibritta*, Calcutta.

Sen, Ramcamal (1836), 'A Report on the Cultivation of Jute and the Manufacture of Gunnies in Bengal', *Transaction of Agricultural and Horticultural Society of India*, Vol. 2, pp.77–80.

Sen, S. (1976), *Muslim Politics in Bengal 1937–1947*, New Delhi.

_____ (1990), *Women and Labour in Late Colonial India: The Bengal Jute Industry*, Cambridge.

Sen, S.P. (1974), (ed.), *Dictionary of National Biography, Vol. IV (s–z)*, Calcutta.

Sen, Shila (1976), *Muslim Politics in Bengal*, New Delhi.

Shehanobis, Chinmohan (1978), 'Bramho Samaj and Toiling People', *Mainstream, Vol. 127*.

Singh, Iqbal (1988), *The Indian National Congress: A Reconstruction, Vol. II, 1919–1923*, Delhi.

Singh, Moni (1988), *Life is a Struggle*, Delhi.

Sinha, Kaliprasanna (1972), *Hutum Panchar Naksha*, Calcutta, 1865, Reprinted, Calcutta.

Stevens, R. (1766), *The Complete Guide to East India Trade*, London.

Tabili, L. (1994), *"We ask for British Justice": Workers and Racial Difference in Late Imperial Britain*, Ithaca.

Thompson, E.P. (1965), 'The Peculiarities of the English', in R. Milliband and J. Saville (eds), *Socialist Register*, London.

——— (1978), 'Eighteenth century English society: Class Struggle without Class', Social History, 3/2 (May 1978), p. 154.

——— (1978), The Poverty of Theory and Other Essays, London.

Tillitson, G.H.R. (1989), The Tradition of Indian Architecture: Continuity, Controversy and Change Since 1850, Yale.

Wallace, D.R. (1928), The Romance of Jute—A History of the Calcutta Jute Mill Industry 1855–1909, Calcutta.

Williams, R. (1977), Marxism and Literature, Oxford.

Yang, Anand (1989), The Limited Raj Agrarian Relations in Colonial India, Saran District, 1793–1920, Berkeley.

Zaidi, A.Z.M., The Encyclopaedia of the Indian National Congress, 1921–1924, India at the Crossroads, Vol. VIII, Delhi, 1980.

Unpublished PhD Theses

Chattapadhaya, S. 'Muzaffar Ahmed: Beyod the Politics of Identity' (A thesis in progress, School of Oriental and African Studies, University of London).

Cox, A.R. (1999), 'Paternal Despotism and Workers' Resistance in the Bengal Jute Industry 1920–1940'. Unpublished PhD thesis, October, pp. 194–214.

Derbyshire, Ian David (1985), 'Opening up the Interior: The Impact of Railways on the North Indian Economy and Society,' University of Cambridge, Cambridge.

Fisher, C.M. (1976), 'Indigo Plantations and Agrarian Society in North Bihar in the Nineteenth and Early Twentieth Centuries,' University of Cambridge, Cambridge.

Gourlay, S.N. (1983), Trade Unionism in Bengal before 1922: Historical Origins, Development and Characteristics, University of London, London.

Guptoo, Nandini (1991), 'The Political Culture of the Urban Poor: The United Province Between the Two World Wars', University of Cambridge, Cambridge.

Hesseltine H.G. (1981), 'The Development of Jute Cultivation in Bengal 1860–1914', University of Sussex, Sussex.

Kudesia, Gyanesh (1992), 'State Power and the Erosion of Colonial Authority in Uttar Pradesh, India, 1930–42', University of Cambridge, Cambridge.

Sen, Samita (1992), 'Women workers in the Bengal Jute Industry, 1890–1940: Migration, Motherhood and Militancy', University of Cambridge, Cambridge.

ELECTRONIC SOURCES

'About the ILO who we are—ILO History', ILO document available on ILO website *http://www.ilo.org/public/english/about/history.htm*.

http://www.kentlaw.edu/ilhs/gompers.html, a website maintained by Illinois Labour History Society.

Index